W9-CLB-232

Nonintervention
and
International Order

Written under the auspices of the
Center of International Studies,
Princeton University.
A list of other Center publications
appears at the back of the book.

R·J·VINCENT

Nonintervention
and
International Order

PRINCETON UNIVERSITY PRESS

PRINCETON, NEW JERSEY

Copyright © 1974 by Princeton University Press
All Rights Reserved
LCC: 72-6526
ISBN: 0–691–05652–8

Library of Congress Cataloging in Publication Data will
be found on the last printed page of this book

This book has been composed in Linotype Times Roman

Printed in the United States of America
by Princeton University Press, Princeton, New Jersey

CONTENTS

What provoked this inquiry was the prevalence of the view that the contemporary world is not a world in which a principle of nonintervention can obtain in international relations. Its ultimate purpose is to reply to the prevailing view and to state a case for nonintervention principally by meeting the arguments of those who would dethrone it. The doctrine is by now a familiar one that international law is no longer confined exclusively to the relations between sovereign states in which the rule of nonintervention had meaning, but also applies to entities other than states. Developments of this sort shake the old assumptions about sovereignty. Specifically, it is in the international law of internal war that the simple doctrine of nonintervention is held to have received a challenge to which it cannot effectively respond. As to the international political environment in which law operates, a postwar world which has witnessed the arrival of nuclear weapons, of an all-enveloping ideological conflict, of transnational relationships which diminish, and of transnational problems which require the further diminution of the significance of state frontiers, has been regarded as one in which the factual basis for a rule of nonintervention has been irremediably eroded. The intention here is finally to inspect and to counter these arguments as they would dismiss the principle of nonintervention. The approach to them is made through the history of the idea of nonintervention as a principle, a theory, and in the practice of states, and the focus is upon the part which the principle played and might be said still to play in the maintenance of international order.

The study was written as a doctoral dissertation for the Department of International Relations of the Research School of Pacific Studies at the Australian National University in Canberra. It was revised for publication during a year I spent as a Visiting Fellow in the Center of International Studies at Princeton University. To Professors Hedley Bull and J.D.B. Miller in Canberra, I owe a great debt for their inspiration, criticism, and encouragement. I should also like to thank the other members of the Department of International Relations in Canberra who helped me with various parts of the book, and in particular Mr. J.L.S. Girling, Dr. Carsten Holbraad, Mr. Geoffrey Jukes, and Sir Alan Watt. To Dr. Hugh Smith now of the Royal Military College, Duntroon, I am grateful for many hours of stimulating discussion and criticism. At Princeton, I should like to thank Professor Cyril E. Black for the generosity of the Center of International Studies, and I owe a special debt to Professor Richard A. Falk who read the manuscript twice and made important criticisms and suggestions.

Professor Julius Stone and Mr. Upendra Baxi of the Sydney University Law School, the late Sir Kenneth Bailey of the Department of Foreign Affairs in Canberra, and Mr. P. Brazil of the Attorney General's Department in Canberra, all found time to see me, and many problems were clarified in discussion with them. My thanks are also due to Professor John Norton Moore of the University of Virginia Law School, Professor P. A. Reynolds of Lancaster University, and Professor Georg Schwarzenberger of University College, London, each of whom read the manuscript and made useful criticisms.

To Angela, above all, my thanks.

R. J. Vincent

Princeton, New Jersey
February 1973

PART ONE

Definition

ONE

DEFINITION: INTERVENTION AND THE
PRINCIPLE OF NONINTERVENTION

Intervention is a word used to describe an event, something which happens in international relations: it is not just an idea which crops up in speculation about them. The event might take a form as significant as the entry of one state into a violent conflict within another state or as apparently insignificant as an ill-chosen remark made by a statesman about the affairs of a foreign state. The fact that the same word is used to describe such diverse phenomena turns the focus of attention from intervention as an event to intervention as a concept, in order to decide what it is that is common to each case. This is the task of definition and three general observations about it arise from these statements. In the first place, because intervention is a word used to describe events in the real world, and not a purely abstract concept, freedom to stipulate an arbitrary definition is limited. Second, because intervention is a term used to describe such a broad range of activities in international relations, it is unlikely that any definition can capture the whole of reality. And in the third place, disagreement about the concept of intervention, about the sorts of activity that are to be called intervention and what it is that makes them similar, casts doubt upon any idea that painstaking research could uncover the essential meaning of intervention.

Without losing sight of these observations, this chapter will attempt to point out the major features of intervention, before going on to say what is meant by the principle of nonintervention. Believing that established usage, however obscure and contradictory, provides the principal clue to the location of intervention as an event in international relations, it will analyze that usage by breaking down the idea of intervention into six component parts. The analysis will distinguish an actor that embarks upon intervention, a target that suffers it, the activity of intervention itself, the types of intervention, the purposes of the activity, and the context in which it takes place. This should provide a crude outline of the sort of animal that intervention is in international relations; and

3

that is the object of the exercise—to fix its place in knowledge about international relations, and not to discover a legal definition which might satisfy those who seek to restrain its occurrence by law.[1]

I

i. Actors

Someone, some entity, or group, undertakes intervention. It might be a state—Britain intervened in Greek affairs when she dispatched a naval squadron to Greek waters in 1850 in search of redress for an alleged wrong done to one of her citizens. It might be a revolutionary group within a state, a group enjoying the tacit support of its government, as was the case with the adventures of Generals Mathews and Jackson in Florida during the second decade of the nineteenth century. It might be a revolutionary group within a state, whose existence and interventionary activity are not only embarrassing to its government but positively dangerous to its survival, as in recent years with the Palestinian Arabs in Jordan.[2]

[1] On the difference between "logical" and "legal" definition, see Julius Stone, *Aggression and World Order*, Berkeley, Calif., 1958, pp. 84–86. On the search for a legal definition in the United Nations General Assembly, see below Chapter Seven, section III. In a recent study, John Norton Moore criticizes the sort of definition to be advanced here as too narrow in not being explicitly related to the values at stake in interventionary situations. He argues that definition ought to be related to the reasons for our concern about intervention, the policies principally at stake being "self-determination, the protection of human rights, and the maintenance of world order." See "The Control of Foreign Intervention in Internal Conflict," in Moore, *Law and the Indo-China War*, Princeton, N.J., 1972, pp. 119–130. While no study of intervention would be adequate unless it took such values into account, this seems to be an exercise separate from the task of definition, involving a discussion of types, purposes, and contexts of intervention once the concept itself has been identified. But see the article at the place cited for a valuable discussion of the problem of definition.

[2] In both these cases of intervention set in motion by a revolutionary group within a state, it is the state itself which is held responsible for the action. Spain looked to the government of the United States to curb the actions of her dissident generals, Israel to the government of Jordan. Any rules about intervention in international relations are applied to states and the organizations established between them. Though some would have them so, revolutionary groups within states are not formal actors in the international system, and rules of international law apply to them only through the intermediary of the state.

Intervention might be the action of a group of states, as when the powers of Europe presided over the separation of Belgium from Holland in the 1830's. And in the modern world, regional and universal international organizations have taken their place as possible intervening actors, even if only at the prompting of a principal power—the Organization of American States in the Dominican Republic and the United Nations in the Congo.[3]

ii. The Target of Intervention

The description of the target of intervention, the thing which is having something done to it by an outside actor,[4] identifies that target not merely as a sovereign state, but traditionally seeks to indicate that part of the target at which the intervention is aimed. Thus customary definitions of intervention distinguish two broad destinations for the activity of intervention: the domestic affairs of a state and its external affairs (the relations it has with another state or states).[5] This is a useful distinction in that it is sensitive to the difference between an "external" act which addresses itself to a state's foreign relations, and an "internal" act which seeks to penetrate and meddle in the domestic arrangements of a state. American intervention in the First World War had as its aim the defeat of Germany. Allied intervention in Russia in 1918 was justified on the same ground, but after the defeat of Germany, a second and internal target of the intervention was revealed to be the defeat of the Russian Revolution.

[3] For the view that the legitimacy of intervention is partly determined by the nature of the intervening actor, see Richard A. Falk, "On Legislative Intervention by the United Nations in the Internal Affairs of Sovereign States," in Falk, *Legal Order in a Violent World*, Princeton, N.J., 1968, pp. 336–353. For a discussion of this view see below, Chapter Eight, section II, and Chapter Nine, section VI.

[4] The target of any intervention is also an actor in international politics, albeit one playing a diminished role because of the outside interference it is suffering. The choice of the term "actors" for those who undertake intervention should not be taken to mean that targets are not also actors in some sense.

[5] W. E. Hall, *A Treatise on International Law*, ed. A. Pearce Higgins, 8th ed. (Oxford, 1924), p. 337; T. J. Lawrence, *Principles of International Law*, ed. P. H. Winfield, 7th ed., London, 1925, p. 119; L. Oppenheim, *International Law*, ed. H. Lauterpacht, 8th ed., 2 vols., London, 1955, Vol. I, *Peace*, p. 305; Ann van Wynen Thomas and A. J. Thomas, Jr., *Non-Intervention*, Dallas, Tex., 1956, p. 71; Charles G. Fenwick, *International Law*, 4th ed., New York, 1965, p. 288, n. 54.

But the distinction between internal and external intervention is not always so clear. Was American intervention in the Lebanon in 1958 internal intervention to shore up a shaky pro-Western regime against threats from within, or external intervention to ward off threats from abroad?[6] Moreover, external affairs are the stuff of international relations, and to identify them as a target for intervention tends to lose any characteristics peculiar to that event in the general clamor of relations between states. It may be that a better view of the target of intervention is afforded by reference to a concept favored by the framers of the Charter of the United Nations—domestic jurisdiction. If there are matters of purely domestic concern, defined either

> geographically as matters taking place within the territory of a state, personally as matters concerning individuals within the jurisdiction of a state, functionally as matters which could be dealt with conveniently and efficiently by states individually, or politically as matters which could be dealt with by states individually without affecting the interests of others,[7]

then it might be said that intervention occurs whenever any of these matters is made the object of intrusion by a foreign state. But neither is this concept altogether helpful, for the boundaries of domestic jurisdiction are themselves hazy, and the confident assertion that any matter is a domestic question might be confounded in time by international practice.[8]

Here, the broad notion of domestic affairs will be relied upon to identify the target of intervention, and it will be taken to exclude the application of the label "intervention" to the entry of a state into a war between other states, and to include as "intervention" the participation of a state in a conflict taking place within another state. To sharpen the perception of the target it may be added that it is the authority structure of the state suffering intervention. In-

[6] Martin Wight, "Western Values in International Relations," in H. Butterfield and M. Wight, eds., *Diplomatic Investigations*, London, 1966, p. 112.

[7] Quincy Wright, *International Law and the United Nations*, Bombay, 1960, p. 63.

[8] In its Advisory Opinion on Nationality Decrees in Tunis and Morocco of February 7, 1923, the Permanent Court of International Justice observed that: "The question whether a certain matter is or is not solely within the jurisdiction of a state is an essentially relative question; it depends upon the development of international relations," cited in M. S. Rajan, *United Nations and Domestic Jurisdiction*, Calcutta, 1958, p. 37.

tervention is directed at the "identity of those who make the decisions that are binding for the entire society and/or to the processes through which such decisions are made."[9]

iii. The Activity of Intervention

An actor intervenes and a target suffers the intervention; the activity of intervention itself is the "doing-word" of the relationship. Intervention might be a "coming-between" or an "interposition." The mediation by a third party of a dispute between two states would conform to this definition, as would a military operation to separate two feuding parties in a civil war or in a war between states. More generally, intervention might be a "stepping-in" or an "interference" in any affair so as to affect its course or outcome.[10] This definition could encompass the situation in which intervention takes place on behalf of one party to a dispute, as well as the activity of coming-between the parties.

Many scholars have sought to define intervention by using the synonym "interference."[11] Not just interference but "dictatorial interference," Oppenheim thought, was the characteristic that set intervention apart from other sorts of activity.[12] Others have identified the imposition of the will of one state on that of another, the attempt to compel or coerce the sovereign will of another state, as the "essence" of intervention.[13] But these definitions are entirely satisfactory only if the words "interference," "dictatorial," and "coercive" are readily understandable in the context of international politics. Interference might be defined as action taken to affect the actions of others, dictatorial interference as action taken to prescribe the actions of others. The crucial, but in international relations elusive, distinction for Oppenheim's definition is that between affecting some action and prescribing its course. The notion of coercion might clarify this distinction by introducing the idea of force. To coerce is to "constrain or restrain by application of superior force or by authority resting on force; to constrain to

<hr>

[9] James N. Rosenau, "Intervention as a Scientific Concept," *Journal of Conflict Resolution*, Vol. XIII, No. 2, June 1969, p. 163.

[10] Both these meanings of intervention—that of "coming-between" and "stepping-in"—appear in the *Oxford English Dictionary*.

[11] See, e.g., Winfield in Lawrence, p. 119; Fenwick, p. 288, n. 54; Hall, p. 337.

[12] Oppenheim, Vol. I, p. 305.

[13] Lawrence, p. 119; Thomas and Thomas, p. 72.

compliance or obedience by forcible means."[14] Coercive interference, then, might identify intervention by its use or threat of force. But this distinction also has its shortcomings; it can be objected that it is at once too inclusive and too exclusive. Too inclusive because in any case of interference by a great power in the affairs of a small power, the small power can plausibly claim that that activity was coercive due to the implicit threat of force which a powerful state can hold over a weak state. Too exclusive because to confine the label "intervention" to activity which uses or threatens force in international relations might fail to capture the reality of dictatorial behavior in spheres like that of international economic relations.

Here, no pretense will be made to encompass the whole field of interventionary activity in a single definition, and intervention will be understood as coercive interference. The use or threat of force will be taken as a guide to the incidence of intervention. And the idea of "stepping-in," of something imported into a situation from outside, will link the use or threat of force to its destination in the authority structure of the target of intervention. Further, if such "stepping-in" is a distinguishing feature of intervention in international politics, so also is "stepping-out" after the objective of intervention has been achieved or it has failed. Though intervention is a perennial feature of international politics in the sense that interventions are always occurring, each intervention is a discrete act; an intervention made permanent becomes something else. Thus Rosenau speaks of one of the defining characteristics of intervention as its "convention-breaking" nature; it breaks an established pattern of conduct in international relations and either terminates in the reestablishment of that pattern or itself becomes conventional.[15] Intervention might take place in the interests of the balance of power, but it is not a permanent feature of relations between states in the sense that the balance of power itself is.

iv. The Types of Intervention

It might be possible to shed light on intervention as a type of activity by setting it apart from other types of activity, by pointing out what it is not rather than indicating what it is. Thus some writers have referred to intervention as a type of activity which is to be distinguished from war; they have sought to place it in a spectrum

[14] *Oxford English Dictionary.*
[15] Rosenau, pp. 161–163.

between war or the aggressive crossing of international frontiers at the one end and mere diplomatic pressure at the other.[16] As to the distinction between intervention and war, Hall wrote that

> . . . regarded from the point of view of the state intruded upon, it [intervention] must always remain an act which, if not consented to, is an act of war. But from the point of view of the intervening power it is . . . a measure of prevention or of police, undertaken sometimes for the express purpose of avoiding war . . . it may be a pacific measure, which becomes war in the intention of its authors only when resistance is offered. . . . Hence although intervention often ends in war, and is sometimes really war from the commencement, it may be conveniently considered abstractedly from the pacific or belligerent character which it assumes in different cases.[17]

Here Hall seems to be saying that the distinction between intervention and war is not of the utmost importance and that intervention can be studied by the use of criteria which do not depend on such a distinction. Clearly, the scale of American intervention in Vietnam makes it difficult to distinguish between intervention and war on the basis of the intensity of the conflict. The difference between diplomatic pressure and intervention may be clearer, though the *caveats* about interference as opposed to dictatorial interference apply here, and it may be preferable to rely on the "convention-breaking" formula to distinguish them rather than on the degree of intensity of the pressure.

Intervention is a type of activity, and there are also types of intervention. Military intervention might be one such type, taking place when troops are dispatched to keep order or to support a revolution in a foreign state, or when military aid is given to a government whose internal position is insecure or which is in conflict with a neighboring state. It has also been argued that the very presence or display of armed force, such as the location of the American Sixth Fleet in the Mediterranean Sea, has an effect on the politics of the littoral states tantamount to intervention in their affairs.[18] Economic intervention might constitute another type of intervention, occurring when strings are attached by the great to aid given to the small or when an economically developed state

---

[16] See, e.g., D. A. Graber, *Crisis Diplomacy*, Washington, 1959, p. 1.
[17] Hall, p. 337.
[18] P. Calvocoressi, *World Order and New States*, London, 1962, p. 17.

denies a contract to an underdeveloped primary-producing state. Various sorts of political intervention might be said to take place when hostile propaganda is disseminated abroad, when moral support is lent to a revolutionary struggle within another state, when recognition is refused to an established government, or when a member-state of the Commonwealth insists on discussing the internal affairs of another member at a prime ministers' conference.

Not all these activities conform to a definition of intervention as coercive interference aimed at the authority structure of a target state, and two doubtful cases of intervention may be singled out for attention. One view has it that intervention is of the nature of the international system, not in the sense that the nature of the system suggests that states will intervene in each other's affairs from time to time, but in the sense that it is built into the system. Where states weak and strong coexist, "[a] Great Power intervenes in the domestic realm of other states . . . by its sheer existence."[19] A similar view holds that the choice of a policy of nonintervention by a state which has the power to intervene is one form of intervention.[20] Certainly the policies of the great are of continuous and anxious interest to the small, certainly the failure of the democracies to intervene in the Spanish Civil War sped the victory of Franco, and certainly it is difficult to define precisely the notion of intervention. But if either of these two views were accepted, it would be difficult to distinguish intervention from international politics in general.

It is not possible to consider any one case as the ideal type of intervention and to measure other posited cases against that ideal type. The job of distinguishing between types of intervention is one of classification and not of definition; it assumes that the genus of intervention has been identified and goes on to locate the various species of that genus. Political, military, and economic intervention might be such species, but they do not define the genus.

v. The Purpose of Intervention

The purpose of intervention is the end toward which it is directed, the thing which it is designed to achieve. At the outset of the Peloponnesian War, the Athenians sent a fleet to aid Corcyra

[19] Manfred Halpern, "The Morality and Politics of Intervention," in Falk, ed., *The Vietnam War and International Law*, Princeton, N.J., 1968, p. 41.
[20] Falk, "On Legislative Intervention by the United Nations," in Falk, *Legal Order in a Violent World*, p. 341.

against Corinth in order that the Corcyrean fleet should not pass into the hands of the Corinthians and turn the balance of power against Athens.[21] France intervened in Syria in 1860 in order to save the Christian Maronite tribes of the Lebanon from the ravages of the Moslem Druses, an act which has been called one of "pure humanity" when the troops dispatched might have been needed elsewhere at any time.[22] The Soviet Union and her allies intervened in Czechoslovakia in 1968 to defend the socialist gains of the Czechoslovak people and the interests of the entire communist movement.

The balance of power, the interests of humanity, and the maintenance of ideological solidarity are but three of the ends which states have pursued by intervention, and it might be argued that the compilation of a catalog of purposes of intervention is of little value in defining intervention, because it would tend to become a general account of states' motives for action in foreign policy. To many international lawyers, however, the purpose served by any intervention has been a fundamental criterion in the assessment of its legality. Thus, if intervention takes place for the purpose of forcing a delinquent state to submit to recognized rules of international law or to punish a breach of the law or to neutralize the illegal intervention of another, then it has been argued that it is lawful activity.[23] At this point, the notion of intervention has become confused in legal thought by the reluctance to call a lawful act "intervention." Whenever an intervention can be said to take place by right, Oppenheim argues that it never constitutes a violation of external independence or territorial supremacy.[24] But his definition of intervention refers to "dictatorial interference" in the internal or external affairs of a state, and dictatorial interference clearly implies a violation of external independence or territorial supremacy. This is the core of the confusion between the use of the word intervention as a description of an event in international relations and its use as a normative expression by international

[21] In R. Warner's translation, chapter 4 of Thucydides' *History of the Peloponnesian War*, Harmondsworth, 1954, is entitled "Athenian Intervention against Corinth."

[22] Sir A. W. Ward and G. P. Gooch, eds., *The Cambridge History of British Foreign Policy 1783–1919*, Vol. II *1815–1866*, Cambridge, 1923, p. 456.

[23] Oppenheim, Vol. I, p. 305; Winfield in Lawrence, p. 119; Hall, p. 342. For a fuller discussion, see below, Chapter Eight, section I.

[24] Oppenheim, Vol. I, p. 305.

11

lawyers. If intervention by right is held not to violate the independence of the target state, a violation which features in most definitions as the thing which above all differentiates intervention from other phenomena, then is it to be understood that intervention by right is not intervention? However difficult it may prove, there can be no objection to attempting to distinguish lawful from unlawful intervention, but the attempt is not advanced by excluding "lawful intervention" from the class of events called intervention.

Like identifying types of intervention, distinguishing between interventions according to their purpose is a task of classification and not of definition.[25] Two factors make the task problematical. In the first place, any one case of intervention might combine several purposes. The purpose of British, French, and Russian intervention in Turkish affairs, culminating in the battle of Navarino in 1827, might be said to have been the achievement of Greek independence. But sympathy for the Greek nation or for Greek co-religionists was combined with abhorrence at Turkish behavior in the Morea, the interest in peace between Greece and Turkey, and the concern of each great power with the action of the others and for the European balance. If this example demonstrates the problem of choosing between different purposes, a second difficulty lies in the choice between different versions of purpose. The real motive of the intervening state, if such a notion is an intelligible one, might differ from the purpose proclaimed in the official justification and from the leisured assessment of the scholar after the event. The task of classification seems to be as hazardous as that of definition.

vi. The Context of Intervention

The incidence of intervention might vary with the nature of the international system. A system that contains within it states widely different in power might witness more frequent interventions than a system of approximately equal states. A revolutionary international system, in which revisionist movements challenge the *status quo* might likewise be a greater encouragement to intervention than a system composed of satisfied, conservative powers. And a system

[25] Though the preoccupation with ideological conflict during the Cold War allowed one writer to define intervention as "the use of force by the United States, directly or indirectly, in order to prevent what is believed to be the likelihood of Communist assumption of power in a state, or in order to overthrow an established Communist regime." H. S. Dinerstein, *Intervention Against Communism*, Baltimore, 1967, p. 3.

in which small states, within which political authority is under constant challenge, exist alongside great powers, might offer opportunities for outside intervention not available in a system composed of states having stable regimes.[26]

Again, the observation that intervention is more likely to occur, or to be more frequent, in one sort of international system rather than another, is not one germane to the task of defining intervention, and its examination can properly be left for later analysis.[27]

From this survey of customary definitions it is now possible to select an approximate definition of intervention as that activity undertaken by a state, a group within a state, a group of states or an international organization which interferes coercively in the domestic affairs of another state. It is a discrete event having a beginning and an end, and it is aimed at the authority structure of the target state. It is not necessarily lawful or unlawful, but it does break a conventional pattern of international relations. This definition will be used as a guide to cases of intervention in history, but it will not be imposed on that history to the exclusion of doctrines of intervention and nonintervention which have not relied upon the notion of coercion. What will be adhered to more strictly is the notion of intrusion in domestic affairs; intervention will not be taken to mean either simply participation in world politics or entry into a war between other states.

II

Intervention having been defined, nonintervention might be said to be the circumstance in which intervention does not occur. But beyond the accident of nonintervention, a state might be said to follow a policy of nonintervention when it chooses not to intervene in a situation where intervention also is a possible policy. Publicists have expounded theories of nonintervention which assert the desirability of states refraining from intervention from the point of view of the achievement of peace between states, or of providing for the best interests of a particular state.[28] And international

[26] For a discussion of intervention in the context of different international systems, see Oran R. Young, "Intervention and International Systems," *Journal of International Affairs*, Vol. XXII, No. 2, 1968, pp. 177–187.

[27] For which, in relation particularly to the differences between a system in which power is polarized and a system displaying a balance of power among many, see below, Chapter Nine, section IV.

[28] See below, Chapter Three.

lawyers have asserted nonintervention as a principle, a rule which states are obliged to adhere to in their relations with each other.[29]

A rule is an imperative which prescribes a particular form of action or restraint as the legitimate form of conduct for a certain class of people or institutions. It identifies a standard of behavior and makes conformity to such a standard obligatory for the class to which it applies. The rule of nonintervention can be said to derive from and require respect for the principle of state sovereignty. Sovereignty can be a statement expressing the idea that "there is a final and absolute political authority in the political community" and that *"no final and absolute authority exists elsewhere."*[30] Where such final and absolute authorities are collected together in international society, it can be said that the recognition by each of them of the others' authority within their own domains—recognition of a principle of state sovereignty—is fundamental to their coexistence. If a state has a right to sovereignty, this implies that other states have a duty to respect that right by, among other things, refraining from intervention in its domestic affairs. The principle of nonintervention identifies the right of states to sovereignty as a standard in international society and makes explicit the respect required for it in abstention from intervention.

The function of the principle of nonintervention in international relations might be said, then, to be one of protecting the principle of state sovereignty. "Protect" here is used metaphorically; it is not the rule itself which functions as protector, it merely indicates or draws attention to that which is to be protected. The will on the part of states to make the rule effective is the force which provides the protection, and that willingness might be encouraged by three extralegal factors. In the first place, states might feel obliged to obey rules out of a sense of moral duty. Second, they might adhere to rules through a calculation that it is in their interests to do so, and third, they might be forced into obedience to rules.[31] An account of the promise of each of these factors as inducements to rule-determined behavior by states will emerge from the study of the practice of states with regard to the principle of nonintervention.

[29] See below, Chapter Two.

[30] F. H. Hinsley, *Sovereignty*, London, 1966, p. 26 (Hinsley's emphasis).

[31] Stanley Hoffman, "International Law and the Control of Force," in Karl W. Deutsch and Stanley Hoffman, eds., *The Relevance of International Law*, Cambridge, Mass., 1968, p. 25.

Pursuing further the idea of the function of the nonintervention principle as protector of state sovereignty, it has been called a "doctrinal mechanism to express the outer limits of permissible influence that one state may properly exert upon another."[32] It might be said to stand at the frontier between diplomatic pressure which is tolerable to the pressured and various degrees of coercion which are not. The idea of frontier, in more than just a geographical sense, is a useful one. The principle of nonintervention might serve to delimit the border between the domain of international law and that of municipal law. In the same way, the matters which Article 2(7) of the Charter leaves to domestic jurisdiction have the principle of nonintervention as their guardian against the extension of the competence of the United Nations. And for long before the San Francisco Conference in 1945, one of the primary roles for the principle of nonintervention was for it to be invoked on behalf of the independence of states against the development or establishment of a superstate.[33]

It might be objected that this notion of frontier or of various frontiers fails to make it clear whether it is the function of the principle of nonintervention to define them or whether the principle shifts to frontiers defined by other criteria. In effect, the two are complementary. To ask what areas the principle of nonintervention protects is equivalent to asking what matters are within the domestic jurisdiction of states.[34] Castlereagh's principle of nonintervention was also a doctrine of intervention. By specifying the circumstances in which Britain would feel obliged to intervene, he pointed out what was meant by the principle of nonintervention.[35] Similarly, during its debates on the question of *apartheid*, the General Assembly's interpretation of Article 2(7) determined the actual limits of South Africa's extreme interpretation of the principle of nonintervention. The frontiers protected by the principle of nonintervention are unclear at any one time, they vary over time, and they are defined differently by different statesmen— Castlereagh or Palmerston, Theodore or Franklin Roosevelt,

[32] Falk, "United States Practice and the Doctrine of Non-intervention in the Internal Affairs of Sovereign States," in *Legal Order in a Violent World*, p. 159.

[33] For Canning on the Holy Alliance, see below, Chapter Four, section II(ii).

[34] Falk, "U.S. Practice and the Doctrine of Non-intervention," p. 159.

[35] See below Chapter Four, section II(i).

15

Khrushchev or Brezhnev. But the idea of frontier remains a helpful one, not least for international law, in establishing the convention that there are frontiers which states must have good reason
to cross. This is not to make the mistake of supposing that any
crossing of frontiers is unlawful, for there may be circumstances
in which it is both lawful and moral to intervene. What follows
will, in large part, examine the place of the principle of nonintervention in international relations by studying the occasions on
which it has been overridden.

PART TWO

The History of the Idea
of Nonintervention

The chapters of this part will consider the history of the idea of nonintervention from three aspects: as a principle, a theory, and in the practice of states. The discussion of nonintervention as a principle will seek the derivation of the rule through the treatises on international law. The study of nonintervention as a theory will examine the doctrines of writers, other than international lawyers, who have urged the principle as a rule of conduct which might serve the interests of a particular state or the interest of all states in peace, or who have speculated about the conditions in which the principle might be workable as a norm of relations between states. Theory will be treated not as an attempt to account for behavior in international relations, but as a proposal about what form that behavior should take. The examination of nonintervention in the practice of states will be concerned with the extent to which states have acted according to the rule, with doctrines developed by statesmen about nonintervention, and with the function the principle fulfilled in their foreign policies.

The uniting thread of these three aspects is the idea of nonintervention as an imperative of international conduct. Tracing the derivation of the principle answers the question: Why is there such an imperative in international law? The inquiry into theories of nonintervention answers the question: Why observe the rule? And the examination of state practice answers the question: Have states in fact observed the rule? These distinctions are not meant to suggest that international lawyers are not also theorists, or that statesmen are pragmatists unblemished by theory—indeed pragmatism is itself a theory—or that theorists are necessarily far removed from the realities of international life. But the chapters will be organized according to the distinction between Christian Wolff's principle of nonintervention as part of his vision of international law, Richard Cobden's espousal of a doctrine of nonintervention as the principle which should have informed the conduct of British foreign policy in opposition to England's actual behavior in international relations, and the principle of nonintervention as it informed the actual conduct of American foreign policy in the hands of John Quincy Adams.

TWO

PRINCIPLE

I

A principle or rule has been so far understood as an imperative which makes a particular form of action or restraint obligatory for a certain class of people or institutions. Thus the principle of non-intervention is an imperative requiring states to refrain from interference in each other's affairs. This rule, we have seen, is implied by the principle that states shall respect one another's sovereignty.[1] And this derivation illustrates the dual function of the principle of state sovereignty—as a principle according to which authority is allocated in international relations, requiring thereby a particular pattern of behavior, and as an hypothesis or proposition in the science of international law, a first principle from which a number of other rules may be derived. We shall see how often international lawyers of whatever school of thought returned to this first principle for their accounts of the international law of intervention.

In discussing the genesis of the principle of nonintervention, it is possible to make a broad distinction between the formulations of the naturalist international lawyers, on the one hand, and the positivist school of international law, on the other. While the Naturalists conceived of law as a body of rules inherent in the nature of man and of the universe, discoverable by the use of "right reason," the Positivists sought rules of international law by observation of the actual practice of states. For the Naturalists, the rights and duties of man, and of states as collections of men, were no more than their natural inheritance as men or states. For the Positivists, on the other hand, a right or a duty could have meaning only if it were sanctioned by custom or by a treaty between states.[2] Perhaps Westlake caught the essence of the distinction between the two schools of thought when he identified an Anglo-Saxon tradition of law which would think primarily of rules and then of rights as

[1] See above, Chapter One, p. 14.

[2] This is only one, and for the present purpose the most important one, of the many distinctions between Naturalism and Positivism. For a list of others see H.L.A. Hart, *The Concept of Law*, Oxford, 1961, p. 253.

measured by them, while the continental tradition would tend to think primarily of rights and then of rules which embodied them.[3]

The significance of this difference of approach with respect to the principle of nonintervention is not that one school asserted the existence of such a rule and the other denied it, for a right to state sovereignty was conceded by both schools, if for different reasons. Indeed, the similarities between the two schools of thought in their arrival at the same destination—a rule of nonintervention—might be more important than the different routes taken thither. If a generalization is at all possible, it would be that the positivist approach, with its greater attention to the actual practice of states, was more tentative in its formulation of rules than a naturalism informed by supposedly immutable law.

i. The Naturalists

Natural law for the lawyer or the political scientist, as opposed to the natural scientist, is about "ought" not about "is." It is about right conduct discoverable by human reason, not about the description of cause and effect in the natural world. There is, however, a third interpretation of the phrase "law of nature" which, although it uses the language of the lawyer, sets out to frame the hypothesis of the scientist. Thus, for Hobbes, a law of nature was "a precept or a general rule, found out by reason, by which a man is forbidden to do that which is destructive of his life."[4] This is clearly an injunction about what men ought to do, but it is also, as Hobbes goes on to explain, an imperative without which (among other imperatives) civil society would be impossible. If this hypothesis is right, if there are certain rules of conduct without which social life would be impossible, then these rules form what has been called the "minimum content of Natural Law"[5] in a sense which is closer to that of the scientist than that of the lawyer. In the fourth place, it is possible to understand the phrase "law of nature" as describing the rules which are said to apply in the hypothetical state of nature before the establishment of civil society. For Hobbes, no such rules could apply in a condition in which every man was at war with every man, but only a right of nature by which every man is at liberty to use his own power to

[3] John Westlake, *The Collected Papers of John Westlake on International Law*, ed. L. Oppenheim, Cambridge, 1914, p. xxvi.

[4] Thomas Hobbes, *Leviathan*, ed. M. Oakeshott, Oxford, 1946, p. 84.

[5] Hart, pp. 188–189. See also below, Chapter Nine, section II.

preserve himself in a situation of *sauve qui peut*.[6] But Pufendorf and later Wolff and Vattel were to imagine a state of nature in which man's natural condition was one of peace not war, where the obligations of natural law were applicable whatever the social circumstances in which man found himself.[7] Hobbes shared with these later Naturalists, the view that kings and persons of sovereign authority existed together in a state of nature; he differed from them in the conclusions he drew from the existence of such a condition.

To identify, then, a naturalist school of thought, is not to impute to its members a oneness of outlook. First, with respect to the nonintervention principle, it is possible to represent such a rule as a "dictate of right reason" which follows from the natural independence of states. In the second place, it can be argued that a rule of nonintervention is an imperative without which a society of sovereign states would be an impossibility. Third and more generally, the notion of a law of nature has been sufficiently elastic to incorporate the view that would deny the possibility of rules operating between states existing in a state of nature and the directly contrary view that states in such a condition are obliged to obey natural law. In spite of these contending opinions about the content of natural law, it is possible to link them together by means of the negative criterion that the differences within the school of thought are less significant, given the present purpose of seeking the origin of the rule of nonintervention, than those which divide the Naturalists from other schools of thought.

From what sources, then, did the Naturalists derive the principle of nonintervention? Grotius, Hobbes, and Pufendorf can be regarded as precursors of the notion because their writings furnished ideas without which the principle could not have found expression in the form which it took in the works of Wolff and Vattel. In particular, Grotius can be taken as a precursor of the notion, because he conceived of international law as a law which existed between sovereign states; Hobbes and Pufendorf, in their radically different ways, contributed the ideas of natural equality and a state of nature.[8]

---

[6] Hobbes, p. 84.

[7] Samuel Pufendorf, *De Jure Naturae et Gentium*, 1688, trans. C. H. and W. A. Oldfather, New York, 1934, Bk. ii, Chap. ii, section 9. For Wolff and Vattel see below, pp. 26–31.

[8] This is not to suggest either that Grotius invented the concept of sov-

The task which Grotius set himself was to treat the law which was concerned with the mutual relations among states or rulers of states in a comprehensive and systematic manner.[9] He appreciated the fact of the separateness of states; the problem was to establish that a common law among them did exist, and the systematic answer to the problem was to be found primarily in the principles of natural law.[10]

Grotius identified the sovereign power as "that power . . . whose actions are not subject to the legal control of another," and observed that "the state is the common subject of sovereignty."[11] He did not draw, from this observation, the conclusion that states had a duty not to intervene in each other's affairs. The closest he came to advancing such a rule was in his denial that states had a right to intervene in the internal affairs of an ally, if the subjects of that ally claimed to have been wronged at the hands of their sovereign.[12] For, he argued, quoting Aristotle, alliances were concerned with preventing the perpetration of wrongs against any one of the allies, not with wrong-doing among the citizens of an allied state.[13]

Two reasons can be offered in explanation of Grotius' failure to accompany his right of sovereignty with a rule of nonintervention expressing respect for that sovereignty. The first is a technical one about the vocabulary of international law. Grotius, it has been argued, had no conception of intervention as an intermediate condition between peace and war; any act of violence by one state upon another was for him an act of war.[14] According to this view,

ereignty, or that Hobbes and Pufendorf were the first to conceive of a state of nature in which all men were equal. Rather, they can all be taken as very good examples of these views, and Grotius can be regarded as the first to have built a system of international law around the assumption of the sovereignty of states.

[9] Hugo Grotius, *De Jure Belli ac Pacis*, 1625, trans. of 1646 ed. by F. W. Kelsey et al., 1925, rept. New York, 1964, Prolegomena, para. 1.

[10] *Ibid.*, Prolegomena, paras. 28 and 30. By a law of nature, Grotius meant ". . . a dictate of right reason, which points out that an act, according as it is or is not in conformity with rational nature, has in it a quality of moral baseness or moral necessity; and that, in consequence, such an act is either forbidden or enjoined by the author of nature, God." *Ibid.*, Bk. I, Chap. I, section x, para. 1.

[11] *Ibid.*, Bk. I, Chap. III, section VII, para. 1.

[12] *Ibid.*, Bk. I, Chap. III, section XXI, para. 7.

[13] *Ibid.*, Bk. I, Chap. III, section XXI, para. 7.

[14] Winfield, "The History of Intervention in International Law," *British Yearbook of International Law*, Vol. III, 1922–1923, p. 132; Thomas and Thomas, *Non-Intervention*, p. 5.

it would be absurd to search for rules about intervention in a treatise which did not treat the matter as separable from the problem of war.

If, on the other hand, the separation of the concept of intervention from that of war is not regarded as a cardinal defining characteristic of intervention, the reason for the neglect of a rule of nonintervention by Grotius must be sought elsewhere. To locate it, it is necessary to return to Grotius' conception of the place of the state in international society. For Grotius, international society was a universal community of mankind; his natural law applied directly to individuals as well as to states.[15] The notion that states were the exclusive members of international society was a formulation of nineteenth-century international law, unknown to the seventeenth century. If the individual is as much a subject of international law as is a state, and if in any dispute his cause can be regarded as a just one, then service rendered on his behalf "is not only permissible, it is also honourable."[16] Though Grotius made a remarkable concession to the sovereign by denying his subjects the right to take up arms when wronged by him, he did not deny the right of others to take up arms on their behalf.[17]

Grotius' conception of international society made it impossible for him to establish a clear rule of nonintervention. At the same time, his assertion that it was possible to imagine a society formed between sovereign states (as well as between individuals) was an essential presupposition for later writers who did develop a principle of nonintervention.

Hobbes thought that all men in their natural condition were equal. The weakest among them had strength enough to kill the strongest either by subterfuge or by joining a confederacy with others.[18] As to faculties of mind, Hobbes found an even greater equality among men than that of strength, for prudence was but experience "which equal time, equally bestows on all men, in those things they equally apply themselves unto."[19] The three principal causes of quarrel inherent in the nature of man were competition, diffidence, and glory, and in a state of nature, the pursuit of these goals led to a war of all against all.[20] For Hobbes the end of this

---

[15] Hedley Bull, "The Grotian Conception of International Society," in Butterfield and Wight, *Diplomatic Investigations*, p. 68.

[16] Grotius, Bk. I, Chap. v, section II, para. 1; Bk. II, Chap. xxv, section VI.

[17] *Ibid.*, Bk. II, Ch. xxv, section VIII, para. 3.

[18] Hobbes, p. 80. [19] *Ibid.*, p. 80. [20] *Ibid.*, p. 81.

conflict could come about only through the establishment of civil society by means of a social contract which transferred men's natural right to govern themselves to the Leviathan in exchange for their security.[21] But states which had not united into an organized community remained in the state of nature, maintaining toward each other a posture of war;[22] the conception of a proper law existing between them in such a situation would be to Hobbes no more than an "inane phrase."[23] Hobbes' denial of international law has importance for the present study in two respects. First, it meant not only a denial of a society among states but also did away with the older notion of a *societas humana* built upon the individual. In the second place, Hobbes' conception of states existing together in a state of nature meant that they were equal not juridically but, like individual men in the state of nature, having equal claim to all goods or things.[24] This latter view opened the way to the doctrine of the absolute equality of states regarded as important by some publicists of the following century and instrumental in their formulations of a rule of nonintervention. The former view, while it did not admit of any sort of international society, can nevertheless be regarded as a progressive doctrine with respect to international law, by its perception of the participants in the international system being states not individuals. Hobbes' contention that a state of nature prevailing between sovereigns was a less miserable condition than that which prevailed among individuals, had the virtue of, at least beginning, to delineate the international environment as *sui generis*.

Pufendorf's state of nature was very different from that of Hobbes. The natural state of man which he imagined was one in which natural law, in the sense of obligatory rules of law, applied.[25] He denied the Hobbesian war of all against all because even those who lived in a state of nature could, should, and frequently did, lead a mutual social life.[26] Pufendorf saw the equality of strength which Hobbes proposed as "more likely to restrain the will to do harm than to urge it on. . . . For . . . neither gains as much from

[21] *Ibid.*, Chap. XVII.   [22] *Ibid.*, p. 83.

[23] A. Nussbaum, *A Concise History of the Law of Nations*, rev. ed., New York, 1954, p. 146.

[24] P. H. Kooijmans, *The Doctrine of the Legal Equality of States*, Leyden, 1964, pp. 71–75.

[25] Pufendorf, Bk. II, Chap. II, section 3.

[26] *Ibid.*, Bk. II, Chap. II, section 5.

25

victory as the one loses who is killed."[27] Nor, he argued, were things so scarce, that struggle for them would always be necessary.[28] Because man could take heed of his reason, the natural state of man was not one of war but of peace, a peace founded upon natural law.[29] The basis of natural law was for Pufendorf, as it had been for Grotius, the necessity for man to be sociable because of his individual helplessness.[30] The Hobbesian right of self-preservation still applied, but it was not to be so emphasized as to eclipse the possibility of social life between men.[31]

Pufendorf thought that since human nature belonged equally to all men and no one could live a social life with a person by whom he was not rated as at least a fellow man, it followed as a precept of natural law, that "every man should esteem and treat another man as his equal by nature, or as much a man as he is himself."[32] He regarded Hobbes' assertion of equality of strength and in faculties of the mind as not only wrong, but also irrelevant, for whatever the differences or similarities in wealth and the goods of body or mind, men were equal in liberty and before the law. This "equality of right" had its origin in the fact that an obligation to cultivate a social life was equally binding on all men, since it was an integral part of human nature as such.[33]

Pufendorf's doctrine of equality is a classical example of the derivation of a prescriptive statement from a descriptive statement; he argued that because men were equal as men, they ought therefore to treat each other as equals, or as much men as themselves. And as Pufendorf drew the same analogy as Hobbes had between men in a state of nature and states in that condition,[34] the principle of equality obtained in the relations between states as it did in those between men. The principle of equality now had a juristic quality as an imperative which men and states ought to observe in their relations with each other, as contrasted with Hobbes' observation that men and states were factually equal.

The principle of nonintervention finds its first explicit manifestation in the writings of Wolff and Vattel, although neither of them used the word "intervention" in the technical sense it was

[27] *Ibid.*, Bk. II, Chap. II, section 8.   [28] *Ibid.*, Bk. II, Chap. II, section 8.
[29] *Ibid.*, Bk. II, Chap. II, section 9.
[30] *Ibid.*, Bk. II, Chap. III, sections 14 and 15.
[31] *Ibid.*, Bk. II, Chap. III, section 16.
[32] *Ibid.*, Bk. III, Chap. II, section 1.   [33] *Ibid.*, Bk. III, Chap. II, section 2.
[34] *Ibid.*, Bk. II, Chap. III, section 23.

to acquire in the works of nineteenth-century publicists.[35] Like Hobbes and Pufendorf before him, Christian Wolff regarded nations as individual free persons living in a state of nature, a condition in which nations, like individuals, used none other than natural law.[36] According to that immutable, necessary law, nations were bound by perfect obligations to themselves and by imperfect obligations to other nations, and from these duties followed natural rights which were imprescriptible.[37] In order to bring this system closer to the real world, Wolff invented a *civitas maxima*, a great society which was supposed to have come about by a quasi-agreement between nations from which the voluntary law of nations could be derived.[38]

Wolff took over Pufendorf's principle of natural equality. He argued that:

> By nature all nations are equal the one to the other. For nations are considered as individual free persons living in a state of nature. Since by nature all men are equal, all nations too are by nature equal the one to the other. . . . Just as the tallest man is no more a man than the dwarf, so also a nation, however small, is no less a nation than the greatest nation. Therefore, since the moral equality of men has no relation to the size of their bodies, the moral equality of nations has no relation to the number of men of which they are composed.[39]

Their rights and obligations were then also by nature the same.[40] Here again rights and duties are derived from the notion that a state *is* equal to another state and therefore *ought* to be treated as such; factual inequalities between states are not considered relevant.

Wolff is taken to be the author of an absolute principle of non-intervention.[41] He did argue that "[b]y nature no nation has the

[35] Winfield, "The History of Intervention in International Law," pp. 132–133.

[36] Christian Wolff, *Ius Gentium Methodo Scientifica Pertractatum*, 1764, trans. Joseph H. Drake, 1934, rept. New York, 1964, Prolegomena, paras. 2 and 3.

[37] *Ibid.*, O. Nippold's introduction, p. xxxix.

[38] *Ibid.*, Prolegomena, paras. 9–12.

[39] *Ibid.*, Prolegomena, para. 16.   [40] *Ibid.*, Prolegomena, para. 17.

[41] Thomas and Thomas, *Non-Intervention*, p. 5; Wight, "Western Values in International Relations," in Butterfield and Wight, *Diplomatic Investigations*, p. 113.

right to any act which belongs to the exercise of the sovereignty of another nation, for sovereignty, as it exists in a people or originally in a nation, is absolute," and that "perfection of sovereignty consists in its exercise independently of the will of any other."[42] States were under an obligation not to interfere in each other's government from which arose a right not to allow such interference.[43] But Wolff also asserted that "[i]n the supreme state [*civitas maxima*], the nations as a whole have a right to coerce the individual nations if they should be unwilling to perform their obligation, or should show themselves negligent in it."[44] This statement might be interpreted as a contradiction of an absolute rule of nonintervention, allowing a right of collective intervention to enforce minimum standards of human conduct.[45] Wolff's system was based primarily on natural law; the fundamental rights of states to equality, sovereignty, liberty, and independence all arose from his account of the natural law, and it was from such natural rights that the duty of noninterference, in turn, arose (though Wolff started from natural obligations and derived from them natural rights rather than vice versa). His invocation of the fictional *civitas maxima* as a midwife for the positive (voluntary) law of nations confused his clear statement of a principle of noninterference.

Wolff's system of international law, built a priori on supposed principles of natural law, is devoid of any reference to the actual practice of states. His rule of nonintervention is the product of abstract reflection, not the result of observation of this practice. Wolff's follower Vattel, also a Naturalist, made more attempt to accommodate his account of international law to the behavior of states.

---

[42] Wolff, Chap. II, para. 255.   [43] *Ibid.*, Chap. II, para. 269.

[44] *Ibid.*, Prolegomena, para. 13.

[45] The resolution of this apparent conflict in the interpretation of Wolff seems to be either that (a) intervention by the *civitas maxima* does not negate an absolute principle of nonintervention, because the rule applies to the relations between states and not between the state and the community of states acting together; or (b) measures taken by states to coerce another state to perform its obligations may amount to reprisals, blockade, or war, but not to intervention; or (c) in the definition of "absolute," is an absolute right one that is prior to any conflicting rights of others, or merely one that always applies in the ideal *civitas maxima* in which every state is acting as it should act? This last interpretation would conform to Wolff's general approach, his greater concern with "ought" than with "is" in the relations between states.

If Wolff's *civitas maxima* was an impotent fiction, his system at least had the value, as Vattel pointed out in his preface,[46] of conceiving of a society of states, not of individuals; Wolff had effected the separation of the two ideas. In place of Wolff's *civitas maxima*, Vattel put the natural liberty of nations, their common welfare, duties, and perfect and imperfect rights as productive of the voluntary law of nations.[47] Both the necessary and the voluntary law of nations were established by natural law, but the former was necessitated by that law, the latter only recommended.[48]

The cornerstone of Vattel's system was the absolute freedom and independence of states, there being by no means the same necessity for a civil society among nations as there was among individuals.[49] Since nations were free and independent by nature, as men were, it was a law of their society that "each Nation should be left to the peaceable enjoyment of that liberty which belongs to it by nature. The natural society of nations can not continue unless the rights which belong to each by nature are respected."[50] Thus Vattel reiterates Wolff's doctrine of natural rights, but adds to it by pointing to a general law requiring respect for those rights. If independence is the right, then the principle of nonintervention would be the rule requiring respect for that right.

Vattel also follows closely the principle of equality as formulated by Wolff:

Since men are by nature equal and their individual rights and obligations the same, as coming equally from nature, Nations, which are composed of men and may be regarded as so many free persons living together in a state of nature, are by nature equal and hold from nature the same obligations and the same rights. Strength or weakness, in this case, counts for nothing. A dwarf is as much a man as a giant is; a small Republic is no less a sovereign State than the most powerful Kingdom.[51]

Here again, states were equal because they were states, just as men were equal because they were men.

[46] E. de Vattel, *The Law of Nations or the Principles of Natural Law*, 1758, trans. Charles G. Fenwick, Washington, 1916, Preface, p. 7a.

[47] *Ibid.*, Preface, pp. 9a–10a.   [48] *Ibid.*, Preface, p. 11a.

[49] *Ibid.*, Introduction, para. 4 and Preface, p. 9a. But this freedom and independence was not freedom from the obligations of natural law. *Ibid.*, Introduction, paras. 7–9.

[50] *Ibid.*, Introduction, para. 15.   [51] *Ibid.*, Introduction, para. 18.

Vattel's insistence on the absolute independence of states as the basis of international law renders that law extremely fragile with respect to its enforcement. "All States," he argued, "have a perfect right to whatever is essential to their existence, hence all Nations may put down by force the open violation of the laws of the society which nature has established among them."[52] But these rights must not be so extended as to prejudice the liberty of nations.[53] Thus the imperative of self-preservation is reasonably urged as the motive for enforcing law, but that enforcement is not reckoned a duty but only an option, and whatever happens, law enforcement must never prejudice the liberty of the offender. Given Vattel's reluctance to sacrifice liberty to the enforcement of law and his unequivocal championship of the absolute independence and equality of states, it is logical that a rule of nonintervention should play a prominent part in his system. He states it thus:

> It clearly follows from the liberty and independence of Nations that each has the right to govern itself as it thinks proper, and that no one of them has the least right to interfere in the government of another. Of all the rights possessed by a Nation, that of sovereignty is doubtless the most important and the one which others should most carefully respect if they are desirous not to give cause for offence.[54]

Despite such a clear statement of the principle of nonintervention, Vattel seems to allow two notable exceptions to the rule: intervention on the just side in a civil war and intervention in the interests of the balance of power.[55]

Vattel's international law can be regarded as a definitive end to the notion of a *societas humana* which had survived since the Spanish school of international law had popularized it in the sixteenth century.[56] Although his system was built upon the natural law, Vattel's emphasis of the independence of states and the im-

[52] *Ibid.*, Introduction, para. 22.   [53] *Ibid.*, Introduction, para. 23.
[54] *Ibid.*, Bk. II, Chap. IV, para. 54.
[55] For a discussion of these exceptions see below Chapter Eight, section I.
[56] F. H. Hinsley, *Power and the Pursuit of Peace*, Cambridge, 1963, pp. 166–167. Hinsley takes the rejection by Vattel of Wolff's *civitas maxima* as evidence for this. But this might as well be seen as the rejection of the idiosyncrasies of a particular author, rather than of a whole tradition of legal scholarship, particularly as Wolff's *civitas maxima* was so different from the old *societas humana*.

plications of such emphasis for the content of international law foreshadowed the positivist treatises of the following century.

ii. The Positivists

In general the positivist international lawyers are to be distinguished by their common search for rules of international law in the actual practice of states. In this approach, there is an implied rejection of the method of natural law which holds those rules to be discoverable by the use of human reason. Both these definitions of positivism are acceptable here; one draws attention to what positivism is, the other says what it is not. The meaning of positivism which is not acceptable here is that which refers to the definition of law advanced by Austin and people of his persuasion, whose view it was that laws, properly so-called, were the commands of the sovereign. According to this view, the expression "international law" is a misnomer for a body of rules which is no more than "positive international morality." The examination of this doctrine is beyond the scope of the present study which is to discover the derivation of the principle of nonintervention in the writings of some positivist international lawyers—Positivists, because their accounts of international law were based on rules arising from custom and treaty and not from the dictates of right reason. Unlike the Naturalists, the Positivists tended to draw a clear distinction between international law as it actually was and opinions about what it ought to be.[57] But naturalist assumptions persisted.

G. F. von Martens recognized the existence of a natural law prevailing between nations living in a state of nature, but deemed it insufficient when nations "come to frequent and carry on commerce with each other."[58] In such a situation the common interests of nations obliged them to "soften the rigour of the law of nature," and to "render it more determinate" by means of express or tacit conventions and by simple custom. The sum of the rights and obligations thus established formed the positive law between nations in opposition to the natural law.[59] In spite of this positivist

[57] Nussbaum, *Concise History*, p. 232.

[58] G. F. von Martens, *The Law of Nations: Being the Science of National Law founded upon the Treaties and Customs of Modern Nations in Europe*, trans. Wm. Cobbett, London, 1829, Introduction, sections 1 and 2.

[59] *Ibid.*, Introduction, section 2. Martens actually refers here to "rights and obligations established between two nations." In section 3 he generalizes the statement to demonstrate a positive law between the majority of European powers.

basis, Martens' law of nations contained significant elements which seem to be borrowed from the Naturalists, especially from Wolff and Vattel. He referred to nations having "inherent rights," and seemed to number among them, those of territorial sovereignty, equality, and liberty, and even a natural right to augment the power of the state by external aggrandizement.[60]

It is not clear whether Martens derives the rule of noninterference from the "inherent right" of a state to territorial sovereignty, or from the same right derived from observation of the practice of states. He merely declares that the internal constitution of the state depends upon the will of that state, "foreign nations having not the least right to interfere in arrangements which are purely domestic."[61] Nor are his permissible exceptions to the rule any guide. By allowing intervention on the just side in a civil contest, he echoes the views of Grotius and Vattel and inclines to a naturalist doctrine. On the other hand, the right to intervention from positive title and the right to intervene on the ground of self-preservation he derives from the practice of European states.[62] What appears sometimes as arch-positivism in Martens' work,[63] is opposed by his apparent acceptance of the doctrine of fundamental rights; it is difficult to ascertain which view prevailed in his arrival at a rule of nonintervention.

This mixture of rights of states derived from the natural law and rules sanctioned by the practice of states did not end with the work of von Martens. It recurs in the writings of the early American international lawyers, James Kent and Henry Wheaton. Kent referred to the "perfect equality, and entire independence of all distinct states" as a "fundamental principle of public law" and criticized the interventions of the Holy Alliance in Naples and in Spain as violations of that principle.[64] He cited Grotius, Vattel, and Rutherforth in support of his view that "no state is entitled

[60] *Ibid.*, Bk. VI, Chap. VIII, section 1; Bk. III, Chap. I, section 1; Bk. III, Chap. I, section 2; Bk. IV, Chap. I, section 2. Nussbaum points to the unmistakable influence of Grégoire's Déclaration des Droits des Gens, submitted to the French Convention in 1793, on Martens' thought, which, Nussbaum argues, led him to stress "rights" of states rather than Wolff's "obligations." *Concise History*, p. 183.

[61] Martens, Bk. III, Chap. II, section 1.

[62] *Ibid.*, Bk. III, Chap. II, section 1.

[63] See his Introduction, section 2.

[64] James Kent, *Commentaries on American Law*, 7th ed., 4 vols., New York, 1851, Vol. I, Pt. I, Lecture II, sections 21 and 23.

to take cognizance or notice of the domestic administration of another state, or of what passes within it as between the government and its own subjects."[65] At the same time, he recognized intervention to preserve the balance of power among neighboring nations as being very frequent and on occasion necessary and just.[66] Kent retreated before the confusions of state practice in his discussion of the permissibility of intervention in civil conflict by arguing rather lamely that "the right of interposition must depend upon the circumstances of the case. It is not susceptible to precise limitations, and is extremely delicate in the application. It must be submitted to the guidance of eminent discretion, and controlled by the principles of justice and sound policy."[67]

While Kent saw the most useful part of the law of nations as being positive law founded on usage and consent, he was unwilling to sacrifice natural jurisprudence, which, he argued, derived its force and dignity from the principles of right reason and which bound every state to conduct itself with justice, good faith, and benevolence.[68] Kent's discussion of the rule of nonintervention reflected his determination to serve two masters in the derivation of law.

Henry Wheaton's account was similar to that of Kent though his definition of international law was less deferential to state practice. For him, international law consisted of "those rules of conduct which reason deduces, as consonant to justice, from the nature of the society existing among independent nations; with such definitions and modifications as may be established by general consent."[69] He made a distinction between primitive or absolute rights of states and conditional or hypothetical rights. The former were held by states because they were states, and they were absolute in the sense of not being limited to particular circumstances. The latter rights were associated with belligerency and neutrality.[70] For Wheaton, the absolute right, which lay at the foundation of all the rest, was that of self-preservation, and it was with reference to this right that he discussed intervention.[71] An

[65] *Ibid.*, Pt. I, Lecture II, section 21 and footnote a.
[66] *Ibid.*, Pt. I, Lecture II, section 21.
[67] *Ibid.*, Pt. I, Lecture II, section 24.
[68] *Ibid.*, Pt. I, Lecture I, section 2.
[69] Henry Wheaton, *Elements of International Law*, rept. of R. H. Dana's 1866 ed., ed. G. G. Wilson, Oxford, 1936, Pt. I, Chap. I, para. 14.
[70] *Ibid.*, Pt. II, Chap. I, para. 60.
[71] *Ibid.*, Pt. II, Chap. I, paras. 61 and 63.

examination of the practice of states, and in particular, of the events following the Congress of Aix-la-Chapelle in 1818, proved to him "the inefficacy of all the attempts that have been made to establish a general and inevitable principle on the subject of intervention," and made him wary of the abuses that were likely to accompany a necessarily vague rule.[72] But despite these reservations, Wheaton attempted to formulate a principle of nonintervention. He observed that

> [e]very state, as a distinct moral being, independent of every other, may freely exercise all its sovereign rights in any manner not inconsistent with the equal rights of other States. . . . No foreign state can lawfully interfere with the exercise of this right, unless such interference is authorized by some special compact, or by such a clear case of necessity as immediately affects its own independence, freedom and security. Non-interference is the general rule, to which cases of justifiable interference form exceptions limited by the necessity of each particular case.[73]

Wheaton, like Kent, tried thus to reconcile a right to independence regarded as by nature absolute, with state practice which recognized no such absolute right.

Sir Robert Phillimore claimed to have based his international law as much on divine as on positive law.[74] In fact, his treatment of the subject made very little reference to natural law except in the introductory remarks about the sources of international law.[75] The positivist emphasis is reflected in Phillimore's discussion of the rights of states in general, and rules about intervention in particular. Unlike Kent and Wheaton, he claimed that as a matter of fact states did recognize one another's independence;[76] therefore, he did not need to derive such a right from natural law. However, merely to show that states had a right to independence from custom or tacit consent was not apparently sufficient for Phillimore. He derived the state's right to independence from the "proposition" that states were recognized as "free moral persons," and the right to equality from the proposition that each state was a "member of

---

[72] *Ibid.*, Pt. II, Chap. I, para. 65. [73] *Ibid.*, Pt. II, Chap. I, para. 72.

[74] Sir Robert Phillimore, *Commentaries Upon International Law*, 2d ed., 4 vols., London, 1871, Vol. I, Pt. I, Chap. III, section XXII.

[75] *Ibid.*, Vol. I, Pt. I, Chap. VIII.

[76] *Ibid.*, Vol. I, Pt. I, Chap. IX, section LX.

a universal community."[77] For Phillimore, the science of international law was mainly constructed on these two presuppositions. From the right to independence, he deduced, among other things, the right to a free choice with regard to the internal constitution and government of the state without the intermeddling of any foreign state, the right of territorial inviolability, the right of self-preservation, and the right to absolute and uncontrolled jurisdiction over all persons and things within the territory of the state.[78]

Phillimore thought that the right of self-preservation was the first law of nations, as it was of individuals. "A society which is not in a condition to repel aggression from without," he argued, "is wanting in its principal duty to the members of which it is composed."[79] This right warranted a state in extending precautionary measures outside her territorial limits, even to the extent of transgressing the borders of her neighbor's territory.[80] By thus reckoning the right of self-preservation as prior and paramount to that of territorial inviolability, Phillimore established a right of intervention on those grounds as superior to the rule of nonintervention. This does not negate the principle of nonintervention as a general rule; however, it does mean that it is overridden when it collides with the higher imperative of self-preservation.

For W. E. Hall, the "ultimate foundation" of international law was the assumption that "states possess rights and are subject to duties corresponding to the facts of their postulated nature."[81] The old doctrine of "natural rights" which for Phillimore were "propositions" had now become "assumptions." Among these assumptions, Hall listed the right of a state to do whatever was necessary to continue and develop its existence, the right to give effect to and preserve its independence, and the right to hold and acquire property.[82]

Hall defined independence as "the power of giving effect to the decisions of a will which is free, in so far as absence of restraint

[77] *Ibid.*, Vol. I, Pt. III, Chap. II, sections CXLV and CXLVII.

[78] *Ibid.*, Vol. I, Pt. III, Chap. II, section CXLV.

[79] *Ibid.*, Vol. I, Pt. III, Chap. X, section CCXI.

[80] *Ibid.*, Vol. I, Pt. III, Chap. X, section CCXIV.

[81] Hall, *A Treatise on International Law*, p. 50.

[82] *Ibid.*, p. 50. Hall argued that "the proprietary character of the possession enjoyed by a state is logically a necessary consequence of the undisputed fact that a state community has a right to the exclusive use and disposal of its territory as against other states." *Ibid.*, p. 53. On property and sovereignty see below, Chapter Nine, section I.

by other persons is concerned."[83] His right of independence followed as "in its largest extent, a right possessed by a state to exercise its will without interference on the part of foreign states . . . and so taken it would embrace the rights of preserving and developing existence."[84]

Absence of interference from other states, then, Hall regarded as a defining characteristic of the right of independence. At the same time, the duty of noninterference, or of respecting the independence of others, he saw as arising out of that right of independence. "A state has entire freedom of external and internal action within the law. To interfere with it, therefore, is wrong, unless it can be shown that there are rights or duties which have priority . . . over the duty of respecting independence."[85] One such incontestable right was that of self-preservation; Hall, like Phillimore, held that the imperative of self-preservation was superior to that of nonintervention.[86]

In the work of T. J. Lawrence, the rights and obligations of states appeared neither as fundamental rights and duties nor as propositions nor as assumptions. States possessed rights and duties by virtue of the law that they had created for themselves. Under Lawrence's unabashed positivism, Wheaton's absolute and conditional rights became the normal and abnormal rights and duties of states.[87] "Just as the law of the land clothes every child under its authority with certain rights which are his through no act of his own, so International Law gives to the states under its authority certain rights which belong to them through the mere fact of subjection to it."[88] There was then no mystery for Lawrence in the derivation of the right of independence, "the right of a state to manage all its affairs, whether external or internal, without control from other states." Such a right was simply conferred on states by the law under which they lived.[89]

Having established that the rights and duties of states were nothing more than rules made by states for the use of states, Lawrence went on to observe that an appeal to the practice of states in order to discover rules on the subject of intervention was

[83] *Ibid.*, p. 55.   [84] *Ibid.*, p. 55.
[85] *Ibid.*, p. 65. On the distinction between independence and nonintervention see below, pp. 40–41.
[86] *Ibid.*, p. 65.
[87] Lawrence, *Principles of International Law*, pp. 112–113.
[88] *Ibid.*, p. 12.   [89] *Ibid.*, pp. 115–116.

useless;[90] "the facts of international intercourse," he wrote, "give no clue to the rules of International Law." Confronted with this difficulty, he advocated a return to first principles "admitted on all sides," such as the right of independence and of self-preservation, from which rules or at least moral precepts regarding intervention could be deduced.[91] Thus, even Lawrence, in order to escape the confusions of state practice, resorted to principles of natural law, or axioms of the science of international law, in order to discover rules applying to intervention. Lawrence rejected a doctrine of absolute noninterference, if it meant simply isolationism, as fatal to the idea of a family of nations. He also discounted it if it meant that a state should take an interest in international relations, but merely resort to moral utterances if other states behaved in a manner of which it disapproved. His answer amounted to a plea for reasonableness in international relations. "[States] should intervene very sparingly, and only on the clearest grounds of justice and necessity; but when they do intervene, they should make it clear to all concerned that their voice must be attended to and their wishes carried out."[92] Perhaps the request for reasonableness was a final admission that intervention was a matter of policy rather than of law.

The positivist international lawyers looked at here, sought in the main to discover the principles of international law in the actual practice of states. Where practice provided but an equivocal guide to principle, refuge was found either in borrowing from the naturalist international lawyers or in the assumptions or first principles upon which the system of international law was supposedly based. Mountague Bernard based his account of the "reason of the rule" of nonintervention on the latter approach.[93] Law, in Bernard's view, was made by the development of principles, their pursuit into detail, and their application to classes of cases. In this way a body of law could accumulate without reference to positive legislation. This law might be contradicted by the consent of nations or be given a positive value exceeding its intrinsic weight by universal acceptance, but acceptance did not, strictly speaking, make law.[94]

[90] *Ibid.*, p. 121.   [91] *Ibid.*, p. 121.

[92] *Ibid.*, p. 135. This statement might be said to reveal Lawrence's admiration for Canning, see below Chapter Four, section II(ii).

[93] Mountague Bernard, *On the Principle of Non-Intervention*, Oxford, 1860.

[94] *Ibid.*, pp. 4–5.

For Bernard, the whole fabric of international law rested on two first principles, the destruction or impairment of which would destroy or impair the system. The first principle was that states were "severally sovereign and independent," the second that they were also members of a community "united by a social tie."[95] The doctrine of nonintervention as a corollary from a cardinal principle of international law, that of sovereignty, had a prima facie claim to a place in the system, and the burden of proof lay with those who would deny it.[96] Admitting, however, that abstract reasoning was always liable to control by positive usage, Bernard examined the commonly advanced justifications for intervention and found them wanting as legitimate exceptions to the principle of nonintervention. The international practice of intervention, he argued, was so diverse as not to allow its classification as settled usage, which was the necessary requirement for a rule to be established. The conclusion which Bernard arrived at was that the exceptions were all inadmissible, and that the principle of nonintervention, so far as he had examined it, was "universally true."[97]

In allowing no exceptions to the rule, Bernard echoed Wolff's absolute principle of nonintervention. Unlike Wolff, Bernard conceived of the rule as a logical requirement of a system based on the principle of state sovereignty, not as an imperative of natural law. It was in this sense that Bernard asserted the universal truth of the nonintervention principle, and as such he set up the rule against the facts of international conduct. But he also wanted to measure the rule against those facts, and he found that while there were exceptions in practice to the principle of nonintervention, none of them was sufficiently consistent to provide a guide to law.

The difficulty with Bernard's account, a difficulty encountered to a greater or a lesser extent by most of the nineteenth-century Positivists, was the distinction between first principles or assumptions and the practice of states. Bernard wanted to argue at once that the general principles were established by universal consent and that those principles could be contradicted by universal consent.[98] He distinguished between the intrinsic weight of first principles and the value given to them by international acceptance, and yet derived them both from the same positivist source. The solution to this dilemma in positivist thought might lie in the

[95] *Ibid.*, p. 7.   [96] *Ibid.*, p. 9.
[97] *Ibid.*, p. 23.   [98] *Ibid.*, pp. 4–5.

notion of a minimum content of natural law, which would logically separate Bernard's "first principles" from international practice.[99]

iii. The Derivation of the Principle of Nonintervention in International Law: Summary and Critique

It might be concluded that the Naturalists established a rule of nonintervention arguing a priori from first principles and that the Positivists, submitting such principles to the bar of practice, accounted for the exceptions to the general rule. The Naturalists might then be criticized for taking too little notice of state practice, and the Positivists for reducing law to a rubber stamp for legitimizing that practice. But such a division is too simple, for we have seen that the principle of nonintervention was advanced with a tenacity varying as much within as between the two schools of thought. However, the more cautious conclusion that reason established the rule and practice modified it does seem tenable, particularly from the texts of the Positivists.[100]

In the writings of the Naturalists and the Positivists, the principle of nonintervention was seen to be closely related to sovereignty or independence or equality, whether these rights were held to be fundamental or axiomatic, presuppositions of the law of nations, or simply rights through customary acceptance. The task here is to examine these ideas as they relate to that of nonintervention

A. THE DOCTRINE OF FUNDAMENTAL RIGHTS

The doctrine which taught that states held certain fundamental rights from their very nature as states had its origin in the work of Wolff. It was fully acceptable to von Martens. It underpinned, if with some reluctance, many of the positivist writings of the nineteenth century, and its influence endured into the twentieth.[101] The objections to the doctrine now seem obvious. The first is that it is impossible to deduce, in so comprehensive a way as the

[99] See below, Chapter Nine, section II.

[100] This generalization applies only to the Positivists referred to in the above text. It would emphatically not apply to modern Positivists like Kelsen.

[101] See, e.g., Elihu Root, "The Declaration of the Rights and Duties of Nations Adopted by the American Institute of International Law," *American Journal of International Law*, Vol. 10, 1916, pp. 211–222; International Law Commission's Draft Declaration on Rights and Duties of States, annexed for the members' consideration to United Nations General Assembly Resolution 375(IV) of December 6, 1949, in *Year Book of the United Nations, 1948–1949*, pp. 948–949.

Naturalists did, prescriptions about the way men or states ought to behave from more or less simple statements of what they are. For law as a normative system guiding the behavior of men in society, or of states in international society, is not the same thing as a law of physics which attempts to describe regularities in the natural world. The second objection applies to the doctrine of fundamental rights in its diluted form held by the Positivists as presuppositions rather than imprescriptible rights. As Kelsen has pointed out, "this version of the natural-law doctrine is as logically impossible as is the classical version of that doctrine. Legal principles can never be presupposed by a legal order; they can only be created in conformity with this order."[102] However, neither of these objections applies to the enterprise of attempting to discover those rules without which social life among men or states would be impossible, and referring to them as fundamental principles.

B. SOVEREIGNTY AND INDEPENDENCE

Sovereignty can be understood as a description of the supreme authority within a political community or as an assertion of the need for such an authority as a provider of order within the state. From the notion of supreme authority can be inferred a denial of any authority above the state, an inference which, if it rendered international law meaningless, might be logically valid but can be shown to be false empirically. Sovereignty might also be interpreted as meaning the exclusion of the authority of other states, but not of international law,[103] and it is in the expression of this idea that the principle of nonintervention has its primary function.

In this sense the idea of nonintervention is close to, if not synonymous with, that aspect of sovereignty which draws attention to its exclusive nature—independence. If sovereignty and independence are not themselves merely two words conveying the same idea, the difference between them might lie between sovereignty in its internal and in its external aspect. Sovereignty in its internal aspect can be regarded as Hinsley's "final and absolute authority in the political community"[104]—a positive concept about power within the state. Sovereignty in its external aspect can be regarded,

[102] Hans Kelsen, *Principles of International Law*, 2d ed., rev. and ed. Robert W. Tucker, New York, 1966, pp. 244–245.

[103] On how this is possible, see C.A.W. Manning, *The Nature of International Society*, London, 1962, pp. 101–103.

[104] See above, Chapter One, p. 14.

if not as *no* authority above the state, then at least as the exclusion of the authority of other states—a negative concept defining sovereignty by what it excludes rather than by what it includes. It is for this aspect of sovereignty that independence is a synonym.[105] In turn, nonintervention is not quite a synonym for independence. If a state has a right to independence, it has a right to conduct its affairs free from the interference of others, and other states have a duty to respect that right. The principle of nonintervention explicitly links the right of one state to independence to the duty of others to respect it and expresses this relation in a rule of international conduct.

C. EQUALITY

Perfect equality is not possible, for two things similar in every other respect will always differ as to their distribution in space.[106] To say that two or more things are equal is to say that they resemble each other in a way which is relevant to the comparison being made between them. Thus two triangles can at once be considered equal in the sense that the sum of their internal angles amounts to two right angles, unequal if their sides are of different lengths. Men are equal as men, unequal as particular individuals. States are equal as states, unequal in most other respects.[107]

Men are equal before municipal law, states are equal before international law. This does not mean that all men or all states have equal rights, for company directors have a greater capacity for rights than have janitors; great maritime states have a greater capacity for rights than small continental ones. What the principle of equality before the law does require is that a janitor and a company director should receive equal treatment by the law if they have committed a similar offense; that a great state should be as circumspect about interfering in the affairs of another state as a small state, for the principle of nonintervention applies equally to both of them. In neither of these cases is actual inequality considered relevant, for the cases themselves are alike. That like cases should be treated equally and unlike ones not is an imperative with-

---

[105] Hans J. Morgenthau defines independence as "that particular aspect of the supreme authority of an individual nation which consists in the exclusion of the authority of any other nation," *Politics Among Nations*, 4th ed., New York, 1967, p. 302.

[106] Kooijmans, *Doctrine of Legal Equality*, p. 8.

[107] *Ibid.*, p. 9.

41

out which law would cease to be law and become mere arbitrariness.

Dickinson distinguished another sort of equality in international law, which posited, if not an arithmetical equality of rights between states, then at least an equal capacity for rights by which states were potentially equal.[108] This sort of equality, according to Dickinson, is what most writers on international law have meant in their discussions of equality.[109] It is a legacy of natural law; Wolff and Vattel thought states as collections of men were by nature equal, as individual men were, and that in consequence they all had the same rights and were under the same obligations. This notion is not only empirically false, but is subject to the same objections as the doctrine of fundamental rights.

The actual inequality of states has led some international lawyers to reject the doctrine of legal equality as a useless, redundant, and even mischievous fiction.[110] Useless because it serves no purpose as a principle from which rules of international law can be deduced.[111] Redundant because it offers nothing which is not already provided by the notion of independence.[112] Mischievous because it is a "spurious application of a nominally democratic principle" to the unsuitable environment of international relations.[113] But the principle of equality before the law has survived the attacks of the deniers. Oppenheim's conception of the member-states of the international community being "equal to each other as subjects of international law,"[114] is carried on in the Charter of the United Nations which bases the organization on the "principle of the sovereign equality of all its Members."[115] The principle of nonintervention, so frequently derived in the treatises of international law from the principle of equality, does at least receive from that principle the idea that it applies equally to all states.

[108] E. D. Dickinson, *The Equality of States in International Law*, Cambridge, Mass., 1920, pp. 4–5.

[109] *Ibid.*, pp. 4–5.

[110] P. J. Baker, "The Doctrine of the Legal Equality of States," *British Yearbook of International Law*, Vol. IV, 1923–1924, pp. 3–4.

[111] *Ibid.*, pp. 3–4.

[112] Westlake, *Collected Papers*, pp. 86–87.

[113] J. L. Brierly, *The Law of Nations*, 6th ed., ed. C.H.M. Waldock, Oxford, 1963, pp. 132–133.

[114] Oppenheim, *International Law*, Vol. I, pp. 22–23.

[115] Article 2(1).

It has been said that the doctrine of fundamental rights betrays its origin in the struggle for independence of the modern state.[116] The dual functions the doctrines of sovereignty, independence, and equality—whether or not they were asserted as fundamental rights —might be said to have performed were that of detaching the emergent states from the pretensions of papal and imperial authority, and at the same time that of drawing attention to their individual existence, each separate from the other.[117] Apart from its attendance as midwife at the birth of the modern state, the doctrine of fundamental rights might be said to have functioned as a protector of weak states from the ravages of the strong.[118] If the weak had no other means of protection, they could at least mark the interventions of the strong with the brand of illegality and make the most of such a feeble weapon by representing intervention as the violation of an absolute or fundamental right. A third function for the fundamental rights doctrine was within the science of international law. Where the Positivists could derive no rule from a confused pattern of state practice, fundamental rights were the first principles to which they could return for guidance.

In each of these functions of the fundamental rights doctrine, the principle of nonintervention finds a place. It features as a doctrine asserted on behalf of the sovereignty and independence of the state against other states and against the existence of any authority above the state, and as a principle which crowned the achievement of a society made up exclusively of states. It is a principle championed by small states against the meddling of the great. And it is a first principle of a society of sovereign states which can be relied upon by international lawyers in the absence of any

[116] C. de Visscher, *Theory and Reality in Public International Law*, trans. P. E. Corbett, Princeton, N.J., 1957, p. 18.

[117] Hinsley speaks of Bodin's attempt to "release international relations from the imperial or universalist framework," *Sovereignty*, pp. 181–182. Kooijmans represents legal equality as having mainly a negative nature, being manipulated as a weapon against universalistic tendencies, *Doctrine of Legal Equality*, p. 56. Philip C. Jessup argues that "independence was a historically convenient concept because it helped to differentiate those political groupings which determined their own policies, especially in international relations," *A Modern Law of Nations*, New York, 1949, pp. 36–37.

[118] Fenwick, *International Law*, p. 225.

clear customary rule.[119] This chapter has examined the principle of nonintervention as an imperative of international law. The next will examine the view that it makes good political sense for states to observe it.

[119] For an expansion of the idea of nonintervention as a "first principle" of international society, see below, Chapter Nine, sections I and II.

THREE

THEORY

A theory of nonintervention will be understood here as a doctrine urged as a means to some particular desired end, such as lasting peace, or the security of states, or the protection of the best interests of a particular state. As such, it will encompass the views of those who, while asserting the need for states to observe the principle of nonintervention if peace between them were to be secured, argued that this was not the only condition having to be met before that end could be achieved. Cobden's espousal of a near-absolute doctrine of nonintervention will first be examined, and then the views of Mill, Kant, and Mazzini, as they departed from Cobden's extreme position.

Richard Cobden's Theory of Nonintervention

Though he wished to see the principle of nonintervention win general acceptance as a rule of international conduct, it was not abstract inference from the premise of the sovereignty of states that led Cobden to espouse it. What he did assume was that no government had the right to involve its people in hostilities except "in defence of their own national honour or interests."[1] Unless this principle were made the rule of all, he thought, there could be no guarantee for the peace of any one country, "so long as there may be found a people, whose grievances may attract the sympathy or invite the interference of another State."[2] Thus Cobden believed that the "national interest" was an intelligible concept, that fidelity to it required states to abstain from participation in the domestic conflicts of others, and that adherence to such a rule was a *sine qua non* of peace among states.

Cobden was a Manchester businessman and later a professional politician who, when he advocated the conduct of foreign policy according to the principle of nonintervention, had in mind the interests of the people of Great Britain. In Cobden's view, this did

[1] Richard Cobden, "England, Ireland and America," 1835, in *The Political Writings of Richard Cobden*, London, 1886, p. 8.
[2] *Ibid.*, p. 8.

not mean that British interests were to be indulged at the expense of other nations, for he combined with his conviction about the rightness for Britain of a policy of nonintervention, a convenient belief in the doctrine of the harmony of interests. "Now the House of Commons is a body that has to deal with nothing but the honest interests of England," he said in a speech to that body, "and I likewise assert that the honest and just interests of this country, and of her inhabitants, are the just and honest interests of the whole world."[3] The fact that the real world was not a place in which concord prevailed could be ascribed to the failure of states to observe the principle of nonintervention, to the interference of aristocratic government in the naturally harmonious relations of peoples. The idea that intergovernmental relations were inimical to good international relations was expressed in Cobden's maxim in praise of American foreign policy: "As little intercourse as possible betwixt the *Governments*, as much connection as possible between the *nations* of the world."[4]

Just as Christian Wolff came closest to advocating an absolute principle of nonintervention among eighteenth-century international lawyers, so among nineteenth-century politicians, Cobden was the nearest to urging an absolute policy of nonintervention. In 1858, he wrote in a letter to a friend:

> You rightly interpret my views when you say I am opposed to any armed intervention in the affairs of other countries. I am against any interference by the government of any one country in the affairs of another nation, even if it be confined to moral suasion. Nay, I go further, and disapprove of the formation of a society or organisation of any kind in England for the purpose of interfering in the internal affairs of other countries. I have always declined to sanction anti-slavery organisations formed for the purpose of agitating the slavery question in the United States.[5]

[3] Speech to the House of Commons, June 5, 1855, in John Bright and James E. Thorold Rogers, eds., *Speeches by Richard Cobden on Questions of Public Policy*, 2 vols., London, 1870, Vol. II, p. 27.

[4] Cobden, "Russia," 1836, in *Political Writings*, p. 216 (Cobden's emphasis). Cobden also used a quotation from Washington's Farewell Address as an introduction to "England, Ireland and America,": "The great rule of conduct for us in regard to foreign nations is, in extending our commercial relations, to have with them as little *political* connection as possible." *Ibid.*, p. 3.

[5] Richard Cobden to Mrs. Schwabe, 1858, in J. A. Hobson, *Richard Cobden, The International Man*, London, 1919, p. 400.

By his advocacy of such a comprehensive prohibition of intervention in the domestic affairs of other nations, or in quarrels between them,[6] Cobden found himself at odds with most of the statesmen of his day who were responsible for the making of British foreign policy. In his speeches and writings, he agitated for acceptance of his doctrine in two main ways. The first was to stress the advantages which would accrue to the people of Britain should their government adopt a policy of nonintervention and to point out the domestic disadvantages of an interventionary foreign policy. The second and more persuasive part of Cobden's argument consisted in trenchant criticism of the interventionary policies of successive governments. Cobden was concerned to show either that the purposes which intervention was intended to serve were spurious or that intervention was an unfitting instrument for their achievement.

That Cobden stressed the material advantage of the British people in order to advance the cause of nonintervention is evidence more of his political acumen than of "a narrow and grovelling commercialism."[7] If adherence to the rule of nonintervention were a necessary, if not a sufficient, condition for international peace, then for Cobden its pedigree was pure, and at the least a foreign policy conducted according to a coherent principle was to be preferred to being "at sea on foreign politics without rudder or compass."[8] But Cobden found his association with the "peace party" more of an embarrassment than a fruitful platform for his views; he thought that the party's dogged insistence on the doctrine of nonresistance allowed no agitation or discussion on secondary details, plans of a more gradualist nature which "might prepare men's minds, step by step, to look upon the abolition of war as a possible thing."[9] For Cobden, the doctrine of nonintervention was one of these modes, one which could be tied to a more concrete conception of interest than that of a vision of future peace.

Cobden's interpretation of the doctrine of the harmony of interests did not lead him to set up this abstraction as the primary goal that Britain ought to pursue in formulating her foreign policy.

---

[6] In the two pamphlets "England, Ireland and America," and "Russia," in which Cobden worked out a large part of his theory of foreign policy, he was concerned to demonstrate the inefficacy of a war against Russia on behalf of the Turks. *Political Writings*, pp. 5–119 and 122–258.

[7] A criticism of Cobden quoted in Hobson, p. 16.

[8] Cobden to Henry Richard, May 27, 1856, in Hobson, p. 145.

[9] Cobden to Henry Richard, November 18, 1851, in Hobson, pp. 81–82.

That goal would be best served by Britain pursuing her own immediate interest which was ultimately the interest of the whole world.[10] But statesmen with whose foreign policies Cobden fundamentally disagreed would also erect the national interest as their guiding motive. What set Cobden apart from them was that his conception of Britain's interest was informed by the interests of the commercial classes. Britain was a manufacturing nation whose well-being was dependent upon trade. Since trade was best served by a peaceful world, Cobden could attach his doctrine of nonintervention to the interests of the manufacturers. In order to show that his policy of nonintervention was more than just a "sterile principle," Cobden was concerned to emphasize that the Palmerstonian principle of intervention was against the interests of "our people in a variety of ways, as in distracting attention from home politics, adding loads of debts and taxation which keep down by their presence the working class and prevent them from rising in the social scale and therefore from rising politically."[11] Thus Cobden's biographer could write that "he has always advocated the principles [sic] of nonintervention, not on grounds of sentiment, philanthropy, or religion, but strictly in the dialect of policy and business."[12]

[10] There are confusions in this doctrine which appear if the argument is taken to any length, e.g., in Cobden's own words: "And if such is the character of free trade . . . that it unites, by the strongest motives of which our nature is susceptible, two remote communities [England and America], rendering the interest of the one the only true policy of the other. . . ." *Political Writings*, p. 225. The imperative of pursuing the national interest seems here to become the imperative of pursuing another nation's interest.

[11] Cobden to Henry Richard, October 15, 1856, in Hobson, p. 171. One of Cobden's criticisms of British intervention in Spain during the 1830's was the cost of the exercise—half a million sterling in 1836 compared to 10,000 pounds spent on establishing Normal Schools. "When the affairs of the British Empire are conducted with as much wisdom as goes to the successful management of a private business," he wrote, "the honest interests of our own people will become the study of the British ministry; and then, and not till then, instead of being at the mercy of a chaos of expedients, our Foreign Secretary will be guided by the principle of non-intervention in the politics of other nations." *Political Writings*, p. 230.

[12] John Morley, *The Life of Richard Cobden*, 2 vols., London, 1881, Vol. II, p. 158. Morley wrote this of Cobden to combat the argument that Cobden's opposition to the Crimean War carried no particular weight because of his well-known opposition to almost every war.

The second means which Cobden adopted to advance his doctrines about international politics was to discredit those of his opposition. These consisted of the "two stock pretences" usually employed to excuse British intervention in the politics of the Continent, the maintenance of the balance of power in Europe and the protection of commerce.[13] To these, Cobden added the particular species of interventionism of his own time, Palmerston's notion that British interference was required to further the cause of liberalism abroad.

Cobden considered the phrase "the balance of power" an "undescribed, indescribable, incomprehensible nothing."[14] The various definitions of the balance of power offered by Vattel, Gentz, and Brougham were, he thought, vague and meaningless if taken separately, confusing and contradictory if taken together. It was not the balance of power which had motivated England's foreign policy but lust for conquest, and if, perchance, any small state had preserved its independence, Cobden attributed that state of affairs to the limits which "nature herself has set to the undue expansion of territorial dominion."[15] The only correct view of the balance of power, Cobden thought, was the literal definition of Francis Bacon's, which interpreted the phrase as meaning a balance of all ingredients of national power from extent of territory to advances in civilization.[16] Bacon's principle of balance required that states see and hinder a potential imbalance before it occurred and disrupted the system; if men were to abide by this rule, wrote Cobden, it would reduce them below the level of brute animals.[17]

Even when he assumed a principle of balance which operated with complete efficiency, Cobden considered its invocation to justify British intervention in Turkey against the spread of Russian power to be wrong. In the first place, he drew attention to that tradition of European thought and practice which placed Turkey beyond the pale of European civilization, outside the system of which the balance of power was a part.[18] Intervention in Turkey on the grounds of balance would not accord with this tradition. Second, to the argument that a Russia in possession of Constantinople would jeopardize the interests of British commerce, Cobden replied by asking why the American possession of New York, "a

[13] *Political Writings*, p. 196.
[14] *Ibid.*, pp. 197–198.
[15] *Ibid.*, p. 201.
[16] *Ibid.*, p. 204.
[17] *Ibid.*, pp. 204–205.
[18] *Ibid.*, pp. 206–209.

port far more commodious than Constantinople," had never been subjected to a similar sort of balance of power calculus.[19] In the third place, Cobden countered the argument that a Russian invasion of Turkey would endanger Britain's colonies by declaring that the Russians (or Austrians) would be "far too abundantly occupied in *retaining* the sovereignty over fifteen millions of fierce and turbulent subjects" to contemplate any further expansion.[20]

Cobden's fundamental objection to the principle of the balance of power, however, was not its vagueness and confusion as a concept or that interventions based upon it did not match the doctrine they were supposed to uphold. Cobden objected above all to the military connotation of the phrase "balance of power," as if conquest could augment the power of a state or intervention check or balance the power of another. Cobden thought that it was through "the peaceful victories of mercantile traffic, and not by the force of arms, that modern states have yielded to the supremacy of more successful nations."[21] The engine of national power and grandeur was "labour and improvement," and to Russian aggrandizement in Poland and the Crimea, Cobden compared the achievements of Watt and Arkwright in England, declaring that it was to these people that England owed her position and not to Wellington or Nelson.[22] If peaceful industry were the true source of the power of the state, it followed that intervention could neither enhance the power of the intervening state, nor balance the power of its opponent.

Thus, for Cobden, if the balance of power meant anything at all, its maintenance would certainly not be served by intervention. The second "stock pretence" which Cobden sought to unmask was that which saw the protection of commerce as requiring an interventionary foreign policy and a large navy. Cobden was not doubtful about the objective of the protection of commerce, as he was about that of maintaining the balance of power. What he was doubtful about was whether military force could ever provide the desired protection. Commerce, he thought, provided its own protection in that force could never prevail against the natural wants and wishes of mankind;[23] in particular British trade could be

[19] *Ibid.*, p. 210.

[20] *Ibid.*, p. 20 (Cobden's emphasis). The posing of this question of potential danger to the British colonies led Cobden to question their retention if so much military power had to be deployed to protect them.

[21] *Ibid.*, p. 79.   [22] *Ibid.*, pp. 147–148.   [23] *Ibid.*, p. 11.

protected and enlarged only by the cheapness of her manufac-tures.[24] Indeed, far from providing protection, standing armies and navies actually detracted from commerce by adding taxation to manufacturers' costs and by tending to repel rather than to attract customers.[25] Cobden's conception of the autonomy of commerce and of the reality of shared interests which brought traders to-gether, meant that he regarded intervention for the protection of commerce as at best an irrelevance and at worst a serious disservice to the interests of the "middle and industrious classes of England."[26]

The third notion which Cobden wished to discredit was that of Britain as carrier of "schemes of universal benevolence," as enforcer of "the behests of the Almighty in every part of the globe,"[27] or as a "gensdarme [sic] whose office it was, gratuitously, to keep in order all the refractory nations of Europe."[28] Whether it was Pitt, Burke, Fox, and Grey sitting in judgment on the French Revolution[29] or the widespread enthusiasm in and out of the parlia-ment of his own time for the cause of liberalism and constitutional-ism in Europe, Cobden wondered at the self-importance of a na-tion which could assume such a store of virtue and wisdom, of God-given power and authority, as to make it feel competent event to discuss these matters so earnestly.[30] Cobden was also impressed by the hypocrisy of Englishmen who, notwithstanding the "em-barrassing weight" of their own colonies, chastised others for their unlawful aggrandizement.[31]

In place of the arrogance of an interfering foreign policy, Cob-den recommended that Britain confine herself strictly to the just interests of her empire, and those interests excluded intervention to maintain peace and order, or to bring truth and justice to the world. Cobden sympathized with the cause of progress and free dom in Europe, and one of his criticisms of the balance of power system was that it erected a barrier in the path of that cause. Be-cause the maintenance of a balance required that the established members of the states system be kept intact against nationalist

[24] Ibid., p. 219.   [25] Ibid., p. 235.

[26] Ibid., p. 34. The justification for the phrase "at best an irrelevance" lies in Cobden's account in "England, Ireland and America," of how little Eng-land's trade was affected by Napoleon's blockade during the Napoleonic Wars. Political Writings, pp. 11–13.

[27] Speech to House of Commons June 5, 1855, in Bright and Rogers, Speeches by Richard Cobden, Vol. II, p. 27.

[28] Political Writings, p. 9.

[29] Ibid., p. 195.   [30] Ibid., pp. 6–7.   [31] Ibid., p. 153.

revolution, Cobden deplored the consequent subordination of the interests of the people of Europe to the perceived interests of their governments.[32] In spite of, and in his own view because of, his sympathy for nationalist movements, however, Cobden could not countenance intervention on their behalf. Such action would contravene the nonintervention principle which, Cobden stressed, would also prevent foreign interference to put down the nationalities.[33]

Cobden's case against interference with the form of European governments was stated most clearly in a speech to the House of Commons in June 1850 opposing a motion in praise of the government's conduct of foreign policy.[34] In the first place, Cobden questioned the wisdom of a Britain which acted as a universal guarantor of constitutional government, pointing out that this would involve the Foreign Office in the reform of "every country on the face of the earth."[35] Second, after asserting that Britain had no right to interfere with any other form of government whether it were republic, despotism, or monarchy, Cobden emphasized the consequences of contravening this principle. A Britain which intervened to further constitutionalism, he argued, must tolerate a Russia which invaded Hungary.[36] On the other hand, a Britain which adhered to the nonintervention principle would not be embarrassed by its own actions when denouncing the illegalities of others. In the third place, Cobden put the nonintervention principle into the mouths of the Hungarian and Italian nationalists, and regarded its efficient operation as the best chance for the achievement of their aspirations. It was not British interference on their behalf that they required, Cobden argued, but the establishment

[32] Cobden to Henry Richard, no date except December (?), in Hobson, pp. 188–190.

[33] Speech to House of Commons, December 22, 1854, in Bright and Rogers, Vol. II, p. 6.

[34] Speech to House of Commons, June 28, 1850, in *ibid.*, pp. 211–229. Cobden directed this speech at those who advocated intervention for constitutionalism and in particular at its chief proponent, Mr. Cockburn, M. P. for Southampton. But Cobden was reluctant to attribute the championship of liberalism against despotism abroad to Lord Palmerston and thus dignify his interventionary foreign policy with high-sounding principles. Rather he wished to represent Palmerston as timid in dealings with the great powers (and in particular Russia) and overbearing to small states (in this instance Greece). See *ibid.*, pp. 227–228.

[35] *Ibid.*, p. 224.   [36] *Ibid.*, p. 225.

of such a principle, among outside powers, as would leave them entirely to themselves.[37]

To this argument that observation of the rule of nonintervention would further the growth of liberalism by preventing intervention against it, Cobden added a more direct one that outside interference on behalf of liberalism simply could not work. It was by the "force and virtue of native elements, and without assistance of any kind" that a people worked out its own political regeneration.[38] Moreover, "[a] people which wants a saviour," wrote Cobden quoting Channing with approval, "which does not possess an earnest and pledge of freedom in its own heart, is not yet ready to be free."[39] Thus intervention was doubly inappropriate as a means to promoting liberalism abroad; outside assistance could not promote a necessarily mature growth, and if such assistance were requested by a people, that very request was evidence of its immaturity and inability to benefit from intervention.

Cobden urged adherence to the nonintervention principle as a policy which would suit the real interests of the British people, not primarily as a rule of international law. His counsel on the grounds of her interest against British intervention to protect Turkey from Russia reveals the difference between the two imperatives. The rule of nonintervention, it can be argued, if it is to function effectively as an ordering device in international society, must admit the legitimacy of counterintervention to uphold the principle of nonintervention. According to international law, Britain might have a right if not a duty to intervene on behalf of the Turks against Russian intervention.[40] The only sanction Cobden would allow was the power of opinion and moral force.

Cobden's faith in the power of moral force in international relations took two forms. In the first place, Cobden thought that opinion alone would establish rules of conduct between nations. Impressed by Russian and Austrian restraint in not interfering in Turkey to claim the Hungarian political refugee, Kossuth, Cobden wrote to John Bright:

> . . . I felt convinced . . . that it was that expression of OPINION from Western Europe scared the despots instantly from their prey. And you are quite right; it is opinion and opinion only

[37] *Ibid.*, p. 226.　　　　　　[38] *Political Writings*, p. 36.
[39] *Ibid.*, p. 230.
[40] See below, Chapter Eight, section I.

53

that is wanting to establish the principle of non-intervention as a law of nations, as absolutely as the political refugee in a third and neutral country is protected now by the law of nations.[41]

By "that expression of opinion," Cobden meant the unanimous expression of indignation from all parties and every shade of opinion as expressed in the newspapers of London and Paris.

The second article of Cobden's faith was the power of example. To those who argued that they were in favor of nonintervention provided other people conformed to the same principle, Cobden replied that he too wished to see the principle universally adopted and that the first step toward it was for Britain to set an example by herself conforming to it.[42] "If England, America and France would proclaim such a law *for themselves*," he wrote, "no other power would dare to violate it. . . . [I]f England and America would first observe the principle themselves, they might afterwards say 'Stop' to Russia, and the word would *then* have as much force as if uttered with the voice of a thousand cannon."[43]

Cobden's hypotheses about the power of persuasion in international relations were not and still have not been put to the test, unlike his faith in the peace-loving nature of the commercial classes of England which was found wanting at the time of the Crimean War. But his refusal to admit even the possibility of force to uphold the law being opposed to force deployed against the law was a weakness in his doctrine which Mill emphasized.[44]

JOHN STUART MILL

Concern that by her words England was misrepresenting the true motive of her foreign policy and that by her deeds she was abusing the habitual principles of that policy led Mill to attempt to clarify

[41] Cobden to John Bright, November 13, 1851, in Morley, *Life of Cobden*, Vol. II, pp. 105–106.

[42] Cobden to Henry Richard, December 5, 1856, in Hobson, *Richard Cobden*, p. 183.

[43] Cobden to Henry Richard, November 9, 1851, in Hobson, pp. 78–79 (Cobden's emphasis). Similar phrases in a letter to John Bright, November 6, 1851, in Morley, Vol. II, pp. 102–103.

[44] Though Mill did not address himself to the speeches and writings of Cobden but rather to a British foreign policy which proclaimed a principle of nonintervention.

the grounds upon which it was justifiable to intervene in the affairs of other countries.[45] Because the British policy of nonintervention was interpreted in other countries as a mere screen for her own aggrandizement and because Britain's actions did not always seem to accord with her professed principles, Mill thought it appropriate to reconsider the whole doctrine of noninterference as a moral question.[46]

In the first place, Mill more forcibly than Cobden made a distinction between rules applicable in the relations of civilized nations and those which were relevant to conduct towards "barbarians." The behavior of the former toward the latter might indeed offend against the great principles of morality but could never violate the law of nations since barbarians had not the rights of a nation. For Mill, criticism of French conduct in Algeria, or that of the English in India, in terms of the principle of nonintervention, or indeed of any customary rule of international law, was mistaken.[47]

In the international relations of civilized nations, Mill reduced the question of the legitimacy of interfering in the regulation of another country's internal concerns to whether in time of civil war a nation is justified in taking part on one side or another. Mill answered the various questions which arose from this problem in some cases according to the customary law of nations, in others by reference to rules of morality or the requirements for their proper operation, and in others by the use of reason or what seemed to him to be sound policy. In the case of a protracted civil war in which neither side could gain a sufficient ascendancy to end it, Mill relied on "admitted doctrine" to justify intervention by

---

[45] J. S. Mill, "A Few Words on Non-Intervention," reprinted from *Fraser's Magazine,* December 1859, in Mill, *Dissertations and Discussions. Political, Philosophical, and Historical,* 4 vols., London, 1875, Vol. III, pp. 153–178. The "words" Mill objected to were those used by statesmen to justify nonintervention by England in continental affairs by reference purely and baldly to the criterion of British interests. This, he thought, left England open to the charge of being an unprincipled meddler in other nations' affairs. What they really meant, according to Mill, was that while England would normally observe the principle of nonintervention, she would overrule it if such action were required by the higher principle of self-defense. The "deed" Mill objected to was the "insane blunder" England seemed to be committing by her attempts to defeat the French-inspired Suez Canal project. *Ibid.*, pp. 162–166.

[46] *Ibid.*, p. 166.   [47] *Ibid.*, p. 168.

neighbors to insist that the contest cease.[48] As to intervention on behalf of a people struggling for liberty against its government, Mill used similar arguments to Cobden to deny its legitimacy. This judgment was not based on a rule of any sort, but upon a conviction that the best test of a people's fitness for popular institutions was a willingness "to brave labour and danger for their liberation."[49]

Assistance to a people kept down by foreign intervention, Mill argued, was a necessary requirement for the proper operation of the principle of nonintervention. Help of this kind did not disturb an indigenous balance of forces but served to redress a balance disrupted by outside intervention. Mill argued the case for counter-intervention in this way.

> The doctrine of non-intervention, to be a legitimate principle of morality, must be accepted by all governments. The despots must consent to be bound by it as well as free States. Unless they do, the profession of it by free countries comes but to this miserable issue, that the wrong side may help the wrong, but the right must not help the right. Intervention to enforce non-intervention is always rightful, always moral, if not always prudent.[50]

By admitting the legitimacy of what might be called humanitarian intervention to bring to an end a deadlocked civil war and by insisting on the legitimacy of counterintervention to uphold the rule of nonintervention, Mill parted company with Cobden's more extreme doctrine of nonintervention.

IMMANUEL KANT

Kant's fifth preliminary article for eternal peace reads: "No state shall interfere by force in the constitution or government of another state."[51] Like Cobden, he held this principle to be an indis-

---

[48] *Ibid.*, p. 172. By "admitted doctrine," Mill clearly meant that of customary international law. He showed it to be a maxim of "what is called international law" by the use of examples of intervention of this type.

[49] Mill did not lay this down as an invariable rule, he merely said that intervention of this sort can "seldom . . . I will not go so far as to say never—be either judicious or right." *Ibid.*, p. 175.

[50] *Ibid.*, p. 176.

[51] Kant, "On Eternal Peace," trans. Carl J. Friedrich in Friedrich, *Inevitable Peace*, Cambridge, Mass., 1948, p. 248.

pensable condition for the achievement of peace among nations. Unlike Cobden, Kant seemed to allow exceptions to the rule of nonintervention in order to make it consistent with other articles that he set forth in his scheme for perpetual peace.

International peace and a law of nations to preserve it, Kant thought, must be based on the freedom and "moral integrity" of each nation.[52] There could be no justification for a state interfering in the constitution of another unless internal dissension had split it into two parts each constituting a separate state. But if the internal strife had not yet reached this stage of anarchy, then interference from outside powers was an infraction of the right of an independent people struggling with its own weaknesses. Interference of this sort, Kant considered, would tend to render the autonomy of all states insecure.[53]

While Cobden agitated against intervention to promote or bring down a particular form of government, Kant appeared to imply an exception to the rule of nonintervention if by intervention a republic could be established or a despotic regime crushed. Kant's first definitive article for perpetual peace declared that "the civil constitution in each state should be republican."[54] To the question whether a republican constitution was the only one which could lead to world peace, Kant replied that it did "offer the prospect of the desired purpose," because the decision to go to war would be in the hands of citizens who would be aware of their real deprivations as a result of war unlike a head of state (i.e., not a citizen) who could find war an amusing diversion.[55]

The solution to this problem in the interpretation of Kant as to which is the more pressing imperative—the rule of nonintervention or an international society made up of republics—seems to lie in regarding republicanism as prior to nonintervention. If it is the nature of the internal order that ultimately determines the character of international society,[56] then rules about international relations must give precedence to rules about domestic society.

[52] *Ibid.*, p. 256, the second definitive article of the eternal peace.

[53] Kant, "On Eternal Peace," in Friedrich, p. 248.

[54] *Ibid.*, p. 250. By a republican constitution, Kant meant one founded on the following three principles: *freedom* of all members of society as men, the *dependence* of all on a single common legislation as subjects, and the *equality* of all as *citizens. Ibid.*, p. 250.

[55] *Ibid.*, pp. 251–252.

[56] This is Karl Loewenstein's interpretation of Kant in *Political Reconstruction*, New York, 1946, pp. 17–20.

57

It is then possible to argue that "Kant restricts and defines non-intervention . . . to the making of a *civil constitution*; conversely, Kant would probably have asserted the right of other powers to intervene when a people is being deprived of its constitution by a totalitarian *coup d'état*."[57] Only in an international society made up of republican nations could a rule of nonintervention apply absolutely.

With regard to the rule of nonintervention, the other problem in Kant is his conception of a "cosmopolitan or world law" set forth in the third definitive article of perpetual peace. He did not make Mill's distinction between civilization and barbarism with respect to the applicability of rules which was a commonplace of the positivist tracts of the nineteenth century. Moreover, Kant's requirement of a *jus cosmopoliticum* seemed to erode the distinction between municipal and international law, and to add a third dimension of world law applying directly to men without consulting the state as intermediary. The nonintervention principle is a rule between states whose applicability is compromised if individual men or groups have recourse to a law beyond the state. Kant's conception of a "public law of mankind" making a "violation of law and right in one place felt in *all* others" seems to restrict the rule of nonintervention to an even narrower field than the requirement of republicanism.[58]

While Mill's thoughts on the principle of nonintervention can be said to have analyzed among other things the requirements for the operation of the rule in the then existing international order, Kant's requirements for perpetual peace seemed to base adherence to the principle on a radical, if not a revolutionary, revision of that order.

JOSEPH MAZZINI

Mazzini's criticism of the doctrine of nonintervention involved at best a feeling with Kant (though for very different reasons) that

---

[57] Friedrich, p. 178 (Friedrich's emphasis of "civil constitution").

[58] Kant, "On Eternal Peace," in Friedrich, pp. 257–259. Kant's concern, in proposing his third definitive article, was with the "inhospitable" conduct of civilized nations towards people outside Europe and North America who were "counted for nothing." Thus Friedrich suggests that Kant "would have restricted the idea of non-intervention in such fashion as to enable the world federalism [Kant's second definitive article on international law] to take positive steps to protect people against imperialism and minorities against abuse." *Inevitable Peace*, p. 48.

its proper functioning would require a revision of the international system. At worst, Mazzini considered the doctrine a mere slogan disguising the machinations of the great powers. Mazzini did not share with Cobden and Mill the conviction that the doctrine of nonintervention as advanced in the Europe of his time had a moral content.

Mazzini saw the origin of the principle of nonintervention as an offspring of the theory of human rights which was the legacy of eighteenth-century thought in Europe.[59] The doctrine of the equality and liberty of all men, as it was applied to states, led to an assertion of a right of nonintervention. According to Mazzini, this product of the "negative and purely critical" spirit of the previous century had originally served a useful purpose.[60] The function of the nonintervention principle had been twofold. In the first place, it was "a useful and righteous protest against the lust of conquest and appetite for war, which had till then characterized the activity of Europe."[61] Second, the principle of nonintervention represented the best way so far evolved by governments to avoid conflict between them.[62]

After the French Revolution, Mazzini thought, the history of the principle of nonintervention demonstrated that it had already made its contribution to "the intellectual progress of the human race" and was now a mere tool of the great powers, a principle invoked to protect their own self-interest.[63] After the Congress of Vienna, Mazzini argued, the rule of nonintervention was to fulfill a function which directly contradicted the cause in whose service it had originated; it became a protector of the legitimist settlement of 1815. The rule was to stand guard over the parceling out of Europe effected at Vienna. It was to allow the governments recognized by that settlement to do as they would with the people within their frontiers, and it was to justify intervention to uphold the *status quo*, should those people attempt to disturb it.[64] This

[59] Gaetano Salvemini, *Mazzini*, trans. I. M. Rawson, London, 1956, pp. 25–27.

[60] Joseph Mazzini, *Life and Writings of Joseph Mazzini*, 6 vols., London, 1891, Vol. 6, Appendix on "Non-Intervention," first publ. 1851, p. 300. Theories of equality and liberty were negative because they begged the question—equality and liberty to what end? critical because they served to protest against a tyrant in the name of freedom. Salvemini, pp. 26–27.

[61] Mazzini, Vol. 6, p. 300.   [62] Salvemini, p. 28.

[63] Mazzini, Vol. 6, p. 300; Salvemini, p. 28.

[64] Mazzini, Vol. 6, pp. 300–301.

interpretation of the function of the nonintervention doctrine after 1815 allowed Mazzini to assert his view of the real meaning of the doctrine in words which were to be echoed by John Stuart Mill eight years later.[65] According to Mazzini, the nonintervention principle now meant "intervention on the wrong side; intervention by all who choose, and are strong enough, to put down free movements of peoples against corrupt governments. It means cooperation of despots against peoples, but no cooperation of peoples against despots."[66] Because of this perversion of its original meaning, Mazzini thought nonintervention to be a discredited doctrine at least among thinking people in Europe. Only in England was the doctrine still respected and this was due to its degeneration into a "kind of selfish indifferentism."[67]

For Mazzini, two sorts of conditions would have to be met if the nonintervention principle were to be an acceptable rule of conduct between nations. In the first place, Mazzini thought that the rule would have to be adhered to absolutely. If the principle of nonintervention were proclaimed by other states as a ground for doing nothing on behalf of Italian independence, then those states should also accept an internal revolution as legitimate and do nothing to put it down.[68] But Mazzini went further than this to demand that the historical record of the rule of nonintervention be put straight. "The same theory which proclaims non-interference as the first law of international politics," he declared, "must include, as a secondary law, the right of interference to make good all prior infractions of the law of non-interference."[69]

Mazzini's second condition for acceptance of the rule of nonintervention was that it should apply between nations. He thought that the rule presupposed a state of things "in which all the due conditions of Nationality have been attended to."[70] Mazzini's theory of nationalism asserted that "God has divided the human race into masses so evidently distinct; each with a separate tone of thought, and a separate part to fulfil."[71] On this view, the rule of nonintervention could play a legitimate role only if it served to protect a God-given order, and that role was no longer a legiti-

[65] See above, p. 56.

[66] Mazzini, Vol. 6, pp. 305–306.

[67] *Ibid.*, Vol. 6, p. 301. This argument was one to which Mill addressed himself in his essay on nonintervention, see above, pp. 54–55.

[68] Mazzini, Vol. 6, pp. 304–305.

[69] *Ibid.*, p. 305.   [70] *Ibid.*, p. 301.   [71] *Ibid.*, pp. 302–303.

mate one if "the inhabitants of Europe were flung together anyhow."[72] For Mazzini, the nation was a more permanent entity than a system of rule, and it was the nation and not the system of rule which should be inviolate.[73]

But apart from his criticism of the abuse of the principle of nonintervention by the great powers and his view of the only conditions in which such a rule could properly operate, Mazzini seemed to repudiate the sort of international society which would embrace the rule as a principle of its existence. He would not have tolerated Cobden's anarchistic conception of international society in which the rule of nonintervention would be of fundamental importance. The very reasons which convinced Cobden of the wisdom of a policy of nonintervention led Mazzini to denounce it as "an abject cowardly doctrine: atheism transplanted into international life, the deification of self-interest."[74] The "atheism"— the political bloodlessness of the rule of nonintervention—was for Cobden its principal asset. Certainly, it would prevent intervention on behalf of liberalism, but it would prevent intervention against it too. But Mazzini, fired by enthusiasm for revolutionary nationalism, could see the rule operating only against this righteous cause. In a similar way to Kant's *jus cosmopoliticum*, Mazzini envisaged an international society in which nations, as a matter of international duty, could combine to counter some glaring wrong being done within an independent nation. He thought it was beginning to be felt in international society that confronted with such a wrong "other nations are not absolved from all concern in the matter simply because there may interpose between them and the scene of the wrong, seas, tracts of continent, and traditional diplomatic courtesies."[75] Furthermore, Mazzini thought, the traditional diplomatic courtesy—the rule of nonintervention—removed "one of the most potent impulses towards progress, which as history teaches us, is almost always fulfilled through acts of intervention."[76]

Both Cobden and Mill addressed their ideas about nonintervention primarily to British foreign policy, Cobden in a long and lonely attempt to persuade its makers into a radical change of course, Mill in a less ambitious attempt to coax them back into what he saw as the mainstream of the British tradition of noninter-

[72] *Ibid.*, p. 303.
[73] *Ibid.*, p. 304.
[74] Quoted in Salvemini, p. 28.
[75] Mazzini, pp. 307–308.
[76] Quoted in Salvemini, pp. 28–29.

vention. Cobden not only laid bare the weaknesses of his opponents' doctrine with inescapable logic but also developed his own theory of foreign policy, and it is in the theory Cobden constructed rather than in the arguments he used to belabor Palmerston that a major flaw can be found. Outside the power of example and of opinion, Cobden's radical anarchism made no provision against the violator of the rule of nonintervention. In affirming the legitimacy of counterintervention to enforce nonintervention, Mill improved on Cobden's theory, but in doing so, he raised a whole series of questions which Cobden's absolute noninterventionism avoided, questions about when the law had been broken, which is the wrong side, and who judges. Concerned neither with the reform of a particular state's foreign policy nor with approximate order in the world as it was but with the conditions for perpetual peace between states, Kant seemed to require the establishment of republican government within states before a rule of nonintervention could operate between them. In requiring that certain conditions be met before the rule could be observed, Mazzini followed Kant; the principle could apply only when international relations were indeed the relations between nations. But this vision remaining unrealized, Mazzini was bitter about the function of the principle in the international politics of his time. Originally a progessive doctrine, it had been turned to the advantage of the great powers and so corrupted that it had come to mean not nonintervention, but intervention and intervention on the wrong side at that.

Each of these theories of nonintervention outlived its author and survives to instruct the contemporary debate about international relations. In the view that nonintervention is for the great powers a disguise for intervention, in the wish to extend the protection of the principle of nonintervention to nations, making it the obverse of the right of self-determination, and in the desire to make good prior infractions of the rule in the campaign against colonialism and racialism, the Third World doctrines of nonintervention pressed at the United Nations bear a striking resemblance to those of Mazzini.[77] Kant's doctrine that the form of government within states determines the nature of order between them has had many followers from Woodrow Wilson's faith in and interference on behalf of constitutional democracy of which Kant might have approved, through the interference of the Russian revolutionaries on

[77] See below, Chapter Seven, sections IV and V.

behalf of the working-class movement of which Kant might not have approved, to the acknowledgment by the founding fathers of the United Nations of some basis in the Kantian relationship by their writing the protection of human rights and fundamental freedoms into the Charter. In the Cold War, Mill's doctrine of counterintervention to enforce nonintervention has seen service on both sides of the battle, and Cobden's doctrine has survived as a protest against it. The recurrence of these different themes will be apparent in the chapters that follow.

FOUR

PRACTICE

In writings on international law and in theories of foreign policy, adherence to the rule of nonintervention has been urged as right conduct for states in their relations with each other. Whether the motive of such urging is the maintenance of a rule of law between states or the advancement of the interests of a particular state, the function of the principle is one of restraint; its purpose is to prevent the state from conducting its foreign relations by a method perceived to be undesirable. This chapter will examine the extent to which the principle can be said to have restrained the foreign policies of three states: France at the time of the Revolution and its aftermath, Britain after the Vienna settlement, and the United States from her independence to the Second World War. Beyond the question of whether these states can be said to have observed the rule for whatever reasons, it will be seen that the principle had functions in more than the one dimension of restraint. The rule formed part of the language of diplomacy. Statesmen developed doctrines of nonintervention and used them to defend their own policies and to criticize the policies of others, to advance their own objectives and to hamper the achievement of the objectives of others, and to communicate their views about the limits of the permissible in international relations. The principle of nonintervention served to legitimize action in international politics, to provide a doctrinal weapon in support of foreign policy, and to offer some guide by which states could predict each other's action or reaction in international relations.

I

Nonintervention in French Revolutionary Doctrine and Practice

It is tempting to regard the ideas of the French Revolution about international relations as following from, and out of the same root as, the Declaration of the Rights of Man. To an extent, this temptation can be justifiably indulged. In the first place, Abbé

Grégoire's Declaration of the Law of Nations submitted to the Convention in June 1793 echoed the Declaration of 1789, substituting the rights of peoples for the rights of men.[1] That this substitution could be made so easily by Grégoire was due, it has been argued, to the natural law doctrine of the eighteenth century.[2] Writers like Wolff and Vattel had already made use of the analogy between man in a state of nature and states in a similar condition in their accounts of international law.[3] Second, Rousseau's ideas about government by consent and sovereignty would be, if put into practice, as significant for the relations between states as for their domestic order. The doctrine of the sovereignty of the people injected into international law the idea of nationality.[4]

Grégoire's declaration was not passed by the Convention; but that body and the Assembly before it did espouse notions about the conduct of foreign policy couched in terms of natural law if not directly inspired by it. Doctrines of this sort were the May 1790 announcement that the French nation would not embark upon wars of conquest and the Decree of April 1793 declaring that the French people would not interfere in the government of other powers. The question whether or not these protestations can be taken as representative of French revolutionary doctrine on international relations depends upon their consistency with other declarations. Are they to be regarded as guiding principles for the French nation or merely as reactions to particular circumstances?

The National Assembly declared on May 22, 1790 that "the French nation will refuse to undertake any war of conquest, and

[1] Among the articles of the declaration is one positing a state of nature among nations, another asserting the inalienable sovereignty of nations, another proclaiming the nonintervention principle. Amos Hershey, *The Essentials of International Public Law and Organization*, New York, 1939, p. 82, n. 34.

[2] Nussbaum, *Concise History of the Law of Nations*, p. 119. This is not, of course, to argue that natural law doctrine was peculiar to the eighteenth century. For the influence of the doctrine on the French Revolution, and for the theoretical antecedents of the Revolution generally, see A. W. Ward, G. W. Prothero, and S. Leathes, eds., *The Cambridge Modern History* (hereafter *C.M.H.*), Vol. VIII, Cambridge, 1904, pp. 1–35.

[3] See above, Chapter Two, pp. 26–31. Nussbaum draws a direct line between Vattel and Grégoire, stating that Grégoire's theses were drawn almost entirely from Vattel's treatise. Nussbaum, p. 158.

[4] *C.M.H.*, Vol. VIII, p. 755.

will never employ its forces against the liberty of any people."[5] Coming as it did, after the Assembly's refusal to take part in a war with England on behalf of Spain over the Nootka Sound incident, this declaration can first be interpreted as "an honest expression of a pacific policy."[6] This "unrevolutionary" interpretation is strengthened by Mirabeau's warnings of the madness of French disarmament in the face of an armed Europe, his concern that France by changing her own political system could not thereby change that of others.[7]

A second interpretation of the Declaration of May 22 places emphasis not on it "honest expression of pacific policy," but on its significance as representative of a "new international law, foreshadowed as early as 1789 when Corsica was admitted as a department of France."[8] On this view, the importance of the declaration was not its pacific character but its assertion that "man's will, freely expressed, was to determine the destiny of the soil."[9] Whereas before international law had been a law between territorial and dynastic states, states which, in their relations, took no account of the wishes of individual men or peoples, the Revolution would liberate nations, as it had men, and make the will of the people the determinant of the subjects of international law. According to this principle, the citizens of other states could change their allegiance by plebiscite. When the National Assembly was confronted with the results of its own declaration by the declared wish of the inhabitants of Alsace and Avignon to join France, it hesitated to annex them for fear of providing the interested powers with a *casus belli*. Thus while the May 22 Declaration can be interpreted as an earnest of a pacific policy, it was not its pacific nature which mattered. The declaration, if it ever became more than mere words, would undermine the very foundations of the old order of public law in Europe.

The difficulties of adhering to the twin obligations of a principle which would liberate subject peoples without taking over responsi-

[5] J. M. Thompson, *The French Revolution*, Oxford, 1947, p. 248. This declaration was included in the Constitution of 1791 at Title VI. See F. M. Anderson, *The Constitutions and Other Select Documents Illustrative of the History of France 1789–1907*, 2nd rev. ed., New York, 1907, rept. 1967, p. 93.

[6] Thompson, p. 248.   [7] *C.M.H.*, Vol. VIII, pp. 188–189.

[8] Georges Lefebvres, *The French Revolution; from its Origins to 1793*, trans. Elizabeth Moss Evanson, London, 1962, p. 196.

[9] *Ibid.*, p. 196.

bility for their protection by armed force were brought home to the French Convention toward the end of the year 1792. On November 19 the Convention was asked to consider the requests of the citizens of Limburg and Mainz for French protection from "the despots who threaten them."[10] The Convention could choose among ignoring the petitions, offering French protection, or guaranteeing the liberty of the neighboring peoples.[11] Infected by the enthusiasm following Dumouriez's victory over the Austrians at Jemappes, the Convention, without referring the matter to the Diplomatic Committee, adopted the following decree:

> The National Convention declares, in the name of the French people, that it will accord fraternity and assistance to all peoples who shall wish to recover their liberty and charges the executive power to give to the generals the necessary orders to furnish assistance to these peoples and to defend the citizens who may have been or who may be harrassed for the cause of liberty.[12]

From this declaration of French intentions toward peoples struggling for freedom followed the Decree of December 15, which was addressed to the financing of French activity not only in the Rhineland but also in the territory captured by Dumouriez's campaigns. It directed the French generals in occupied countries to proclaim immediately the sovereignty of the people, the suppression of all established authority, and the placing under the protection of the French Republic of all goods belonging to the public treasury.[13] "This famous decree," according to Lefebvre, "instituted the dictatorship of revolutionary minorities under the protection of French bayonets, and undertook to secure the fortunes of other peoples without consulting them, at their expense."[14] By the policy of annexation and of *guerre aux châteaux, paix aux chaumières*, "France thus ceased to be the volunteer, and became the mercenary of the cause of 'freedom.' "[15]

The French Convention, by its reaction and perhaps overreaction to events forced upon its notice, had carried two declarations, which together with the forcible opening of the Scheldt by French gunboats were to lead to war with England.[16] Of the December 15

[10] *C.M.H.*, Vol. VIII, p. 300.
[11] Lefebvre, p. 273; *C.M.H.*, Vol. VIII, p. 300.
[12] Anderson, p. 130. [13] *Ibid.*, pp. 130–133.
[14] Lefebvre, p. 277. [15] *C.M.H.*, Vol. VIII, p. 257.
[16] The French defended the opening of the Scheldt by reference to

Decree "[m]ore even than all the previous transactions," Pitt said in the House of Commons seven years later, "it amounted to a universal declaration of war against all thrones, and against all civilized governments."[17]

The Decree on Nonintervention of April 13, 1793 has to be read, then, against the background of these momentous decrees of the last months of the previous year, as well as the circumstances that immediately provoked its proclamation. The new decree aimed at reciprocal nonintervention between France and the other European states:

> The National Convention declares in the name of the French people, that it will not interfere in any manner in the government of the other powers; but it declares at the same time, that it will sooner be buried under its own ruins than suffer that any power should interfere in the internal regime of the Republic, or should influence the creation of the constitution which it intends to give itself.[18]

At the time of the passing of this declaration, France was not only split by internal dissension, but her armies in the Low Countries, on the Rhine, and on the Moselle were in a disastrous condition.[19] Danton, who was at this time controlling French foreign policy, sought to repair the international situation by reopening contacts with England and Prussia, and by disavowing the decrees of November 19 and December 15. Addressing the Convention, he said:

> It is time the National Convention should make it known to Europe that France knows how to combine with republican virtues statesmanship. In a moment of enthusiasm you passed a decree, the motive of which was certainly noble, since you bound yourselves to protect nations resisting their tyrants. This decree would logically imply an obligation to assist an insurrec-

---

natural law. *C.M.H.*, Vol. VIII, p. 300. Nussbaum points out that the law of nature might better be interpreted as dictating that the Scheldt be open to all nations and not just to France, p. 120.

[17] Quoted in Thompson, p. 338. The causes of the outbreak of war between France and England in February 1793 are a matter of controversy which is not relevant here.

[18] Anderson, pp. 133–134.

[19] A. H. Beesly, *Life of Danton*, London, 1899, p. 235.

tion in China. . . . Let us pass a resolution that we will not meddle with our neighbour's affairs.[20]

Thus Danton invoked the doctrine of nonintervention as a tactical device in the war against the powers, a device which together with the diplomatic contacts did "little more than increase the assurance of the victorious coalition."[21]

For Danton, the doctrine of nonintervention was not, as it was for Grégoire, a matter of principle traceable from natural law and consistent with French revolutionary ideals. Danton invoked it as a weapon from the French nation's desperately weak armory to function not as a stick with which to beat the European powers, but as a shield against their further advance. Nor can the Decree on No Conquest of May 1790 be regarded, according to traditional international law, as amounting to a declaration of nonintervention; it would rather represent annexation by plebiscite—a pacific action having a clear interventionary effect. However, the doctrine of national sovereignty from which the doctrine of no conquest arose, could be interpreted as carrying with it a rule of nonintervention once the will of the people had become the informing principle of statehood. In this sense French revolutionary doctrine would take on the same quality as that of Kant and Mazzini, both of whom based adherence to the principle of nonintervention on the prior fulfillment of another condition.[22] But nowhere in French revolutionary thought is this sort of doctrine spelled out. Indeed, in the 1793 Constitution which failed to pass the Convention, the Decree on Fraternity of November 19, 1792 and the Decree on Nonintervention of April 13, 1793 appear next to each other, no explanation being offered for their apparent inconsistency.[23] In the fervor of the successful Revolution, France proclaimed a doctrine of intervention in the name of the new order but retreated behind the principle of nonintervention in an attempt to safeguard her security when it was threatened by the forces of the Old Regime. It was after the Revolution had become the Empire and after the defeat of the Empire in 1815 that the traditional British

[20] *Ibid.*, pp. 236–237.
[21] A. Fugier, "La Révolution Française et L'Empire Napoléonien," in Pierre Renouvin, ed., *Histoire des Relations Internationales*, 7 vols., Paris, 1953–1957, Tome IV, 1954, p. 85.
[22] See above, Chapter Three, pp. 56–61.
[23] Articles 118 and 119 of the Constitution, Anderson, p. 183.

doctrine of nonintervention was worked out more closely than hitherto, and opposed to the interventionary doctrines of the European powers.

II

NONINTERVENTION IN BRITISH DOCTRINE AND PRACTICE

Action according to the principle of nonintervention had always been a possible policy for Great Britain in her relations with Europe. Indeed, her insular position, reinforced by a powerful navy, suggested the seductive policy of total abstention from participation in continental affairs, an isolationism which would interpret the nonintervention principle absolutely. But because such a policy presaged ultimate disaster if it ignored the threat of single-power hegemony in Europe, a British interest in a European balance of power went hand-in-hand with the requirement of naval supremacy. The principle of balance and that of nonintervention were consistent with each other at least in the sense that both were concerned to protect the independence of the several European states by preventing the aggrandizement of any one power beyond its own frontiers.[24] For Britain, this concern with the independence of states and with a balance between them stopped short of the continental preoccupation with the form of government established within states. The threat to British security was the power which revealed its aggressive intentions by forcible intervention in the affairs of other states, not the power which was supposed to be aggressive because of the nature of its internal institutions. British faith in the singularity and inviolability of her institutions led her not only to discount any threat to her security emanating from the mere existence of a particular social system in another state but also to deny the validity of a principle of interference which had as its object the form of government within states.[25] The distinction between political threats and social threats and between the external conduct of states and their internal affairs has been

[24] In other senses, however, the two principles are not consistent with each other. For a discussion of them see below, Chapter Nine, section III.

[25] For these reasons the British doctrine of noninterference has been called the "reverse side of the belief in the uniqueness of British institutions" expressing the conviction that "threats to British security were political, not social in nature." Henry A. Kissinger, *A World Restored*, London, 1957, p. 34.

fundamental in British foreign policy. Thus in 1792 Pitt saw the danger from France not in her revolution but in her threat to the Scheldt and thereby to the "political system of Europe, established by solemn treaties and guaranteed by the consent of all the Powers."[26] Even when Britain dispatched troops to Lisbon in 1826, Peel could argue in a debate in the House of Commons three years later that such conduct was not intervention in Portugal's internal affairs because it was undertaken not to maintain any political institution, but to honor treaty commitments and to uphold the independence of Portugal.[27] Britain's *laissez-faire* attitude to forms of government in other states did not mean she would refrain from intervention if pressing imperatives like the maintenance of the balance of power required it; what it did mean was that she could admit intervention only as an exception not as a rule of international conduct.

The British principle of nonintervention could then be regarded as an expression of a *laissez-faire* ideology. As a guide to conduct, it was not necessarily inconsistent with the traditional British pursuit of a European balance of power. It could also be advocated as an instrument for the achievement of another objective of British policy—the maintenance of European peace. For Britain, commitment to this objective was not a mere pious aspiration; it was founded in the interests of a satisfied nation, with no territorial ambitions in Europe, whose well-being as a commercial power did not benefit from European conflict. The rule of nonintervention, if observed by states, would contribute to peace to the extent that it removed one instrument of conflict between them. Thus Britain could espouse the rule not only as a guide to the conduct of her own foreign policy but also as a beneficent principle of European international relations.

If nonintervention was a possible policy for Britain, it was also actual, at least in the sense that it was widely held to be a precept of foreign policy. The doctrine of noninterference in the internal affairs of other countries has been referred to as "an axiom of British politics since the accession of the House of Hanover."[28]

[26] Quoted in *C.M.H.*, Vol. VIII, p. 304.

[27] Donald Southgate, *The Most English Minister*, London, 1966, p. 10. That the existing government did benefit by Canning's intervention does not alter the fact that his motive for intervention was the preservation of Portuguese independence, and not the survival of constitutional government.

[28] C. K. Webster, *The Foreign Policy of Castlereagh, 1815–1822*, London, 1947, p. 53.

It was a doctrine of "British politics" in the sense that it was not the preserve of any one party or faction in the spectrum of political allegiance. During a House of Lords debate in 1849, Lord Derby declared nonintervention to be "the one principle of sound policy in which on both sides of the House there was a universal and unanimous concurrence."[29] That the doctrine was at one time held to be a "Whig principle,"[30] or attached at another to the famous Tory names of Pitt, Castlereagh, and Canning, or related at a third to Cobden and the Peace Party, serves to demonstrate its political promiscuity.

This widespread adherence to the principle of nonintervention can be explained in part as a recognition by all parties of the objective situation of Britain—an island power facing a powerful Europe and cherishing her unique institutions. The persistence of the principle is perhaps better explained by its flexible nature, which allowed politicians of vastly different color to interpret the rule in their own way and to use it as a lever for their various conceptions of the British interest. In Whig thought, the principle of nonintervention could be related to the doctrines of 1688 by which "all power held by Sovereigns may be forfeited by misconduct, and every nation is the judge of its own internal government."[31] For the Tory, the beauty of the principle was that it eschewed doctrine in favor of interests, that it restricted the activities of the ideologue in foreign policy. For the Radical, a policy of nonintervention meant a Britain at peace and flourishing commercially.

While advocacy of a policy of nonintervention was ubiquitous in British political thought, it did not constitute a consensus of it. In the Lords debate mentioned above, Derby's enthusiasm for nonintervention was opposed by Lord Lansdowne's quip that a declaration against interference in the concerns of foreign nations was only fit for a place "among the neat maxims at the head of a schoolboy's copy-book" and that any practical statesman would treat it with "perfect contempt."[32] There was no lack of discussion about the desirability of a policy of nonintervention; indeed, it formed a focal point of the British debate on foreign policy. But it

[29] Quoted in Bernard, *On the Principle of Non-Intervention*, p. 2.

[30] By Sir Henry Bulwer, British envoy to Madrid 1843–1848. Southgate, p. 189.

[31] Lord John Russell to Queen Victoria, January 11, 1860, explaining his Italian policy, cited in R. W. Seton-Watson, *Britain in Europe, 1789–1914*, Cambridge, 1945, p. 404.

[32] Bernard, p. 2.

was not a debate which took place according to party alignment; the principle of nonintervention found support and met opposition among all political groupings.

This section will look at the part played by the principle of nonintervention in the foreign policies of Castlereagh, Canning, and Palmerston.[33] It will examine the way in which these statesmen interpreted the rule, the extent to which they can be said to have acted in accordance with it, and the function the rule fulfilled in their diplomacy.

i. Castlereagh

The settlement of 1814–1815 had laid low for the time being the specter of revolution in Europe. Yet it was the issue of what was to be done in the event of its resurgence which divided Britain from the continental powers, and led to the demise of the congress system after Verona in 1822. A need to conserve the new European order was generally recognized among the victorious allies, but there were differences of view as to what constituted that order. One school of thought dominant in Britain held that it was sufficient for international tranquillity to uphold the territorial settlement of 1815; to this imperative, the other school of thought typified by Austria added the requirement of preserving the dynastic arrangements legitimized by the Congress of Vienna. Both these views can be explained in terms of the interests of their principal proponents. For Austria, a vulnerable international position between France and Russia, and a sensitive internal sovereignty over a multinational empire gave her a twin interest in the sanctity of frontiers and the legitimacy of thrones. For Metternich, the Chancellor of Austria, revolution was a threat because it might spread by contagion to the Austrian domain. It was the more dangerous because its spread was not left to chance but was advanced by an international conspiracy against the dynastic order. Moreover, a direct relation was traced in Austrian thought between

[33] These three to illustrate three different conceptions of the principle of nonintervention: Castlereagh, sympathetic to the Old Guard of Europe, but using the principle to restrain their schemes from a position within the alliance; Canning, using the principle to separate Britain from the alliance, and delighting in it as a weapon against both the Old Guard and the constitutionalists; and Palmerston, erring from Canning's middle way in the opposite direction to Castlereagh and interpreting it as defining the outer limits of permissible British action against the Old Guard and for constitutionalism in Europe.

revolution within a state and its propensity to aggress beyond its frontiers. This analysis led Austria to assert a right, if not a duty, to intervene in states torn by social upheaval, in order to forestall an otherwise inevitable challenge to the whole European order.[34]

The Austrian doctrine of prophylactic intervention stemmed from the view that territorial and dynastic integrity were interdependent, that the one could not be preserved without attention to the other. In British thought, the two ideas were separated and only one of them taken as fundamental to the conservation of the new order. The British perception that she was politically but not socially vulnerable meant that she shared with the continental powers the view that protection of the territorial settlement was a legitimate subject for European concern, but parted company with them on the dynastic question. In one of its senses, the British doctrine of nonintervention meant that she would act to meet an immediate danger demonstrated by actual aggression, but not a potential danger whose existence was a matter of conjecture. It was not that British foreign-policy makers were unconcerned about revolution in other states—some of Castlereagh's antirevolutionary outbursts were as virulent as Metternich's—but the existence of revolution did not by itself justify a policy of intervention.

For Britain to go as far as she did in committing himself to the Vienna settlement which allowed no frontier to be altered "without touching a Treaty to which Britain was a party"[35] was a new, if not a radical, departure in foreign policy. But Castlereagh's attachment to the alliance and his belief in the efficacy of conference diplomacy did not prevent him from setting limits to the activities of the allies by attempting to control them from within. When the Treaty of Alliance was being redrafted at Paris toward the end of 1815, the Tsar proposed that the allies support both Louis XVIII and the liberal constitution which he had granted the year before.[36] This Castlereagh could not accept; it was "too strong and undisguised an interference of the Allied sovereigns in the internal concerns of France."[37] Castlereagh's draft, which in large part became the Treaty of November 20, 1815, declared the main object of the alliance to be the protection of Europe against

---

[34] On Austrian thought, see Carsten Holbraad, *The Concert of Europe: A Study in German and British International Theory 1815–1914*, London, 1970, pp. 15–34.

[35] Webster, p. 51. [36] *Ibid.*, p. 53.

[37] Quoted in *C.M.H.*, Vol. x, Cambridge, 1907, p. 12.

French attack. Revolution in France was not to be considered a *casus foederis* unless it should prove to be aggressive.[38] Thus Castlereagh upheld the British doctrine of nonintervention by directing the attention of the allies to the external activities of France and not to her internal politics.[39]

Castlereagh restated this doctrine at the Congress of Aix-La-Chapelle in 1818. In a reply to a Russian memorandum which would have bound each state to guarantee not only the frontiers but also the governments of all other states, he disparaged the idea of an "Alliance Solidaire" which implied "the previous establishment of such a system of general government as may secure and enforce upon all kings and nations an internal system of peace and justice."[40] Such a system was premature; in the Europe of 1818 it would mean that "force was collectively to be prostituted to the support of established power without any consideration of the extent to which it was abused."[41] For Castlereagh, the only practicable arrangement was one in which each state was left to rely for its security upon the justice and wisdom of its own particular system.[42] Castlereagh's mission was to persuade Alexander and his ministers to "descend from their abstractions,"[43] and to further the British view of the alliance as an instrument of peace, not of reaction, whose function was to mediate, not to dictate.[44]

The fullest exposition of the way in which Castlereagh interpreted the principle of nonintervention came in the State Paper of May 5, 1820, a document which has been taken to express the "foundations of British foreign policy."[45] This paper was formulated in cabinet as a response to a Russian dispatch drawing the attention of the allies to the revolution in Spain and anticipating the need for their interference.[46] It is significant for three reasons: first, it contained the British definition of the permissible perimeter

[38] Webster, p. 54.

[39] With one significant exception, viz. the engagement to exclude the Bonaparte family from the throne of France, justified on the ground that their return would certainly lead to aggressive war. See Webster, p. 54.

[40] Quoted in *ibid.*, p. 51.   [41] Quoted in *ibid.*, p. 51.

[42] *Ibid.*, p. 51.

[43] *Cambridge History of British Foreign Policy* (hereafter *C.H.B.F.P.*), Vol. II, p. 27.

[44] *Ibid.*, p. 31.

[45] Harold Temperley and Lillian M. Penson, eds., *Foundations of British Foreign Policy*, Cambridge, 1938, p. 48.

[46] Webster, p. 228.

of alliance activity; in the second place, it conveyed Castlereagh's conception of how the game of European diplomacy was to be played or his theory of international relations; and third, it delineated the circumstances in which Britain would feel obliged to intervene. The principle of nonintervention defined or was defined by each of these aspects of Castlereagh's foreign policy.[47]

In Castlereagh's view, nothing was more likely to impair or even to destroy the real utility of the alliance than any attempt to push its obligations beyond its original conception. It was an alliance formed to subdue France and then to protect the ensuing territorial settlement. "It never was, however, intended as an Union for the Government of the World, or for the Superintendence of the Internal Affairs of other States." The alliance could be kept together so long as it did not assume as a matter of course, a collective jurisdiction whenever a great political event like the one in Spain presented a future and speculative danger to Europe. Further, Castlereagh doubted whether unanimity or concurrence between the powers on all political subjects was either possible or desirable. The different position, institutions, and habits of thought of the powers rendered them essentially different; in view of this, the allies could find a common interest only if they limited themselves to the genuine overlap of their separate interests. For Castlereagh, the principle of nonintervention could be identified with the legitimate boundary of the objects of the alliance. Action beyond that boundary violated the principle.

Castlereagh saw the "Game of Public Safety" in Europe, as taking place between a "Western Mass" consisting of France and Spain and an "Eastern Mass" made up of Russia and Germany. The problem was to protect the latter against revolutionary dangers from the former. The solution of Russian and German armed intervention was impracticable because it left unsolved the problem of self-government after the intervening forces had withdrawn, and it also subjected the intervening armies to the danger of revolutionary contamination. Secure in their own power, the eastern states should leave those of the west to work out their own political processes. Moreover, to reduce the principle of interference to a system was not only physically impracticable but also morally reprehensible such that no state with a representative system of government could act upon it nor tolerate intervention

[47] The following summary of Castlereagh's State Paper is taken from the text in *C.H.B.F.P.*, Vol. II, pp. 623–633.

to direct the course of experiments in representative government in other states. Thus Castlereagh drew a distinction between representative and autocratic government, but unlike the eastern powers, he did not base his foreign policy or his conception of world order on the survival of one and the fall of the other. He reiterated in 1820 his assertion at Aix-La-Chapelle in 1818 that each state must rely for security on its own political system. He rated the political independence of the state higher than the nature of the political order within it and thus opposed his principle of noninterference to the continental doctrine of ideological interference.

Of the actual position in Spain, Castlereagh wrote that "there is no portion of Europe of equal magnitude, in which such a Revolution could have happened, less likely to menace other States with that direct and imminent danger, which has always been regarded, at least in this country, as alone constituting the case which would justify external interference." The British principle of noninterference was not absolute. Britain would be found in her place when there was actual danger to the European system, but could not act on "abstract and speculative Principles of Precaution."

For Castlereagh, nonintervention was not just a principle which adorned formal statements of the British position in European international politics, it was also a policy she could follow in her relations with Europe. Nonintervention was a practicable policy for Britain and also, Castlereagh argued, for Europe, and he sought to demonstrate this by stressing the impracticability of intervention. At Aix one of Castlereagh's objections to the allied assertion of a right to intervene in the internal affairs of other states was his doubt about their competence to judge what was "legal" in another state.[48] In his State Paper of May 5, 1820, Castlereagh (apart from his general critique of allied intentions) raised particular objections arising from the nature of the situation in Spain. In the first place, because there was no governing authority with which foreign powers could communicate, intervention in such an unsettled situation would probably compromise both the allies and the king of Spain and weaken the efforts of Spaniards of good intention.[49] Second, on the authority of the Duke of Wellington's memorandum, Castlereagh pointed out that the Spanish nation was "of all the European People, that, which will least brook any interference from Abroad."[50] Their national character, rendering

[48] *Ibid.*, p. 29. [49] *Ibid.*, pp. 624–625. [50] *Ibid.*, p. 624.

them "obstinately blind to the most pressing considerations of public safety,"[51] would make the position of the king the more threatened by the suspicion of foreign interference. Castlereagh's third objection to intervention in Spain was that such a policy could not be legitimized domestically if there were no immediate danger to other states.[52]

It followed that Wellesley, the British minister at Madrid, was instructed by Castlereagh to abstain from any interference, including advice on affairs in Spain, unless the king's life were in danger or an attack on Portugal countenanced.[53] Later in 1820, when revolution took place in Portugal, the traditional ally of Britain, Castlereagh was concerned to point out that England's guarantee did not apply "to the question of authority now pending between Sovereign and subject."[54] His policy of nonintervention reflected the old distinction between internal and external affairs; Britain wanted to be friendly to Portugal "without reference to the state of its political institutions."[55]

The policy of nonintervention which Castlereagh pursued toward Austrian activity in Germany and Italy was less ingenuous. When Metternich asked for the moral support of the powers for his putting down of constitutionalism in the German states contained in the Carlsbad Decrees of 1819, Castlereagh replied that "we are always pleased to see evil germs destroyed without the power to give our approbation openly."[56] His excuse for inaction was that the expression of any opinion would be an intervention in the internal affairs of the German Confederation.[57] Again, after the revolution in Naples of July 1820, Castlereagh's nonintervention allowed Austrian repression. In terms of the principles of May 5, Castlereagh conceded an Austrian right to intervene because the Neapolitan revolution was at once more dangerous and less justified than that in Spain. Because of the dangers to Europe of collective allied action, Castlereagh positively encouraged Austria to act against the Neapolitan rebels unilaterally.[58] In neither of these cases was the political independence of other states the prime motive for Castlereagh's policy of nonintervention. Indeed, by failing to counterintervene, Britain could be said to have degraded the principle of state independence. Her main concern was

[51] Ibid.
[54] Ibid., pp. 250–251.
[57] Ibid., p. 194.
[52] Ibid., p. 625.
[55] Ibid., p. 254, n. 2.
[58] Ibid., p. 262.
[53] Webster, p. 233.
[56] Ibid., p. 192.

to forestall the collective action of the allies by encouraging the most interested power to intervene on her own.

Sound policy for England, the principle of nonintervention was also urged by Castlereagh as a guide to the conduct of the other European powers; he advised them in terms of the rule. The purpose of the State Paper of May 5 was not only to explain British inaction in Spain but also to forestall the intervention of others by a strong statement of the British attitude. The particular objections to intervention in Spain, arising from the peculiar nature of the situation there, gave Castlereagh good reason for British nonintervention. By rehearsing these objections in the state paper, it was his intention to demonstrate to the European powers the follies of intervention. Castlereagh's objective was to make general the British interpretation of the limits of the alliance. The extent to which he would pursue this objective beyond the giving of advice was left unclear. The threat of British counterintervention to offset intervention by the eastern powers was not made explicit, but the attention of those powers was drawn to Britain's traditional interest in the affairs of the peninsula. In Portugal also, while making clear the British policy of nonintervention, Castlereagh emphasized that no other state would be allowed to interfere either. In particular, he sought to disabuse the King of Portugal of the "delusive hope that the Holy Alliance will undertake a crusade for the reestablishment of the old system in Portugal."[59] With respect to the revolution in Naples, Castlereagh interpreted the rule of nonintervention in a different way. Britain would not interfere with what she regarded as justifiable intervention by Austria to put down the revolution, but she wished to localize the dispute and oppose any European principle of intervention.[60]

Affairs in Spain and Italy led Castlereagh to invoke the principle of nonintervention to restrain allied suppression of revolution. Revolution in Greece led him to invoke the same principle to restrain Russian support for rebellion. If in the former cases the rule of nonintervention expressed British separation from the alliance, in the latter case the same rule was consistent with the restatement of alliance principles against Russia. The Greek rebellion was a national movement undertaken in the name of Christianity against an Islamic power, whose credentials as a member of the European system were disputed. Sympathy for coreligionists and the possi-

[59] *Ibid.*, p. 252.   [60] *Ibid.*, pp. 267 and 270.

bility of expansion at the expense of the Turk made Russian intervention a probability. For Castlereagh, the overriding consideration was the danger to the balance of power if Russia advanced in the Balkans. To forestall this, Castlereagh and Metternich had to convince the Tsar that the Greek revolt belonged in the same dangerous category as the revolutions in the west. A Castlereagh who had been accustomed to playing down the danger of revolution, now emphasized it and appealed to the alliance principles in their widest manifestation, for in the one case of Greece, they were in perfect unison with the British principles of nonintervention and the balance of power.[61]

When invocation of the nonintervention principle failed to prevent the intervention of another power, Castlereagh could still use it to protest against that action and to defend his own policy. The State Paper of May 5 at once criticized the attitudes of other states and justified the British position. Later in 1820, after the revolution in Naples, Castlereagh's refusal to comply with Metternich's suggestion that diplomatic relations with that state be broken off was defended on the ground that such an action would be unwarranted interference in the internal affairs of Naples.[62] But, in spite of British efforts to avoid it, a conference convened at Troppau "to define by a general proposition the principles on which the allies would intervene in Naples."[63] On November 19, 1820, Austria, Russia, and Prussia issued a protocol of this sort sanctioning a general principle of intervention.[64] Castlereagh's protest against this document was contained in a dispatch to Stewart, the British Minister at Vienna. The Troppau Doctrine of interference appeared to Castlereagh to make the alliance into a superstate and the allies into "armed guardians of all thrones";

[61] On the Greek rebellion and the European reaction, see Webster, pp. 349–382, and Kissinger, *A World Restored*, pp. 286–311.

[62] Kissinger, p. 254.

[63] *C.M.H.*, Vol. x, p. 27. Britain sent a delegate, but one of mere ambassadorial rank, to the conference.

[64] The Troppau Protocol read: "States which have undergone a change of government, due to revolution, the results of which threaten other States, *ipso facto* cease to be members of the European Alliance, and remain excluded from it until their situation gives guarantee of legal order and stability. If, owing to such alterations, immediate danger threatens other States, the Powers bind themselves, by peaceful means, or if need be by arms, to bring back the guilty State into the bosom of the Great Alliance." *C.H.B.F.P.*, Vol. ii, pp. 37–38.

Britain could not consent "to charge itself as a member of the Alliance with the moral responsibility of administering a general European Police of this description."[65]

These objections were repeated in a circular sent by Castlereagh on January 19, 1821 to all British ambassadors. This dispatch set out to reply to a Holy Alliance Circular of December 8, 1820 which had implicated Britain in the activities at Troppau and had not remained secret.[66] Again Castlereagh criticized the general principle of interference and the "federative system in Europe" which it implied, again he recognized an Austrian but not an allied right to intervene in Naples, and again he stressed that the right of intervention was an exception to general principles which could not be reduced to a rule.[67]

Internationally, Castlereagh used the nonintervention principle to restrain the activities of the Holy Alliance; domestically the principle was used to restrain Castlereagh from too "European" a foreign policy. A tradition of nonintervention in British foreign policy provided a Parliament which tended to isolationism with doctrinal ammunition against Castlereagh's European posture.[68] This ammunition was also available at cabinet level. The need for Britain to legitimize her foreign policy domestically was explained by Castlereagh in the May 5 State Paper. In the first place, he pointed out that dictatorial intervention in the affairs of Spain would be unpopular in Britain and would lead to the embarrassment of the government. Second, excitement of public sentiment by unnecessary interference abroad distracted the people from internal problems of greater importance. Third and most importantly, Castlereagh stressed that constant and ineffectual meddling by Britain in Europe would so sour the public mind as to encourage total abstention from European affairs. "The fatal effects of such a false step," he wrote, "might be irreparable when the moment at which we might be indispensably called upon by Duty and Interest to take a part should arise."[69] Britain had then to take her principle of action not merely from the expediency of the case but from those maxims which a popular and national government had imposed on her.[70]

[65] Webster, p. 304. [66] *Ibid.*, pp. 306 and 320.
[67] *Ibid.*, pp. 322–323.
[68] On the "isolationism" of the British Parliament, see *ibid.*, pp. 20–21.
[69] *C.H.B.F.P.*, Vol. II, pp. 628–629.
[70] *Ibid.*, p. 632.

Sometimes this domestic constraint operated only to affect the mode of legitimization of a policy which was to be undertaken anyway. After Napoleon's escape from Elba and his overthrow of Louis XVIII, there was no doubt in Castlereagh's mind of the need for a Bourbon restoration, but he could not justify war with Napoleon on that basis. To make the war a popular one, Castlereagh needed to stress that it was to be fought against a Napoleon who had lost the support of the French people.[71] Here the doctrine of noninterference operated not to prevent intervention, but to stop its taking place for the wrong reasons.[72] At another time the doctrine enforced a muted reaction from Castlereagh to a policy of which he approved but public opinion disliked—the Austrian action at Carlsbad in 1819.[73] Constraints such as these were irritants for Castlereagh but not major obstacles to his making of foreign policy.

Objections to Castlereagh's policy, in terms of the doctrine of nonintervention, were more significant when they came directly from cabinet than when they issued from Parliament. In his dispatches from Aix in 1818, when Castlereagh referred more than once to the maintenance of the Congress system of diplomacy, Canning, who was suspicious of continental entanglements and objected to the great power system, pointed out that "our true policy has always been not to interfere except in great emergencies and then with commanding force."[74] Not only at Aix but during the whole of his tenure of the Foreign Office, Castlereagh had to consider a cabinet and a Parliament which thought of an alliance as directed against a particular enemy, and not as a permanent instrument for peace.[75]

This problem confronting Castlereagh is illustrated by the distinction he drew between policy and its legitimation, both internationally and domestically. Of the Troppau Protocol, he said to Esterhazy, the Austrian minister in London: "You would have

[71] Webster, *The Foreign Policy of Castlereagh, 1812–1815*, London, 1931, p. 443.

[72] Kissinger, *A World Restored*, p. 178.

[73] See above, p. 78.

[74] Webster, *Castlereagh, 1815–1822*, p. 147.

[75] *Ibid.*, pp. 147–148. This attitude in Parliament could be turned to advantage by Castlereagh in the actual conduct of his diplomacy. Thus, at Aix, he could throw on Parliament "the onus of obstructing the complete realisation of the Tsar's ideal" and bargain on that basis for a position acceptable to the British government. *C.H.B.F.P.*, Vol. II, p. 27.

done better to have acted first and talked afterwards."[76] Even after the dispatch of December 16 was sent to Stewart, Castlereagh told the Russian ambassador that he was not opposing the aims and intentions of the allies but the issue of an official document, and he warned Lieven that if the protocol were made public, Britain would have to issue a counterblast.[77] This happened on January 19 and was forced on Castlereagh by the publication in the British press of the Holy Alliance Circular of December 8. The need for Castlereagh to issue this counterblast as a palliative for domestic opinion caused Esterhazy to liken him to a "great lover of music who is at Church; he wishes to applaud but he dare not."[78] Castlereagh's desire to maintain the alliance foundered on the rock of Metternich's insistence that intervention in Naples be sanctioned by the principles of the Holy Alliance. The British doctrine of noninterference presaged the end of the Alliance, not because it precluded any intervention, but because it disallowed intervention on grounds which were domestically intolerable. In this case at least, the domestic legitimation of action in international relations was more significant for Europe than action itself.

It is possible to regard Castlereagh's interpretation of the principle of nonintervention as the keystone of a coherent system of foreign policy. It meant that Britain would intervene if an immediate threat to her security evidenced by aggression presented itself, but she would not do so on abstract and speculative principles of precaution. Into this definition could be fitted the distinction between the internal and external affairs of a state, only the latter being the proper subject for the concern of others. In turn, Britain's concern with the territorial settlement of 1815 was consistent with her interest in the external affairs of states; her lack of concern with the dynastic order of 1815 was consonant with the view that internal affairs were not a matter for international adjudication. In each of these three aspects, the nonintervention principle expressed the outer limits of legitimate allied conduct. For Castlereagh, the principle had the practical advantage of flexibility. In the Spanish case, it was used to prevent allied intervention on behalf of the throne of Spain. In Naples it was used to prevent the participation of any other power in the Austrian intervention, in Germany it excused inaction, and in Greece it served to prevent a Russian upset of the balance of power.

[76] Webster, *Castlereagh 1815–1822*, p. 302.
[77] *Ibid.*, p. 305.   [78] *Ibid.*, p. 326.

ii. Canning

In a speech to the House of Commons on April 14, 1823, Canning took as the text for his own foreign policy the principle of non-intervention laid down "with all the qualifications properly belonging to it," by Castlereagh in May 1820.[79] But if Castlereagh had used the nonintervention principle to define the outer limits of the alliance from a position within it, Canning used the principle to bring the alliance to an end and to place Britain outside it. Canning espoused an "English" policy compared to Castlereagh's "Europeanism." He objected to the alliance system of congress diplomacy, where Castlereagh disputed only its methods.[80] Furthermore, Canning made his "Englishness" the basis for popular support and he mobilized opinion in favor of his attitude to the European "Areopagus."[81]

Canning's separation of Britain from the Europe of the Holy Alliance did not lead him to campaign abroad for the acceptance of British principles of government. He shared Castlereagh's concern for the independence of states within the framework of the Vienna settlement,[82] but he was even less concerned with the nature of government within states than Castlereagh. He thus drew once more the traditional distinction between the internal and external affairs of states, and declared British neutrality with respect to the former. To this Canning added a new interpretation of the nonintervention principle by stating the British position as "one of neutrality not only between contending nations, but between contending principles."[83] So long as arbitrary governments did not violate the rights of free states, Britain was quite ready to live in amity with them,[84] and for this *laissez-faire* attitude, Canning had a special reason. Britain would lose her preponderating influence if free states with institutions comparable to her own were established on the continent.[85] Intervention to uphold constitutionalism was out of the question for a Britain whose proper position was the *via media* between "Jacobinism" and

---

[79] *C.H.B.F.P.*, Vol. II, pp. 622–623.

[80] Temperley, *The Foreign Policy of Canning, 1822–1827*, London, 1925, p. 44.

[81] Temperley and Penson, *Foundations of British Foreign Policy*, pp. 65–66.

[82] Temperley, pp. 464–465.   [83] Temperley and Penson, p. 66.

[84] *Ibid.*, p. 86.   [85] Temperley, p. 458.

"Ultraism."[86] Adherence to the principle of nonintervention was then fundamental for a Canning, who, suspicious of both despotism and democracy, based his policy on a middle course between them.[87]

Canning's objection to the principle of interference was more thoroughgoing than Castlereagh's, and his use of the nonintervention principle to underline his opposition to the congress system tended to an isolationism which Castlereagh could not have countenanced. However, their appreciation of the limits for Britain of a policy of nonintervention was similar; Castlereagh would intervene when threatened by "direct and imminent danger," while Canning would intervene "in great emergencies and then with commanding force."

During Castlereagh's years at the Foreign Office, Canning had been a consistent advocate of a policy of nonintervention for Britain. When Austria intervened to put down revolution in Naples in 1821, Canning, from the back benches of the House of Commons, urged "neutrality in word and deed."[88] Neutrality in word because it would be a fraud for England to mention support when she intended none; neutrality in deed, first because of the absurdity of going to war over the pedantic state papers of the Holy Allies and second, because the democratic principles of the rebels were not those of Britain anyway.[89] Furthermore, a policy of nonintervention recommended itself because the interference of strangers became sooner or later an object of jealousy, and the cause for which it was undertaken would be retarded rather than advanced thereby.[90] In office himself, Canning practiced what he had preached to Castlereagh. Foreseeing an allied project of interference in the Spanish struggle, Canning instructed Wellington at the Congress of Verona "frankly and peremptorily to declare, that to any such interference, come what may, His Majesty will not be a party."[91] But if Canning would not share in an allied interference, he would not counter it by force either. When France marched on Spain in the spring of 1823, Canning declared an "honest neutrality" for England.[92] Canning maintained this position against a French request for support from Britain and a request from the rebels for a guarantee of their constitution. "The

---

[86] *Ibid.*   [87] *Ibid.*, p. 43.
[88] Speech of March 20, 1821, cited in *ibid.*, p. 46.
[89] *Ibid.*   [90] *Ibid.*   [91] *Ibid.*, p. 65.
[92] *Ibid.*, p. 87.

very principle on which the British government so earnestly dep-
recated the war against Spain," wrote Canning to A'Court, the
British minister at Madrid, "was that of the right of any Nation
to change or to modify its internal Institutions."[93] Exercise of a
right of guarantee would lead "to an intermeddling with the affairs
of the guaranteed state, such as to place it, in fact, at the mercy
of the Power who gives the guarantee."[94] While uncertainty prevailed in Spain, Canning's instructions to A'Court were that he
avoid the appearance of advising or controlling, or of being the
setter-up or puller-down of successive ministries.[95]

At the outset, Canning shared the attitude of Castlereagh toward the continuing turmoil in Portugal—the desire to carry on good
relations without reference to Portuguese political institutions.
Thus Canning rejected the frequent appeals from the Portuguese
liberals for British military intervention against the reaction-
aries.[96] In Canning's view, such an intervention would be a measure of internal police and not of external defense and, as such,
could not be legitimized in terms of the principle of nonintervention.[97] Thus Thornton, the British minister at Lisbon, who had
supported the Portuguese requests for intervention, was rebuked
by Canning, and rebuked again for an offense against another
British interpretation of the doctrine of nonintervention. Thornton
was informed by Canning that his attendance at conferences, with
Portuguese ministers and the ambassadors of the Holy Alliance,
which discussed the internal affairs of Portugal, was "wholly out
of your Province and entirely disapproved by your Court."[98] But
to bring about the demise of French influence at Lisbon, Canning
himself was prepared to override the principle of nonintervention
and intrigue in Portuguese domestic policies for the removal of
the French party.[99] Canning repeated this policy of intervention
in 1826 when British forces were sent to fight in Portugal; this
time, however, Canning could justify an interventionary policy
in terms of the principle of nonintervention.[100]

The other exception to Canning's general policy of nonintervention was his reaction to the Greek rebellion, which culminated after

[93] September 18, 1823, cited in *ibid.*, Appendix II, p. 540.
[94] *Ibid.*   [95] *Ibid.*, p. 95.
[96] *Ibid.*, pp. 196, 198, and 201.
[97] *Ibid.*, p. 198. This did not, however, preclude the sending of a naval
squadron to the Tagus.
[98] *Ibid.*, p. 204.   [99] *Ibid.*, p. 208.
[100] See below, pp. 88–89.

Canning's death in the Battle of Navarino in which the Turkish and Egyptian fleets were destroyed in 1827. Castlereagh's policy toward the rebellion against Turkish rule in Greece had been to isolate the conflict from European international politics by welding the nonintervention principle to the antirevolutionary principles of the Holy Alliance.[101] The inability of the Turks to protect British commerce, popular sentiment in favor of the Greeks, and the ever-present threat of Russian intervention made Castlereagh's course impossible for Canning.[102] The imperative of the balance of power and the expedient of satisfying it by restraining Russia by cooperation rather than by opposition led Canning to interfere on behalf of the Greeks. First he recognized their status as belligerents and finally acted as midwife for their independence. In this case, the principle of nonintervention was judged by Canning to be inferior to the principle of balance and to the opportunity of splitting Russia from the Holy Alliance.

Like Castlereagh, Canning viewed nonintervention as not only a policy for England but also as a principle to be urged on other states or in terms of which others were to be persuaded to do England's bidding. Canning's instructions to Wellington at Verona meant the separation of Britain from the Alliance. They were also intended to forestall collective allied intervention in Spain by making British opposition clear[103] (but leaving the action which would follow from actual allied intervention deliberately vague). If Canning succeeded in forestalling collective intervention, he had still to prevent French intervention in the name of the alliance without going to war against her. His aim was to persuade France to conform to the principle of nonintervention by stressing the popular agitation in England against French intentions and by introducing a doubt into the mind of the French *chargé d'affaires* as to whether England would remain neutral if France marched on Spain.[104]

These warnings failed. Canning accepted perforce the *fait accompli* of the French attack on Spain but took the opportunity to warn France against a permanent military occupation of Spain, the appropriation of any part of the Spanish colonies, and the violation of the territorial integrity of Portugal.[105] In October 1823

[101] Though Castlereagh himself was prepared to recognize Greek belligerent status when the situation required it. *C.H.B.F.P.*, Vol. II, p. 45.
[102] Temperley, pp. 319–337.
[103] *Ibid.*, p. 74. [104] *Ibid.*, p. 80. [105] *Ibid.*, p. 83.

Canning cemented this warning by wringing from Polignac, the French ambassador in London, a declaration that France had "no intention or desire to appropriate to Herself any part of the Spanish Possessions in America."[106] In July 1824 Canning's formidable attitude to the threat of French intervention in Cuba on behalf of legitimist Spain caused France to give a pledge that French troops would not land in Cuba.[107] Where vital British interests were threatened, Canning was prepared to uphold the principle of nonintervention by the counterthreat of British military action; in other cases he was prepared to use diplomacy but not the threat of force for the same purpose.

Portugal was a vital interest. Canning's policy of nonintervention in Portuguese affairs depended upon the prevention of intervention by others. In 1824 the threat to send Hanoverian troops to Portugal prevented French military activities there and allowed Canning to maintain his policy of nonintervention.[108] In 1826, when the king of Portugal died, his heir, the emperor of Brazil, gave Portugal a constitution. The legitimists of the Holy Alliance were thus placed in a dilemma, for a sovereign of whom they approved had granted a constitution of which they disapproved. If logic could forestall allied intervention, Canning's was the victory, for he could use the legitimists' own argument of legality emanating from the sovereign to show that there was no ground for intervention against the constitution.[109]

The principle of nonintervention could be invoked in defense of British inaction in European politics, in protest against the policies of other states, and, by implication at least, as a justification when Britain did interfere in European politics. As a British principle counseling interference only in great emergencies and then with commanding force, it could be used as a reason for Britain to hold aloof from the conflicts of others. The physical impossibility of intervention against the French invasion of Spain would thus justify the British policy of neutrality. British intervention in Portugal, however, was defended not on grounds of interest, but on those of duty, and the principle of nonintervention was upheld as a European imperative and not as a British expedient. In December 1826, when Portuguese deserters supporting the absolutist Miguel attacked Portugal with Spanish arms and equipment, Canning decided that the *casus foederis* of the

---

[106] *Ibid.*, p. 115.
[107] *Ibid.*, pp. 170–171.
[108] *Ibid.*, pp. 202–203.
[109] *Ibid.*, pp. 368–370.

ancient British alliance with Portugal had occurred. In the House of Commons, Canning justified his sending of troops by pointing out that they were sent "not to rule, not to dictate, not to prescribe constitutions—but to defend and preserve the independence of an Ally."[110] This was intervention to uphold the principle of non-intervention; it was launched to protect territorial integrity not to guarantee a constitution. Canning's defense satisfied the traditional British concern with refraining from intervention in the internal affairs of other states, though the Holy Alliance considered his distinction between defending territorial integrity and supporting constitutionalism to lack substance.[111]

Canning also used the nonintervention principle to criticize the policies of other states. He went further than this to use the rule as a weapon with which to beat the Holy Allies. Thus his instruction to Wellington at Verona irrevocably separated Britain from the allies and destroyed the congress system, and the process was legitimized by reference to the nonintervention principle. Canning made this weapon the more potent as he based it upon popular support. Castlereagh had foreshadowed British separation from the European despots; Canning brought the congress system to an end and looked for support for his policy in public opinion.[112] In his view, opinion was stronger than armies, and he feared a war of opinion more than a war of armies. But if opinions were to collide, then Britain had the superior strength.[113] When the French king opened Parliament in 1823 with a speech which reiterated the principles of the Holy Alliance, Canning took this as his cue publicly to declare British opposition to the allied doctrine of interference.[114] After the French intervention in Spain, Canning again denounced France in Parliament and went as far as to trust that Spain "may come triumphantly out of the struggle."[115] But he would go no further. Like Castlereagh, Canning would not countenance British intervention on behalf of constitutionalism; unlike Castlereagh, he loudly publicized his opposition to the legitimist interventions of the allied powers.

Neutrality between contending principles as well as between

[110] *Ibid.*, p. 380.   [111] *Ibid.*, p. 385.
[112] Temperley and Penson, *Foundations of British Foreign Policy*, pp. 65–66.
[113] *Ibid.*, pp. 66–67.
[114] Temperley, *Foreign Policy of Canning*, p. 78.
[115] Quoted in *ibid.*, p. 87.

contending nations was the basis of Canning's foreign policy, and it was a policy designed to maintain Britain's unique position in the world. If the principle of nonintervention was the dogma which expressed this policy, Canning also elevated the rule to a central place in his international theory. Adherence to the rule would safeguard the independence of states, and it was that independence upon which the peace of the world depended.[116] But in practice Canning was not always faithful to his doctrine of independence. In Portugal it had been maintained by the sending of troops, but in Spain the policy of nonintervention excused his failure to react to French intervention. The shortcomings of the doctrine of independence were revealed in a third case, when the Greek rebellion confronted Europe with a choice between the creation of an independent Greece, or the maintenance of the integrity of the Turkish Empire. If Canning's interpretation of the principle of nonintervention was thus as flexible as Castlereagh's, it reflected the primacy of interest over doctrine. In this sense, one of Canning's interpretations of the principle was consistent—the rejection of ideological intervention as a possible policy for England in favor of constitutions or as an actual policy of the Holy Allies against them.

iii. Palmerston

For Castlereagh, the nonintervention principle had defined the outer limits of permissible conduct for an alliance of which Britain was a member; in Canning's case, the principle represented the middle way between despotism and democracy; for Palmerston, the principle drew the outer limits of permissible conduct for Britain as a champion of liberalism as well as an opponent of the European despots. Palmerston regarded Canning as his master, but he interpreted the master in a way which suited his own policy.[117] In his first major foreign policy speech to the House of Commons on June 1, 1829, he criticized the nonintervention policy of Wellington and Aberdeen toward Portugal; he regarded their legalistic attitude as an abuse of Canning's principle in that it favored the absolutist Miguel.[118] In Palmerston's view, Canning would never have allowed the balance of power in Portugal to

---

[116] *C.M.H.*, Vol. x, pp. 37–38; *C.H.B.F.P.*, Vol. ii, pp. 622–623.
[117] Temperley and Penson, p. 88.
[118] Southgate, *The Most English Minister*, p. 12.

turn against him in this way.[119] Palmerston also chose to overlook Canning's distinctions between intervention to uphold independence and intervention in favor of constitutions. To his mind, the whole history of relations between England and Portugal had been one of intermeddling by the former, and for the Wellington government to take shelter now behind the principle of nonintervention was to make the navy of England "the subservient tool of tyranny."[120] Palmerston's desire to "keep England on the side of liberal opinions"[121] was made explicit soon after his arrival at the Foreign Office. In the House of Commons on August 2, 1832, he said: "Constitutional States I consider to be the natural allies of this country; and . . . no English Ministry will perform its duty if it be inattentive to the interests of such States."[122] Palmerston's method of fulfilling this duty was to advertise his support for constitutional states and thereby to sway public opinion to their cause. He inherited from Canning the belief that the power of opinion was superior to that of physical strength, but he wielded that power on behalf of a cause, support for which Canning had declared to be against the interests of England.[123]

Palmerston interpreted the principle of nonintervention in a way which allowed him to act as the moral guardian of European liberalism. His assertion that there was nothing in the principle of noninterference which disallowed intervention if what passed in a neighboring state concerned the interests of England,[124] differed from the interpretations of Castlereagh and Canning only in degree (Palmerston did not emphasize the "great emergency" requirement stressed by his predecessors). What was new in Palmerston's interpretation of the principle was contained in his explanation to William IV of the action the cabinet intended to take in protest against Austrian repression of liberalism in Germany. Palmerston explained that the cabinet objected on principle to interference by force of arms which subjected the will of an independent nation to the military dictation of a powerful neighbor and led to the destruction of the balance of power. On the other hand, an interference which consisted merely of friendly advice and which was designed to prevent the collision of arms was sanctioned by international law and consistent with the independence

[119] *Ibid.*, p. 13. [120] Quoted in *ibid.*, p. 12.
[121] Temperley and Penson, p. 100. [122] *Ibid.*, p. 101.
[123] *Ibid.*, p. 100. [124] *Ibid.*, pp. 91–92.

of states.[125] For Palmerston then, the nonintervention principle proscribed only military intervention. Apparently clear, this doctrine could imperceptibly become one of intervention and not of nonintervention. When in the following year Metternich was again concerned with putting down constitutionalism in Germany, Palmerston's riposte went as far as to claim that "[w]hatever affects the general condition of Europe . . . is a legitimate object of solicitude to England, and a proper subject for the exercise of her moral influence in the first place, or even for her armed interference if she should think the occasion require it."[126] Fifteen years later, Palmerston was to defend his interference in Portugal in even more exaggerated terms, referring to a Britain "at the head of moral, social and political civilisation" whose duty, whose vocation it was not to enslave but to set free.[127]

Palmerston's enthusiasm for the spread of liberalism had its doctrinal root in the belief that constitutional reform averted revolution.[128] He thought that the state's natural condition was one of freedom and that anything that stood in the way of achieving this condition was necessarily a conspiracy.[129] It followed that British interference on behalf of liberalism was a "good" policy in that it sought to reinforce a natural tendency, and a practical policy in that it avoided revolutionary disruption. It was also, in Palmerston's view, an advantageous policy for Britain. It countered the pretensions of the eastern powers more successfully than did reliance on a nonintervention principle which allowed the asymmetry of unanswered legitimist intervention.[130] Canning's neutrality in the ideological dispute gave way to Palmerston's participation in it; Canning's objection to intervention as a method of conducting foreign policy was replaced by Palmerston's greater concern with the objectives or principles for which intervention was undertaken.

Palmerston, however, did not sacrifice traditional British interests like the balance of power for an ideological crusade, and while he spoke of a "duty to set free," he acted only according to the imperative of British interests.[131] But his conception of British in-

[125] Palmerston to William IV, August 5, 1832, cited in C. K. Webster, *The Foreign Policy of Palmerston, 1830–1841*, 2 vols., London, 1951, Vol. II, pp. 799–800.

[126] *Ibid.*, Vol. I, p. 358.

[127] Seton-Watson, *Britain in Europe*, p. 254.

[128] *Ibid.*, p. 460.   [129] Southgate, p. 108.   [130] *Ibid.*, pp. 53–54.

[131] *Ibid.*, pp. 43–45 and 237; Webster, *Palmerston*, Vol. I, p. 100.

terests was wider than that of Castlereagh or Canning and included a commitment to liberalism on the ground that a liberal state meant an independent state which meant in turn a pro-British state.[132] It was in this sense that Palmerston meant that it was England's real policy to be "the champion of justice and right."[133]

If Palmerston's interpretation of the nonintervention principle lay in the distinction he made between "friendly advice" which was permissible and "armed interference" which was not, in his actual policy he was not always faithful to either precept. On some occasions he followed a policy of nonintervention which precluded even the giving of advice. During the Polish insurrection in the early 1830's, Palmerston, preoccupied as he was with the problem of Belgian independence, looked to a quick victory for the Russian forces which had intervened to repress the revolution. The principle of balance prevailed over that of independence to the extent of a reluctance on the part of Palmerston even to enter a protest against the Russian action.[134] Similarly, when Austrian troops intervened in Modena and Parma to put down revolution there in 1831, Palmerston would not criticize Metternich. If the rule of nonintervention required counterintervention to uphold it, Palmerston side-stepped this logic by stating that his concern was more with avoiding a Franco-Austrian war than with "the abstract and not easily definable principles upon which interference and noninterference should depend."[135] When Russia interfered on Austria's behalf to repress the revolution in Hungary in 1849, Palmerston's concern with a strong Austria in the European balance again led him to encourage rather than to protest the Russian action.[136]

At other times, Palmerston strayed from the principle of nonintervention, as he defined it, in the opposite direction, by using armed force to interfere, notably in Portugal and in Spain. To events in Portugal he was especially sensitive since he had criticized the Wellington government for allowing the absolutist Miguel

[132] Southgate, p. 108.   [133] Seton-Watson, p. 459.

[134] It was the cabinet which insisted that the Tsar be informed that, in the British view, he was still obliged to uphold the constitution. Webster, *Palmerston*, Vol. I, p. 189.

[135] Southgate, p. 45.

[136] *The New Cambridge Modern History* (hereafter *N.C.M.H.*), Vol. X, ed. J.P.T. Bury, Cambridge, 1960, p. 264. It was only after Hungary had been restored to Austria that Palmerston protested against Austrian inhumanity.

to come to power. But in 1831 the urgency of problems elsewhere and the inheritance of nonintervention made action difficult. Palmerston would have liked to intervene on behalf of Pedro, the supposed liberal and the legitimate ruler of Portugal, but the nonintervention principle persuaded him that the "thing ought to be done in a decent manner,"[137] and Grey pointed to the lack of justification for a British assisted invasion of Portugal against a *de facto* ruler.[138] In reply to Pedro's constant requests for British help in the ensuing years Palmerston then had to plead neutrality and nonintervention. This, however, was merely a formal posture; the nonintervention policy was used to justify British connivance at Pedro's expedition against Miguel,[139] and it never precluded support for the constitutionalists at Lisbon. In 1834, when Palmerston and Grey were finally convinced of the need to interfere with armed force in Portugal, the cabinet again rejected the plan and caused Palmerston to achieve his objects by a "veiled intervention" —the negotiation of the Treaty of Quadruple Alliance.[140] By the terms of the treaty signed in April 1834, the queens of Spain and Portugal were to assist each other in expelling the Portuguese and the Spanish pretenders (Miguel and Carlos) from the peninsula. England was to blockade the ports and French armed assistance was also promised.[141] Thus by a *"coup de main,"* Palmerston had legitimized a policy of interference which had been barely disguised by verbal allegiance to the nonintervention principle, and at the same time had set up what he regarded as a "powerful counterpoise to the Holy Alliance of the East."[142]

To the civil war in Spain, Palmerston's attitude was even less reserved than it had been in Portugal. He admitted his policy to be interference based on the treaty of 1834, and he went further to assert the right of outside countries to take part with either of the belligerents in a civil war.[143] British ships attacked and blockaded Spanish ports, arms were supplied to the government forces, and Spain was allowed to recruit a legion of 10,000 men in Britain.[144]

---

[137] Webster, *Palmerston*, Vol. I, p. 242.

[138] *Ibid.*, p. 244.   [139] *Ibid.*, p. 245.

[140] Temperley and Penson, p. 103.

[141] *Ibid.*, p. 103; Webster, *Palmerston*, Vol. I, p. 393.

[142] Webster, *Palmerston,* Vol. I, p. 397.

[143] Speech to the House of Commons, June 24, 1835, cited in Temperley and Penson, p. 104.

[144] Southgate, pp. 101–102.

Palmerston's justification for his action was extravagant. He spoke of an obligation to improve Spanish institutions and to help her acquire the "inestimable privileges of representative government."[145] He followed in Spain the doctrine which he was to lay down in 1844 in relation to Greece, "that if any nation should be found not fit for constitutional government, the best way to fit such a nation for it would be to give it to them."[146]

On other occasions, Palmerston was true to his own doctrine of nonintervention. Dissatisfied with the Italian settlement between Austria and France in 1859, he protested to both powers on the ground of self-determination for Italy and proposed that the disputed territories be annexed to Piedmont. Palmerston intended no military intervention, but he was determined to give advice, to express an opinion, and even to threaten action in the belief that "the threat would make the action unnecessary."[147] Again in 1864, when Austrian and Prussian troops took over Schleswig-Holstein, Palmerston's reaction was to take a middle course between "an ignominious silence" and "broadsides of shot and shell,"[148] a policy which was to lead to a vote of censure in the House of Commons and represented internationally the nemesis of Palmerston's devious doctrine of nonintervention.

The principle of nonintervention could be used as a rule in terms of which to guide or coerce the actions of others in either of two ways. First, an attempt could be made to avert the intervention of another state by the suggestion that she follow the principle of nonintervention or by the threat of counterintervention if she executed the policy. Second, once an intervention had taken place, the rule of nonintervention could justify and be upheld by counterintervention to discipline the intruding state. Palmerston made use of the principle in both these senses. Though with respect to the latter method, he preferred to discipline by words rather than action. In attempting to forestall intervention Palmerston, on several occasions, used the rule of nonintervention as a "ring-holding" device. When Piedmont, located in a sensitive position between France and Austria and threatened in 1831 by attack from French extremists, took fright at what she supposed to be a Whig policy of nonintervention, Palmerston set out to reassure her. France was informed that her toleration of the extremists on the Piedmontese border was inconsistent with a policy of nonintervention, and at

145 *Ibid.*, p. 103.   146 *Ibid.*, p. 104.
147 *Ibid.*, p. 465.   148 *Ibid.*, p. 514.

the same time Austria was left in doubt as to the British reaction to a French initiative.[149] It was Palmerston's policy to uphold the independence of Piedmont by making both France and Austria uncertain of the British reaction to intervention. In Portugal, Palmerston was less tentative; he made it very clear that any intervention from Spain or the Holy Alliance would provoke British counterintervention.[150] In 1848 and again in 1859 Palmerston demonstrated his concern for Italian independence. In 1848 he warned Metternich that Britain could not view with indifference "any aggression whatever" on the rights and territories of Rome or Turin.[151] In 1859 Austria and France were merely "formally requested" to refrain from armed interference in Italy.[152]

Palmerston stated the logic of counterintervention more clearly than either Castlereagh or Canning. Changes in internal constitution and form of government were matters with which England had no business to interfere by force of arms, but the attempt by one nation to seize and appropriate the territory of another was a different matter. Because such action might endanger other states by upsetting the balance of power, Britain held herself at liberty to resist it on the principle of self-defense.[153] Palmerston rarely made use of this doctrine to the extent of employing armed force, though his activities in Portugal and Spain could be justified in terms of counteracting the support, both material and moral, which the eastern powers gave to the absolutists in the peninsula.[154] More often Palmerston's method of counterintervention was to answer armed bands by dispatches in the belief that protest, even if ineffective, was to be preferred to "tacit acquiescence" in the wrongs of others.[155]

For Palmerston, the rule of nonintervention did not play a major part, as it had done for Castlereagh and Canning, in the criticism of others and in the defense of his own actions. It provided the rationale for his counterinterventionary protests, and his objections to Austrian activity in Germany and Italy were couched in terms of the independence of states and the desirability of nonintervention. But Palmerston surrendered Canning's middle ground be-

[149] Webster, *Palmerston*, Vol. I, pp. 202–203.
[150] *Ibid.*, p. 246.   [151] Southgate, p. 204.   [152] *Ibid.*, p. 466.
[153] Palmerston to Clanricarde, January 11, 1841, informing the Tsar of the "obligations of the British constitution," cited in Temperley and Penson, pp. 135–138.
[154] Webster, *Palmerston*, Vol. I, p. 238.
[155] *Ibid.*, pp. 359 and 367.

tween contending principles and contending nations, and as a result, criticism and justification were framed in the language of
participation in the ideological battle rather than that of abstention
from it. Palmerston found it "impossible not to fancy one saw
a settled design on the part of the Austrian government to put
down constitutional freedom wherever it exists and to cherish
bad government wherever it is to be found," and he traced symp-
toms of this from the Vistula to the Tagus.[156] Thus he objected
more to the ends than to the means of Austrian foreign policy.
Confronted, in his view, by a universal conspiracy against constitutionalism on the part of the Holy Alliance, Palmerston replied
in defense of his own conduct by claiming himself a universal
reference. His continual interference in Portugal was justified by
a supposed obligation to come to the aid of struggling liberalism
everywhere.[157] His penchant for giving advice to others and expressing an opinion on their conflicts was justified on the ground
of England's great power status which meant that "no event . . .
bearing on the balance of power, or on the probabilities of peace
or war" could be a matter of indifference to her.[158]

This aptitude for lecturing gave other powers the opportunity
to criticize Palmerston according to the nonintervention principle.
In 1848, when the Spanish government was advised to adopt constitutional methods, her premier found this "offensive to the dignity of a free and independent nation" and demanded that the
British ambassador leave the country.[159] In the same year, Schwar-
zenberg reacted to Palmerston's protests about Austrian repression
in Lombardy by repudiating all interference in Austrian affairs
and pointing out to Palmerston that Austria did not presume to
advise him on his policy in Ireland.[160] In 1832 even Metternich
objected in terms of the nonintervention principle to Palmerston's
protest against his policy in Germany.[161]

As well as forming part of the language of international relations, the rule of nonintervention was an important weapon in the
hands of Palmerston's domestic critics throughout his years as
foreign secretary and later as prime minister. In parliament, the
principle was the instrument of Tory and Radical dissent. In
1850, when Palmerston dispatched a naval squadron to Greek
waters to obtain redress for an alleged wrong done to a British citi-

---

[156] *Ibid.*, p. 235.
[158] Quoted in Southgate, p. 463.
[160] *Ibid.*, p. 262.

[157] Seton-Watson, p. 254.
[159] Seton-Watson, p. 254.
[161] Southgate, p. 53.

zen, Don Pacifico, his action brought on a motion of censure in the House of Commons. In the ensuing debate, Gladstone opposed the principle of nonintervention to the Palmerstonian spirit of interference, fearing that the attachment of England to a party within foreign countries would encourage other powers to behave in the same way to the ultimate detriment of freedom and peace.[162] Cobden also stressed the power of example, and the consequent danger of British departure from the rule of nonintervention, restating his doctrine that the spread of liberalism depended more upon peace, commerce, and education than on the labors of cabinets and foreign offices.[163] Peel looked back with favor to Fox, Pitt, Grenville, Canning, and Castlereagh whose policy it had been not to intervene in the affairs of others.[164] Again, in 1864, when Disraeli moved a vote of censure over Palmerston's threats without performance to Germany on the Schleswig-Holstein question, support for the motion from all parties was expressed chiefly in the language of nonintervention. Lord Robert Cecil drew the threads of the debate together with his view that if Cobden had been at the Foreign Office instead of Russell, Britain's position would be more dignified and she "would at least have been entitled to the credit of holding out in the name of England no hopes which she did not intend to fulfil."[165]

The nonintervention principle also provided the palace with the language for disagreement with Palmerston's foreign policy. In 1848 the queen objected to Palmerston's system of diplomacy in Spain and Portugal "which makes the taking up of party politics its principal object."[166] In 1859 Victoria warned Palmerston that a proper neutrality involved abstention from the advice he was giving to the powers on the management of Italian affairs.[167] Whatever the motive of the royal advice to Palmerston, the principle of nonintervention was thought to be the most effective vehicle for conveying it.

Palmerston's response to criticism varied: sometimes it was a matter of parliamentary tactics, at other times he had an acute reply to a particular argument, and at still other times he formulated a doctrine of his own to counter the noninterventionists. As a parliamentary tactician, he survived the Don Pacifico debate by fixing

---

[162] Seton-Watson, p. 280.
[163] *Ibid.*, p. 282 and above, Chapter Three, pp. 45–54.
[164] Seton-Watson, p. 283.   [165] Quoted in *ibid.*, pp. 456–457.
[166] Southgate, p. 198.   [167] *Ibid.*, p. 463.

his *Civis Romanus Sum* argument to a clause in the preamble of Lord Stanley's motion of censure which suggested that British subjects abroad were entitled to the protection of the laws of the country in which they resided. By pointing to the fallibility of this doctrine and exaggerating it, Palmerston was able to side-step the major issue.[168] A later attempt to turn the debate on a motion of censure in his favor was less impressive; in the Schleswig-Holstein debate of 1864, Palmerston "took away the breath" of his audience by totally ignoring the arguments of his critics and basing his defense on what the government had done for national prosperity.[169] To the argument that his activity in Turkey in 1839 was an offense against the rule of nonintervention, Palmerston replied that "true political wisdom consists not in enunciating a policy in sonorous terms, but in applying to each question as it occurs the rules of common-sense and prudence."[170] The Cobdenite argument that the true interest of England was in commerce not the balance of power and that the promotion of liberalism abroad did not aid the expansion of commerce Palmerston stood on its head: the freedom of commerce depended upon attention to the balance of power and the adoption of liberal constitutions led to the development of commercial ties.[171]

On a number of occasions, however, domestic criticism acted as a constraint to Palmerston's conduct of foreign policy, particularly when the criticism was manifest at cabinet level. In his policy toward Portugal and Spain in the 1830's, Palmerston was restrained by an unwilling cabinet.[172] In 1859 Palmerston's draft advice to Austria and France on Italy was made less offensive by the intervention of the queen and the tailoring of the cabinet.[173] The palace and the cabinet combined again in 1864 to deflate the

[168] *Ibid.*, pp. 271–272. [169] *C.H.B.F.P.*, Vol. ii, p. 580.
[170] A. G. Stapleton, *Intervention and Non-Intervention*, London, 1866, pp. 72–74. Stapleton criticizes this defense as a casting aside of the recognized established principles of international law. He also censures Palmerston's interventionary foreign policy in general because it separated the moral from the physical strength of Britain—irresistible when combined—and advanced the establishment of the law of force throughout Europe. He also used the Cobdenite argument that Palmerston's intervention had set the example for Russian intervention in Hungary in 1849, and French intervention in the Papal States in 1850. The book as a whole is a neo-Canningite syllabus of Palmerston's errors.
[171] Southgate, p. 141.
[172] Webster, *Palmerston*, Vol. i, pp. 243 and 428.
[173] Southgate, p. 465.

bombast of Palmerston and Russell in the interests of avoiding war with Germany over Schleswig-Holstein.[174]

It is possible to read into Palmerston's foreign policy a certain logical coherence in the following manner: he interpreted the doctrine of nonintervention in a way which allowed him to support the growth of liberalism abroad, in order to avert revolutionary upheavals, which by inviting outside intervention would upset the balance of power. In practice, Palmerston, while he would have accepted that the factors were interrelated, never conformed to the logic of such a system. True, he confronted Metternich's support for crowns with British advocacy of liberalism, but he rarely allowed ideology to predominate over the principle of balance and the maintenance of the territorial system.[175] The nonintervention principle was not an invariable rule but a device to be used when the opportunity presented itself.

This opportunism was reflected in Palmerston's definition of the principle of nonintervention. The distinction between armed interference and the giving of friendly advice allowed him to support the liberal cause without committing British armed force to its survival. He worked out the logic of counterintervention, used it in his policy towards Spain and Portugal, left the option open to use it elsewhere, but did not stake the British reputation on the universality of its application.[176] He could define the rule as strictly as had Canning when it suited his purpose, and he used it as an excuse for accepting Louis Napoleon's supposedly illiberal coup in France.[177]

The reaction from Palmerston's interfering foreign policy after the Commons' debate of 1864 led succeeding ministries to interpret the principle of nonintervention in a way which owed much

---

[174] *Ibid.*, pp. 515–518.

[175] For the view that the policy of actively encouraging the liberal cause against the Holy Alliance died with Canning, and the placement of Palmerston in the tradition of Castlereagh, see Hinsley, *Power and the Pursuit of Peace*, p. 222.

[176] Seton-Watson calls the formation of the Quadruple Alliance, Palmerston's "idea of non-intervention," *Britain in Europe*, p. 183. Similarly Webster says that the difference between the doctrine of nonintervention as it was interpreted in the 1820's, and the 1830's, was that in the earlier years Britain had put forward the doctrine, but had stood aside when it was disregarded, and in the later years Britain had interpreted the doctrine as giving her a "right to protect the Liberal Movement if the Eastern Powers attacked it." *Palmerston*, Vol. II, pp. 787–788.

[177] Southgate, p. 287.

to Cobden and meant virtual abstention from continental affairs.[178] But although it was thought that Palmerston had been overfree with his advice to foreign powers, the distinction he made between armed interference and the giving of opinion lived on.

To speak of a British doctrine of nonintervention, then, is not to suggest that there was one doctrine of nonintervention which each incumbent of the Foreign Office felt it his duty to observe. The form the doctrine took and the sort of action it was held to require varied with the statesman interpreting it. Castlereagh laid the theoretical foundation of the doctrine of nonintervention in his State Paper of May 5, 1820, distinguishing between actual and speculative menaces to the European system, external and internal affairs, and between the maintenance of the territorial settlement and of the order within the territories. Canning took this paper as the basis for his own foreign policy but added to it a neutrality and an isolation from Europe which set him apart from Castlereagh. Palmerston, in turn, claimed Canning as his master in foreign policy. But by developing a doctrine of nonintervention which allowed him to express opinions and give advice to foreign states on their domestic affairs, he departed from his master and from that part of Castlereagh's paper which had doubted the wisdom of giving advice on the ground that unsupported by force it was more likely to be held in contempt than heeded.

Further, the doctrine of nonintervention was variously interpreted within the foreign policies of each of these statesmen. For Castlereagh, it would exclude the intervention of any power in Spain, but in Naples it merely excluded collective intervention by the eastern powers not the unilateral intervention of Austria. For Canning, it meant a response in Portugal but none in Spain. Palmerston lectured both Austria and France on the Italian question in 1859, but, more faithful to the principle of balance than that of nonintervention, he would utter no protest against Russian intervention in Hungary in 1849. Measured against Cobden's principle of nonintervention, the doctrines of Castlereagh, Canning, and Palmerston were all doctrines of intervention. Cobden equated British interests with nonintervention. Where Castlereagh and Canning made no such equation, but conceived of fundamental interests which might require intervention, if only exceptionally, they allowed themselves a greater flexibility in diplomacy than Cobdenism could provide. This was the more true of Palmerston

[178] Temperley and Penson, pp. 305–306.

as he disparaged abstract principle in favor of common sense and prudence.

If the doctrine of nonintervention was available to each of these statesmen for his own interpretation according to his conception of British interests and to the situation which confronted him, to what extent can a principle of nonintervention be said to have restrained the foreign policies of any of them? In the first place, there was a domestic constraint. A British tradition of nonintervention, however ill-defined, had at least to be taken account of in the formulation of foreign policy, and departure from it required justification before a Parliament which was in part the guardian of the tradition. Second, the existence of this tradition provided a broad conception of what British interests generally were, and this conception was the inheritance of each foreign minister. Castlereagh's State Paper of May 5 gathered together the threads of an old tradition and restated it as the British position against the European allies, and in so doing he added to the tradition to be passed on to his successors. In this sense, the tradition itself constrained the maker of foreign policy because it provided his framework for action in international relations. Third, there was an external constraint encouraging adherence to the principle of nonintervention. In some cases, Britain had no choice but to refrain from intervention if she wished to avoid war with other great powers. Attention to the balance of power in Europe meant that Britain should not only act against the power which upset it but also that she should not herself upset it by a policy of intervention. Further, as Palmerston discovered, the "British" principle of nonintervention could be turned against his own interference. If it can be said that to the extent that Great Britain observed the principle of nonintervention, it was an adherence dictated by her interests, there is no need on that account to disparage the principle as a mere disguise for interest, for it is as a protection of interests that rules exist. But if the essence of law is that it should have the power to compel an actor in any circumstance against his will, then Britain was not restrained by the rule in this essential sense.

III

NONINTERVENTION IN AMERICAN DOCTRINE AND PRACTICE

If British ideas about international relations played some part in contributing the principle of nonintervention to the body of international law, that contribution was supplemented and strengthened by a United States practice which claimed the doctrine of nonintervention as the basis of its foreign policy. The full extent of the contribution was demonstrated when, in the twentieth century, the United States doctrine of nonintervention merged with Latin American doctrine in the proclamation of a near-absolute principle of nonintervention as a formal rule of inter-American public law. This section of the chapter will look at the birth and growth of the United States doctrine, at the practice of the United States measured against the principle of nonintervention, and at the functions performed by the doctrine of nonintervention in American foreign policy.

i. The American Doctrine of Nonintervention

American doctrine will be examined here through three phases: the origin of the idea of nonintervention in the thoughts of the Founding Fathers and its relation to isolationism; the working out of the rule at the time of Latin American independence and its relation to the Monroe Doctrine; and the adoption of the principle as a rule of law in the American hemisphere and its relation to the Latin American doctrine of nonintervention.

A. ORIGINS

"Nonintervention" has been used as a generic term encompassing the various American doctrines that have counseled aloofness from European politics and as a synonym for any one of them.[179] The interest here is in the doctrine holding that the United States should not interfere in the domestic affairs of other sovereign states. The roots of this doctrine may be traced to the ideas about foreign policy current during Washington's second term as president and more generally to that collection of ideas forming the "isolationist's ideal."[180]

This ideal, expressing the "natural desire of every people for

[179] For use as a generic term, see Charles E. Martin, *The Policy of the United States as Regards Intervention*, New York, 1921, pp. 58–59. For use as a description for noninterference in the wars of others, see Thomas A. Bailey, *The Diplomatic History of the American People*, 5th ed., New York, 1955, p. 6.

[180] This phrase is Albert K. Weinberg's in "The Historical Meaning of the American Doctrine of Isolation," *American Political Science Review*, Vol. xxxiv, No. 4, August 1940, p. 540.

maximum self-determination,"[181] was reinforced in the United States by her sense of escape from a corrupt Old World, by the perception of extreme geographical distance from the rest of the world, and by a jealous regard for her novel institutions.[182] The ideal was seen also as an interest. Arguing that dependence on Britain meant involvement in European wars, Thomas Paine, writing in 1776, urged that it was "the true interest of America to steer clear of European contentions."[183] The ideal and its expression in terms of interest were rewarded on April 22, 1793, with Washington's Proclamation of Neutrality which announced that the United States was to be impartial in the war between France and the European coalition. Made in the face of massive popular support for the French cause, this policy of separation from Europe received its famous defense in Washington's Farewell Address three years later.[184] Repudiating "inveterate antipathies against particular nations and passionate attachments for others" as productive of a variety of evils—the incitement of jealousy at home and abroad, the perception of imaginary shared interests with other nations, involvement in the quarrels of others—Washington laid down the great rule of conduct for America in regard to foreign nations "in extending our commercial relations to have with them as little *political* connection as possible." The controversies of Europe were remote to the concerns of the United States, and nothing was to be gained by surrendering the advantages of her distant situation and interweaving her destiny with that of any part of Europe. It was America's true policy to avoid permanent alliances with any portion of the foreign world.

It might be said that the doctrine of nonintervention has one of its roots in this advice of Washington's that the United States should make her actual isolation the guide to her conduct in foreign relations—nonintervention in the internal affairs of other states being part of the broader doctrine of noninvolvement with them.[185] But, although Washington in his address made much of

[181] *Ibid.*

[182] Louis J. Halle, *American Foreign Policy: Theory and Reality*, London, 1960, pp. 1–33.

[183] Quoted in Bailey, p. 4.

[184] The quotations following are taken from the extracts from the address in Henry Steele Commager, *Documents of American History*, 5th ed., New York, 1949, pp. 169–175.

[185] Not just part of it, Julius Goebel argues, but in its beginnings nearly identical with it. He locates the origin of the doctrine of nonintervention

American remoteness from the concerns of Europe, the United States was not in fact isolated from them; Washington was referring to the situation which ought to obtain rather than to the real situation. The open agitation of France against Jay's Treaty with England, and on behalf of the election of the supposedly pro-French Jefferson to the presidency, was in Washington's mind when he prepared his address. In view of this, it is possible to regard the address not merely as an isolationist tract advising the United States to steer clear of foreign quarrels, but as a declaration of the independence of American foreign policy, an assertion of national sovereignty against French interference in her domestic affairs.[186] This immediate purpose of rallying the nation against European interference might be detected in Washington's phrase: "[a]gainst the insidious wiles of foreign influence . . . the jealousy of a free people ought to be *constantly* awake." Herein, a second root of the doctrine of nonintervention might be discerned, complementing the doctrine

---

in the debate in the cabinet before the publication of the Proclamation of Neutrality. The principals in this debate, Hamilton and Jefferson, were agreed that the attitude of the United States toward the war in Europe should be one of neutrality; they disagreed about the recognition of France, whose minister was on his way to Philadelphia, and about the status of the 1778 Treaty with France. Hamilton argued that the treaty was void because of the radical change in the government of France since its ratification, and he advocated that the French minister be received with the reservation that future considerations might render the treaty suspended. Jefferson thought the treaty still valid, it being an action taken in the name of the French nation, an authority which did not vary with the form of government. He proposed unconditional acceptance of the French minister as an envoy of a government based on the will of a nation. Hamilton was concerned that any action or declaration by the United States which showed sympathy with France would be regarded by the European enemies of France as an interference, and would give them cause to regard the United States as an enemy. Hamilton thought that "[t]he military stipulations they [the treaties] contain are contrary to that neutrality in the quarrels of Europe which it is our true policy to cultivate and maintain." It is in this doctrine of nonparticipation in European affairs that Goebel sees the first flowering of the doctrine of nonintervention—they were the same, or nearly so, because the European states were the only places where the question of American interference could come up. It was only later, he adds, during the South American struggle, that the doctrine of nonintervention expanded to assume the form in which it is most generally understood. *The Recognition Policy of the United States*, New York, 1915, pp. 106–112.

[186] Samuel Flagg Bemis, "Washington's Farewell Address: A Foreign Policy of Independence," *American Historical Review*, Vol. xxxix, No. 2, January 1934, pp. 263–268.

of nonparticipation with a doctrine addressed to the protection of the sovereignty of the United States against outside interference.[187]

If the germ of the idea of reciprocity, of a rule of nonintervention to be observed by the United States in her foreign policy and an expectation that other states would observe the same rule in their relations with the United States, can be traced to the Farewell Address, it can be said that Jefferson provided the conception of rights on which this reciprocity could be based. In an instruction to Pinckney, the American representative in London, about the American attitude to revolutionary France, he wrote:

> We certainly cannot deny to other nations that principle whereon our own government is founded, that every nation has a right to govern itself internally under what form it pleases and to change these forms at its own will; and externally to transact business with other nations through whatever organ it chooses, whether that be a King, Convention, Assembly, Committee, President or whatever it be. The only thing essential is the will of the nation.[188]

Jefferson's idea of a right of all states to govern themselves according to whatever principles they choose may be said to imply a duty of nonintervention.[189]

[187] This protective concern with the independence of the United States was well expressed by John Adams when he wrote that "our form of government, inestimable as it is, exposes us more than any other, to the insidious intrigues and pestilent influence of foreign nations. Nothing but our inflexible neutrality can preserve us. The public negotiations and secret intrigues of the English and French have been employed for centuries in every court and country of Europe. . . . If we convince them that our attachment to neutrality is unchangeable, they will let us alone; but as long as a hope remains, in either power, of seducing us to engage in war on his side and against his enemy, we shall be torn and convulsed by their manoeuvres." Quoted in J. B. Moore, *A Digest of International Law*, 8 vols., Washington, 1906, Vol. VI, pp. 11–12.

[188] Instruction of December 30, 1792, cited in Goebel, p. 104.

[189] Like Goebel, Charles E. Martin seems to find the origin of the American doctrine of nonintervention in the cabinet debate which led to the Proclamation of Neutrality. Unlike Goebel, he takes Jefferson as its originator and not Hamilton. Where Hamilton argued that the carrying out of the military stipulations of the treaty with France would breach neutrality in favoring the French, Jefferson argued that the abrogation of the treaty would be a breach of neutrality against France, giving the French a just cause for war against the United States. Martin takes Jefferson's acceptance of the right of revolution, and his application of a *de facto* test for the recognition of a

Though each of these doctrines—the doctrine of nonparticipation in the affairs of others, the assertion of American independence against the interference of others, and Jefferson's theory of the right of nations to choose their own form of government—can be regarded as precursors of the American doctrine of nonintervention, and taken together they provide all the elements of such a doctrine, the particular question whether or not the United States should interfere in the domestic affairs of another state had not yet confronted American statesmen. The independence movement in Latin America posed the particular question.

B. THE DOCTRINE OF NONINTERVENTION AND THE MONROE DOCTRINE

Just as the French Revolution had forced Washington into a difficult foreign-policy decision in 1793, so the revolution in Latin America against Spanish rule, in the first decades of the nineteenth century, confronted the American statesmen of the time with a similar dilemma. Similar but more complex, because the choice of policy now involved, as well as Europe and the United States, an additional group of Latin American actors. Both the doctrine of nonintervention and the Monroe Doctrine can be traced from the policy adopted. What follows will examine the evolution of the doctrine of nonintervention from the Spanish American revolution to its acceptance as an established principle of American foreign policy in the administrations that followed Monroe's, and it will distinguish the differences and similarities between the doctrine of nonintervention and the ideas contained in the Monroe Doctrine.

From 1811 until recognition in 1822, the official policy of the United States toward the struggle between Spain and her Latin American colonies was one of neutrality.[190] Thus Madison and

_____

government within another state, to be the first statement of the American policy of nonintervention. *Policy of US as Regards Intervention*, pp. 41–46.

[190] In fact, it was a neutrality favorable to the rebel cause, so that nonbelligerency rather than neutrality was the accurate description of American policy. Spain could object to such a policy not only because the neutrality was not impartial but also because American recognition of the belligerency of the rebels (which was concurrent with the Proclamation of Neutrality of September 1811) could be regarded as intervention in Spanish affairs. C. C. Griffin, *The United States and the Disruption of the Spanish Empire 1810–1822*, New York, 1937, pp. 97–98; A. P. Whitaker, *The United States*

after him Monroe took the same attitude to a foreign war as had Washington in 1793; this time, however, the foreign war was legally a civil conflict. For Washington, the neutrality doctrine had meant nonparticipation in an international war, for Madison and Monroe, it now meant abstention from interference in the internal affairs of another power. When American recognition of the new states came in 1822, Monroe's Secretary of State, John Quincy Adams, defended it as "an obligation of duty of the highest order" and Monroe himself spoke in terms of the duty of recognition.[191] This transition from neutrality to recognition of statehood, while dictated by practical considerations, could at the same time be justified in theory. The settled policy of the United States not to interfere in the conflicts of others was in no way inconsistent with America's taking notice of the outcome of those conflicts. Armed with the Jeffersonian *de facto* doctrine, Adams could reply to Spanish protests by asserting that American recognition was the mere acknowledgment of existing facts.[192] By her neutrality, the United States would not interfere in the issue of the Latin American war of independence, but a fortiori she would not interfere by refusing to recognize governments which were, in her view, legitimate expressions of the will of the people.

The abstention of the United States from active participation in the conflict in South America and the long delay before recognition of the insurgents were not policies which commanded a consensus within America. The Spanish objection that American policy was too favorable to the rebels confronted Monroe and Adams internationally; at home they had to face the criticism, principally from Henry Clay, that their policy was insufficiently favorable to the insurgents. While the debate between Adams and

---

and the Independence of Latin America 1800–1830, New York, 1962, pp. 194–199.

[191] Whitaker, pp. 375–376. Adams derived this obligation from his non-colonization principle which he had advanced in 1821. See below, pp. 109–110.

[192] Adams argued that two principles were involved in the matter of the independence of a nation—one of right and one of fact. Right depended on national self-determination, and fact on its successful achievement. At the same time, he asserted that American recognition of Latin American independence was not intended to violate any right of Spain. Goebel relates the Spanish position to the doctrine of monarchical legitimacy, and the Adamsonian argument to democracy and republican government—to which the *de facto* principle is an inevitable counterpart. *Recognition Policy of the U.S.*, p. 141.

Clay can be regarded as merely the natural antagonism of two presidential aspirants, the issues raised in it were of fundamental importance to American foreign policy. Sympathy for the cause of Latin American independence was not the point at issue, though Adams' credentials on this matter, at least at the outset, were dubious;[193] rather the dispute was about the principles which should guide American policy toward the revolutionaries.

Clay's criticism of the administration was that its failure to recognize the rebels' claim to independence was not in accord with public opinion in the United States. He argued that the Latin American rebels be supported by all means short of war in order to encourage the cause of freedom everywhere, and he advocated the formation of a counterpoise to the Holy Alliance to advance national independence and liberty by the force of example and moral influence.[194] Adams parodied these arguments of Clay, and took the parody as a text for destruction at an Independence Day speech in Washington in 1821, representing Clay's views as a call to arms. He made use of the same platform to criticize an article in the *Edinburgh Review* of May 1820, which had called for American cooperation with British liberals for the cause of reform and liberty in Europe.[195] To these sorts of arguments Adams had two replies. In the first place, he questioned the possibility of an American role as the judge of the righteous cause in a civil war.[196] Second, he spoke of an "inevitable tendency" of direct interference, even if undertaken in the cause of liberty, to degenerate into mere power and dominion, so that these forces rather than liberty provided the foundation of government.[197] He might have added Monroe's argument that if the revolting colonies could not beat Spain of their own accord, then they did not deserve to be free.[198]

For Adams the two great principles on which American foreign policy ought to be conducted were the anticolonial principle and the principle of nonentanglement. In Adams' view, the anticolonial principle provided a solid basis for the right of the United States to independence and settled the question of the justice of

[193] Bemis, *John Quincy Adams and the Foundations of American Foreign Policy*, New York, 1949, pp. 342–343.
[194] Speech at Lexington, Kentucky, May 19, 1821, cited in Whitaker, p. 345.
[195] Whitaker, pp. 344–369.
[196] Adams to A. H. Everett, December 29, 1817, cited in Griffin, p. 138.
[197] Whitaker, pp. 361–363, and especially p. 362, n. 34.
[198] Monroe to Jackson, December 21, 1818, cited in Whitaker, p. 211.

the struggle for independence in South America.[199] His principle of nonentanglement allowed the United States to be the "well-wisher to the freedom and independence of all" but the "champion and vindicator only of her own."[200] Impressed by the similarity of the situation which confronted him and that which faced Washington in his second term, Adams restated the principles of the Farewell Address and made them universal. Though the ideas of Adams were thus firmly in the isolationist tradition, his application of them to conflict within states as well as to international conflict, presaged the emergence of the doctrine of nonintervention, which he was to establish when he assumed the presidency.

Monroe's message to Congress of December 2, 1823 expressed the attitude of the United States to Europe, to the newly independent states of Latin America, and to the relations between these groups of powers. The message contained three declarations of principle. First, the American continents were not to be considered as subjects for future colonization by any European power. In the second place, the message reiterated the traditional American policy of abstention from the affairs of Europe. Third, Monroe warned the European powers against any interposition in any portion of the American Hemisphere.[201] This two worlds doctrine of Monroe was at once the confirmation of America's traditional policy of isolation and a radical departure from it: traditional in its intention to abstain from European affairs, novel in its apparent extension of United States protection to the whole of the American hemisphere.[202]

It is possible to regard the two worlds doctrine as nothing more than the assertion of a hemispheric principle of nonintervention by which the rule applied between continents rather than between states. The reciprocal respect required for such a rule to operate was hinted at by Adams in his description of the purpose behind the American response to threats of Russian intervention in the Americas in 1823. His view was that an America which disclaimed all intention of propagating her principles by force in Europe or of interfering with European political affairs could declare her "expectation and hope" that the European powers would equally

[199] Whitaker, pp. 359–361.

[200] Quoted in Bemis, *John Quincy Adams*, pp. 364–365.

[201] See the extract from Monroe's message in D. Perkins, *Hands Off: A History of the Monroe Doctrine*, Boston, 1948, pp. 390–392.

abstain from the attempt to spread their principles in the American Hemisphere.[202]

As well as this intercontinental doctrine of nonintervention, the Monroe Doctrine espoused a specific principle of nonintervention in three areas of interstate relations. In the first place, the stipulation that America should abstain from European politics included a specific undertaking not to interfere in the internal concerns of any of its powers. This undertaking was a product of the influence of Adams, who prevailed upon Monroe to exclude from his message any commitment to sustain liberty in Spain or Greece. Any course other than complete nonentanglement would not conform with Adams' conception of the interests and traditions of the United States.[203] Second, Monroe's message declared that America had not and would not interfere with the existing colonies or dependencies of any European power. This commitment to nonintervention, which could be shown to be inconsistent with the noncolonization principle, seems to be part of Adams' attempted bargain by which the United States would refrain from interference in Europe if this would keep the Europeans out of those parts of the Americas that were not still colonies. Third, the message suggested that it was American policy to leave the parties to the dispute in Latin America to themselves in the hope that other powers would pursue the same course. All references to the doctrine of nonintervention in Monroe's message, then, appear to have been related to the rather feeble aspiration that the European powers would follow American example in observing the rule.[204]

If the Monroe Doctrine contained elements of the doctrine of nonintervention, it also contained elements which were contrary to that doctrine as it was informed by the isolationist tradition. The assertion that any attempt by the European powers to extend their system to the American hemisphere would be considered dangerous to American peace and safety has itself been regarded as an interventionary act on the part of the United States: inter-

[202] *Ibid.*, p. 49. Elsewhere, Perkins refers to "an appealing, if perhaps a specious, logic in the view-point that the United States, in keeping out of European affairs, had a right to demand a like forbearance from Europe with regard to the Americas," "John Quincy Adams," in Bemis, ed., *The American Secretaries of State and their Diplomacy*, Vol. IV, New York, 1958, p. 71.

[203] Whitaker, pp. 486–487; Bemis, *John Quincy Adams*, pp. 388–389.

[204] For further treatment of the notion of reciprocity, see below, pp. 131–136.

ventionary because any European interference was objected to, irrespective of its legitimacy in international law.[205] Moreover, if fidelity to the hemispheric principle of nonintervention required a forcible response from the United States when any Latin American state was under threat from a European power, then this would depart from a doctrine of nonintervention that was closer to Cobden than to Mill. The Monroe Doctrine also remained silent on the principles which were to govern the United States in her relations with Latin America. While concerned with Latin America, the Monroe Doctrine was aimed at Europe; it remained to be seen whether the doctrine of nonintervention which was to apply between hemispheres would also be taken as an interstate rule within one of them.

In the decades that followed the announcement of the Monroe Doctrine, the idea that the United States should not intervene in the internal affairs of other nations, became a familiar part of American doctrine on foreign policy. The doctrine of nonintervention was invoked not merely to criticize the actions of other states, and particularly the European powers, it was also announced as the official policy of the United States toward the Latin American states.[206] Practice had thus hardened into an accepted political doctrine and doctrine in turn came to be defended on legal grounds. In 1842 Secretary of State Webster wrote:

> The great communities of the world are regarded as wholly independent, each entitled to maintain its own system of law and government, while all in their mutual intercourse are understood to submit to the established rules and principles governing such intercourse. And the perfecting of this system of com-

[205] Thomas and Thomas, *Non-Intervention*, p. 13.

[206] Adams, in his annual message to Congress of 1827, declared that towards Latin America the United States was "disclaiming alike all right and all intention of interfering in those concerns which it is the prerogative of their independence to regulate as to them shall seem fit." Cited in Graber, *Crisis Diplomacy*, p. 56. In 1829, Secretary of State van Buren wrote in a dispatch to the American minister in Colombia: "It is the ancient and well-settled policy of this country not to interfere with the internal affairs of any foreign country. However deeply the President might regret changes in the governments of the neighboring American States, which he might deem inconsistent with those free and liberal principles which lie at the foundation of our own, he would not, on that account, advise or countenance a departure from this policy." Cited in Moore, *Digest*, Vol. VI, p. 14.

munication among nations, requires the strictest application to the doctrine of nonintervention of any with the domestic concerns of others.[207]

C. THE DOCTRINE OF NONINTERVENTION AS A PRINCIPLE OF AMERICAN INTERNATIONAL LAW

At the Inter-American Conference for the Maintenance of Peace, held at Buenos Aires in December 1936, the United States was one of the High Contracting Parties which declared "inadmissible the intervention of any one of them, directly or indirectly, and for whatever reason, in the internal or external affairs of any other of the Parties."[208] That the United States should accept a rule of nonintervention as a guide to her relations with other American states was not of great significance; such a doctrine had a long pedigree. What was remarkable was that the United States should bind herself by treaty to the observation of an apparently absolute rule of nonintervention, allowing none of the exceptions with which she had increasingly indulged herself. By signing and ratifying such a protocol, it seemed that the United States had finally succumbed to the Latin American doctrine of nonintervention.

The assertion of the principle of nonintervention as a fundamental rule of international law has been an article of faith with the Latin American republics ever since the time of Bolivar.[209] It made sense, given the weakness of the Latin American states compared with the European powers and with the United States, that they should proclaim the doctrine of complete equality of sovereign states and derive from it an absolute rule of nonintervention, in order to compensate for patent factual inequality. Economic backwardness and political instability in Latin America combined to produce two interesting interpretations of the doctrine of nonintervention. First, the Argentinian jurist, Carlos Calvo, laid down the doctrine that disputes arising from contracts involving foreign nationals should be settled in the courts of the country concerned. Calvo had in mind the European interventions in Latin America to enforce private financial claims, and he wished to proscribe the

[207] Quoted in Moore, *Digest*, Vol. VI, pp. 15–16.

[208] Article I of the Protocol relative to nonintervention, cited in J. W. Gantenbein, *The Evolution of our Latin American Policy: A Documentary Record*, New York, 1950, p. 778.

[209] Thomas and Thomas, pp. 55–56.

appeal of foreign nationals to their home country for defense of their rights.[210] This doctrine asserted the illegality of interventions which the European powers had always considered lawful. In the second place, Latin American jurisprudence was concerned to outlaw the intervention of foreign states to protect the lives and property of their nationals when civil order crumbled sufficiently to threaten them. The problem for Latin American diplomacy was to involve the United States in an American international law which would contain a guarantee not only that the United States would refrain from intervention in the countries to her south, but would also support those countries against non-American intervention whatever the provocation.[211]

The reluctance of the United States to be drawn into such a position was demonstrated at the first International Conference of American States at Washington in 1889. In response to a Latin American initiative to have a variant of Calvo's doctrine incorporated as American international law, the delegate of the United States to the committee on international law objected to the phrase "American international law" and dissented from the resolution on the ground that national courts might not provide "substantial justice."[212] This difference of outlook was characteristic of the conferences which took place before the First World War; the reluctance to debate important issues and the mutual mistrust between the two Americas did not create an environment encouraging to the growth of neighborliness and an American international law. This, after all, was the age of United States intervention in Latin America. After the war, in the international euphoria provided by the establishment of the League of Nations and the Permanent Court of International Justice, the project for an American international law came almost to a standstill. At the same time, there was considerable nongovernmental enthusiasm for such a scheme among eminent international lawyers from both the United States and Latin America, whose collective voice was made more effective through the mouthpiece of the recently formed American Institute of International Law and the funds of the Carnegie Endowment. It was largely the work of these private individuals and institutions, and the sympathetic response from

[210] *Ibid.*, pp. 56–57.

[211] Bemis, *The Latin American Policy of the United States*, New York, 1943, pp. 237–238.

[212] *Ibid.*, p. 233.

Secretary of State Hughes, which brought the project and, in particular, the doctrine of nonintervention to the attention of the delegates to the sixth International Conference of American States held at Havana in 1928.[213]

But sympathy and willingness to discuss important issues at Havana could not resolve the conflict of perceived interests between the United States and the Latin American republics. The United States was unwilling to eschew its residual right to intervene to protect its nationals in any American republic whose government was unable to fulfill this function. Acting under instructions from the State Department, Hughes, the leader of the American delegation at Havana, could not accept the unqualified doctrine that "no state has a right to interfere in the internal affairs of another."[214] The stand taken by Hughes at Havana was a rearguard action. At Montevideo in 1933, the United States signed, and later ratified, the Convention on the Rights and Duties of States. Article 8 read: "No state has the right to intervene in the internal or external affairs of another."[215] The reservation attached to signature that the United States would follow the law of nations as generally recognized and accepted—the last attempt to avoid the full implications of an American international law—disappeared with the acceptance of the Buenos Aires Protocol in 1936. Franklin Roosevelt's Good Neighbor Policy had extended to the international legal relations of the American states.

The acceptance by the United States of the Latin American doctrine of nonintervention gave the Latin Americans good cause to congratulate themselves upon a sweeping diplomatic victory. But a victory for the one party did not necessarily mean a defeat for the other. While Latin American persistence played a signifi-

[213] At the Fifth International Conference of American States held at Santiago in 1923, Professor Alvarez, the most prominent Latin American advocate of an American international law, had put the reasons for an American doctrine of nonintervention in a way which could not be unattractive to traditional United States doctrine on foreign policy. In a report to the juridical committee, he wrote: "The States of America, even before reaching a mutual agreement, have proclaimed certain regulations or principles different and even contradictory to those prevailing in European countries, and which these latter are compelled to respect in our Continent, for instance, non-intervention and non-occupation of territories of the states of America by ultra-continental countries." Cited in *ibid.*, p. 243.

[214] *Ibid.*, pp. 248–252.

[215] Cited in Gantenbein, pp. 759–763.

cant part in the acceptance by the United States of the legal rule of nonintervention, the United States could find ample doctrinal justification for adherence to the rule in her own diplomatic history.[216] But the most persuasive reasons for this radical change in United States foreign policy between the administrations of the two Roosevelts lies not in doctrine, or in Latin American persistence, but in the changed interests, perceived and real, of the United States. It will be one of the tasks of the next section to examine the practical considerations that led the United States to bind herself to an apparently absolute principle of nonintervention.

ii. Nonintervention in United States Practice

The intention in this section is to comment on the extent to which the United States can be said to have conducted her foreign policy according to the principle of nonintervention, and on the reasons which compelled obedience to it or divergence from it in her relations with four distinct areas: the North American continent, Latin America until the end of the First World War, Europe, and the Far East. It will conclude by drawing attention to the inherent difficulties in a policy that attempts to adhere meticulously to the rule of nonintervention which were revealed by United States relations with Latin America in the interwar period.

A. THE NORTH AMERICAN CONTINENT

The principle of nonintervention was not generally persuasive as a guide to American policy toward those territories which stood in the path of her expansion to fill the continent of North America in the first half of the nineteenth century. The practical advantages to be had from the acquisition of territory were considered superior to the abstract advantages which were supposed to flow from a policy of self-restraint. The strategic importance of Florida to the United States led to frequent American attempts to buy it from Spain, or to acquire it by peaceful negotiation. At the same time, American immigrants took advantage of the weakness of Spanish authority and provoked rebellion in Florida with a view to persuading the United States herself to intervene against Spain.[217] In 1810 West Florida was declared an independent republic by rebellious American immigrants, and President Madison accepted her request

[216] Bemis, *Latin American Policy*, pp. 227–228.
[217] Graber, p. 35.

to join the United States, justifying the acquisition by a dubious reference to the Louisiana Purchase.[218] In 1812 and again in 1818, filibustering expeditions led respectively by Generals Mathews and Jackson were carried out in Florida with the tacit support of the administrations in Washington. The first adventure was disavowed by Congress, but John Quincy Adams defended Jackson's action as taken in self-defense and he advised Spain to "control or cede" the territory of East Florida.[219] Unable to control, Spain ratified the cession of Florida in 1821.

The expansion of the United States into every part of the North American continent was not, however, an inevitable process; mere contiguity did not presage annexation. President Van Buren's reluctance to involve the United States in a war with Britain led him to enforce vigorously the neutrality laws against Americans who were supporting the Canadian insurrectionists in their unsuccessful uprising of 1837.[220] In other cases, the United States refrained from intervention because such a step was unnecessary. The joint occupation arrangement which the United States had with Britain in respect of the Oregon territory allowed American immigration into the area, a decisive factor when the frontier on the forty-ninth parallel was negotiated with Britain in 1846.[221] In Texas too the establishment of *de facto* independence from Mexico did not require the official support of the United States, and for nine years from 1837 until 1846, America asserted her neutrality in the dispute between Texas and Mexico, refusing the Texan request for annexation.[222] War between the United States and Mexico came after annexation, over the disputed extent of Texan territory.

In all the areas on the continent of North America which the United States annexed in the first half of the nineteenth century, three factors were significant to varying degrees. In the first place, American immigration into Oregon, Texas, California, and Florida created a climate of opinion within the United States which was in the immigrants' favor when the question of annexation was

[218] Bailey, *Diplomatic History*, pp. 163–164.

[219] *Ibid.*, pp. 171–172.   [220] *Ibid.*, pp. 208–209.   [221] *Ibid.*, pp. 242–245.

[222] Though the neutrality laws were enforced with far less vigor than had been the case with regard to Canada, and in Bailey's judgment, the Texan revolution "would probably not have succeeded without American support." One reason for the American reluctance to annex Texas was the slavery question. Annexation, it was feared, would increase the political power of slavery, set South against North, and possibly split the Democratic Party. Bailey, pp. 252–253.

raised. This was consistent with the second factor—Manifest Destiny—which taught that "the proper dominion" of the United States was the continent of North America.[223] This doctrine was in turn reinforced by a third factor which was indeed a part of Manifest Destiny—the desire to exclude other powers from the American continent—and it was the threat of a British guarantee of an independent Texas which in part precipitated annexation.[224] In competition with these weighty factors the principle of nonintervention, while not ignored, was overridden by a more alluring doctrine.

B. LATIN AMERICA TO 1918

For the greater part of the nineteenth century, the principle of nonintervention played a role as significant in directing the policy of the United States toward the emergent and new states of Latin America as it had been insignificant on the continent of North America. Though an early declaration of United States neutrality toward the war between Spain and her American colonies, and then a neutrality imperfectly adhered to, might have been taken by Spain as interference in her internal affairs, Adams' policy did at least prevent the premature recognition of Latin American independence and the active participation of the United States in the war against Spain. For a number of reasons, abstention from open intervention was sound policy for the United States. In the first place, premature recognition would have furnished Spain with a *casus belli* against the United States, which might have meant war with Britain as well.[225] Second, the economic interests of the United States were not involved as trade with South America was not significant.[226] In the third place, the negotiations for the Spanish cession of Florida to the United States might have been imperiled by too energetic a policy toward Latin America.[227] Finally, it could even be argued that by not doing anything to provoke European intervention, the United States was not only keeping out of war herself but also promoting the cause of freedom in Latin America

---

[223] This was the view of John Quincy Adams: the actual phrase "Manifest Destiny" was not coined until 1845. Bemis, *Latin American Policy*, p. 74.

[224] *Ibid.*, pp. 82–83 and 86.

[225] Bemis, *John Quincy Adams*, p. 343.

[226] Perkins, "John Quincy Adams," p. 39.

[227] Goebel, *Recognition Policy of the U.S.*, p. 142.

by holding the European powers at bay.[228] The risks contained in this policy of nonintervention, namely, the possibility of alienating American public opinion and of incurring the ill-will of the Latin American insurgents, were small compared to the risks involved in an interventionary policy.[229] When the United States decided to recognize five of the new states in 1822, it was in response to the completion of the war for independence in most Latin American countries, when failure to recognize that situation would have been an unfriendly act toward the new states, and against the American interest in cultivating good relations with the new states to the exclusion of the European powers.

The independence of the Latin American colonies being achieved, the United States declared and conformed to a policy of nonintervention respecting it. In following that policy in its isolationist mode—failing to respond to the interventions of the European powers in Latin America—the United States did not interpret Monroe's warning that such action would be taken as a manifestation of an unfriendly disposition toward the United States as requiring any positive American reply. It was not until the end of the century that new interpretations of the Monroe Doctrine coincident with the growth of American power turned the policy of nonintervention into one of intervention, and the threat to the independence of the Latin American states then seemed to come as much from the United States as from across the Atlantic.

In 1895, Secretary of State Olney, commenting on the boundary dispute between Venezuela and British Guiana, foreshadowed the age of imperialism in United States foreign policy by asserting that she was "practically sovereign" on the American continent.[230] Three years later, the United States intervened in the civil war between Cuba and Spain on behalf of Cuba's struggle for independence. The factors which had restrained the United States from interfering in a previous Cuban insurrection were no longer significant;[231] in 1898 President McKinley was swept into war with Spain

[228] Whitaker, *U.S. and Latin America*, pp. 210–211.

[229] Bailey, pp. 165–167.   [230] See below, pp. 133–134.

[231] In 1873, for example, Spanish capture of the *Virginius*, which flew the American flag, on the high seas, might have given the United States cause for war, but a mood of introspection, a decrepit navy, and doubts about the character of the *Virginius*, among other things, prevented intervention. Bailey, p. 423.

by a frenzied public opinion.[232] While the doctrine of nonintervention might have influenced McKinley sufficiently for him to advance elaborate justifications for American intervention, it could not assuage a public bent on war.

The victory of the United States in the Spanish-American War and the consequent acquisition of territory in the Caribbean and in the Pacific provoked renewed interest in the construction of an Isthmian canal.[233] Two obstructions stood across the path of such a project. The first was the Clayton-Bulwer Treaty of 1850 by which the United States and Britain had agreed to cooperate in constructing a canal and never to fortify or exercise exclusive control over it.[234] This obstacle was finally surmounted by the Hay-Pauncefote Treaty of 1901, leaving the second problem of selecting and negotiating the location of the canal. Colombian reluctance to ratify a treaty extorted from her minister in Washington threatened to frustrate the enterprise, until a successful revolution in Panama allowed the United States to obtain by a treaty with the new state the territory in which to build the canal. The United States Navy acted as midwife at the birth of the state of Panama by preventing Colombian troops from landing to stamp out the rebellion. A few days later the United States offered her guarantee of the new state by recogizing Panama. President Theodore Roosevelt justified this action as taken in the "interests of collective civilization," though eight years later he was to boast that he "took the Canal Zone and let Congress debate."[235] Roosevelt's anxiety to take the Canal Zone because of its perceived strategic importance to the United States, a conception of American interests perhaps reinforced by the forthcoming presidential election, meant that the doctrine of nonintervention rated a low priority.

If Roosevelt's action in Panama had been naked and perhaps unnecessary imperialism, his intervention in the Dominican Republic in 1904 could be represented as both justifiable and necessary. Two years earlier Roosevelt had not invoked the Monroe Doctrine to counter the collective intervention of Britain, Germany, and Italy in Venezuela to enforce the collection of debts,

[232] See Halle, *American Foreign Policy*, pp. 176–214.

[233] The spoils of the Spanish-American War were the Philippines, Guam, and Puerto Rico. Acquisition of these territories encouraged a hitherto hesitant America to proceed with the annexation of American Samoa (1899), and Hawaii (1898).

[234] Bailey, p. 291.   [235] *Ibid.*, pp. 544–545.

120

because he did not "guarantee any state against punishment if it misconducts itself."[236] Since then, however, The Hague Court of Permanent Arbitration had handed down a verdict in the Venezuela case that the intervening powers had a right to payment of claims ahead of those who had not expressed their interests by force.[237] This legal sanction of the use of force confronted Roosevelt when the Dominican Republican defaulted on its debts with a choice between allowing European intervention or intervening himself to preclude such action. By occupying the Dominican customhouses, collecting revenues, and instituting a customs receivership, Roosevelt opted for American intervention.[238] The doctrine of nonintervention was overridden when action was thought necessary to combat the principle of European intervention.

Roosevelt's acquisition of the Panama Canal Zone and his doctrine of preventive intervention left a legacy which was enthusiastically accepted by his successor, President Taft. As Taft's Secretary of State, Knox, put it,

> the logic of political geography and of strategy, and now our tremendous national interest created by the Panama Canal, make the safety, the peace, and the prosperity of Central America and the zone of the Caribbean of paramount interest to the Government of the United States. Thus the malady of revolutions and financial collapse is most acute precisely in the region where it is most dangerous to us. It is here that we seek to apply a remedy.[239]

One remedy lay in the use of American capital to impose a financial order and thereby, in Taft's view, a political orderliness in the Latin American states.[240] Another remedy was the use of American marines in an attempt to fashion a political order in Nicaragua after the revolution in 1909. This intervention was to involve the United States intimately in Nicaraguan affairs for

[236] Annual message to Congress, December 3, 1901, cited in Gantenbein, p. 360.

[237] Bemis, *Latin American Policy*, p. 151.

[238] Thomas and Thomas, p. 34.

[239] Speech of January 19, 1912, cited in Bailey, p. 582.

[240] *Ibid.*, p. 583. This is the much vaunted "dollar diplomacy" of Taft's, which, Bemis argues, was an "easily misusable journalistic alliteration" tending to obscure the real motive of America's protective foreign policy. *Latin American Policy*, p. 166.

more than twenty years. The widening horizon of United States security diminished the relevance of the doctrine of nonintervention for her relations with Central America.

Taft's policy towards the revolution which erupted in Mexico in 1911 had been one of nonintervention and recognition of the *de facto* government in Mexico City. His successor, Woodrow Wilson, declared, at the outset of his administration, his intention to lend American influence "of every kind" to the realization of republican principles in Latin America.[241] Following this doctrine, Wilson refused to recognize the Huerta regime in Mexico because it had taken power unconstitutionally, and avowed it to be the policy of the United States to force the usurper out of office.[242] Armed intervention followed in 1914 and Wilson succeeded in attaining his objective of ridding Mexico of Huerta. But Huerta's fall and the succession of Carranza did not bring order to Mexico. In 1916 United States forces entered Mexico again in hot pursuit of Carranza's rival, Villa, who had carried out raids in American territory. It was preoccupation with events in Europe rather than a settled state of affairs in Mexico, which brought Wilson's policy of intervention there to an end with the *de jure* recognition of Carranza's government in 1917. Wilson's declaration of Latin American policy also sanctioned armed intervention in Haiti in 1915 and in the Dominican Republic in the following year to establish an American order after revolutionary uprisings. Thus Wilson carried the logic of "protective imperialism" much further into practice than its inventor, Roosevelt, and justified his policy by reference to the universal value of constitutional government, and to an American devotion to its development.[243]

In spite of his vigorous interventionary policy in Central America and the Caribbean, Wilson saw himself as a noninterventionist.[244] He repudiated the Dollar Diplomacy of his predecessors.[245] It was only with "infinite distaste" that he had resorted to armed interference in Mexico.[246] Yet his enthusiasm for constitutionalism, if it were to be indulged, led to a policy of intervention, particu-

[241] "Declaration of Policy with Regard to Latin America," March 11, 1913, cited in Gantenbein, pp. 94–95.

[242] Thomas and Thomas, p. 46.

[243] See, for example, address by Wilson at Mobile, Alabama, October 27, 1913, cited in Gantenbein, pp. 97–98.

[244] Bemis, *Latin American Policy*, p. 178.

[245] Bailey, pp. 594–596.

[246] Bemis, *Latin American Policy*, p. 178.

larly, as it happened, in those countries which were located in areas strategically important to the United States. Wilson might have been a noninterventionist by conviction, but conviction served only to make his policy of intervention a course reluctantly pursued; it did not prevent it.[247]

C. EUROPE

Though the United States had always taken the doctrine of nonintervention into account in her relations with Latin America, it was in those relations that her interpretation of the doctrine evolved from a nonparticipation informed by the isolationist tradition, through preventive intervention against the real or perceived threat of European interference in Central America and the Caribbean, and thence to the Wilsonian brand of intervention on behalf of constitutionalism. In her relations with the European powers throughout the nineteenth century, the United States maintained a policy of nonintervention free of any of the corollaries added to it in inter-American relations.

Adams had laid the doctrinal foundations for such a policy in 1821 by restating the nonentanglement principle of Washington and Jefferson in response to a suggestion that the United States should support liberal principles in Europe.[248] It was Adams who refused the request of the Greek insurgents for American aid in 1823, and his influence led to the incorporation of the principle of nonintervention in the Monroe Doctrine. Projects of interference in the internal affairs of European states were likely to provide the United States with powerful opponents. They would prejudice the survival of what little there was in the Adamsonian principle of reciprocity, and any support the United States would be able to lend was not likely to affect a situation within a European state to any significant degree.

A challenge to Adams' principle was presented by the revolution in Hungary in 1848. American sympathy for the uprising inspired the sending of a diplomatic mission to recognize the revolutionary government, but the revolt was suppressed before it arrived.[249] When, however, the leader of the failed revolution ar-

[247] In Graber's view, Wilson saw no contradiction between nonintervention and support for constitutionalism, because pressure to protect a foreign country from dictatorship was not to his mind intervention at all. *Crisis Diplomacy*, p. 198.

[248] See above, pp. 109–110.   [249] Bailey, p. 285.

rived in the United States in 1851, it was made clear to him that the sympathy which made him a hero in the eyes of the American public could not lead to armed intervention on his behalf.[250] In his message to Congress of 1852, President Fillmore emphasized the allegiance of the United States, whether she be weak or strong, to the nonintervention doctrine, and Senator Clay pointed out to Kossuth that the war which would follow from American intervention would serve the interests of neither Hungary nor the United States.[251]

When the United States did make a decisive entry into European international politics, it was not to intervene in the domestic affairs of a state but to assist in the defeat of Germany. That task being achieved, the place which American involvement earned for the United States in European politics and under Wilson's guidance in the international organization established after the war was spurned by the American Congress, and during the interwar years the doctrine of nonintervention in the domestic affairs of states rested once more within the broader doctrine of isolation from Europe. The nonintervention doctrine defended the failure of the United States, along with Britain and France, to respond to the intervention of other powers in the Spanish Civil War, and it was uttered as a protest against the German conquest of Czechoslovakia in 1939.[252] But though Roosevelt's protests against the behavior of Germany and Italy were couched in the language of involvement, of global concern at threats to the peace anywhere, it was not until after the Second World War that the American doctrine of nonintervention was tested against American participation in European politics.

D. THE FAR EAST

In the Far East the United States conducted her foreign relations according to a method "peculiar to the region";[253] a method quite alien to the doctrine of nonintervention as it was interpreted in either the European or the Latin American case. In policy toward Latin America, where the doctrine of nonintervention had laid down at the outset a rule requiring respect for the independence of the new states, in the Far East the claiming of extrater-

[250] *Ibid.*, p. 287.   [251] Graber, pp. 120–121.
[252] *Ibid.*, p. 187.
[253] A. Whitney Griswold, *The Far Eastern Policy of the United States*, New York, 1938, p. 5.

ritorial rights and the gaining of ends by gunboat diplomacy paid little attention, even formally, to the right of the nations of the area to independence. Whereas toward Europe, the doctrine of nonintervention was in part a repudiation of the old European methods of balance of power politics and at the same time a warning against entanglement with the European powers, in the Far East the United States was ready not only to entangle herself with the European powers but also to act according to the precepts of the balance of power. Two primary factors can be adduced to account for the lapsing of the doctrine of nonintervention in relations with the Far East: one is that the peculiar nature of the region required peculiar methods in the conduct of American relations with it; the other that America herself had a particular interest in the region which, in combination with the first factor, led to a wholly different style of diplomacy. These factors can be illustrated by reference to Caleb Cushing's mission to China to secure a trade treaty in 1844 and to the mission of Commodore Perry to Japan in the years 1853 and 1854.

The United States shared the view of the European powers that if trade privileges were to be gained in China and Japan, then the threat or use of force was an indispensable means to that end, mere argument being unavailing without an imposing show of power.[254] If the United States were to secure and maintain a part of the trade of the area, then forcible intervention was the behavior required of her. In the tradition of positivist international law, the justification for that behavior lay in placing China and Japan beyond the pale of civilization, where the rules of the law of nations did not apply. Cushing, including China among the states that did not recognize the law of nations, wrote in a dispatch to the secretary of state:

From the greater part of Asia and Africa individual Christians are utterly excluded, either by the sanguinary barbarism of the inhabitants, or by their phrenzied bigotry, or by the narrow-minded policy of their governments; to the courts the ministers of Christian governments have no means of access except by force and at the heads of fleets and armies; as between them and us there is no community of ideas, no common law of nations, no interchange of good offices; and it is only during the present generation that treaties, most of them imposed by

[254] Tyler Dennett, *Americans in Eastern Asia*, New York, 1941, p. 263.

force of arms or by terror, have begun to bring down the great Mohammedan and Pagan governments into a state of inchoate peaceful association with Christendom.[255]

But it was not just trade privileges to be gained that led the United States to involve herself in the Far East. With the expansion of the United States to the west coast of the North American continent at mid-century, the "Far East" became for the United States the "Farthest West"—not a remote area of which it was safe to take little notice, but an immediate area of concern for American security, particularly in view of the progressive eastward extension of the British Empire.[256] It was this political consideration, or the consideration that the political and the commercial were inextricably linked together, that was uppermost in the mind of Commodore Perry. He foresaw a time when the United States would be involved with Great Britain in a contest for the control of the Pacific, and for him, the task for American foreign policy was to secure ports of refuge against such a time.[257] He wrote:

> Though it does not belong to the spirit of our institutions to extend our dominion beyond the sea, positive necessity requires that we should protect our commercial interests in this remote part of the world [in particular, the Lew Chew Islands, south of Japan], and in doing so, to resort to measures, however strong, to counteract the schemes of powers less scrupulous than ourselves.[258]

Though Perry's designs ran ahead of official American policy, the protection of American interests in Asia involved the United States in the politics of balance, lest her failure to do anything to counteract the policy of the European powers should give them a decisive advantage at her expense. If the rule of nonintervention were held to apply at all in American relations with the Far East, it was very much a conditional application. But the doctrine did encourage Secretary of State Seward to inform the American representative at Ningpo in 1862 that despite the peculiarities of the Chinese situation it was his "duty to act in the spirit which governs us in our intercourse with all friendly nations, and especially to lend no aid, encouragement, or countenance to sedition or rebellion against the Imperial authority."[259]

[255] Cited in *ibid.*, p. 164.
[257] *Ibid.*, p. 273.
[259] Quoted in Graber, p. 111.
[256] *Ibid.*, pp. 176–179.
[258] Quoted in *ibid.*, p. 274.

The problems raised by taking the principle of nonintervention as a day-to-day guide to diplomatic conduct were demonstrated during the administration of Franklin D. Roosevelt. Adherence to the rule of nonintervention in relations with Latin American states was a fundamental part of Roosevelt's Good Neighbor Policy, and the United States proclaimed that adherence by signing and ratifying the 1936 Buenos Aires Protocol on nonintervention.[260] After the First World War, a number of factors had contributed to the formulation of this new policy of self-denial. In the first place, the possibility of European intervention in Latin America, which had entered so frequently into the calculations of prewar administrations, was no longer so persuasive a guide to policy. In consequence, the Monroe Doctrine, a basically defensive and reactive dogma, became less informative as a signpost for the policy-makers.[261] Second, the view gained currency in both unofficial and official circles that the clumsy weapon of forcible intervention in the affairs of Latin American states was too expensive and failed to achieve its intended objective of educating those states in the ways of constitutionalism.[262] In the third place, the resentment in Latin America caused by American intervention increasingly came to be regarded as contrary to the national interest of the United States.

This new conception of the national interest, which found expression in the Good Neighbor Policy and in the refurbishing of the principle of nonintervention, was informed not only by a negative assessment of intervention as costly, unnecessary, or ineffective but also by a positive calculation. Roosevelt was motivated

[260] See above, p. 113.

[261] Bryce Wood, *The Making of the Good Neighbor Policy*, New York, 1961, pp. 3–6.

[262] *Ibid.*, p. 7. The lesson that intervention was ineffective, Wood argues, had to be learned twice. His experience in the Nicaragua case led Stimson, Hoover's Secretary of State, to doubt the wisdom of intervention because "electoral supervision and bandit fighting were time-consuming and expensive, difficult and embarrassing." On April 18, 1931 Stimson went as far as to say that "general protection of Americans" could not be undertaken in Nicaragua because it would lead to "difficulties and commitments which this Government [did] not propose to undertake." The succeeding Roosevelt Administration learned Stimson's lesson in Cuba, which inclined Cordell Hull and Sumner Welles to the view that a consistent policy of nonintervention could not be maintained unless the United States refrained from interference as well. *Ibid.*, pp. 47, 41–42, and 133. On the distinction between "intervention" and "interference" see below, p. 128.

by the conviction that by promoting good-will the Good Neighbor Policy would increase trade and make possible the creation of "a kind of hemispheric partnership" which would serve a strategic purpose.[263] But adoption of a policy of nonintervention did not mean that the United States had lost interest in the protection and fair treatment of her citizens or their property in Latin America. It did mean that her interests in this respect were to be pursued not by intervention, but by the expectation of reciprocity, of a Latin American response in kind to the neighborliness of the United States.[264]

In her policy toward Latin American states after Roosevelt became president in 1933, the United States distinguished between the external affairs of those states which could be legitimately influenced and their internal affairs which could not.[265] This distinction led to the formulation of a doctrine of noninterference to complement that of nonintervention.[266] The policy of nonintervention required that the United States refrain from the use of armed force in her relations with Latin American states. By the doctrine of noninterference, the United States denied to herself that influence which had been formerly wielded in party and revolutionary politics which were now allocated to the realm of domestic affairs.[267] The United States would no longer interfere to inculcate democratic habits or to preserve order, because this sort of interference led too easily to that armed intervention which Roosevelt was determined to avoid.

The policy of noninterference put advice or the expression of opinion on domestic affairs out of official bounds for American diplomats, but the frontier of the permissible was hard to define. Practicing diplomats, confronted with the everyday business of conducting relations with the state to which they were accredited,

[263] *Ibid.*, pp. 129 and 131.

[264] *Ibid.*, pp. 7–8. Wood stresses that the American policy of nonintervention was not conditional on such reciprocity but that fair treatment of nationals was an expected response. *Ibid.*, pp. 159–161.

[265] This distinction is implied in an address by Roosevelt of December 28, 1933, cited in Gantenbein, *Evolution of Latin American Policy*, pp. 165–166. Wood argues that by foreign affairs the United States meant economic policy, the treatment of American nationals and property, and later, hemispheric defense. *Making of Good Neighbor Policy*, pp. 136–137.

[266] Welles, in a speech of October 19, 1936, referred to intervention and interference as separate phenomena. Cited in Gantenbein, pp. 172–173.

[267] Wood, p. 137.

sought from the State Department a more flexible interpretation of noninterference. In 1934 the minister to Nicaragua argued in a dispatch to the department that it was in harmony with the Good Neighbor Policy to use personal contacts and the expression of personal views in an attempt to avert disorder.[268] Again in 1936 the minister to El Salvador pointed out that the powerful influence of the United States was an established fact in Latin America and that failure to use it constructively might become a sin of omission and subject to misinterpretation. He urged the utility of peaceful, diplomatic cooperation by the United States in the service of liberalism and order.[269] To both these communications, Sumner Welles, the Assistant Secretary of State, was at first sympathetic. He seemed to think that an official policy of noninterference was consistent with an informal policy of influence in the interests of peace and order.[270] But by April 1936, Welles's view had changed radically. An instruction to ministers in Central American states sent at the end of the month, required them "to abstain from offering advice on any domestic question, and, if requested to give such advice, they should decline to do so."[271] Thus the problem of defining the limits of the permissible was solved by making noninterference in domestic affairs absolute.

Not quite absolute however; the United States left open the option of collective intervention if life and property were threatened by a breakdown of order in a Latin American country.[272] Furthermore, the Latin American conception of what constituted "domestic affairs" was broader than that of the United States. Consequently, the Latin American states could style more acts as interventionary than would appear so under the United States doctrines of nonintervention and noninterference. To the United

[268] *Ibid.*, pp. 142–143.
[269] *Ibid.*, p. 145.
[270] *Ibid.*, p. 143.
[271] Instruction of April 30, 1936, cited in Wood, p. 148. This instruction pointed out, as a rationale for noninterference, the connection between advice, perception of intervention, and actual intervention. The reason for Welles's conversion, Wood suggests, was the advice of Duggan, Chief of the Division of Latin American affairs, that abstention from any interference was to be preferred on three grounds: (a) that no action is better than action whose consequences cannot be foreseen; (b) that the opinion of a minister is usually taken to be the considered judgment of his government; and (c) that because ministers varied in ability, it would be unwise to give them discretion in particular cases. *Ibid.*, pp. 146–147.
[272] Bemis, *Latin American Policy*, pp. 277 and 292–293.

States, the welfare of American corporations in Latin American states was an external affair, but to the Latin Americans it was domestic; United States action on their behalf was in her view legitimate influence, but to the Latin Americans it constituted that indirect intervention which had been outlawed at Buenos Aires.[273] Difficulties about definition, then, plagued the Roosevelt Administration in its attempt to adhere to both nonintervention and noninterference. A century earlier, definition of the policy of nonintervention had been a comparatively uncomplicated task for a state which had lacked the power to exercise an interventionary option. The problem was more complex in the 1930's for a state which, while its influence was undeniable, had nevertheless chosen to deny to itself a particular method of exercising it.

iii. The Function of the Principle of Nonintervention in American Foreign Policy

Nonintervention was a doctrine the United States proclaimed for herself, and a policy she followed with a fidelity that varied according to time, place, and circumstance. This section will point out the part played by the principle of nonintervention as a doctrine which the United States would have others adhere to, as a principle in terms of which the actions of others were criticized and the policy of the United States defended and as a landmark of the domestic debate about foreign policy in the United States.

A. GUIDANCE AND COERCION

As well as taking the nonintervention principle as one of the standards which informed her own conduct of foreign affairs, the United States wished to encourage others, and especially Europeans, to abide by it. This objective could be pursued in three ways. In the first place, other states could be warned off intervention in the American hemisphere by the threat, however credible or explicitly stated, of counterintervention. Second, the rule could be upheld by counterintervention against the power which had ignored the warning. In the third place, the intervention of outside powers could be forestalled by the preventive intervention of the United States. In time, the Monroe Doctrine came to be associated with each of these policies; its original concern was confined to the first of them.

Monroe's message of 1823 stated that the interposition of any

[273] Wood, pp. 159–167.

130

European power for the purpose of oppressing or controlling the destiny of the newly independent Latin American states would be viewed as a manifestation of an unfriendly disposition toward the United States. There was no direct threat of counterintervention here, and Adams preferred to rely upon his notion of reciprocity. His response to the threat of intervention by the Holy Alliance to restore Spanish rule in Latin America was to desire a *quid pro quo* for American good behavior in Europe. His purpose, as it was explained to the cabinet on November 21, 1823, was for the United States to disclaim "all interference with the political affairs of Europe" and to declare her "expectation and hope that the European powers will equally abstain from the attempt to spread their principles in the American hemisphere, or to subjugate by force any part of these continents to their will."[274]

In the two decades after Monroe's message, before it came to be known as the Monroe Doctrine, its pronouncements and thus Adams' hope for reciprocity were ignored by the European powers, and the United States took little notice of the contravention. Her weakness, preoccupation with internal politics, and a feeling that her interests were not involved led the United States to be indifferent, or at least passive, in response to European adventures in the American Hemisphere at this time.[275] In 1842, however, President Tyler specifically invoked the Adams doctrine in regard to the Texan question, and in the same year he warned the European powers of American displeasure if they attempted to acquire the Hawaiian Islands.[276] When this warning was ignored by a British officer in the following year, the United States entered a vigorous protest and later stated that she might even feel justified in intervening by force to prevent European conquest.[277] By 1845 American interest in the acquisition of Texas, California, and Oregon, to the exclusion of European states, strengthened by the knowledge of French and British interference in La Plata, induced President Polk to restate emphatically the principles of 1823. In his annual message to Congress, he denied the applicability of the European balance of power principle to the North American continent, affirmed the legitimacy of annexation by consent, and declared that

[274] Allan Nevins, ed., *The Diary of John Quincy Adams, 1794–1845*, New York, 1929, p. 306.
[275] Perkins, *Hands Off*, pp. 66–75.
[276] Bemis, *Latin American Policy*, p. 99; Garber, pp. 49–50.
[277] *Ibid.*, p. 50.

no European colony or dominion should be planted on the North American continent with the consent of the United States.[278] Polk was primarily concerned with keeping Europe out of North America; it took European activity in Central America to encourage the United States to apply the Monroe Doctrine with more force to a wider area.[279]

The United States was reluctant to counterintervene militarily to uphold the rule of nonintervention when European powers violated it.[280] Either weakness ruled out such a course, or her interests did not warrant it, or her warnings were effective—intervention being prevented thereby rather than countered. Counterintervention any way was a last resort; the United States could first attempt to achieve her objectives by diplomatic means. When acquisition of California provoked renewed American interest in an Isthmian canal, the British claim to sovereignty over the eastern terminus of the proposed canal route in Nicaragua presented a difficulty. Any conflict over the Canal Zone was averted by signature of the Clayton-Bulwer Treaty in 1850. But the treaty was ambiguous and in 1852, when Britain, in her view legitimately, declared the Honduran Bay Islands a Crown Colony, the seeds of conflict were sown once more. President Pierce, when he took office in 1853, rejected "the idea of interference or colonization on this side of the ocean by any foreign power beyond present jurisdiction as utterly inadmissible" and in so doing he inaugurated a diplomatic debate which was to last until Britain returned the Bay Islands to Honduras in 1860.[281] The United States had not counterintervened against Britain in Central America but had made her position clear in the diplomatic negotiations which were the alternative to intervention.[282]

[278] Perkins, *Hands Off*, pp. 79–81.

[279] Originally the Monroe Doctrine had been applied to the whole of the American hemisphere. Polk chose to stress its particular relevance to North America without denying its hemispheric applicability. See *ibid.*, p. 80.

[280] The doctrine of nonintervention in its simple (Cobdenite) sense could itself be used to justify American failure to uphold the rule of nonintervention by countering the intervention of others.

[281] Perkins, *Hands Off*, pp. 98 and 101.

[282] The episode could be regarded as a British, not an American, diplomatic victory because Britain secured recognition of the Clayton-Bulwer Treaty and not the Monroe Doctrine as the established rule of law in Central America. Clarendon's position was that the Monroe Doctrine was

The American reaction to the debt-collecting intervention of Britain, France, and Spain in Mexico in 1861 was one of studied caution. The recognized legitimacy of such an operation and the American preoccupation with the Civil War made counterintervention impossible. The furthest Secretary of State Seward was prepared to go was to state unmistakably the American position, to reiterate the Monroe Doctrine without mentioning it by name, and to make the American position more clear as the French intention to set up an empire in Mexico, under Maximilian, itself became more obvious.[283] It was not until victory for the North in the Civil War seemed probable that the United States directed her attention to ridding Mexico of the French.[284] After Appomattox Seward, while still cautiously avoiding threats of force, referred more pointedly to the sympathy of Americans for the "Republicans of Mexico" and to their "impatience" with the "continued intervention of France."[285] By November 1865 Seward was regretting French unreadiness to remove the cause of disharmony between the United States and France, and by January 1866 the French were persuaded to withdraw from Mexico.[286] The American attitude, French public opinion, and the political situation in Europe joined to encourage this decision, and once more the need for forcible counterintervention was obviated by the success of diplomacy.[287]

If Seward had been reluctant to invoke the Monroe Doctrine in the 1860's, by the 1890's Secretary of State Olney was not only prepared to resurrect the doctrine but also to add a notorious corollary. Referring to the boundary dispute between Britain and Venezuela which Britain refused to arbitrate, Olney asserted a doctrine of American public law which required the United States

---

the dictum of the person who announced it, not an international axiom which regulated the conduct of European states. Bailey, p. 293, n. 25; Perkins, *Hands Off*, p. 100.

[283] Perkins, *Hands Off*, pp. 124–127.

[284] On April 4, 1864, for example, Congress passed a resolution declaring it not to be the policy of the United States to acknowledge "any monarchical Government erected on the ruins of any republican Government in America under the auspices of any European power." Cited in Perkins, *Hands Off*, pp. 127–128.

[285] *Ibid.*, p. 132.   [286] *Ibid.*, pp. 134–135.

[287] As to American earnestness, Bemis seems to suggest that if the French troops had not been withdrawn, the United States would have put them out by force. *Latin American Policy*, p. 112.

"to treat as an injury to itself the forcible assumption by an European power of political control over an American state."[288] Such injury justified American interposition, which, in this case, took the form of insistence upon peaceful arbitration, and Olney demanded a British decision on whether she would consent to submit to it.[289] Not content with this extension of the Monroe Doctrine, Olney added a boast that the United States was "practically sovereign on this continent, and its fiat is law upon the subjects to which it confines its interposition."[290] Salisbury, in his capacity as British foreign secretary, was slow to reply to Olney's note, and when he did, it was to argue that the Monroe Doctrine was irrelevant to the case at issue, and unsound anyway as a principle of international law.[291] President Cleveland took this as his cue to suggest the sending of a boundary commission to Venezuela to report on the matter. Cleveland wrote to Congress: "When such report is made and accepted, it will in my opinion, be the duty of the United States to resist by every means in its power as a willful aggression upon its rights and interests the appropriation by Great Britain of any lands or the exercise of governmental jurisdiction over any territory which after investigation we have determined of right belongs to Venezuela."[292] Cleveland was less cautious about threatening the use of force than Seward had been; but as with Seward, his policy was helped by a greater European interest in events elsewhere. British attention to the Venezuela problem, muted anyway by a placid public opinion, was diverted to the deteriorating situation in South Africa by a German declaration of support for the Boers, and the Venezuela case went to arbitration.[293]

[288] Olney to Bayard (U.S. Ambassador to Britain), July 20, 1895, cited in Gantenbein, p. 350.

[289] *Ibid.*, pp. 347, 351, and 354.

[290] Quoted in Bemis, *Latin American Policy*, p. 120.

[291] Perkins, *Hands Off*, pp. 177–178.

[292] Special message to Congress, December 17, 1895, cited in Gantenbein, p. 358.

[293] Bailey, pp. 486–489. I have taken the Venezuela case as an example of American counterintervention if not to uphold the rule of nonintervention then to uphold the Monroe Doctrine. It has also been regarded as conforming to one of Oppenheim's categories of intervention, viz. "[d]ictatorial interference of a third state in a difference between two states, for the purpose of settling the difference in the way demanded by the third state." George B. Young, "Intervention under the Monroe Doctrine: The Olney Corollary," *Political Science Quarterly*, Vol. LVII, No. 2, 1942, pp. 279–280.

A third method by which the United States encouraged others to respect the nonintervention principle and the Monroe Doctrine was that of preventive intervention. The best illustration of this policy came during Theodore Roosevelt's administration when American violation of the principle of nonintervention was held to be justified by its exclusion of outside powers and thereby its protection of the Monroe Doctrine. Roosevelt's policy had been foreshadowed as early as 1843 when Secretary of State Legaré spoke of interfering by force to prevent the Hawaiian Islands being conquered by a European power.[294] Again in 1848 President Polk suggested the annexation of Yucatán in Central America in order to exclude the European powers.[295] In the late 1850's, the threat of European intervention in the Mexican Civil War led not only Senator Houston but also President Buchanan to advocate preventive intervention because in Buchanan's words, "[i]t is a duty which we owe to ourselves to protect the integrity of Mexico's territory against the hostile interference of any other power."[296] The Roosevelt Corollary to the Monroe Doctrine which was to justify United States intervention in the Dominican Republic in the following year was enunciated in his 1904 message to Congress: "Chronic wrongdoing, or an impotence which results in a general loosening of the ties of civilized society, may in America, as elsewhere, ultimately require intervention by some civilized nation, and in the Western Hemisphere the adherence of the United States to the Monroe Doctrine may force the United States, however reluctantly, in flagrant cases of such wrongdoing or impotence, to the exercise of an international police power."[297] Roosevelt's successors in the presidency made use of his corollary to justify interventionary policies—Taft in Nicaragua and Wilson in Haiti. In the latter case, the notion of preventive intervention was taken a step further by the application of the Monroe Doctrine to European financial control over an American state, which could be said to "impair its independence."[298]

The interpretations of the Monroe Doctrine and the corollaries attached to it expanded with the growth of American power. A

[294] Graber, p. 50.   [295] Perkins, *Hands Off*, p. 90.

[296] Quoted in *ibid.*, p. 114.

[297] Cited in Gantenbein, p. 362. This American assumption of responsibility was encouraged by the European powers rather than being suspected by them. See Perkins, *Hands Off*, pp. 232–234.

[298] *Ibid.*, pp. 265–266.

tentative warning to European powers not to intervene in the American Hemisphere, in time, became a license for the United States to interfere in the affairs of other American states. This growth was reflected in an American attitude to European intervention which moved from warning to the threat of coercion and thence to prevention.

B. CRITICISM AND DEFENSE

The nonintervention principle and the Monroe Doctrine could be used together and served the same purpose as diplomatic weapons of criticism or protest against European interference in the American hemisphere. Before Monroe had read his message to Congress in 1823, Jefferson advised him to "protest against the atrocious violations of the rights of nations by the interference of any one in the internal affairs of another so flagitiously begun by Bonaparte, and now continued by the equally lawless Alliance calling itself Holy."[299]

The defense of her own actions was more complicated for the United States because the nonintervention principle and the Monroe Doctrine, as separate imperatives, frequently counseled divergent courses of action. The two remained consistent so long as the United States had no alternative but to refrain from intervention. They could be made to appear consistent so long as the United States was counterintervening and not initiating intervention, and thereby upholding the nonintervention principle as well as the Monroe Doctrine.[300] But when the Monroe Doctrine was interpreted in such a way as to justify American initiation of intervention, it was no longer consistent with the principle of nonintervention.

When the United States followed a policy of nonintervention, it was a simple enough matter to explain such a policy choice by reference to the principle of nonintervention. The purpose of in-

[299] Quoted in Graber, *Crisis Diplomacy*, p. 56. The nonintervention principle was not exclusively American property, and she was criticized by Austria in terms of the rule in 1849 over the intention to recognize the Hungarian insurgents. The Monroe Doctrine also was the subject of diplomatic debate—both Clarendon in 1853 and Salisbury in 1895, we have seen, questioned its legitimacy as a principle of international law.

[300] There was no attempt, however, to spell out this consistency or to represent the intervention of the United States as undertaken to uphold the rule of nonintervention. The Monroe Doctrine or the right of self-defense fulfilled the function of justification.

voking the rule was not only to explain policy to both the international and the domestic audience but also to justify the policy by attaching it to a tradition of foreign policy. Frequently the nonintervention principle provided the United States with an excuse for inaction in circumstances which seemed to warrant some sort of American response. Thus the rule of nonintervention could be used to fend off Latin American requests for the alliance of the United States or for her interference on their behalf against European powers.[301] The rule was also used to exempt the United States from invitations to join the European powers in debt-collecting expeditions in Latin America.[302] During the Civil War, the necessarily feeble reaction of the United States to French intervention in Mexico, was presented as the proper policy required by the nonintervention principle.[303]

On the other hand, when the United States practiced intervention and legitimized it in terms of the Monroe Doctrine, the principle of nonintervention was still referred to as a rule to be taken into account in the measurement of policy. In presenting his plan for intervention in Mexico to Congress in 1859, Buchanan admitted its inconsistency with the nonintervention principle but asked whether the present case did not constitute an exception.[304] Again, when President Roosevelt "took" the Canal Zone in 1903, he argued that departure from the generally observed principle of nonintervention was "justified and even required in the present instance."[305] In both these cases there was an admission of intervention and a plea of extenuating circumstances. President Wilson's use of the principle was different; seeing himself as a noninterventionist, he seemed not to regard his activity in Mexico up until 1917 as interventionary, and he invoked the rule of nonintervention in 1917 as a reason why the United States could not intervene in Mexico by force of arms.[306] By narrowing the definition of intervention, Wilson saved himself the embarrassment of violating the principle of nonintervention.

[301] In 1859 Secretary of State Cass went so far as to invoke the principle of nonintervention to excuse the failure of the United States to render good offices in a dispute between Venezuela and France. Moore, *Digest*, Vol. VI, p. 17.

[302] As in the case of Mexico in 1860. See Graber, p. 106.

[303] *Ibid.*, p. 98.   [304] *Ibid.*, p. 122.

[305] Quoted in *ibid.*, p. 138. Here Roosevelt was referring to the premature recognition of Panama.

[306] *Ibid.*, pp. 171–172.

In the critical armory of the United States, both the principle of nonintervention and the Monroe Doctrine were available as weapons with which to beat the European powers. In defense their roles were not as simple. It is possible to distinguish one phase of American foreign policy during which the nonintervention principle served as an excuse for ignoring the Monroe Doctrine. In the imperialist phase, on the other hand, the Monroe Doctrine and its corollaries were used to justify the overriding of the nonintervention principle.

C. THE DOMESTIC DIMENSION OF FOREIGN POLICY

As well as its function in international relations, the nonintervention doctrine played a fundamental part in the domestic justification of foreign policy. Washington had asserted the wisdom of neutrality toward European wars and nonentanglement in European affairs against a public opinion which enthusiastically favored the French in the wars of the Revolution. In subsequent years, when American statesmen perceived it to be in the interest of the United States to refrain from intervention, they could look back to Washington for doctrinal support. In his Fourth of July oration of 1821, John Quincy Adams pitched his argument against intervention unmistakably in the language of the Farewell Address. In this speech, by his influence on the Monroe Doctrine, and in his view of the proper relations of the United States with Latin America, Adams solidified the tradition of nonentanglement and addressed it directly to interference in the domestic affairs of other states. As usage established the rule and tradition supported its continuation as the fixed, wise, and settled policy of the United States, it was available to various administrations to justify failure to translate popular sympathy for foreign causes into a policy of intervention. Thus President Fillmore's invocation of the doctrine against the enthusiasm inspired by Kossuth's visit to the United States in 1851. Throughout his two terms of office, President Grant, encouraged by Secretary of State Fish, used the doctrine of nonintervention to stave off domestic pressure for intervention in and annexation of Cuba.[307]

The doctrine of nonintervention was also available to critics of the conduct of foreign policy. When John Quincy Adams, as President, decided to send delegates to the Panama Congress of

[307] See, e.g., 1869 message to Congress, cited in Gantenbein, pp. 441–442.

American Republics in 1826, his decision was fiercely criticized in Congress in terms of nonentanglement and isolation.[308] In 1898, when the United States acquired Hawaii and the Philippines, the administration was accused not merely of ignoring the traditions of American foreign policy but of violating the reciprocal principle of nonintervention contained in the Monroe Doctrine. Now, it was argued, every European power had a right to acquire dominion in the American hemisphere.[309] When the Roosevelt Corollary was attached to the Monroe Doctrine, a critic asked whether the Latin American states would not prefer to do their own business in their own way without intervention or intermediary.[310] The doctrine of nonintervention was a constraint on administrations which would depart from it, and a justification for administrations which would not.

As in the case of the "British" doctrine of nonintervention, it might be more accurate to refer to American doctrines of nonintervention than to one doctrine held, if not held to, from the outset. Though it could be represented as such by interested parties, the doctrine was not an ex cathedra teaching of the Founding Fathers which the United States could ignore only to her cost for as long as she had a foreign policy. Nor is it wholly true to say that these teachings and the doctrine of nonintervention as part of them persisted as the ideal while intervention became increasingly the reality with the growth of international relations and the corruption of the United States by international politics; for, as frequently, nonintervention was the imposed reality and intervention the dream. In fact, as shown by its development in relations with Latin America, the doctrine of nonintervention meant abstention from any intervention in 1827; it allowed a response to the intervention of outside powers in 1895, intervention against the threat of European interference in 1904, and support of every kind for republican principles in 1913. By 1936 it was taken to mean noninterference as well as nonintervention.

Though the interpretation of the doctrine of nonintervention changed with the growth of American power and the consequent expansion of her interests, it is a facile view which asserts that the United States refrained from intervention when it was her interest

<hr>

[308] Perkins, *Hands Off*, pp. 71–72.
[309] *Ibid.*, pp. 193–199.   [310] *Ibid.*, pp. 242–243.

to do so and supported such a policy by reference to the principle of nonintervention, but that when interest demanded intervention excuses were found for contravention of the principle. For the doctrine of nonintervention was not just invoked or disregarded as interest determined, it formed part of the calculation of interest. Common to all the interpretations of the doctrine in relations with Latin America was the estimation that the rights of the states of the area to independence had to be taken into account, even if that right was to be overridden by a prior imperative. In policy toward the European states, the doctrine of nonintervention did not merely justify abstention from interference in their internal affairs, but, particularly in the hands of John Quincy Adams, it provided an account of what the American interest was in that area of foreign relations. In this respect, the ideas of the Founding Fathers were important in providing one persuasive account of what American interests were and in being available to support the argument of nonintervention as it was deployed for or against the policy of any administration. And though none of these constraints prevented Roosevelt from taking the Canal Zone, it is not possible to infer from that action alone that the principle of nonintervention played no part in restraining American behavior in foreign relations.

From this brief survey of French foreign policy after the Revolution, of the foreign policy of Britain after the Vienna settlement, and of American foreign relations from their beginnings to the Second World War, it is possible to draw three conclusions about the place of the principle of nonintervention in international relations. In the first place, if by analogy from the domestic model of law it is of the essence of rules of law that they should be obeyed when it is against the interests of those to whom they apply to obey them, that the rules should be applied impartially, and that a sanction should be almost automatically available against the rule-breaker, then the principle of nonintervention and the international law of which it was a part failed to capture that essence. The rule of nonintervention did not persuade Palmerston to act against the perceived interests of Britain in Spain and Portugal however much it might have convinced him of the need to do the thing in a decent manner. President Cleveland, when he warned the British against aggression in Venezuela, made it clear that a response would be forthcoming after "*we* have determined" the right of the matter. And the want of impartiality made the notion of sanction or the upholding of the law, a doubtful one. Canning's intervention in Portugal, unimpeachable according to his doctrine of nonintervention, was not, in the minds of the statesmen of the eastern powers, an impartial vindication of Portuguese independence.

A second and less pessimistic conclusion is that while the principle of nonintervention might not have fulfilled the requirements for a rule of law on the domestic model, there is no call to dismiss it as a mere slogan. Though the French use of it at a time of extreme weakness might be said to have been desperate and ineffective opportunism, the doctrines of nonintervention elaborated by Castlereagh and Canning, by John Quincy Adams and by Franklin D. Roosevelt were not mere polished justifications of their countries' interests, but a study in and a statement of those interests—accounts of the rule as they would have it observed in international relations. The felt need on the part of statesmen to state positions and establish principles of international conduct renders the account of international relations somewhat less dismal than the Hobbesian war of all against all. This leads on to a third conclusion about the function of the principle of nonintervention in international relations as a rule in terms of which to persuade and coerce and to criticize and defend both internationally and domestically. It was not just a principle to be pulled out, as occasion demanded, from a bagful of principles made available to statesmen by international lawyers; doctrines of nonintervention were a means by which states could communicate to each other their views about what was tolerable and what was not in international relations and the circumstances in which they would feel obliged to intervene. Though the variation in doctrine from state to state and within one state over time made the function of the principle as a legal restraint problematical, it was not thereby deprived of its function in the language of diplomacy.

PART THREE

The Principle of Nonintervention in Contemporary World Politics

FIVE

SOVIET DOCTRINE AND PRACTICE

It is to the ideas of the French Revolution that a Soviet international lawyer has recently looked for the origin of the principle of noninterference, tracing its course thereafter through the recognition and subsequent abuse of the principle by the European and American "bourgeois" states in the nineteenth and twentieth centuries, to the Soviet initiative on behalf of the inadmissibility of intervention in the General Assembly of the United Nations in 1965.[1] This chapter will trace the course of the nonintervention principle in Soviet doctrine and practice, from its uneasy position in a revolutionary perspective on international relations, through the response to the milieu in which the Soviet state had to operate, to its consecration as a shibboleth of Soviet foreign policy.

I

In its urging of "a just and democratic peace . . . without annexations . . . and without indemnities," the Decree on Peace passed by the Second All-Russian Congress of Soviets on November 8, 1917, echoed the plea for national liberty entered by the French National Assembly in May 1790.[2] The French doctrine of national sovereignty, the view that the will of the people should determine the destiny of the nation, found its Russian expression in the assertion that any nation had the right to choose freely "the constitutional forms of its national existence."[3] The proclamation of a right to national self-determination, if no longer novel in 1917, was nonetheless revolutionary.

Thus far, the Russian Revolution had a significance across state frontiers; it might redraw them, including her own, according to the principle of self-determination, but would not do away with

[1] D. Levin, "The Non-Interference Principle Today," *International Affairs* (Moscow), November 1966, pp. 21–25.

[2] For the Decree on Peace, see Jane Degras, ed., *Soviet Documents on Foreign Policy*, 3 vols., London, 1951, 1952, 1953, Vol. I, *1917–1924*, pp. 1–3. On the French decree, see above, Chapter Four, pp. 65–66.

[3] Degras, Vol. I, p. 1.

them. But the Revolution went further; its constituency was made up of workers not bourgeois, its guiding principle one of class not of nation. In 1913 Lenin had related the attitude to be assumed toward the question of self-determination to the theory about the two stages of revolution. As the Revolution moved from the first stage of national struggle against national oppression to the second stage of the breaking down of national barriers and the international unity of capital, so the Marxist position was to shift from upholding the principle of self-determination to upholding the principle of internationalism.[4] In the same year Stalin had declared the aim of socialist policy to be the breaking down of national barriers and the uniting of peoples "in such a manner as to open the way for division of a different kind, division according to classes."[5] At the Third All-Russian Congress of Soviets in January 1918, Stalin affirmed that "the principle of self-determination must be an instrument in the struggle for socialism and must be subordinated to the principles of socialism."[6] In the light of these statements, Lenin's famous injunction to turn the imperialist war into a civil war could be said to be a misnomer, for a civil war presupposes a national environment for its fighting. What appeared to be advocated was a transnational conflict between classes as opposed to the international war between states.

Though the appeal to the "class-conscious workers" of Britain, France, and Germany, contained in the Decree on Peace, was a hint at rather than a strident call for social revolution, the two imperatives of peace and of revolution were inextricably mixed up in bolshevik thought.[7] The decree asked for help in bringing "to a successful end the cause of peace, and, together with this, the cause of the liberation of all who labour and are exploited from every kind of slavery and exploitation."[8] On December 19, 1917, Trotsky was more explicit. The People's Commissariat for Foreign Affairs issued an appeal to the toiling, oppressed, and exhausted peoples of Europe condemning the war and its authors and urging the workers and soldiers to "wrest the business of war and peace from the criminal hands of the bourgeoisie and take it into their own hands."[9] The banner under which this was to be done was that of peace and the social revolution.

[4] See E. H. Carr, *The Bolshevik Revolution 1917–1923*, 3 vols., Harmondsworth, 1966, Vol. 1, p. 431.

[5] Quoted in *ibid.*, p. 432.   [6] Quoted in *ibid.*, p. 272.

[7] See Carr, Vol. 3, pp. 18–19.   [8] Degras, Vol. I, p. 3.

[9] Text in *ibid.*, pp. 18–21.

Thus the principles of peace and self-determination which conformed with the inheritance of the French Revolution were bound up with but overridden by the principle of proletarian revolution which did not. The world revolution, upon which the survival of the one in Russia was thought to depend, would not only dispatch the *ancien régime*, it would also rewrite the language of world order. If men were to be citizens of the world, if their allegiance was to be to class and not to nation, then little sense could be made of the notion of foreign policy or indeed of international relations. Hence Trotsky's appreciation of his role as people's commissar for foreign affairs, "I will issue a few revolutionary proclamations to the peoples of the world and then shut up shop."[10] The principle of nonintervention might find a place in French revolutionary thought as the desirable norm in a world of national, popularly sovereign states; in Russian revolutionary doctrine which had substituted class for nation it appeared to find no place at all.

II

Such heady doctrine notwithstanding, from the outset the Bolsheviks were prepared to mix politics with ideology. The Decree on Peace was an act as much inspired by the shop which Trotsky wanted to shut as by postrevolutionary fervor. It took account of radical opinion, particularly in the United States, and addressed itself to it.[11] It struck no chord among the governments of the allied states, however, and the promise of peace to the Russian soldiers and peasants had to be honored.[12] On November 21, 1917, the Council of People's Commissars directed General Dukhonin, the commander-in-chief, to propose an immediate armistice and the opening of peace negotiations with the hostile armies.[13] On the same day, Trotsky addressed a note to the allied ambassadors in Petrograd extending the armistice proposal to all belligerent nations and their governments.[14] This was a foreign policy, albeit one of weakness; Russia was behaving as a state in a world of states.

When Trotsky arrived in Petrograd on January 20, 1918, from the adjourned peace negotiations with the central powers at Brest-

[10] Quoted in Carr, Vol. 3, p. 28.   [11] *Ibid.*, pp. 22–23.

[12] Louis Fischer, *The Soviets in World Affairs*, 2 vols., London, 1930, Vol. I, pp. 16–18.

[13] Text in Degras, Vol. I, pp. 3–4.   [14] Text in *ibid.*, p. 4.

Litovsk, the issues of war or peace, revolution or accommodation, were raised in stark relief. The hardening of the German line at Brest and the failure of the revolution to take root in Germany or elsewhere presented the Bolsheviks with three possible courses of action. In Lenin's summation, the first was to sign a separate, annexationist peace, the second was to wage a revolutionary war, and the third was to declare the war ended and demobilize the army but not to sign the peace.[15] Lenin opted for the first course in his theses on a separate and annexationist peace of January 20, 1918.[16] In them, he argued the need for time to consolidate the success of the Revolution in Russia "during which the hands of the Socialist Government must be absolutely free for the job of vanquishing the bourgeoisie in our own country first." In the crucial thesis, Lenin justified this position:

> The situation of the Socialist revolution in Russia must form the basis of any definition of the international tasks of our Soviet state, for the international situation in the fourth year of the war is such that it is quite impossible to calculate the probable moment of outbreak of revolution or overthrow of any of the European imperialist governments (including the German). That the Socialist revolution in Europe must come, and will come, is beyond doubt. . . . But it would be a mistake to base the tactics of the Russian Socialist Government on an attempt to determine whether the European, and especially the German, Socialist revolution will take place in the next six months (or some such brief period), or not.

Lenin's case for a separate and annexationist peace was to prevail but not before Trotsky's formula of "no war, no peace" had been tried at Brest and had failed with the German advance, and not before Lenin had fought for the acceptance of the German terms in the Central Executive Committee and for their ratification at the Seventh Party Congress.[17] The need for a breathing space legitimized the acceptance of the Brest peace of March 3, 1918.

The breathing space did not last long. Allied intervention in the

[15] Quoted in Fischer, Vol. I, pp. 48–49.

[16] Text in Degras, Vol. I, pp. 34–39, from which the quotations following are taken.

[17] For an account of the debates preceding acceptance, see Fischer, Vol. I, pp. 48–75. For extracts from the text of Lenin's speech to the Seventh Party Congress, see Degras, Vol. I, pp. 57–61.

Russian Civil War began in Murmansk in June, and continued in August in Siberia through Vladivostok and in the North through Archangel. The rationale asserted in defense of this intervention was its contribution to the prosecution of the war against Germany.[18] With the conclusion of the war against Germany, therefore, Soviet Russia might hope for a cessation of the allied intervention. On the other hand, the ending of the World War might intensify allied interest in the Civil War; Lenin is reported to have said to Chicherin at this time, "[n]ow *das Weltkapital* will start an offensive against us."[19] Whatever the forecast it was in the interests of the Soviets to take the initiative for an armistice, and on November 8, 1918 the Sixth Congress of Soviets proposed that negotiations for the conclusion of peace be opened.[20] On the day before Christmas, Litvinov renewed the plea for an end to intervention in a telegram to President Wilson. He asked how foreign countries, which had never dreamed of interfering with Tsarist barbarism and militarism, could feel justified in interfering in a Russia of working people "aiming at nothing but their own happiness and international brotherhood, constituting no menace to other nations."[21] Wilson's reply was to send an American diplomat to talk to Litvinov, talks which produced an assurance from Litvinov that the Russian revolutionary propaganda would end with the making of peace.[22] Wilson used the results of these talks to support Lloyd George's call for a Russian truce made at the Peace Conference of Paris in January 1919. An invitation to attend a conference at Prinkipo was extended to all groups exercising power in Russia. The Soviet government, accepting the invitation, took the opportunity to define its attitude.[23] It declared itself "so anxious to secure agreement on the cessation of hostilities" that it was prepared to make "weighty concessions" to the allies on the debt question, on interest on loans, and on the exploitation of natural resources in Russia. The Soviet government was also prepared, if necessary, "to include in the general agreement with the Allied

[18] Fischer, Vol. I, pp. 124–125.

[19] Quoted in *ibid.*, p. 150. For evidence of escalation in allied activity in Russia at this time, see W. H. Chamberlin, *The Russian Revolution 1917–1921*, 2 vols., London, 1935, Vol. II, pp. 152–154.

[20] Text of the resolution in Degras, Vol. I, p. 123.

[21] Text of the telegram in *ibid.*, pp. 129–132.

[22] Carr, Vol. 3, p. 118.

[23] Text of Chicherin's reply of February 4, 1919, in Degras, Vol. I, pp. 137–139, from which the quotations following are taken.

Powers an undertaking not to interfere in their internal affairs." This was a declared willingness to adhere to a rule of nonintervention at least as regards the dissemination of hostile propaganda; the offer was made as part of a package deal for peace.

The package was not at this time acceptable to the allies. But with the waning fortunes of the anti-Soviet armies in the Russian Civil War, a shift in the British attitude evoked a quick response from the Soviets.[24] On December 5, 1919 the Seventh Congress of Soviets listed the repeated overtures for peace made by the Soviet government and renewed the call for immediate negotiations.[25] In diplomatic correspondence, the "inviolable" principle of national self-determination was emphasized, together with respect for the independence and sovereignty of states.[26] The reciprocity implied by any rule of noninterference was perceived and stressed. "If our capitalist partners abstain from counter-revolutionary activities in Russia," said Radek, "the Soviet Government will abstain from carrying on revolutionary activities in capitalist countries."[27] In the negotiations for a trade treaty between the Soviet and British governments, Krasin combined earlier Soviet positions and made noninterference both conditional and reciprocal; conditional on an agreement resuming economic and commercial relations between the two countries, and reciprocal in that Soviet abstention from propaganda and interference in England's political life required a similar undertaking from England with regard to Russian affairs.[28]

The outbreak of war between Poland and Soviet Russia in April 1920 interrupted the *rapprochement* which had been developing between Russia and Britain in the early months of the year. At the conclusion of the war in October, the desirability of an agreement had increased for both sides. For the Soviets the persistent expectation of revolution in the west had been disappointed and the situation at home was desperate.[29] In Britain, the perception of Russia as a supplier had now been joined by another of her as a

[24] Carr, Vol. 3, pp. 156–157.

[25] Text of the resolution in Degras, Vol. I, pp. 176–177.

[26] See, e.g., the Declaration of the Council of People's Commissars to the Polish government and the Polish nation, January 28, 1920, in *ibid.*, pp. 179–180.

[27] Quoted in Carr, Vol. 3, p. 165.

[28] As reported in Narkomindel statement on Anglo-Russian negotiations, July 9, 1920. Text in Degras, Vol. I, pp. 191–194.

[29] Carr, Vol. 3, pp. 272–273. On the situation in Russia, see Chamberlin, Vol. II, pp. 430–449.

market.[30] The Anglo-Soviet Trade Agreement was signed in London on March 16, 1921. Its preamble contained a detailed prohibition of propaganda and other hostile action against each other's institutions. For England, these institutions included those of the British Empire and especially India and the independent state of Afghanistan. The Soviets acquired a particular commitment from Britain with regard to the independent countries which were formerly part of the Russian Empire.[31] This agreement on mutual nonintervention was the condition and symbol of the Soviet acceptance of a role as a state in a world of states, and of the acceptability of this role to at least one of the states of the old order.[32] Revolutionary doctrine could not comfortably accommodate a rule of nonintervention, but her years as a target for intervention had modified the Soviet position; doctrinal justification for acceptance of such a rule would follow.

III

By accepting her position as a state, Soviet Russia did not abandon her position as wellspring of the world revolution. As well as merely calling for revolution, the Council of People's Commissars appropriated two million rubles to be put at the disposal of the foreign representatives of the Commissariat for Foreign Affairs for the "needs of the revolutionary international movement."[33] Sections for international propaganda were set up in the Soviet government soon after the revolution.[34] Trotsky used the peace negotiations at Brest-Litovsk as a platform from which to speak revolution to the world.[35] Even after the signature of the Brest peace and Joffe's appointment as ambassador to Berlin, Soviet propaganda in Germany continued to flow. Indeed, acting in "perfect bad faith," Joffe made every attempt to bring about the downfall of the imperial government.[36]

[30] Carr, Vol. 3, p. 286.

[31] Preamble to the agreement quoted in *ibid.*, p. 288.

[32] Fischer calls the agreement "the Soviet acceptance of the *status quo* ... a pledge not to spread the revolution by armed force." *Soviets in World Affairs*, Vol. I, p. 296.

[33] For calls to revolution see, e.g., the Appeal of Sovnarkom to the Moslems of Russia and the East, December 3, 1917, in Degras, Vol. I, pp. 15–17. For the decree appropriating rubles, see *ibid.*, Vol. I, p. 22.

[34] Carr, Vol. 3, pp. 29–31.   [35] Fischer, Vol. I, pp. 42–46.

[36] *Ibid.*, pp. 75–76.

With the allied intervention in the Russian Civil War in the summer of 1918, explicit commitment to world revolution and propaganda on its behalf were the two serviceable instruments in a Soviet armory weak in the conventional weapons of war. Full use had to be made of them. On August 1, 1918, the Council of People's Commissars turned to the toiling masses of England, America, France, Italy, and Japan in the name of the solidarity of the workers of the world, and of the international revolution, against the bandits of international imperialism.[37] Propaganda at this time assumed its "crudest and most outspoken form."[38]

The revolutionary strand in Soviet foreign policy was formalized in March 1919 with the creation of the Communist International. Invitations to the First Congress were sent at the same time as Soviet noises for peace were being heard at Paris. The invitation included a Soviet opinion of the aims and tactics of the International, enjoining the proletariat to seize political power immediately by mass action "right up to open armed conflict with the political power of capital."[39] The Comintern platform adopted by the First Congress referred to an International "which subordinates so-called national interests to the interests of the international revolution."[40] In the first months of its existence, the Comintern failed to honor its revolutionary promise. The Soviets, in their almost total isolation, made little effort to direct the activities of Communists in other countries, and saw events in them according to the revolutionary climate in Russia. Thus both Trotsky and Zinoviev prophesied the imminence of a Soviet Europe.[41] Such misplaced optimism apart, the significance of the establishment of the Comintern was its establishment; it remained a monument to the revolutionary aspirations of its designers.[42]

The Comintern in 1920 was a more effective organization than it had been in 1919. Its prestige was greater and the summer of the year brought with it the highest hopes for world revolution.[43]

[37] Text of the Appeal in Degras, Vol. I, pp. 88–92.

[38] Carr, Vol. 3, p. 99.

[39] Text of the invitation of January 24, 1919, in Degras, ed., *The Communist International 1919–1943, Documents* (hereafter *Comintern Documents*), 3 vols., London, 1956, 1960, 1965, Vol. I, *1919–1922*, pp. 1–3.

[40] Text of the platform of March 4, 1919, in *ibid.*, pp. 17–24.

[41] F. Borkenau, *The Communist International*, London, 1938, p. 165.

[42] See Carr, Vol. 3, pp. 130 and 152.

[43] On the reasons for the changes see *ibid.*, pp. 170–181. But as Borkenau points out: ". . . the biggest effect which the Russian revolution ever had

The Second Comintern Congress assembled in Moscow at the same time as the dramatic advance of the Red Army into Poland. It was in the context of the enthusiasm generated by this state of affairs that Zinoviev called for the Comintern to become, not a mere propaganda association as it had been at its foundation, "but a fighting organ of the international proletariat."[44] Another delegate demanded that the Comintern grow from a series of national parties to "a single Communist Party having branches in different countries."[45] On July 24, 1920 the Congress approved twenty-one conditions of admission to the Communist International which required, among other things, that each party conduct propaganda in favor of the proletarian revolution, that underground organization be prepared for the coming civil war, that reformists be broken with, that iron military discipline be established in the party ranks, and that all decisions of Comintern be accepted as binding.[46] This program for revolution was the fullest statement of the communist onslaught on the old order.

The July theses were a triumph for the principles of international socialism and of tightly centralized control over the inferior principle of national self-determination. The latter principle had already been compromised by Soviet activity in the Baltic states, in the Ukraine, and elsewhere.[47] In October 1920 Stalin rejected the demand of the border regions for secession from Russia "because it contradicts the essential interests of the popular masses," interests which would render secession "at this stage of the revolution profoundly counter-revolutionary,"[48] In policy toward the peoples of Asia, on the other hand, the Soviets could espouse the principle of national self-determination as a sound weapon against the imperialists, and justify it by placing colonial emancipation in the stage of bourgeois revolution.[49] Support for national freedom against the oppression of the imperialists was the general line pursued in Soviet relations with Asia from the December 1917 Appeal

---

upon Europe was achieved before there was a Communist International." *Communist International*, p. 93.

[44] Quoted in Carr, Vol. 3, p. 194.   [45] Quoted in *ibid*.

[46] Text of the conditions in Degras, *Comintern Documents*, Vol. I, pp. 168–172.

[47] Carr, Vol. 1, pp. 277–278.

[48] Quoted in Elliot R. Goodman, *The Soviet Design for a World State*, London, 1960, p. 229.

[49] Carr, Vol. 3, pp. 234–235.

to the Moslems of Russia and the East onward.[50] It occasionally shaded into a proletarian rather than a national revolutionary appeal, but at the Second Comintern Congress, Lenin reaffirmed the need for "the closest union between Soviet Russia and all the national and colonial liberation movements."[51] At the Baku Congress of the Peoples of the East in September 1920, Zinoviev evoked a tumultuous reaction when he summoned his audience to a holy war against British imperialism, but it was a call against oppression rather than for the proletarian revolution.[52]

While the distinction between support for proletarian revolution in Europe and support for bourgeois national revolution in Asia was significant in Soviet doctrine and practice, support for either was unwelcome to the old order. The slogan of national self-determination might strike a Wilsonian chord in the United States and among liberal opinion in Europe, but the self-consciously revolutionary pronouncements of the Soviet regime and of the Comintern seemed inimical to established principles of international conduct like that of nonintervention.

IV

A dual foreign policy, then, was partly imposed on and partly fashioned by the Soviets, so long as the world revolution failed to materialize. The need to provide for the security of the Soviet state in a hostile world and the need to champion the revolution which was the legitimation of the new regime, caused the Soviets to attempt to come to terms with the capitalist governments at the same time as trying to undermine them.[53]

But in Soviet doctrine, the serving of one master did not exclude the simultaneous serving of the other. The goal of international socialism required support for the revolution and for the interests of the Russian state, indeed the two were regarded as mutually

[50] Text of the Appeal in Degras, *Soviet Documents*, Vol. I, pp. 14–16.

[51] Text of the Theses on National and Colonial Question adopted by the Congress in Degras, *Comintern Documents*, Vol. I, pp. 138–144. For shading into proletarian appeal see Appeal from Chicherin to the workers and peasants of Persia, August 30, 1919, in Degras, *Soviet Documents*, Vol. I, pp. 161–164.

[52] Extracts from Zinoviev's speech cited in X. J. Eudin and R. C. North, *Soviet Russia and the East 1920–1927*, Stanford, 1957, pp. 165–167.

[53] Carr, Vol. 3, pp. 32–33.

dependent. A party manifesto written to explain acceptance of the German terms at Brest stated: "By upholding Soviet power we render the best and most powerful support to the proletariat of all countries in its unprecedentedly difficult and onerous struggle against its own bourgeoisie. There could be no greater blow now to the cause of socialism than the collapse of Soviet power in Russia."[54]

The twin imperatives of Soviet foreign policy, arguably, were compatible and interdependent; they were not indistinguishable. The various situations in which the Soviet state found itself led to differences in emphasis. When the Brest Peace with Germany was signed, the demand for national security was uppermost; during allied intervention in the Civil War and again while the Polish War lasted, the call to revolution was stressed. With the New Economic Policy and the signature of the trade agreement with Britain, national security was emphasized once more.[55]

It is possible to establish this dualism as a theme of Soviet foreign policy between the two wars containing a revolutionary motif which led to interference with the affairs of other states and a motif of accommodation which proclaimed noninterference at the formal diplomatic level. The Revolution legitimized action on its behalf through the Communist Parties, the activities of the Comintern being considered immune from the constraint of the principle of nonintervention.[56] The security of the state legitimized acceptance of the rule as a passport to the establishment of relations between governments and as a shield against intervention in Russia.

The role of the Comintern as the carrier of the international revolution was cemented at its Second Congress with the laying down of the ideological principles which were to govern communist policy. Objections to the "strict international centralization

[54] Quoted in *ibid.*, p. 67.

[55] Borkenau puts the duality in this way: "There is hardly a leading man in world affairs who did not regard the communists alternately as hopeless and insignificant Utopians and as dangerous, unscrupulous, and hard-boiled realists. In reality they are both at the same time." *Communist International*, p. 180.

[56] This freedom was asserted, not only because of the superior claims of the revolution in the legitimation of action, but also because the Comintern was held to be a nongovernmental international organization and thus not liable to those obligations which applied only to subjects of international law. Adam B. Ulam, *Expansion and Coexistence*, London, 1968, p. 130.

of the communist movement" established at the Second Congress were rejected by the Third Congress.[57] Each Congress thereafter, except the Seventh and last in 1935, specifically reaffirmed the need for central direction of and iron discipline in the Comintern. The Fourth Congress in November 1922 called upon the Executive Committee of Comintern to become an international proletarian organization "built on the principle of the strictest democratic centralism."[58] The Fifth Congress in June 1924 instructed "the Executive to demand more emphatically than before iron discipline from all sections and all party leaders."[59] The program of the Comintern adopted at the Sixth Congress in September 1928 required, among many other things, that: "international communist discipline must be expressed in the subordination of local and particular interests to the common and enduring interests of the movement, and in the execution without reservation of all decisions made by the leading bodies of the Communist International."[60] The relationship of the Comintern to its member parties as one of superior to inferior was defined by the Comintern Presidium in 1929 during a dispute with the Czechoslovak Communist Party. Relations between the Comintern and its sections, it declared, "are not relations between two partners who are negotiating with each other but are based on the principle of international proletarian discipline."[61]

This relationship was a formal one, it was contained in the statutes of the Comintern adopted at its Fifth Congress. Decisions of the Executive Committee of Comintern (ECCI) were binding on all sections, and the Executive Committee had the right to expel from the Comintern parties, groups, or individual members "who acted contrary to the programme, the statutes, the decisions of the world congress, or the ECCI"; it also had the right to send delegates to individual sections to supervise the execution of the Comintern line.[62] In the light of these provisions, it seems pedantic

[57] In the Resolution of the Congress on the Report of the Executive Committee, extracts in Degras, *Comintern Documents*, Vol. I, pp. 227–229.

[58] In the Resolution of the Congress on the Report of ECCI, in *ibid.*, Vol. I, pp. 378–379.

[59] In the Resolution of the Congress on the Report of the ECCI, in *ibid.*, Vol. II, *1923–1928*, p. 106.

[60] In the Program of the Comintern, cited in *ibid.*, Vol. II, p. 525.

[61] Quoted in Kermit E. McKenzie, *Comintern and World Revolution 1928–1943*, London, 1964, p. 33.

[62] In Statutes of Comintern, July 1924, Degras, *Comintern Documents*, Vol. II, pp. 119–120.

to speak of Comintern interference in the affairs of national Communist Parties and more accurate to describe such Comintern activity as the normal operation of a political party within its legitimate domain.[63] But in those national parties, the notion of outside interference seemed to survive and force Comintern leaders to deal with it. Bukharin said that nine-tenths of the significance of the Fourth Congress of Comintern consisted in this, that it "interfered" in the affairs of the national sections.[64] At the same Congress, Zinoviev wrote: "It is obvious that the Executive must 'interfere' in the affairs of practically every party. . . . It took an active part in the preparations for every congress and conference of its principal parties. . . . Representatives of the Executive attended practically every important congress and gave them ideological direction."[65] At the Seventh Comintern Congress, Pieck, a German Communist who was a high official in the Comintern, went as far as to concede that the ECCI would "refrain from intervening in the internal organizational affairs of the sections," but, he added, "[t]he Executive will, of course, continue to intervene if the work of our sections betrays serious defects."[66] National parties as well as the states in which they were formed seemed, on this evidence, to have found the activities of the Comintern interventionary.

As to the motif of accommodation in Soviet foreign policy between the wars, the principle of nonintervention became a slogan adorning statements on international relations.[67] But espousal of the principle also had more concrete functions. It had been one of the keys to the agreement with Britain in 1921 which had ended the isolation of the Soviets. An equally elaborate prohibition of intervention formed the fifth article of the Franco-Soviet Nonag-

[63] The crucial question here is the definition of "legitimate," or rather, the identification of the set of standards to which the legitimation referred. The Comintern standards were those of "international proletarian discipline." The states in which the communist parties were located, however, might not adopt a similar code. These states could regard Comintern direction of national parties as an interference in what were conventionally regarded as internal affairs—the domestic political process.

[64] Quoted in Degras, *Comintern Documents*, Vol. I, p. 375.

[65] Quoted in *ibid.*, p. 436.

[66] Quoted in *ibid.*, Vol. III, *1929–1943*, p. 353.

[67] See, e.g., Litvinov's speech at the League Assembly on the entry of the USSR into the League of Nations, September 18, 1934, cited in Degras, *Soviet Documents*, Vol. III, *1933–1941*, pp. 92–93; and Stalin's interview with Roy Howard, March 5, 1936, in *ibid.*, pp. 164–169.

gression Pact signed in November 1932, which, with the other nonaggression pacts signed by the Soviet Union in the same year, registered her urgent need for peace.[68] In treaties between the Soviet Union and the states on her frontiers, inclusion of a rule of nonintervention had another function—it was to provide a legal barrier against their being used as bases for intervention in the Soviet Union.[69]

The rule was also used as justification for foreign policies which seemed ideologically unpalatable. In September 1933 Litvinov defended the attempt to maintain good relations with Hitler by saying: "We do not interfere in the internal affairs of Germany, as we do not interfere in that (sic) of other countries, and our relations with her are conditioned not by her internal but by her external policy."[70] Molotov's defense of the Soviet-German Non-aggression Pact in 1939 was similar:

> . . . people ask, with an air of innocence, how could the Soviet Union consent to improve its political relations with a State of a fascist type? Is that possible, they ask. But they forget that it is not a question of our attitude towards the internal regime of another country but of foreign relations between two States. They forget that our position is that we do not interfere in the internal affairs of other countries and correspondingly do not tolerate interference in our own internal affairs.[71]

[68] Article 5 of the treaty is cited in Max Beloff, *The Foreign Policy of Soviet Russia 1929–1941*, 2 vols., London, 1947, 1949, Vol. I, *1929–1936*, pp. 23–24.

[69] *Ibid.*, Vol. I, p. 12. See, e.g., the Nonaggression Treaty between USSR and Afghanistan, August 31, 1926, paragraph III of which reads in part: "The high contracting parties, mutually recognizing their State sovereignty, undertake to refrain from any armed or unarmed intervention in the internal affairs of the other contracting party and they will refrain completely from assisting or participating in any intervention by a third or several third Powers which might take steps against the other contracting party. The contracting parties will not permit and will prevent on their territory the organization and activity of individuals prejudicial to the other contracting party, or which are aimed at the overthrow of the political regime of the other contracting party, or which make attempts on its territorial integrity, or which assemble and recruit forces against the other contracting party." Text in Degras, *Soviet Documents*, Vol. II, *1925–1932*, pp. 130–133.

[70] Quoted in Beloff, Vol. I, p. 98.

[71] In a speech by Molotov to the Fourth (Special) Session of the Supreme Soviet on the Negotiations with Britain and France and the Nonaggression Pact with Germany, August 31, 1939, cited in Degras, *Soviet Documents*, Vol. III, p. 367.

At the same time, Stalin criticized "the non-aggressive countries," particularly England and France, for their misuse of the policy of nonintervention. By adopting such a policy and rejecting the policy of collective security, these countries had connived at aggression and given free reign to war. The ultimate rationale behind this policy, Stalin thought, was the desire of the noninterventionists to lure the other powers into an exhausting war and then to appear on the scene and "dictate conditions to the enfeebled belligerents."[72] Its adoption as a slogan of Soviet foreign policy clearly did not blind Stalin to the diverse functions of the principle of nonintervention.

The distinction made between a revolutionary strand in Soviet foreign policy which led to intervention through the Communist Parties, and a national security strand which led to nonintervention at the government level, is an oversimplification. In the first place, the activities of the Comintern on behalf of the revolution were not restricted to the Communist Parties. Borodin's activities in China from 1923 to 1927 were guiding a bourgeois revolution by a nationalist party, the Kuomintang.[73] There was doctrinal basis for this sort of support in the theory that the anti-imperialist revolution was to come first in Asia and in the united front strategy adopted by the Third Comintern Congress. In the second place, the distinction is misleading if it suggests that the Comintern remained the chaste carrier of revolution. As the Comintern grew older, it became increasingly the creature of the Russians, not only because of their financial dominance or their prevailing voice in the ECCI, but also because in Russia the revolution had happened and homage to the revolution could be paid only to Russia.[74] During the 1930's, when the Comintern became the instrument of Soviet foreign policy, the revolutionary strand appeared to lose any separate identity.[75]

If it is dangerous to identify the Comintern with intervention, it is the more so to identify the demands of national security with adherence to the rule of nonintervention. Soviet intervention in the Transcaucasian Republics in 1920 and 1921 was as much about

[72] In Stalin's Report to the Eighteenth Congress of the CPSU, in *ibid.*, Vol. III, pp. 318–319.

[73] For an account of Soviet intervention in China at this time, see Fischer, *Soviets in World Affairs*, Vol. II, pp. 632–679.

[74] See Borkenau, *Communist International*, p. 416.

[75] See *ibid.*, p. 419.

national security as about the encouragement of revolution.[76] Similarly, the establishment and consolidation of Soviet influence in Outer Mongolia from 1921 was not an intervention solely inspired by the Revolution.[77] But Soviet intervention in the Spanish Civil War arose from a choice among options more complicated than those presented by the filling out of frontiers. The Popular Front had won an electoral victory in Spain in February 1936; in July the Nationalists revolted against it. Ideological solidarity demanded support for the Spanish Left, particularly as it represented the fulfillment of the new Comintern strategy of the united front. The prestige of the Soviet Union as the leader of the world revolution was involved in the war in Spain.[78] At the same time, preservation of the good relations so recently established with Britain and particularly with France seemed to demand acceptance of the agreement on nonintervention in Spain which those powers were canvassing.[79] A third pressure was the perceived need to counteract German and Italian intervention in the Civil War on Franco's behalf by coming to the aid of the Republican government. Britain and France wanted to keep the peace in Europe by avoiding a confrontation between the powers. The Soviet Union sought the same end by her emphasis on collective security and the thwarting of the aggressive powers in Spain.[80] In effect, the Soviet Union attempted to respond to each of these pressures upon her. She signed the nonintervention agreement and maintained her seat on the Nonintervention Committee but continually pointed to the futility of asymmetrical adherence to it.[81] She intervened on behalf of the Republicans, protesting the action's conformity with international law at the same time as trying to hide

[76] See Carr, Vol. 1, 343–354.

[77] See Carr, Vol. 3, pp. 505–509 and 512–516.

[78] David T. Cattell, *Communism and the Spanish Civil War*, Berkeley, Calif., 1956, p. 71.

[79] Cattell, *Soviet Diplomacy and the Spanish Civil War*, Berkeley, Calif., 1957, p. 16.

[80] *Ibid.*, p. 37.

[81] See, e.g., Statement on the Soviet Attitude to Nonintervention: Note from the Soviet Ambassador in London to the Chairman of the Nonintervention Committee, October 23, 1936, in Degras, *Soviet Documents*, Vol. III, pp. 212–213, and Reply to the British Proposal on Volunteers for Spain: Note from Litvinov to the British Ambassador in Moscow, January 15, 1937, in *ibid.*, pp. 233–234.

its existence.[82] She intervened at all levels in the Spanish Civil War, but not to establish communist rule which would have prejudiced the other goals of Soviet foreign policy that the united front was carefully cultivating.[83] The questions of intervention and nonintervention were not asked and answered in terms of any simple dichotomy between world revolution and national security.

The principle of nonintervention was a popular phrase among the writers of Soviet diplomatic documents between the wars, and any discomfort to its espousal caused by the activities of the Comintern could be avoided by the claim that such matters were beyond the competence of the Soviet government. This convenient distinction apart, the difficulties of adhering to such a rule when other states ignored it or preferred their own definitions of it, difficulties illustrated during the Spanish Civil War, were instructive for international politics after the Second World War.

V

The establishment of communist regimes in the East European states during and after the Second World War and the victory of the revolution in China in 1949 transformed the problem of communist interrelations from one between parties to one between states. Yugoslavia and Albania apart, and with variations in degree from country to country, the Soviet Army played an important part in the establishment of communist regimes in Eastern Europe.[84] This was not the revolution of the proletariat and the establishment of their dictatorship any more than it was the preliminary bourgeois revolution. Tito's coinage, "People's Democ-

[82] Cattell, *Communism and the Spanish Civil War*, pp. 73 and 75. The legal opinion of the Soviet Union was that "the fulfillment by other States of the orders of a legitimate government which they have recognized, including orders for war materials, cannot be regarded as intervention, but that, on the contrary, the supplying of arms to rebels against a legitimate government and the arbitrary recognition of their leaders as a government must be regarded as flagrant intervention, inconsistent with international practice," in Reply to the Anglo-French proposal for mediation in the Spanish Civil War: Note from Litvinov to the British and French Ambassadors in Moscow, December 9, 1936, in Degras, *Soviet Documents*, Vol. III, pp. 227–228.

[83] Cattell, *Communism and the Spanish Civil War*, pp. 208–212.

[84] On the communist seizure of power in Eastern Europe see H. Seton-Watson, *The East European Revolution*, London, 1950, pp. 167–229.

racy," was the phrase used to describe the process of evolution toward communism in the new entities and they became "People's Democracies" in the communist lexicon.[85] In relations between the Soviet Union and the People's Democracies, Lenin's principle of national self-determination was not applicable because it belonged in the province of the bourgeois revolution. Neither was the higher principle of international socialism, not primarily because of the inferior status of the People's Democracies, but because of the strength of national feeling within them and of the need for the Soviet Union to feel her way carefully in the postwar international environment.[86] The definition adopted for relations between the Soviet Union and the People's Democracies was a compromise. Formally, they were to be based on mutual recognition of the principles of sovereignty, equality, and noninterference in domestic affairs. On the other hand, their designation as People's Democracies placed them at a less advanced stage in the building of communism than the Soviet Union, giving the latter an ideological entrée for the control of the former.[87]

It was not long before the Soviet Union made use of this entrée. The establishment of the Cominform in September 1947 was the Russian reply to that diversity in Eastern Europe which had arisen from the reluctance to establish total Soviet control. Its declared function was the exchange of information between the member parties; it had none of the Comintern's pretensions to being the bearer of revolution. Indeed, Zhdanov, one of the Soviet delegates to the inaugural meeting of the Cominform, referred to the positive side of the dissolution of the Comintern: "in that it once and for all put an end to the slanderous allegations by the enemies of Communism and of the working-class movement that Moscow was interfering in the internal affairs of other countries and that the

[85] F. Borkenau, *European Communism*, London, 1953, p. 484. Zbigniew K. Brzezinski, *The Soviet Bloc*, revised and enlarged ed., Cambridge, Mass., 1967, pp. 25–32. Brzezinski describes the Soviet conception of the People's Democracies as a hybrid between the forms of the old bourgeois state and the forms of the socialist state as created by the USSR, "a form of permanent revolution in which the transitional phase developed a distinct institutional identity," *ibid.*, pp. 31–32.

[86] For Stalin's 1920 view on drawing East Europe together in a confederation and for his appreciation of the tactical situation there after 1945, see David J. Dallin, *Soviet Foreign Policy after Stalin*, London, 1962, pp. 21–23.

[87] Brzezinski, pp. 367 and 108–109.

Communist parties of the various countries acted not in accordance with the interests of their peoples but on orders from abroad."[88] But, Zhdanov argued, the dissolution of the Comintern should not be taken to mean breaking off all connection between the Communist Parties, which would be "wrong, harmful and at bottom unnatural."[89] Zhdanov also stressed the need for the Communist Parties to take the lead in resisting imperialist plans for expansion and aggression in a world arena divided into two main camps.[90] Though the speech also contained expressions of Soviet deference to the principles of sovereignty and equality in international relations, the element of guidance to "brotherly" parties was clear.[91] A new set of rules for communist international relations was being established. The Soviet-Yugoslav dispute was to demonstrate that they existed and could be broken, its aftermath was to clarify what they were.

The roots of Soviet-Yugoslav conflict lay in Tito's fashioning of an independent revolution. In retrospect, the Yugoslavs could trace the increasing incidence of Russian misdeeds from the Soviet Union's reluctance to give aid to Yugoslavia during the war and failure to support the Yugoslav claim to Trieste just after it, through its attempts to subvert the party and the army in Yugoslavia, to its veto of the Yugoslav dream of a Balkan federation in January 1948.[92] The Soviet Union could trace an antithetic course in Yugoslav behavior from their parochial identification of Yugoslavia's own interests with those of international communism, through their obstinate refusal to provide information for the representatives of the Soviet Union, to their failure to make a low enough genuflection to the Russians at the foundation of the Com-

[88] Quoted in Gunther Nollau, *International Communism and World Revolution*, London, 1961, p. 219. This statement of Zhdanov's echoed that of Stalin's at the time of the dissolution of the Comintern: "It exposes the lie of the Hitlerites to the effect that 'Moscow' allegedly intends to intervene in the life of other nations and to 'Bolshevize' them." Quoted in Gabriel Kolko, *The Politics of War: The World and United States Foreign Policy, 1943–1945*, New York, 1968, p. 36.

[89] Quoted in Nollau, p. 218.

[90] Quoted in *ibid.*, pp. 218 and 221. The two-camps doctrine seemed to be a signal for the drawing together of the one camp against the aggressive tendencies of the other.

[91] Adam B. Ulam, *Titoism and the Cominform*, Cambridge, Mass., 1952, pp. 50–51.

[92] See *ibid.*, pp. 69–95.

inform.[93] Some of these issues were ventilated in the correspondence between the central committees of the Communist Parties of the Soviet Union and of Yugoslavia which took place in the first six months of 1948.[94] The real points at issue, however, were obscured in an ideological tirade from the Russians and in the injured innocence of the Yugoslav replies, replies which failed to meet the Soviet requirements and resulted in the expulsion of the Yugoslavs from the Cominform. There were some clues. The Soviet letter of May 4, 1948 went back to 1945 to find evidence of an anti-Soviet attitude on the part of the Yugoslavs and warned of the danger of underestimating "the experiences of the CPSU [Communist Party of the Soviet Union] in matters relating to the development of socialism in Yugoslavia."[95] It seemed that Yugoslavia's primary sin was insubordination.

The new rules governing the relations between the Soviet Union and the People's Democracies were emerging. The East European states were privy to the details of the Soviet-Yugoslav dispute, having received copies of the Soviet letters; and they were gathered together to legitimize the view that the Yugoslav party had "placed itself . . . outside the ranks of the Information Bureau."[96] By December the content of the relationship was spelled out in a phrase reminiscent of the Comintern: "The attitude toward the Soviet Union is now the test of devotion to the cause of proletarian internationalism."[97] The Soviet experience was to be the model for the People's Democracies and their progress was to be measured in terms of their conformity to the model.[98] The principle of sovereignty was still proclaimed, but in practice it was shown to be inferior to the principles allowing Soviet control of Eastern Europe.[99] Doctrines about the sovereignty of states and nonintervention in internal affairs now seemed more the preserve of the Yugoslavs.[100]

[93] *Ibid.*, pp. 53–54 and 117.

[94] See generally, *The Soviet-Yugoslav Dispute*, Royal Institute of International Affairs, London, 1948.

[95] *Ibid.*, pp. 36–37 and 42.   [96] *Ibid.*, p. 69.

[97] Quoted from the Cominform Journal of December 5, 1948, in Hamilton Fish Armstrong, *Tito and Goliath*, London, 1951, p. 90.

[98] Brzezinski, pp. 67–83.   [99] *Ibid.*, p. 82.

[100] In the first draft of the April 13, 1948 letter to the CPSU, Tito included a paragraph reminding Soviet citizens in Yugoslavia that they were in a "brotherly independent country and that they should not interfere in that country's internal life." Later, Tito was to criticize the Kremlin for

After the passing of Stalin, the relaxation of Soviet control over the People's Democracies was accompanied by a renewed emphasis on the governing principles of sovereignty and nonintervention in internal affairs. The abolition of the mixed companies, which had been the instrument of Soviet economic hegemony in Eastern Europe, was taken as evidence of that cooperation which "embodied the new type of international relations between the countries of the Socialist camp," and one of the factors lending "vital power" to these relations was the observance of the rule of noninterference.[101] Khrushchev heralded the *rapprochement* with Yugoslavia with a reaffirmation of the nonintervention principle, among others, as the basis of Soviet relations with other countries.[102] In July 1955 at a Plenum of the Central Committee of the CPSU, Mikoyan went as far as to admit that the Soviet Union under Stalin had interfered in Yugoslavia's internal affairs and went on to establish Soviet interference as a general criticism of Stalinist policy toward the People's Democracies.[103] New rules were again being formulated. The touch of Moscow was to be lighter in Eastern Europe and Soviet leadership was to be placed on a new basis of mutual cooperation.[104]

In his address to the Twentieth Party Congress, Khrushchev made this new basis for relations clearer, but still left undefined the outer limits of permissible conduct for the People's Democracies. He recognized that "[a]longside the Soviet form of reconstructing society on socialist lines, we now have the form of People's Democracy," a recognition that different forms of transition to socialism were possible and legitimate.[105] The effect in Eastern Europe of this acknowledgment of diversity, and of Khrushchev's "secret" speech on Stalin, was unsettling.[106] Even more so was the placing of the Soviet imprimatur on Titoism in

---

basely attacking the young revolution in Yugoslavia. "It was intervention in the true sense of the word, such as the October Revolution had had to endure." Vladimir Dedijer, *Tito Speaks*, London, 1953, pp. 347 and 391.

[101] *Pravda*, November 13, 1954, quoted in Dallin, *Soviet Foreign Policy after Stalin*, p. 196.

[102] In his speech at Belgrade Airport, May 26, 1955; text in R. Bass and E. Marbury, *The Soviet-Yugoslav Controversy, 1948–1958: A Documentary Record*, New York, 1959, pp. 51–54.

[103] Dallin, pp. 230–231.   [104] Brzezinski, pp. 181–182.

[105] N. S. Khrushchev, *Report of the Central Committee of the CPSU to the Twentieth Party Congress*, Moscow, 1956, p. 43.

[106] Brzezinski, pp. 198–206.

a Declaration on Soviet-Yugoslav relations in June 1956.[107] The Poznan riots which broke out in Poland towards the end of June signaled the dangers of rapid liquidation of Stalin's legacy and brought a change of emphasis from the Soviet leaders. A *Pravda* editorial of July 16, 1956 spoke of "the principle of international proletarian unity" as the guide for the Marxist parties of the working class.[108] In Warsaw, Bulganin criticized misguided attempts "to weaken the international ties of the Socialist camp under the banner of the so-called 'national peculiarities.' "[109]

These warnings came too late to prevent the unfolding of events in Poland and in Hungary. In Poland the slow process of cautious response to the demands for reform, which had been going on since the death of Stalin, was jolted by the Twentieth CPSU Congress and rendered untenable in the aftermath of the Poznan riots. Gomulka's resurrection and his subsequent election to the First Secretaryship of the Polish Party demonstrated the rout of the pro-Soviet wing of the Central Committee by the "national communist" wing. On October 19, heeding the warnings of the pro-Soviet faction, a Soviet delegation arrived in Warsaw to confer with the Polish Central Committee. The delegation left the following day without swaying the Poles from their new line, and apparently satisfied that the situation in Poland did not require Soviet armed intervention.[110] On the same day, Gomulka blamed the cult of personality for the inequality in relations between the Soviet Union and the People's Democracies, and looked forward to relations based on respect for rights of sovereignty which was "how it is beginning to be."[111] In Hungary, three days later, military intervention occurred. The course of Hungarian history since 1953 had witnessed a more explicit division between the old

[107] Text of the declaration of June 20, 1956, in P. E. Zinner, ed., *National Communism and Popular Revolt in Eastern Europe*, New York, 1956, pp. 12–15. The third paragraph of the declaration reads in part: ". . . the path of socialist development differs in various countries and conditions . . . the multiplicity of forms of socialist development tends to strengthen socialism . . . any tendency of imposing one's opinion on the ways and forms of socialist development is alien to both."

[108] Cited in *ibid.*, p. 27.

[109] Quoted in Dallin, pp. 339–340.

[110] On the situation in Poland and Soviet-Polish relations at this time, see Brzezinski, pp. 239–268.

[111] In his address to the Central Committee of the Polish United Workers Party, October 20, 1956, cited in Zinner, pp. 225–231.

166

Stalinists and the new national communists than had been the case in Poland.[112] When Rakosi took the Soviet-Yugoslav Declaration of June 20 as his cue for adopting a Stalinist road to socialism, Mikoyan was sent from Moscow to explain the content of the new diversity to the Hungarian leaders. Rakosi's subsequent resignation led to a compromise regime which eschewed Stalinism without embracing Nagy. The compromise failed. Violent disorder in Budapest produced an appeal for Soviet assistance and on October 24, Soviet troops were used in quelling the uprising.[113] Nagy, whose return to power on the previous day seemed to match the return of Gomulka in Poland, called repeatedly for order and arranged a cease-fire on October 28.[114] With the beginning of the withdrawal of Soviet troops on the following day it seemed that the Russians were content to allow Nagy to manage the situation as best he could. But the stifling of the revolution was only temporary. On October 30 Nagy announced the restoration of a multiparty system and a coalition government, and followed this on November 1 with a proclamation of the neutrality of Hungary.[115] The second Soviet military intervention followed. The Soviet justification for her action was that it had taken place, at the request of the Hungarian government, to restore order against the forces of reaction supported by the imperialist powers.[116]

It might be concluded from these events of 1956 that Khrushchev's new order could accommodate a Gomulka whose road to socialism was paved with statements of Polish friendship for the Soviet Union, but not a Nagy whose pretension to neutrality and a plurality of parties, in the Soviet view, put him on a road away from and not towards socialism. But this is too simple. The first Soviet intervention in Hungary occurred before Nagy's statements of October 30 and November 1 and cannot be explained just in

[112] Imre Nagy had developed an ideology of national communism which went as far as to advocate Hungarian neutrality between the power blocs without moral distinction between them, a quite different approach from Gomulka's cautious adoption of domestic diversity. See Brzezinski, pp. 219–222.

[113] The authorship of the request for help is still disputed, though the consensus is that it came from below the top echelons of party and government. Nagy, in an address on October 31, 1956, denied any responsibility for it; text in Zinner, pp. 458–459.

[114] See Zinner, pp. 408, 409–411, 416–418, and 428.

[115] Texts in *ibid.*, pp. 453–454 and 463–464.

[116] *Pravda* editorial, November 4, 1956, cited in Zinner, pp. 498–505.

terms of the ideological apparatus Khrushchev had been building since the Twentieth Party Congress. The coming of the Hungarian crisis so soon after the one in Poland may have put a premium on firm Soviet action by frightening her leaders with a domino theory of "counterrevolution." Moreover, the Hungarian party did not keep control of the situation in the same way as had the Polish party, nor did it manage the united front which the Poles had presented to the Russians. Two further considerations made intervention in Hungary more likely than in Poland. In the first place, Poland's freedom to leave the bloc was limited by the fact that of the major powers only the Soviet Union recognized her postwar frontiers, whereas Hungary had no such constraint; and second, intervention in Hungary was easier. Smaller than Poland and having only one-third of its population, Hungary had three Soviet divisions stationed on its territory where only two were in Poland.[117]

Thus, if by her action, the Soviet Union was demonstrating the limits of the permissible in the People's Democracies, the limits remained a matter of conjecture. Evidence of uncertainty and division in the ranks of the Soviet leadership casts doubt upon any idea that the Soviet Union was applying a clear set of rules for socialist international relations.[118] And the doctrine developed in support of the action was as equivocal. On October 30 the Soviet government announced that the policy of peaceful coexistence found

> its deepest and most consistent expression in the mutual relations among the socialist countries. United by the common ideals of building a socialist society and by the principles of proletarian internationalism, the countries of the great commonwealth of socialist nations can build their mutual relations only on the principles of complete equality, of respect for territorial integrity, state independence and sovereignty, and of non-interference in one another's internal affairs. Not only does this not exclude close fraternal cooperation and mutual aid among the countries of the socialist commonwealth in the economic, political, and cultural spheres; on the contrary, it presupposes these things.[119]

[117] I am indebted for these two considerations to Mr. Geoffrey Jukes.
[118] On division in the Soviet ranks see Brzezinski, p. 229.
[119] In "Declaration by the Government of the USSR on the Principles of Development and Further Strengthening of Friendship and Cooperation

The declaration went on to say that the Soviet Union was prepared to review the question of the expediency of the further presence of Soviet advisers in the People's Democracies and the question of the stationing of Soviet troops. Coming as it did after the Polish crisis and the first intervention in Hungary, this statement seemed to represent a real attempt at conciliation and recognition of the autonomy of the People's Democracies. It seemed that Gomulka and Nagy were receiving the stamp of legitimacy from Moscow.[120] A few days later, the second intervention in Hungary occurred and the all-encompassing nature of the doctrine of proletarian internationalism was again demonstrated. After the second intervention, the emphasis on nonintervention which was characteristic of the October 30 Declaration changed to an emphasis on "international working-class solidarity." An article in the Moscow periodical *Kommunist* stressed that

> the principle of co-existence is the principle of the peaceful association of countries which have differing and opposing social and economic systems. It is not difficult to see that it would be a great mistake to carry this principle of co-existence over to the reciprocal relations between similar Socialist states or to the relationships between Communist parties, which have a common aim and a common ideology.[121]

This change of emphasis did not mean a return to Stalin's infallible orthodoxy. Gomulka, in his November talks with the Soviet leaders in Moscow, insisted on the formula of "full equality and regard for state sovereignty" in relations between socialist countries.[122] The Chinese provided the doctrine to meet the new situation with the theory of fundamental and nonfundamental contradictions.[123]

Between the Soviet Union and Other Socialist States," text in Zinner, *National Communism and Popular Revolt*, pp. 485–489.

[120] Not only from Moscow, but from many members of the bloc who supported the declaration, see Zinner, pp. 489–496. Brzezinski argues that the Soviet declaration was "obviously designed to prevent a Hungarian defection from the Soviet bloc," *Soviet Bloc*, p. 229. In summary, the declaration might be said to have recognized the diversity prevailing, but aimed to prevent its further spread.

[121] Cited in Nollau, pp. 284–285.

[122] See the communiqué on the talks, November 18, 1956; text in Zinner, pp. 306–314.

[123] On this, see J. M. Mackintosh, *Strategy and Tactics of Soviet Foreign Policy*, London, 1962, pp. 195–196, from which the following summary of the article in *People's Daily*, December 29, 1956, is taken.

Fundamental contradictions occurred between captalism and communism and within capitalism, nonfundamental contradictions occurred between Communists. The "Great Power chauvinism" of the Soviet Union in her relations with the People's Democracies and the excessive nationalism of the latter were nonfundamental contradictions. But the Hungarian crisis became a fundamental contradiction when Hungary opted for a future away from the communist bloc and thus justified Soviet intervention. Having provided justification, the Chinese built a model for socialist international relations consisting in "ideological and political unity while recognizing the possibility of limited local diversity."[124] This was the solution adopted by the twelve ruling Communist Parties in their conference at Moscow in November 1957. The Soviet Union was recognized to be at the head of the socialist countries, though Gomulka's preference "first and mightiest socialist power" was also used. The five principles of equality, territorial integrity, independence, sovereignty, and nonintervention were balanced by "fraternal mutual aid" as a "striking expression of socialist internationalism."[125] The Soviet Union maintained her leading position, but her leadership was complicated and its nature changed by the persistence of Gomulka among the led.

Tito's "revisionism" was an added complication. Having established her primacy in the communist bloc, the attempt to combine unity with it led the Soviet Union to a new emphasis as between the recently balanced principles of nonintervention and socialist internationalism. It emerged as a criticism of what was regarded as wrong emphasis in the Draft Program of the Yugoslav League of Communists.[126] An article in *Kommunist* found fault with the Draft Program for reducing proletarian internationalism exclusively to the principles of equality and noninterference in internal affairs, so that "the necessity for strengthening the unity and cooperation of the Socialist countries and the Marxist-Leninist Parties is buried in oblivion." "Under certain conditions," the article went on, "proletarian internationalism demands the subordination of the interest of the proletarian struggle in one coun-

[124] Brzezinski, p. 280.

[125] From the 1957 Moscow Declaration, text in G. F. Hudson, R. Lowenthal, and R. MacFarquhar, *The Sino-Soviet Dispute*, London, 1961, pp. 46–56.

[126] Text of the Program of April 1958 in V. L. Benes, R. F. Byrnes, and N. Spulber, *The Second Soviet-Yugoslav Dispute*, Indiana, 1959, pp. 29–91.

try to the interests of the struggle on a world-wide scale."[127] Clearly, for the Soviet Union, the principle of nonintervention was not absolute, it had to be measured in a scale of competing imperatives.

With different stress according to the various situations in which the Soviet Union found herself, the principle of nonintervention was now part of Soviet doctrine on international relations between Socialist states and those between states with different social systems. The Sino-Soviet split, disguised until 1960 and undisguised thereafter, affected the place of the nonintervention principle in both these categories of relations. The Chinese objection to Khrushchev's doctrine of peaceful coexistence, flowing from a different perception of the place of peace and war in communist ideology, forced the Soviet Union into a sharper definition of the doctrinal position of the rule of nonintervention and even into a concession that its domain was restricted by the principle of support for wars of national liberation. On the other hand, in relations among socialist states, the main outcome of the Sino-Soviet dispute was practical before it was doctrinal. The Chinese challenge to Soviet ideological leadership and the break-up of unity in the bloc tended to make the relations between socialist states conform to that norm of nonintervention which Chinese doctrine was trying to undermine in another sphere of relations.

At the Twentieth Party Congress, Khrushchev had proclaimed peaceful coexistence as a fundamental principle of Soviet foreign policy. The victory of the socialist over the capitalist system would be won by a superior mode of production, not through armed interference. War was no longer "fatalistically inevitable" though as long as capitalism survived it might try to unleash war.[128] In his speech to the Twenty-First Congress in 1959, Khrushchev went further to suggest that "even before the complete victory of socialism on earth, while capitalism still remains in part of the world, there will be an actual possibility of excluding world war from the life of society."[129] During his visit to Peking in September 1959, Khrushchev espoused a method of conducting international relations of which Cobden would have approved: "The socialist countries . . . fire the hearts of men by the force of their example in

[127] Text of this article of April 1958 in Bass and Marbury, *The Soviet-Yugoslav Controversy*, pp. 142–166.

[128] Khrushchev, pp. 38–42.

[129] Extract from the speech in Hudson, Lowenthal, and MacFarquhar, pp. 56–57.

building socialism, and thus lead them to follow in their footsteps. The question of when this or that country will take the path to socialism is decided by its own people. This, for us, is the holy of holies. . . ."[130] On his return to Moscow, Khrushchev, reporting to the Supreme Soviet, stressed that peaceful coexistence was not something to be desired or not desired, it was an "objective necessity" stemming from the "present situation in the world."[131]

The comprehensive Chinese response to the Soviet position came in an article in the Peking journal *Red Flag* in April 1960.[132] It asserted that "as long as the imperialist system still exists, the most acute form of violence, namely war, has by no means ended in the world." Peaceful coexistence between countries with two different systems was not denied, but at the same time support for revolutionary wars of the oppressed nations against imperialism had to be forthcoming because they were just wars. As against the Soviet emphasis on peaceful coexistence and the possibility of local war leading to nuclear conflict, the Chinese stressed the justice of wars of national liberation and the view that support for armed struggle would weaken imperialism and its capabilities for war.[133]

The Moscow Conference of the Eighty-One Parties in November 1960 did not resolve the differences between the Soviet Union and China. Rather, it ventilated those differences among the members of the communist world. The statement issued by the conference contained both views with the Soviet line predominating, but not so greatly as to prevent the Chinese from deriving doctrinal comfort from the document in the years to come.[134] Though

[130] From September 30, 1959, speech in Peking, extract in *ibid.*, pp. 61–63.

[131] Quoted in D. S. Zagoria, *The Sino-Soviet Conflict 1956–1961*, Princeton, N.J., 1962, p. 281.

[132] Text of the article "Long Live Leninism" in Hudson, Lowenthal, and MacFarquhar, pp. 82–112, from which the quotations following are taken. The persistent tone of the article is the Chinese fidelity to Leninist orthodoxy, in marked and perhaps deliberate contrast to Khrushchev's references to the differences between the modern age and Lenin's time.

[133] See Zagoria, p. 255.

[134] Text of the 1960 Moscow Statement in Hudson, Lowenthal, and MacFarquhar, pp. 177–205. The 1960 polemics established a pattern for the doctrinal debate between China and the Soviet Union. The same issues were argued, though with much greater intensity, during the 1963 correspondence between the two states. The Soviet Union emphasized the all-pervasive imperative of peaceful coexistence, the dangers and ravages of nuclear war, and the significance of the "world socialist system" (as opposed to singling

he made no concessions to Chinese enthusiasm for wars of national liberation at the conference, Khrushchev, in his postconference report, clarified the Soviet position in a way which amounted to such a concession.[135] It was the duty of Communists to fight against world war and against local war which might develop into "world thermonuclear and missile war." But wars of national liberation were not only justified, they were inevitable. They could not be identified with wars between countries, with local wars, "because the insurgent people are fighting for the right of self-determination, for their social and independent national development." The Communists supported such "sacred war" and had allowed it to prevail in Vietnam by threatening counterintervention against the imperialists.[136] This careful admission of the duty to uphold internal wars of national liberation appeared to modify the duty of nonintervention in the internal affairs of other states. Arguably, on the other hand, and strictly in terms of Khrushchev's logic in this report, this national liberation modification did not restrict the range of the nonintervention principle but maintained it. The reference to Vietnam pointed out the effect of the communist attitude in preventing intervention by the threat of counterintervention, and thus in upholding the principle of nonintervention (though it was not stated in quite these terms). If Cobden could have approved of Khrushchev's doctrine of the power of example in international relations, Mill could have approved of his account of the need for counterintervention.

The Chinese challenge to Soviet ideological authority and leadership was not a challenge to the idea of leadership itself, but rather to its nature. The Chinese attitude evolved from sponsorship of Soviet leadership according to the "unity in diversity" formula of 1957 to the announcement in 1964 that the CPSU, through its

---

out one of its components—the national liberation struggle) in the struggle against imperialism. The Chinese accepted peaceful coexistence, but wanted it limited to its proper sphere, argued that the emergence of nuclear weapons did not alter the law of class struggle or the necessity of social and national revolutions, and emphasized revolutionary struggle as against peaceful competition. See in particular the letter from CCP to CPSU, June 14, 1963, and the Soviet "Open Letter," July 14, 1963. Texts in W. E. Griffith, *The Sino-Soviet Rift*, London, 1964, pp. 259–325.

[135] Text of Khrushchev's Report on the Moscow Conference in Hudson, Lowenthal, and MacFarquhar, *Sino-Soviet Dispute*, pp. 207–221, from which the quotations following are taken.

[136] This, written in 1961, refers to the First Indochina War.

revisionism, had forfeited its position as head of the international communist movement.[137] In 1960 the Soviet Union was still the "universally recognized vanguard" if not the head of the movement; by 1961 the only CPSU leadership recognized by China was that over the Soviet people, and in 1963 China, in her June 14 letter to the CPSU, staked what amounted to her own claim to be the repository of doctrinal purity in the movement.[138] The Soviet response to the challenge was first to modify doctrine about stages in the development of communism, in order to fend off any claim of the Chinese to be superior in this respect as a result of the development of the communes. According to Khrushchev's speech at the Twenty-First CPSU Congress, all bloc countries would make the transition to communism "more or less simultaneously," a formula vague enough to accommodate precocity in the bloc and to allow, at the same time, continued Soviet assertion of superiority.[139] But at the 1960 Moscow Conference, the CPSU delegation proposed that the formula "that the Soviet Union stands at the head of the socialist camp" be not included in the statement because leadership from a single center was "both impossible and unnecessary."[140] This represented a Soviet refusal to accept the challenge on Chinese terms, a preference for unity through compromise as against an ideological split.[141] But this Soviet attempt to remain aloof from the ideological debate in order to preserve a façade of unity within the bloc was productive of diminishing returns. Since unity in the communist world was defined in terms of ideology, and not by the mere coincidence of political interests, it was not possible for the Soviet Union to patch it up by dwelling on the latter. Hence the Chinese challenge was at length accepted

[137] See Brzezinski, *Soviet Bloc*, p. 420.

[138] The "universally recognized vanguard" formula was used in the 1960 Moscow Statement. Chou En-Lai's recognition of CPSU leadership over the Soviet people was in his speech to the 22nd CPSU Congress on October 19, 1961. Text in Alexander Dallin, ed., *Diversity in International Communism*, New York, 1963, pp. 45–54. The CCP letter to the CPSU, June 14, 1963, is in Griffith, pp. 259–288.

[139] Zagoria, pp. 130–132. At the Twenty-Second Party Congress, this doctrine was no longer in vogue. Instead Khrushchev spoke of the Soviet Union as "the first to enter on the path of full-scale construction of communism." Khrushchev's Report to Twenty-Second Congress, October 17, 1961, text in A. Dallin, pp. 4–32.

[140] In Khrushchev's Report on the 1960 Moscow Conference; text in Hudson, Lowenthal, and MacFarquhar, pp. 207–221.

[141] See Lowenthal, *World Communism*, New York, 1964, pp. 256–257.

and at the Twenty-Second CPSU Congress the Soviet reply took the form of a bitter attack on Albania. From there, the dispute developed through the open break in 1963 to one between "the restorers of capitalism" and "the petty-bourgeois Trotskyists."[142]

Leadership and unity were correlative phenomena. The Chinese challenge to Soviet leadership and doctrinal authority presaged an end to a unity which could be restored only if the challenge were totally vanquished or totally victorious. Soviet power prevented the latter, the limitations to her power prevented the former. Because of its failure, the Chinese challenge to Soviet leadership, undertaken in the name of her brand of ideological unity, led to increased diversity in the bloc. The East European states were among the beneficiaries of the Sino-Soviet split, their range of autonomy was increased and their heightened importance to a Moscow embattled in the East improved their political leverage.[143] The erosion of Stalin's "two camps" doctrine by the indications of a Soviet-American *détente* and increased stability in Europe, had a similar effect, and the rationale for bloc solidarity was now less persuasive. But the loosening of Soviet control did not mean its abandonment. That there were residual limits to permissible diversity in Eastern Europe was demonstrated by the events in Czechoslovakia in 1968.

The Soviet invasion of Czechoslovakia on August 21, 1968 was forcible testimony to the continued existence of these limits; the rules had been broken but their content was not clear. The events of 1956 appeared to have legitimized national roads to socialism so long as they remained within the bloc and adhered to one-party rule. Czechoslovakia's road to socialism in 1968 seemed to have understood these rules. In her foreign policy, she was "almost embarrassingly anxious to please the Soviet Union" and the draft party statutes of August 10 had explicitly disavowed factionalism in the party.[144] But the same draft statutes would allow an outvoted group to maintain its minority views, a doctrine prejudicial to the leading role of the party.[145] This incipient democratization

---

[142] See Brzezinski, p. 427.   [143] See *ibid.*, pp. 434–435

[144] Philip Windsor and Adam Roberts, *Czechoslovakia 1968*, London, 1969, pp. 16 and 61.

[145] *Ibid.*, p. 61. It has been pointed out that the abandonment of the leading role of the party together with the abolition of censorship were the two main points of criticism of Czech leaders contained in Soviet and Warsaw Pact charges. See Leopold Labedz, "Czechoslovakia and After," *Survey*, No. 69, October 1968, p. 8.

added to the liberalization which found one of its expressions in less rigorous censorship appeared to be the crucial factors provoking intervention.[146] From the Soviet point of view, the danger of Czechoslovakia seemed to lie not in the 1956 problem of Hungarian defection from the bloc, but in the unsettling effects of a reformist and revisionist force within it.[147] The view that Czechoslovakia's most grievous fault lay in internal liberalization rather than in any error of foreign policy seems to be strengthened by the Soviet Union's respect, however grudging, for Romania's independence. Since the late 1950's, Romania had developed not merely an independent foreign policy of "partial alignment" with the other bloc members, but also a coherent doctrine for its legitimation.[148] But in Romania the leading role of the party was not in question.[149]

The initial attempt by the Soviet Union to justify intervention as a response to a request for urgent assistance from Czechoslovakian party and government leaders was discredited by a statement from those leaders that the intervention occurred without their knowledge.[150] The alternative and elaborate Soviet defense of her own and allied action, which was to become famous as the "Brezhnev Doctrine," was contained in a *Pravda* article of September 26, 1968.[151] It set out to answer the allegations that the measures taken to "defend the socialist gains of the Czechoslovak people" contradicted "the Marxist-Leninist principle of sovereignty

[146] The distinction between liberalization and democratization, between a measure of relaxation, reversible, and conceded from above, and a less easily reversible measure allowing participation from below, is Philip Windsor's in Windsor and Roberts, pp. 9–10 and 26.

[147] Lowenthal, "The Sparrow in the Cage," *Problems of Communism*, Vol. XVII, No. 6, November–December 1968, p. 11.

[148] Robert L. Farlow, "Romanian Foreign Policy: A Case of Partial Alignment," *Problems of Communism*, Vol. XX, November–December 1971, pp. 54–63.

[149] One motive that did go beyond the domestic in Czechoslovakia, Lowenthal argues, was the "Soviet preoccupation with West Germany [which] stood at the beginning of the chain of events that ended with the Soviet occupation of Czechoslovakia." "The Sparrow in the Cage," p. 7.

[150] For the Soviet claim to an invitation, see Tass statement of August 21, 1968; text in Windsor and Roberts, pp. 176–177. For the Czechoslovak Presidium Statement of the same date, see *ibid.*, pp. 174–175.

[151] Excerpts from the article in *Problems of Communism*, Vol. XVII, No. 6, November–December 1968, p. 25, from which the quotations following are taken.

and the right of nations to self-determination." In its most out-spoken passage the article argued:

There is no doubt that the peoples of the socialist countries and the Communist parties have and must have freedom to deter-mine their country's path of development. However, any de-cision of theirs must damage neither socialism in their country, nor the fundamental interests of the other socialist countries, nor the world-wide workers' movement, which is waging a struggle for socialism. This means that every Communist party is responsible not only to its own people but also to all the socialist countries and to the entire Communist movement. Whoever forgets this is placing sole emphasis on the autonomy and independence of Communist parties. . . .

Each Communist party is free to apply the principles of Marxism-Leninism in its own country, but it cannot deviate from these principles. . . .

In concrete terms this means primarily that no Communist party can fail to take into account in its activities such a decisive fact of our time as the struggle between the two antithetical so-cial systems—capitalism and socialism. . . .

The article went on to revive that old transformation of the prin-ciple of national self-determination into the principle of socialist self determination which had been engineered by Lenin and Stalin in the years after the Revolution. By the use of this device, the invasion was represented as a struggle on behalf of Czechoslo-vakian sovereignty against the export of counterrevolution from outside and against those who would deliver the country to the imperialists. The allied soldiers were in Czechoslovakia to defend socialist gains, they were not interfering in the country's internal affairs.[152] Those who asserted the contrary were measuring events with the yardsticks of bourgeois law and "laws and the norms of law are subordinated to the laws of the class struggle."[153]

---

[152] This protestation of nonintervention was a constant theme of Soviet statements on Czechoslovakia. It appeared, for example, in the First Mos-cow Communiqué of August 27, 1968, a day after the conclusion of the Soviet-Czechoslovak talks; text in Windsor and Roberts, pp. 178–181. It also constituted Article 2 of the Soviet-Czechoslovak Treaty of October 16, 1968; text in *ibid.*, pp. 193–200.

[153] In June 1969, *Rude Pravo* endorsed the Brezhnev Doctrine. It said that the presence of Soviet troops did not endanger Czechoslovakian sov-ereignty, nor did it interfere in her internal affairs. The troops were there

In one sense there was little that was new about the Brezhnev Doctrine. The principles of sovereignty, independence, and non-interference had always been set alongside the interests of international communism as defined by the Soviet Union.[154] The emphasis on the latter in the Brezhnev Doctrine was an echo of the similar emphasis after Hungary in 1956 and during the second Soviet-Yugoslav dispute in 1958. What was new was the extent of the emphasis, the range of the injunction against damaging socialism. The freedom of socialist countries to determine their own paths of development meant freedom to conform with, but not to deviate from, Marxist-Leninist principles defined by the Soviet Union. Furthermore the determination of the content of the principle of sovereignty according to bloc allegiance in a divided world was made explicit in a way unfamiliar since Stalin's time.[155] Here lay the kernel of the Soviet defense. If a state whose sovereignty was defined by its membership of the socialist system was threatened by counterrevolution, then action in its defense did not deny its sovereignty, did not interfere in it, quite the contrary, it upheld it. Such action was not destructive but protective, not aggressive but defensive. In the light of this sort of argument, de-veloped logically from the false premise of the "export of counter-revolution from outside," the Soviet protestations of noninterference when she was clearly intervening in Czechoslovakian affairs become explicable.

The principle of nonintervention was a constantly repeated slogan purporting, among other principles, to govern the relations between socialist states. For the Eastern European states, it defined the perimeter of permissible independence from the Soviet Union,

---

for the defense of the western frontiers. The paper warned against "a purely abstract interpretation of sovereignty," and against a nationalistic interpretation of it, stressed its relatedness to membership in one of the world systems, and asked if the American version of sovereignty in Latin America or Asia were to be preferred. Cited in *The Times*, June 24, 1969.

[154] This is not a formulation the Soviets would accept. Brezhnev has described the artificial opposition of the principle of proletarian internationalism to the principles of independence, sovereignty, and equality, as "bourgeois propaganda." See L. I. Brezhnev, "For a Greater Unity of Communists, For a Fresh Upsurge of the Anti-Imperialist Struggle," Speech to International Meeting of Communist and Workers' Parties in Moscow, June 7, 1969, Moscow, 1969, p. 37.

[155] See, e.g., O. Pavlov, "Proletarian Internationalism and Defence of Socialist Gains," *International Affairs* (Moscow), October 1968, pp. 11–16.

it marked the threshold between matters within their domestic competence and matters of international socialist concern. But the perimeter was neither stable nor clearly signposted. Its extent varied from the minimal independence allowed by Stalin to Khrushchev's legitimation of national roads to socialism. At one time it was drawn so as to include a Yugoslavia asserting sovereignty and independence within the bloc, at another it excluded that country for its overemphasis of the same principles. The Sino-Soviet dispute expanded the area enclosed by the nonintervention principle, the Brezhnev Doctrine contracted it. And the persistence of a Romania as independent as she is demonstrates the fallibility of any generalizations about the content of the rules that apply in the communist international system.

The Soviet doctrine of nonintervention as applied to socialist international relations was then relative rather than absolute in two senses. Understood as a discrete principle, it was cut across by competing imperatives of Soviet foreign policy embodied in phrases like "fraternal aid," "mutual assistance" and "proletarian internationalism." Understood as a principle applying to states but having a content determined by the system to which those states belonged, its application was subjected to the unpredictable demands of the system as defined by its dominant power, the Soviet Union.

VI

As well as providing a somewhat elusive guide to the relations between socialist states, the principle of nonintervention was proclaimed as part of the formula of "peaceful coexistence" which governed the relations between states with different social systems. In Soviet statements about foreign policy, the principle of peaceful coexistence is almost invariably connected with the name of Lenin.[156] This ideologically legitimizes while it also confuses the differences between Lenin's conception of peaceful coexistence as

[156] The origin of the idea of peaceful coexistence has been variously attributed to Trotsky, Lenin, Chicherin and Stalin. Franklyn Griffiths argues that the slogan apparently began with Trotsky on November 22, 1917, as "peaceful living together," that it was used in various contexts by Chicherin, Lenin, and Stalin, and that it received official sanction in December 1927 as "peaceful coexistence." "Origins of Peaceful Coexistence, A Historical Note," *Survey*, No. 50, January 1964, pp. 195–196.

179

a temporary expedient and Khrushchev's conception of it as a *sine qua non* of contemporary international relations.[157] Khrushchev's speech to the Twentieth Party Congress, placed a new emphasis on the requirement of peace over the requirement of revolution. For Khrushchev, there was no other way but that of peaceful coexistence, the alternative was "the most destructive war in history"; there was no third way.[158] At the Twenty-Second Party Congress, Khrushchev stressed that peaceful coexistence was not an "unstable truce between wars" but the "mutual renunciation of war as a means of settling disputes between states."[159] In his speech to the International Meeting of Communist and Workers' Parties in 1969, Brezhnev sounded like Khrushchev when he pointed out that peaceful coexistence "is not reduced simply to the absence of war between socialist and capitalist states" but that it "opened up broader possibilities for expanding relations between them."[160] When Brezhnev and Nixon, at their Moscow meeting in May 1972, decided upon the basic principles that were to guide the relations of the Soviet Union and the United States, they adopted Khrushchev's formula in declaring that they would proceed "from the common determination that in the nuclear age there is no alternative to conducting relations on the basis of peaceful coexistence."[161] Ideological differences were not obstacles to the development of normal relations based on the five principles of peaceful coexistence.

The renunciation of war in the doctrine of peaceful coexistence does not, however, mean the renunciation of conflict. The struggle between the proletariat and the aggressive forces of imperialism would continue as an "intense economic, political and ideological struggle."[162] As an article in *Pravda* put it in 1962, "peaceful coexistence does not exclude revolutionary changes in society but presupposes them, does not slow down the world revolutionary

[157] See Ivo Lapenna, "International Law viewed through Soviet eyes," *Year Book of World Affairs*, Vol. 15, 1961, p. 215.

[158] Khrushchev, *Report to Twentieth Party Congress*, p. 40.

[159] Report to Twenty-Second Party Congress, cited in A. Dallin, *Diversity in International Communism*, p. 18.

[160] Brezhnev, p. 52.

[161] Text of Basic Principles of May 29, in United States *Department of State Bulletin*, Vol. LXVI, No. 1722, June 26, 1972, pp. 898–899.

[162] In Khrushchev's Report on the 1960 Moscow Conference, cited in Hudson, Lowenthal, and MacFarquhar, *Sino-Soviet Dispute*, p. 214.

process but accelerates it, does not preserve the capitalist order but deepens the disintegration and collapse of imperialism. . . ."[163] Moreover, after Khrushchev's recognition of the inevitability of wars of national liberation in 1961, support for them was included under the rubric of peaceful coexistence. National liberation and social revolutions occurred within states, they were caused by internal factors; they could not serve as an obstacle to peaceful coexistence between states.[164] If this defense of wars of national liberation rather obviously misses its mark by blandly ignoring the problem of international support for them, the idea that they should be supported was one cautiously espoused, in Brezhnev's time as in Khrushchev's. The phrases are vague: "support for," "moral and material help," "militant alliance between," "active cooperation with."[165] And the responsive nature of such support against the aggressive acts of imperialism is emphasized, the call being for resolute *counteraction*.[166]

Thus peaceful coexistence was a canvas or a series of canvases upon which was painted the one fixed image of the abolition of wars between states; the area remaining was filled up with the perceived imperatives of the moment of creation. At one time the need for anti-imperialist struggle is emphasized, at another the requirements of coordinating measures for reducing the danger of war, and expanding trade, technical and cultural ties. The principle of nonintervention was a recurrent theme; the struggle against capitalism was to be won without resort to armed interference in the internal affairs of other states. But support for wars of national liberation, raising the prospect of intervention however carefully the doctrine was enunciated, was often included on the same peaceful coexistence canvas as the nonintervention principle. Seemingly, the Soviet Union wanted simultaneously the avoidance of

[163] Article of January 17, 1962, cited in A. Dallin, p. 629.

[164] See G. Starushenko, "The National Liberation Movement and the Struggle for Peace," *International Affairs* (Moscow), October 1963, pp. 4–5.

[165] Brezhnev, p. 51. B. Ponomaryov, "Under Banner of Marxism-Leninism and Proletarian Internationalism," *World Marxist Review*, Vol. 14, No. 6, June 1971, p. 13.

[166] D. Baratashvili, "International Law Principles of Peaceful Coexistence," *International Affairs* (Moscow), February 1972, p. 21; B. Gafurov, "The Soviet Union and the National Liberation Movement," *International Affairs* (Moscow), July 1971, pp. 17–21 (my emphasis).

potentially disastrous war and at least some connection with the revolutionary spoils necessary to the esteem of the first revolutionary power.[167]

These difficulties involved in deciding upon the precise meaning of the doctrine of peaceful coexistence are compounded by confusion about the status of the doctrine as normative or descriptive. Peaceful coexistence might be a factual statement: states with different social systems coexist and for the most part they have done so peacefully.[168] Or it might be an aspiration, a depiction of a desirable future condition of international relations.[169] Again, in Khrushchev's conception, it might be an objective necessity of contemporary international politics about which states have no choice if they wish to survive. Or it might define international law "as the international code of peaceful coexistence."[170] It is to the Soviet international law of nonintervention that the next section will be addressed.

VII

Soviet international lawyers, like their bourgeois counterparts, derive the principle of nonintervention from the principle of state sovereignty.[171] Unlike those counterparts, they hold that its prohibition of intervention is absolute, that it permits no exceptions.[172] Not only aggressive wars but also indirect, economic, and ideolog-

[167] For the attempted resolution of this apparent contradiction in Soviet international law, see below, section VII.

[168] See Henry Pachter's argument for this conception of peaceful coexistence in "The Meaning of Peaceful Co-existence," *Problems of Communism*, Vol. x, No. 1, January–February 1961, pp. 1–8.

[169] See John Keep, "Soviet Foreign Policy, Doctrine and Reality," *Survey*, No. 40, January 1962, p. 20.

[170] Y. Korovin, "International Law Today," *International Affairs* (Moscow), July 1961, pp. 18–21.

[171] See F. I. Kozhevnikov, ed., *International Law*, Moscow, n. d., p. 112.

[172] See A. Piradov, "The Principle of Non-Interference in the Modern World," *International Affairs* (Moscow), January 1966, pp. 53–58. It is absolute in another sense, too, a sense akin to Mountague Bernard's formulation of the principle (see above, Chapter Two, pp. 37–39). In spite of the arch-positivism of Soviet international law, Levin can assert that the imperialist crimes of intervention "could not shake the legal force of the non-interference principle as one of the cornerstones of international relations." This is law through deduction from first principles not law from state practice and agreement. See "The Non-Interference Principle Today," *International Affairs* (Moscow), November 1966, p. 21.

ical aggression are proscribed. So also is intervention arising from unequal treaties on military aid or from the establishment of aggressive military blocs which are "used as a screen for gross interference in internal affairs."[173] The ability of Soviet international lawyers to maintain such a doctrine without flinching is explicable in terms of what has been described as the standard Soviet definition of intervention: "Intervention [is] the armed invasion or interference of one or several capitalist states in the internal affairs of another state, aimed at the suppression of a revolution, seizure of territory, acquisition of special privileges, establishing its domination, etc. . . ."[174] If intervention were the exclusive sin of the capitalists, then it made sense for Communists to assert an absolute principle of nonintervention.

The rule of nonintervention forms an integral part of each of the two categories of Soviet international law—the law of the "Socialist Commonwealth" and the law pertaining to the relations of states with different social systems—which were developed as a response to Khrushchev's proclamation of the political principles of socialist internationalism and peaceful coexistence. Socialist internationalism is the guiding principle of the international law of the socialist states.[175] This principle encompasses the principles of full equality of states, respect for territorial integrity, sovereignty and independence, and nonintervention in internal affairs. But what sets the principle of socialist internationalism apart from that of peaceful coexistence, what provides its claim to be the foundation of norms of a "new, higher, socialist type," is the "community of interests and goals" between the socialist states, "the close bonds of international socialist solidarity."[176] The principle of noninter-

[173] Piradov, pp. 55–57.

[174] B. N. Ponomarev, ed., *Dictionary of Political Terms*, Moscow, 1958, cited in B. A. Ramundo, *The (Soviet) Socialist Theory of International Law*, Washington, D.C., 1964, p. 87, n. 307.

[175] See Kozhevnikov, p. 20. Socialist internationalism and proletarian internationalism are frequently used as interchangeable terms, but Jamgotch argues, from Soviet texts, that proletarian internationalism applies to relations between the CPSU and communist parties and working people in all countries, while socialist internationalism applies only to the higher order of relations among ruling-party states. N. Jamgotch, *Soviet-East European Dialogue*, Stanford, 1968, pp. 94–95.

[176] G. I. Tunkin, "The 22nd Congress of the CPSU and the Tasks of the Soviet Science of International Law," *Soviet Law and Government*, Winter 1962/1963, cited in Ramundo, p. 6. These higher principles were not always formulated in this way; sometimes the preferred expression was "mutual

vention shared in, "harmoniously combined with," and was defined by, the requirements of socialist internationalism:

> The independence of states and nations in the socialist commonwealth is dialectically connected with fraternal mutual assistance, socialist international division of labour, broad exchange of experience in economic and state organization, the coordination of national economic plans and specialization in production. Similar measures cannot be effected in the capitalist world. All of this imparts special features to the principle of nonintervention, giving it new content which goes beyond the general democratic nature of the principles [sic].[177]

The new content of socialist internationalism consists not merely of legal principles and rules, but rules "of a much higher type compared with general international law—socialist international law principles and rules."[178] If the nonintervention principle had meaning only in the context of these higher principles, then they clearly provided an avenue for escape from the restraint of the principle. The rule of nonintervention as a mere legal principle must give way before a doctrine which asserts common interests and aspirations above the law.[179]

Inferior to the lofty principle of socialist internationalism but still claimed as a new and progressive principle of Soviet international law is that of peaceful coexistence between states with different social systems. Its explication as a legal formulation was borrowed from the *Pancha Shila*, the five principles contained in the Sino-Indian Treaty on Tibet of April 1954. Soviet international law adopted the principles of mutual respect for territorial integrity and sovereignty, nonaggression, nonintervention, equality and

---

assistance" or "the indestructible friendship and fraternal cooperation of the socialist countries." See E. Korovin, "Proletarian Internationalism in World Affairs," *International Affairs* (Moscow), February 1958, pp. 25 and 29.

[177] V. M. Shurshalov, ed., *International Legal Forms of the Collaboration of Socialist States*, Moscow, 1962, cited in Ramundo, pp. 40–41.

[178] Tunkin, "Forty Years of Coexistence and International Law," *Soviet Year Book of International Law 1958*, Moscow, 1959, cited in Ramundo, p. 19.

[179] On the mixture of considerations of power, ideology, and law, in rule-making for socialist international relations, see K. Grzybowski, *The Socialist Commonwealth of Nations*, New Haven, 1964, p. 263.

mutual advantage as the content of the principle of peaceful co-existence.[180]

At the same time as proclaiming the principle of nonintervention as part of peaceful coexistence, Soviet international law affirms the legitimacy of support for just wars of national liberation. "Peaceful coexistence means abstention from armed force in relations between states so long as wars of national liberation and the struggle against aggression and colonialism are not involved."[181] That the two doctrines can be held together is facilitated by the Soviet definition of sovereignty. As well as that of state sovereignty, Soviet international law recognizes a right to national sovereignty, a right of each nation to self-determination and independent development whether or not it has its own statehood.[182] The principle of nonintervention, far from being a barrier against support for such entities, is extended to them, so that any action against them by the states within which the rebellion is taking place can be rendered interventionary.[183] Support for the armed struggle against colonialism does not contradict the principle of peaceful coexistence, it is an affirmation of it, because it upholds a fundamental aspect of peaceful coexistence—the right of all peoples to be masters in their own house.[184]

In its more extreme manifestations, the Soviet concept of sovereignty goes beyond the consecration of the principle of self-determination. Sovereignty has been defined as the "inalienable right of nations to build their social and state life on the most progressive principles" and as the "right of nations to throw off colonial servitude."[185] In this mode, it is a right apprehended only in relation to the Soviet state, other "democratic" states, and the oppressed and exploited; it does not extend to a regime brought

---

[180] Kozhevnikov, p. 16.

[181] Kozhevnikov, ed., *International Law*, Moscow, 1964, cited in Ramundo, *Peaceful Coexistence*, Baltimore, 1967, p. 116.

[182] Kozhevnikov, p. 98.

[183] For the view that the principle of nonintervention extends to peoples and nations fighting for the exercise of their right to self-determination, see Piradov, "Principle of Non-Interference," p. 58.

[184] George Ginsburgs, " 'Wars of National Liberation' and the Modern Law of Nations—The Soviet Thesis," in H. W. Baade, ed., *The Soviet Impact on International Law*, New York, 1965, p. 95.

[185] Y. Korovin, "Sovereignty and Peace," *International Affairs* (Moscow), September 1960, p. 7.

about by aggression or constantly threatening it.[186] Colonial rule is just such a regime and so participation in the struggle against it is defense against aggression.[187] The rationale is counterintervention not intervention, a rationale made possible by a conception of sovereignty which encompasses values other than mere independence and extends to entities other than states. But if the manipulation of the notion of sovereignty is insufficient legal justification for supporting wars of national liberation, then such support may always be taken to arise from the principle of proletarian internationalism, again a remedy plucked from above the law.[188]

Notwithstanding these extensive interpretations of the right of sovereignty, the proclamation of nonintervention, a bourgeois principle made progressive by the touch of the Soviet Union, reflects an increasing Soviet perception of international relations as the relations of states.[189] This is not to suggest, however, that the vague aspirations contained in the slogans of Socialist internationalism and peaceful coexistence add anything concrete to the body of international law. Moreover, the existence of "Marxism-Leninism" as a corpus for the legitimation of Soviet action above international law, makes the latter an uncertain guide to Soviet action.

VIII

That states should behave according to the principle of nonintervention is now a familiar part of Soviet doctrine about international relations. But the asserted content of the principle has changed with time and circumstance, and the terms of its proclamation have varied with the market at which it is directed. From the first years of the revolution, it has been deployed as a legal barrier

[186] M. Chakste, "Soviet Concepts of the State, International Law and Sovereignty," *American Journal of International Law*, Vol. 43, No. 1, 1949, p. 32.

[187] Ramundo, *Peaceful Coexistence*, p. 123.

[188] For justification of this sort see V. Trukhanovsky, "Proletarian Internationalism and Peaceful Coexistence," *International Affairs* (Moscow), August 1966, p. 56.

[189] For the idea of nonintervention as a "bourgeois democratic principle which has become more progressive" see Ramundo, *Soviet Theory of International Law*, p. 25. For the upgrading of the role of the state in recent Soviet thought on international relations see W. Zimmerman, *Soviet Perspectives on International Relations, 1956–1967*, Princeton, N.J., 1969, p. 80.

against outside intervention in the Soviet Union and later any-where in the communist world. Apart from this defensive function, it was used to buttress Soviet initiatives in foreign policy. As a formula of socialist international relations, it gave quasi-legal expression to the area of domestic competence allowed to the East European states. In the international relations of peaceful coexistence, it served to demonstrate the difference between the principles guiding the action of the Soviet Union and the aggressive imperialism of the capitalist powers. As part of peaceful coexistence, the slogan of nonintervention was conspicuously attributed to its inventors in the underdeveloped world, establishing thereby the Soviet credentials as friend of the new states, not exploiter.

In the Soviet view the rule of nonintervention, apart from its value as a slogan, has a genuine content: nonintervention is the desirable situation in relations between the socialist countries themselves, and between them and the capitalist states. But there are other desirable ends, the pursuit of which is prior to the lesser principle of nonintervention, and in terms of which the principle tends to be defined. In socialist international relations, shared interests and goals unite the socialist states in a close communal tie expressed in norms of a type higher than those that apply in relations outside that community, and the principle of nonintervention has to be interpreted against the background of these higher norms. In relations between states with different social systems, the principle of nonintervention as part of peaceful coexistence might be held, in any instance, to be inferior to the principle of proletarian internationalism applying between Communist Parties, or to the principle of international proletarian solidarity uniting the working classes of the world. If, in her actual relations with states outside the socialist system, the Soviet Union made much less use than she might have of these theoretical loopholes in the doctrine of nonintervention, one of the purposes of the next chapter will be to examine the response of the United States to both the doctrine and the practice of the Soviet Union.

187

SIX

UNITED STATES DOCTRINE AND PRACTICE

By the end of the Second World War, the United States had repudiated isolationism, a repudiation symbolized by the much-vaunted conversion of Senator Vandenberg. In August 1943 he had been the motive force in the drawing-up of the Mackinac Charter which pledged Republicans to "responsible participation by the United States in postwar cooperative organization among sovereign nations to prevent military aggression and to attain permanent peace with organized justice in a free world."[1] In his speech of January 10, 1945, Vandenberg announced that he did not believe that "any nation hereafter can immunize itself by its own exclusive action."[2] The foreign policy debate was now to be about the nature and extent of American participation in world politics and not about the desirability of participation per se. This chapter will examine the fate of the doctrine of nonintervention in a United States foreign policy, which, having had involvement in world politics forced upon it, could no longer afford the principle of nonintervention a comfortable nicke in the broader doctrine of isolationism. In Europe, in Latin America, in the Middle East, and in the Far East, the actions and perceived intentions of "international communism" modified the American tradition of nonintervention as it had variously applied to these areas.

I

American participation in world politics did not necessarily mean the abandonment of action according to the principle of nonintervention. Indeed, during and after the war, much American foreign policy energy was spent in attempts to build a new international politics of cooperation on the basis of the United Nations, a vision which eschewed the old order of spheres of influence,

---

[1] Cited in Joseph M. Jones, *The Fifteen Weeks*, New York, 1955, p. 122.
[2] Cited in D. F. Fleming, *The Cold War and Its Origins 1917–1960*, 2 vols., London, 1961, Vol. I, *1917–1950*, p. 274.

balance of power, and exclusive alliances.[3] Acceptance by the world of the new order seemed to be the price demanded by the United States for her abandonment of isolationism and assumption of responsibility in international relations. The history of United States foreign policy from Roosevelt's death to Truman's message to Congress of March 12, 1947 announcing aid to Greece and Turkey, is the history of the blurring of the vision of a new order with the increased perception of Soviet intransigence.[4] As the vision was eclipsed, so the doctrine of nonintervention, which had its roots in reflection about American relations with Europe, was modified with the apprehension of a change in the nature of those relations.

The American image of the Soviet Union as an intransigent and self-seeking power, having to be cajoled into the American pattern of international cooperation, was formed early in the Truman Presidency. The democratic institutions and free elections, prescribed for Poland and the East European states at Yalta, meant something different in Moscow from the Washington interpretation. That the American interpretation was not realized could be taken as evidence of a Soviet desire to dominate Eastern Europe and of Soviet infidelity to international agreements.[5] Suspicion about Soviet motives was reinforced by her failure to withdraw troops from Iran by the agreed date in March 1946, by her pressure on Turkey for a change of the regime governing the Straits, and by communist aid to the insurgents in the Greek Civil War. As early as August 1945 after the Potsdam Conference, Truman had come to the conclusion that the Russians were planning world

[3] See M. Donclan, *The Ideas of American Foreign Policy*, London, 1963, pp. 12 and 20–25. For the argument that these elements of the old order were eschewed because they interfered with the American design for world economic hegemony, see Kolko, *The Politics of War*, pp. 242–279.

[4] For the view that any idea that cooperation with the Russians was possible had died already with Roosevelt, see Gar Alperovitz, *Atomic Diplomacy: Hiroshima and Potsdam*, New York, 1965, p. 30. Kolko argues that the fear in the West of the Left and Bolshevism was beyond negotiation, and thus goes further back than Alperovitz in locating the source of the allied intention not to cooperate with the Russians. *The Politics of War*, pp. 13–42. For a critique of these, and other, revisionist views of the origins of the Cold War, see J. L. Richardson, "Cold War Revisionism: A Critique," *World Politics*, Vol. xxiv, No. 4, July 1972, pp. 579–612.

[5] For the range of attitudes in the cabinet on these questions, see Harry S Truman, *Memoirs*, 2 vols., London, 1955, 1956, Vol. i, *Year of Decisions, 1945*, pp. 80–82.

conquest.[6] In November, Secretary of the Navy Forrestal noted in his diary a summary of State Department dispatches which referred to Soviet high-handedness, unilateral action, and aggressive pressure everywhere from Western Europe to Korea.[7] With the predictions of the imminent collapse of Greece early in 1947, the signs of the previous two years were pieced together to form a picture of an aggressive Soviet Union about to break out unless checked. At a White House meeting on February 27, Acheson spoke of the Soviet Union's most persistent and ambitious efforts to encircle Turkey and Germany, and thus lay three continents open to Soviet domination.[8] The Soviet aim, in Acheson's view, was the control of the eastern Mediterranean and the Middle East, and if this aim were achieved, further Soviet penetration would be limitless.[9]

Having built an image of an aggressive Soviet Union the United States responded to it in the only manner considered appropriate. From the American Embassy in Moscow in 1945, Harriman was advocating a "tough" policy with Russia.[10] On April 23 Truman followed this advice by speaking to Molotov on the Polish question in a fashion to which Molotov was unaccustomed.[11] In a memorandum read to Secretary of State Byrnes on January 5, 1946, Truman took the view that "how many divisions have you?" was the only language the Russians understood and declared himself "tired of babying the Soviets."[12] On March 5, 1946 Truman sponsored Churchill's "Iron Curtain" platform at Fulton, Missouri.[13] Strong diplomatic pressure was brought to bear on the Soviet Union to remove her troops from Iran and a similar re-

[6] According to *ibid.*, Vol. I, p. 342. Two months later, as Truman records it in his memoirs, he linked together the Soviet activity in Iran and the threat of a communist coup in Greece and surmised that "this began to look like a giant pincers movement against the oil-rich areas of the Near East and the warm water ports of the Mediterranean." *Ibid.*, Vol. I, p. 460.

[7] W. Millis, ed., *The Forrestal Diaries*, London, 1952, p. 119.

[8] Jones, p. 139.

[9] *Ibid.*, p. 140. See this work generally for the crisis atmosphere prevailing in Washington at this time, and the widespread view that a Russian "breakthrough" was imminent.

[10] See Millis, *The Forrestal Diaries*, pp. 55–57. For Harriman's special visit to Washington in April to ensure that Truman understood that Stalin was breaking his agreements, see Truman, Vol. I, pp. 72–75.

[11] *Ibid.*, p. 85.

[12] *Ibid.*, pp. 491–493.

[13] Truman, *Memoirs*, Vol. 2, *Years of Trial and Hope, 1946–1953*, p. 100.

sponse to Soviet policy toward Turkey was accompanied by the sending of a gunboat to the eastern Mediterranean. It was not then surprising that the United States should take up the burden which Britain could no longer bear in Greece. What was surprising was the nature and extent of the doctrine formulated to justify the action.

The note informing the American government that Britain could no longer afford to support the governments of Turkey and Greece was delivered on February 21, 1947. On the previous day, a cable had arrived from the three American officials investigating the situation in Greece declaring Greece to be on the verge of a total collapse which would mean a takeover by armed communist bands.[14] American aid was offered, but with the offering the United States asked what was to her the central question: "Which of the two systems currently offered the world is to survive?"[15] Truman's message to Congress announcing aid spelled out the problem.

> At the present moment in world history nearly every nation must choose between alternative ways of life. The choice is too often not a free one.
>
> One way of life is based upon the will of the majority, and is distinguished by free institutions, representative government, free elections, guarantees of individual liberty, freedom of speech and religion, and freedom from political oppression.
>
> The second way of life is based upon the will of a minority forcibly imposed upon the majority. It relies upon terror and oppression, a controlled press and radio, fixed elections, and the suppression of personal freedoms.
>
> I believe that it must be the policy of the United States to support free peoples who are resisting attempted subjugation by armed minorities or by outside pressures.[16]

The Truman Doctrine received its theoretical imprimatur in Kennan's strategy of containment.[17] Kennan saw the political ac-

[14] Jones, p. 131.

[15] Forrestal's words of March 5, 1947, in Millis, *The Forrestal Diaries*, p. 245.

[16] Text in *Department of State Bulletin* (hereafter *DSB*), Vol. XVI, No. 403, March 23, 1947, pp. 534–537.

[17] In the 'X' article on "The Sources of Soviet Conduct," *Foreign Affairs*, July 1947, reprinted in George F. Kennan, *American Diplomacy 1900–*

tion of the Soviet Union as a "fluid stream which moves constantly, wherever it is permitted to move, toward a given goal," but the stream accepted and accommodated itself to unassailable barriers. The answer for the West was to contain Soviet pressure "by the adroit and vigilant application of counter-force at a series of constantly shifting geographical and political points, corresponding to the shifts and maneuvers of Soviet policy." The fruit which this policy might bear for the West, if pursued with sufficient strength and resourcefulness, was the internal decay of Soviet power. Truman depicted a world of two systems and committed the United States to the defense of one of them; Kennan rationalized this commitment in a theory which posited the importance of drawing and holding the line against communism. If the doctrine of containment, which was to become a dominant myth of American foreign policy, was the American acceptance of the principle of the balance of power, it was an extravagant interpretation of that principle.[18]

Intervention was foreshadowed in the theory of containment as its instrument if the line were under threat. But it would be counter-intervention, the application of counterforce to force, action against a movement first and on behalf of one only second, to uphold rather than undermine the independence of states. The Truman Doctrine was even, in Rostow's revealing phrase, part of an American "counteroffensive," not merely holding the line but doing ideological battle beyond it. Yet in the American view this was a response to action not its initiation.[19]

1950, New York, 1952, pp. 89–106, from which the quotations following are taken.

[18] For a critique of Kennan's doctrine and an alternative suggestion for United States foreign policy within the politics of balance, see Walter Lippmann, *The Cold War*, New York, 1947. The suggestion that containment became a dominant myth of American foreign policy does not mean that it excluded other, conflicting or complementary, myths, such as Acheson's "negotiations from strength" or Dulles' "containment plus" or "liberation." Nor did Kennan remain convinced of his theory of internal change in the Soviet Union. See Coral Bell, *Negotiations from Strength*, London, 1962, pp. 25–34.

[19] W. W. Rostow has the Truman Doctrine as the beginning of the American counteroffensive in his *The United States in the World Arena*, New York, 1960, pp. 207–208. James P. Warburg, on the other hand, speaks of "Truman's offensive" and "Stalin's counteroffensive" culminating in the foundation of the Cominform in October 1947. *The United States in the Postwar World*, London, 1966, pp. 43–63. This is entirely plausible, par-

The American response to revolution was itself revolutionary. The American championship of the new order of the United Nations did not bring power politics to an end, but the American perception of this truth did not persuade her to return to the old methods of conducting international politics. Confronting Soviet power everywhere, interpreting the motive of that power as an ideological one, accepting the ideological challenge and responding in kind, the United States turned the relations between states into a struggle about ways of life within them. The Monroe Doctrine had been concerned about the American way of life and the exclusion from it of the old European order—and had implied counterintervention to maintain the exclusion. The Truman Doctrine committed the United States to the logic of counterintervention, not only in the Americas, but all over the world.

II

The specter of international communism, of the intrusion of an alien system into the American Hemisphere, was to lead to a reaffirmation of the Monroe Doctrine by the United States and to the formal acceptance of the doctrine as a hemispheric principle by all members of the inter-American system. But the building of the foundations of hemispheric solidarity had begun in the years before the Second World War and accelerated with its outbreak. It was not at that time a response to the threat of communism. The Havana Meeting of Foreign Ministers in 1940 declared "that any attempt on the part of a non-American State against the integrity or inviolability of the territory, the sovereignty or political independence of an American State shall be considered as an act of aggression against the States which sign this declaration."[20]

When war came to the hemisphere after Pearl Harbor, the practice of the idea of hemispheric solidarity transformed the Good Neighbor Policy into the Good Partner Policy; the policy of "live and let live" changed into "one for all and all for one."[21] A partnership in which the United States was a very senior partner was

---

ticularly from the Soviet viewpoint, and reflects the manner of the American acceptance of the Soviet challenge. But still, to the United States, the Truman Doctrine was the acceptance of a challenge not the issue of one.

[20] Article xv of the Final Act of the meeting, cited in *DSB*, Vol. III, No. 61, August 24, 1940, p. 136.

[21] Roosevelt's words quoted in D. M. Dozer, *Are We Good Neighbors?* Gainesville, Florida, 1959, pp. 112–113.

different from mere propinquity, and the United States requirements for the prosecution of the war prejudiced that scrupulous
adherence to the principle of nonintervention which had characterized the Latin American policy of the Roosevelt administration
in the years before the war. A new awareness of the significance,
for the other American states, of United States action or nonaction,
raised the question of whether her influence, which existed willy-
nilly, should not be employed as a force for democracy and against
dictatorship. Such a policy would have the United States intervening, not merely to hold the ring against undesirable forces from
outside, thereby preserving a negative hemispheric solidarity by
exclusion, but more to infuse that hemispheric solidarity with a
positive ideological oneness.

For a time, the United States government appeared to have
adopted this doctrine. In October 1944 a State Department instruction to embassies in the other American states referred to "a
greater affinity and a warmer friendship for those governments
which rest upon the periodically and freely expressed consent of
the governed."[22] In February 1946 the State Department produced
a memorandum on "The Argentine Situation" disapproving of the
"fascist-totalitarian practices" of the Argentine government and
looking forward to its defeat in the forthcoming elections. This
allowed that government to mount a victorious election campaign
on the slogan "Braden or Perón."[23] Earlier Secretary of State
Byrnes had stated that "the policy of nonintervention in internal
affairs does not mean the approval of local tyranny."[24] Much was
made of the Good Neighbor Policy as "the application of democracy to international affairs."[25] But the most explicit plea for a
democratic hemisphere came from Uruguay, not from the United
States. The Uruguayan Foreign Minister Larreta, in a note to the
other American republics of November 22, 1945, urged that "paral-
lelism between democracy and peace must constitute a strict rule of

[22] Cited in *ibid.*, p. 213.

[23] Perón was the effective head of the government, Braden the U. S.
Ambassador in Buenos Aires. *Ibid.*, p. 215.

[24] "Neighboring Nations in One World," address by Byrnes, October 31,
1945, cited in *DSB*, Vol. xiii, No. 332, November 4, 1945, p. 709.

[25] "The Good Neighbor Policy—An Application of Democracy to International Affairs," address by Truman, March 3, 1947, in *DSB*, Vol. xvi,
No. 402, March 16, 1947, pp. 498–499. This vague phrase could be
stretched from the one extreme of upholding nonintervention as a democratic principle to the other justifying intervention for democracy.

action in inter-American policy."[26] The war, Larreta argued, had demonstrated that the concept of the interdependence of democracy and peace had "acquired the force of an absolute truth." The principle of nonintervention, he said, was not a shield behind which "crime may be perpetrated, law may be violated, agents and forces of the Axis may be sheltered, and binding obligations may be circumvented," and the legitimacy of multilateral action against such situations was not ruled out by the principle of nonintervention. In reply to the Uruguayan note, Secretary of State Byrnes appeared to accept the Larreta Doctrine, citing parts of it with approval, but the parts which were to receive the warmest United States patronage were the advocacy of multilateral action and the taking of such action against threats to security such as the entrenchment of "Nazi-Fascist ideology in the Americas."[27] If opposition to such oppression and support for democracy were but different aspects of the same policy, nevertheless the United States chose to make more of action in response to oppression than of action for the promotion of democracy. The principle of nonintervention was still proclaimed, and it was to apply with particular force to unilateral intervention. Should competing imperatives be deemed prior to the rule, then the proper response was the joint action of the American republics.

This combination of a rule of nonintervention with exceptions justifying collective action was formally expressed in the Inter-American Treaty of Reciprocal Assistance signed at Rio in 1947, and in the Charter of the Organization of American States signed at Bogotá in 1948. Article 15 of the Charter seemed to prohibit intervention absolutely, but its range was narrowed by the statement in Article 19 that measures adopted for the maintenance of peace and security in accordance with existing treaties did not constitute a violation of articles prohibiting intervention.[28] Articles 3

[26] Note published in *DSB*, Vol. XIII, No. 335, November 25, 1945, pp. 864–866, from which the following quotations are taken.

[27] Byrnes' reply in *DSB*, Vol. XIII, No. 336, December 2, 1945, p. 892. For the points emphasized by the United States, see remarks by Assistant Secretary Braden in a radio broadcast "What Is Our Inter-American Policy?" text in *DSB*, Vol. XIV, No. 341, January 6 and 13, 1946, pp. 26–32. Dean Acheson, at this time Under Secretary of State, describes Byrnes in his memoirs as the "sole supporter" of the Larreta Doctrine. *Present at the Creation*, New York, 1969, p. 188.

[28] Article 15 of the Charter of the Organization of American States reads: "No State or group of States has the right to intervene, directly or indirectly,

and 6 of the Rio Treaty constituted the relevant exceptions. In Article 3 the parties agreed that an armed attack on one American state was to be considered an attack on all, and each one undertook to assist in meeting the attack.[29] Article 6 went further to call for a meeting of the Organ of Consultation to agree on the measures to be taken "if the inviolability or the integrity of the territory or the sovereignty or political independence of any American State should be affected by an aggression which is not an armed attack." The peace and security of the hemisphere were now, at least formally, the responsibility of all the American republics and not just of the United States.

The assumption that democracy within American states was a necessary condition for peace between them informed the framing of both the Rio Treaty and the Charter of the Organization of American States. It was part of the idea of continental solidarity. Article 5(d) of the Charter "reaffirmed" the principle that "the solidarity of the American States and the high aims which are sought through it require the political organization of those States on the basis of the effective exercise of representative democracy." More an aspiration than an operative rule, this principle did not presage intervention on the sole ground that an American regime was undemocratic.[30] But the Bogotá Conference was concerned with hostile political movements having their origin outside the hemisphere; "the political activity of international communism" was now condemned and played the role in continental solidarity once filled by "Nazi-Fascist ideology."[31] The Fourth Meeting of Consultation

---

for any reason whatever, in the internal or external affairs of any other State. The foregoing principle prohibits not only armed force but also any other form of interference or attempted threat against the personality of the State or against its political, economic and cultural elements."

[29] For the view that it was official American doctrine that an internal revolution, aided and abetted from outside and involving the use of armed force, constituted an armed attack, see A. A. Berle, *Latin America—Diplomacy and Reality*, New York, 1962, pp. 95–96.

[30] Perhaps all that could be done on the basis of this principle alone was to exclude the offending state from the inter-American system as happened to Cuba in 1962.

[31] The condemnation of communism was contained in Resolution 32 of the Final Act of the Bogotá Conference. The resolution declared in part that "by its anti-democratic nature and its interventionist tendency, the political activity of international communism or any other totalitarian doctrine is incompatible with the concept of American freedom, which rests upon two undeniable postulates: the dignity of man as an individual and the sovereignty of the nation as a state." Cited in U. S. Department of

of Ministers of Foreign Affairs of American States in 1951 spoke of vigorous preparation of military planning for the common defense against the aggressive activities of international communism.[32]

The official reaction of the United States to the perceived threat of an extension of communism to the Americas was spelled out by Assistant Secretary Miller in 1950.[33] Any such attempt at extension in any portion of the hemisphere, Miller said, would be considered "dangerous to our peace and safety." The actions of the United States during the era of protective intervention had "accomplished an objective equally vital to all states of the Western Hemisphere." The difference in 1950 was that the objective would be pursued jointly and not by the United States alone. The doctrine of nonintervention had never proscribed "the assumption by the organized community of a legitimate concern with any circumstances that threatened the common welfare." Such collective action did not represent intervention, rather it was "the corollary of nonintervention."

Miller's statement of the position of the United States was generalized into an inter-American doctrine and brought within the meaning of Article 6 of the Rio Treaty at the Tenth Inter-American Conference at Caracas in 1954. Secretary of State Dulles supervised the passing of a resolution which declared:

> [t]hat the domination or control of the political institutions of any American State by the international communist movement, extending to this hemisphere the political system of an extracontinental power, would constitute a threat to the sovereignty and political independence of the American States, endangering the peace of America, and would call for a Meeting of Consultation to consider the adoption of appropriate action in accordance with existing treaties.[34]

State, *Peace in the Americas: A Résumé of Measures Undertaken Through the OAS to Preserve Peace*, Publication 3964, Washington, D.C., October 1950, pp. 25–26.

[32] In Resolution VIII of the Final Act of the Meeting, *DSB*, Vol. xxiv, No. 615, April 16, 1951, pp. 608–609.

[33] "Non-Intervention and Collective Responsibility in the Americas," address of April 26, 1950, *DSB*, Vol. xxii, No. 567, May 15, 1950, pp. 768–770, from which the quotations following are taken.

[34] In Declaration of Solidarity for the Preservation of the Political Integrity of the American States Against International Communist Intervention," annex A to W. G. Bowdler, "Report on the Tenth Inter-American Conference," *DSB*, Vol. xxx, No. 774, April 26, 1954, pp. 638–639.

Again on the initiative of Dulles, the resolution also stated that the declaration was made in relation to dangers originating outside the hemisphere and was "designed to protect and not to impair the inalienable right of each American State freely to choose its own form of government."

The passage of the resolution, with the one dissenting vote of Guatemala, was a triumph for Dulles. Though Dulles denied it at Caracas, it seemed that the triumph was required in order to legitimize action against the Arbenz regime in Guatemala which not only tolerated the participation of Communists in politics but also had given them important posts in the administration.[35] Between the Caracas Conference in March and the overthrow of Arbenz in June, the United States made much of communist influence in Guatemala and the threat it presented to the hemisphere.[36] As it happened, the successful ouster of Arbenz by Castillo Armas made action according to the American doctrine of collective response unnecessary, but not before a Soviet veto in the Security Council had prevented reference of the matter to the Organization of American States, and the United States had denied the competence of the United Nations.[37] Armas' success, then, was indebted to the impotence of international organization. It owed more to the assistance of the Central Intelligence Agency, both in the training and equipment of Armas' men in Honduras and Nicaragua, and in the execution of the operation.[38]

It seemed that the doctrine of collective response had fallen at the first hurdle, the United States holding that aspect of the Caracas Declaration to be inferior to its anticommunist aspect. When, too late for it to be effective, a meeting of the Council of the Organization of American States was convened, the representative of the United States took the opportunity to paint a dramatic picture of the relentless advance of international communism in the

[35] See P. B. Taylor, "The Guatemalan Affair: A Critique of United States Foreign Policy," *American Political Science Review*, Vol. L, No. 3, September 1956, pp. 792–793. On communism in Guatemala see R. J. Alexander, *Communism in Latin America*, New Brunswick, N.J., 1957, pp. 350–364.

[36] See generally U. S. Department of State, *Intervention of International Communism in Guatemala*, Publication No. 5556 Washington, D.C., August 1954.

[37] Taylor, pp. 798–805.

[38] See D. Wise and T. B. Ross, *The Invisible Government*, New York, 1964, pp. 165–183.

Balkans, in Korea, in South East Asia, and now an attack on the Americas.[39] Dulles spoke of the choice of Guatemala as a "nesting place" for international communism in the Americas, which constituted a direct challenge to the Monroe Doctrine. What concerned him was "not the power of the Arbenz government . . . but the power behind it."[40] Communism in Guatemala was not distinguished from the objectives of international communism, and the United States intervened subversively in Guatemala to overthrow a regime tarred with the brush of the international movement. Officially, the United States represented the Guatemalan affair as a civil war in which Guatemalan patriots arose to challenge the communist leadership.[41] Officially, then, the United States did not need to call upon the Caracas Declaration; unofficially she violated it by taking unilateral action in defense of the Monroe Doctrine.[42]

In Cuba in 1961, the United States followed the precedent established in Guatemala of unilateral intervention against the menace of communism in the Western Hemisphere. Castro's democratic revolution had been "betrayed" to the Communists, American property in Cuba was expropriated in 1960, and Castro had turned Cuba away from the United States to forge political and economic links with the Soviet Union.[43] The Eisenhower Administration, in its last year of office, made the decision to prepare the ground for an invasion of Cuba by anti-Castro exiles, and the Central Intelligence Agency was directing the preparation in Guate-

[39] Statement of U.S. representative J. C. Dreier before OAS Council, June 28, 1954, *DSB*, Vol. xxxi, No. 785, July 12, 1954, pp. 45–47.

[40] "International Communism in Guatemala," address of June 30, 1954, in *ibid.*, pp. 43–45.

[41] Lodge, in the Security Council of the United Nations, argued that it was "clearly a civil war." Contrary to the evidence then available, this seemed to be an attempt "to offer a rationale for O.A.S., rather than U.N., action," Taylor, p. 803. Eisenhower, in his memoirs, admitted U. S. involvement at a crucial stage in the conflict in the form of the supply of aircraft to the insurgents. *Mandate for Change, 1953–1956*, London, 1963, pp. 425–426.

[42] That the Monroe Doctrine remained the doctrinal bulwark against intervention from outside the hemisphere was made clear by Dulles in a news conference statement: "The Declaration of Caracas and the Monroe Doctrine," March 16, 1954, *Intervention of International Communism in Guatemala*, pp. 10–11.

[43] On Castro's ideological evolution and the American reaction see Theodore Draper, *Castro's Revolution*, New York, 1962, particularly section II, pp. 59–113.

mala after the March 1960 decision.[44] From Eisenhower, Kennedy inherited the invasion force and the perception of Castro's regime as an outwork of international communism. Kennedy showed little sign of disapproval of his inheritance. "The United States," he said, "would never permit the establishment of a regime dominated by international communism in the Western Hemisphere."[45] Kennedy had taken up an extreme anti-Castro position in the campaign for the Presidency, a position which seemed to spring as much from personal antipathy for Castro as from its vote-catching potential.[46]

Beyond presidential idiosyncrasy, the conversion to communism of a country so long considered vital to the security of the United States seemed to make a response in Cuba even more important than it had been in Guatemala.[47] In Cuba, moreover, the hold of the Communists was more secure than it had been in Guatemala, and Castro's revolution was more of a beacon to Latin American radicals than its tame counterpart in Guatemala.[48] Nor was Castro content merely to preach by example; his attempts to create the revolution in other American republics seemed to give the United States an excuse for action against him for the matter was now an international one, and not protected by the rule of nonintervention.[49] A State Department White Paper summarized these pressures into a "grave and urgent challenge" which resulted from "the fact that the leaders of the revolutionary regime betrayed their own revolution, delivered that revolution into the hands of powers alien to the hemisphere, and transformed it into an instrument employed with calculated effect to suppress the rekindled hopes of the Cuban people for democracy and to intervene in the internal affairs of other American Republics."[50] Action was not only required but required urgently. The exile brigade was anxious to move, its host, the Guatemalan government, was under domestic

[44] For an account of the build-up to the Bay of Pigs, see Wise and Ross, pp. 23–50.

[45] Quoted in H. L. Matthews, *The Cuban Story*, New York, 1961, p. 225.

[46] Kennedy's "deep feeling against Castro" is noted in Theodore Sorensen, *Kennedy*, London, 1965, p. 341.

[47] See R. Carr, "The Cold War in Latin America," in J. Plank, ed., *Cuba and the United States*, Washington, D.C., 1967, p. 165.

[48] *Ibid.*, p. 165.

[49] On Castro's attempts to create revolution in other American republics see T. Szulc, "Exporting the Cuban Revolution," in Plank, pp. 69–97.

[50] Cited in Draper, pp. 92–93.

pressure to make it move, and Russian military assistance to Castro would soon make his overthrow a technical impossibility.[51] In April the operation began. It was a "perfect failure."[52]

Before the operation, Kennedy, in an announcement which radically narrowed the scope of the doctrine of nonintervention, said that "there will not be, under any conditions, an intervention in Cuba by the United States Armed Forces."[53] In terms of this doctrine, which excluded the possibility of Americans fighting Cubans, it was just possible for Kennedy to assert that "the basic issue in Cuba is not one between the United States and Cuba. It is between the Cubans themselves."[54] But this assertion, by choosing to emphasize the absence of American combat forces, conveniently neglected another possible emphasis on the fact that the exile brigade was "organized, trained, armed, transported and directed" by the Central Intelligence Agency.[55]

After the operation, Kennedy introduced another modification of the doctrine of nonintervention, not necessarily narrowing its scope but questioning that collective response to its violation which had become part of the doctrine in the Rio and Bogotá treaties:

> Any unilateral American intervention, in the absence of an external attack upon ourselves or an ally, would have been contrary to our traditions and to our international obligations. But let the record show that our restraint is not inexhaustible. Should it ever appear that the inter-American doctrine of noninterference merely conceals or excuses a policy of nonaction—if the nations of this hemisphere should fail to meet their commitments against outside Communist penetration—then I want it clearly understood that this Government will not hesitate in meeting its primary obligations, which are the security of our Nation.[56]

Perhaps this was bravado after a disastrous intervention; perhaps again it was merely Dulles' Guatemalan policy made doctrinally explicit; however, Kennedy's reaction to the Cuban

---

[51] Sorensen, p. 329; Draper, p. 99.

[52] Draper, p. 59.

[53] *The Public Papers of the Presidents of the United States, John F. Kennedy, 1961*, Washington, 1962, p. 258.

[54] *Ibid.*, p. 259.

[55] Sorensen, p. 327.

[56] "The Lessons of Cuba," address of April 20, 1961, *DSB*, Vol. XLIV, No. 1141, May 8, 1961, pp. 659–661.

situation made inroads into the twin pillars of the inter-American principle of nonintervention. The absolute prohibition of intervention was now reduced to the exclusion of the commitment of armed forces, and the principle of collective action to uphold the rule was held by the United States to be inferior to an interpretation that "the nations of this hemisphere had failed to meet their commitments against outside Communist penetration."

President Johnson's reaction to the revolution in the Dominican Republic in April 1965 breached Kennedy's Cuban doctrine of abstention from commitment of American armed forces, but it bore out Kennedy's other declaration "that our restraint is not inexhaustible." The democratically elected government of Juan Bosch had been overthrown in September 1963 in a military coup which resulted in a new government under Reid Cabral. On April 24, 1965 a rebellion led by pro-Bosch "constitutionalist" military officers was successful in overthrowing Cabral but failed to gain the support of the majority of the armed forces. This majority opposed the rebellion and was soon dubbed "loyalist."[57] Conflict between the two groups for the Cabral succession continued, their fortunes fluctuating. On April 28 American forces landed and were subsequently heavily reinforced until the establishment of an inter-American force enabled some of them to be withdrawn.

Johnson first justified the intervention on the ground that it was necessary to protect American lives, the United States having been informed by "military authorities" in the Dominican Republic that these were in danger.[58] By April 30 the rationale had extended from the protection of American lives to keeping order. Ambassador Bunker, addressing a Meeting of Consultation of American Ministers of Foreign Affairs, said:

> We are . . . faced with an immediate problem of how to restore law and order in order to protect not only the citizens of foreign countries . . . but also to stop the excessive vandalism which many people are wreaking on their fellow Dominican citizens. . . . We are not talking about intruding in the domestic affairs of other countries; we are talking simply about the ele-

[57] "Loyal" to whom or what was not clear since they were anti-Bosch and did not seek a return of Cabral.

[58] Statement by Johnson, April 28, 1965, *DSB*, Vol. LII, No. 1351, May 17, 1965, pp. 738–739. By "military authorities" Johnson meant the loyalists. He thus seemed to have taken sides in the conflict by deciding to anoint one faction with authority.

mentary duty to save lives in a situation where there is no authority able to accept responsibility for primary law and order.[59]

On the following day, Johnson spoke of United States forces having "the necessary mission of establishing a neutral zone of refuge" in Santo Domingo in the terms called for by the resolution of the Organization of American States.[60]

The first intimation that United States troops had any other function than that of protecting life and keeping order came from Johnson on the same day as Bunker's statement to the foreign ministers. "There are signs," Johnson said, "that people trained outside the Dominican Republic are seeking to gain control."[61] On May 2 these people were Communists and the revolution had taken "a tragic turn."[62] Communist leaders, many of them trained in Cuba, had joined the revolution and taken increasing control so that "what began as a popular democratic revolution . . . was taken over and really seized and placed into the hands of a band of Communist conspirators." "The American nations cannot," Johnson declared, "must not, and will not permit the establishment of another Communist government in the Western Hemisphere."[63] On May 4 Johnson linked the protection of American lives with resistance to communist gains in a statement emphasizing the defensive role of the United States: "We are not the aggressor in the Dominican Republic. Forces came in there and overthrew the government and became alined with evil persons who had been trained in overthrowing governments and in seizing governments and in establishing Communist control, and we have resisted that control and we have sought to protect our citizens against what

[59] Statement of April 30, 1965, cited in *ibid.*, pp. 739–741. Bunker's "elementary duty" of humanitarian intervention could also sound like the assumption of that international police power so despised by Latin Americans in an earlier period of inter-American relations.

[60] Statement of May 1, 1965, cited in *ibid.*, p. 743.

[61] Statement of April 30, 1965, cited in *ibid.*, pp. 742–743.

[62] Statement by Johnson, May 2, 1965, cited in *ibid.*, pp. 744–748, from which the quotations following are taken.

[63] For evidence that the United States, through her embassy, the Central Intelligence Agency, and military attachés in Santo Domingo, had taken an anti-constitutionalist stand from the outset of the revolution, and had worked for the establishment of a military junta in order to prevent a communist takeover, see T. Draper, *The Dominican Revolt*, New York, 1968, pp. 53–65, 72–79, and 97–124. For evidence that the president himself was contemplating armed intervention from the outset see *ibid.*, pp. 80–86.

would have taken place."[64] But it was not just American citizens who were being protected by the intervention, for, Johnson said, "we know that when a Communist group seeks to exploit misery, the entire free American system is put in deadly danger."[65] After the introduction of the anticommunist theme on May 2, there were many variations on it.[66] Even before that introduction, Johnson had defined the goal of the United States in the Dominican Republic as being to permit the people of that country "to freely choose the path of political democracy, social justice and economic progress."[67] Some weeks later, Rusk amended this image to one of defending democracy, rather than making its establishment possible.[68]

The United States defense of her intervention in the Dominican Republic ranged, then, from protection of the lives of nationals, through the maintenance of order, to anticommunism and the safeguarding of democracy. However plausible these justifications in the light of actual American behavior, they had to be brought into line with the conventions of the inter-American system and in particular the principle of nonintervention and the doctrine of collective action in response to its violation. The doctrine of collective action by the Organization of American States was satisfied in part by the creation of an inter-American force to keep the peace in the Dominican Republic. But before the creation of the force, the United States had acted unilaterally "to give the inter-American system a chance to deal with the situation in the Domin-

[64] Remarks of May 4, 1965, *DSB*, Vol. LII, No. 1352, May 24, 1965, pp. 816–822.

[65] Address of May 28, 1965, *DSB*, Vol. LII, No. 1356, June 21, 1965, pp. 989–992.

[66] One variation had it that the revolution had been taken over by the communists necessitating an American response. A later variation was that American intervention had prevented such a takeover. See Rusk's television interview of May 28, 1965, *DSB*, Vol. LII, No. 1355, June 14, 1965, pp. 947–949; Draper, pp. 133–142 and 159–174.

[67] Statement of May 1, 1965, *DSB*, Vol. LII, No. 1351, May 17, 1965, pp. 743–744. The Dominicans, it seems, were to be free to choose political democracy, but not another system.

[68] In a news conference on May 26, he spoke of "extremist elements . . . attempting to capitalize on the anarchy and the disorder to seize control of the mobs and to try to assert a position of power that would destroy the democracy of the Dominican Republic," *DSB*, Vol. LII, No. 1355, June 14, 1965, p. 939.

204

ican Republic."[69] Far from precluding collective action, the United States argued, the continued military presence of the United States served the purpose of "preserving the capacity of the O.A.S. to function in the manner intended by the O.A.S. Charter."[70]

It remained to accommodate the American action to the principle of nonintervention. The Legal Adviser to the State Department argued that the external communist threat to the Dominican Republic was "by no means fancified" and constituted "the very kind of threat" which the Latin American foreign ministers had had in mind when they declared at Punta del Este in 1962 that "the principles of communism are incompatible with the principles of the inter-American system."[71] Apparently unsatisfied with the force of this justification, Meeker went on to belittle "a fundamentalist approach" which might say that "despite the exigencies of the situation on April 28, the doctrine of nonintervention precludes the United States from sending troops into Santo Domingo." Eschewing such "fundamentalism," Meeker urged a look at the facts. If United States troops had withdrawn after the evacuation of citizens, Meeker surmised, there would have been anarchy, no foothold for the Organization of American States, and possibly, another thirty years of darkness for the Dominican Republic.[72] "In the tradition of the common law," he said, "we did not pursue some particular legal analysis or code, but instead sought a practical and satisfactory solution to a pressing problem," and he referred to the role of "experiment and innovation" in the creation

[69] Statement of Ambassador Stevenson to the United Nations Security Council, May 11, 1965, *DSB*, Vol. LII, No. 1353, May 31, 1965, pp. 883–885.

[70] L. C. Meeker, Legal Adviser to the State Department, "The Dominican Situation in the Perspective of International Law," address of June 9, 1965, *DSB*, Vol. LIII, No. 1359, July 12, 1965, pp. 60–65.

[71] This and the quotations following are taken from Meeker's address. His Punta del Este reference was to the Eighth Meeting of Consultation of Ministers of Foreign Affairs in January 1962, which met to "consider the threats that might arise from the intervention of extracontinental powers directed toward breaking American solidarity." The meeting did not urge intervention against communism. It did urge cooperation to strengthen the capacity of the member states to counteract dangers to peace and security "resulting from the continued intervention in this hemisphere of Sino-Soviet powers." Texts of resolutions in *DSB*, Vol. XLVI, No. 1182, February 19, 1962, pp. 278–282.

[72] Having advocated "looking at the facts," then, Meeker proceeded to examine what might have happened, not what did happen.

of international law. This legal defense revealed an impatience with the law as it stood and an admiration for political remedies snatched from beyond the law. In its dependence on the achievement of good purposes, international agreements notwithstanding, the argument resembles the Soviet assertion of higher principles of socialist internationalism prevailing over mere international law.[73]

After the immediate crisis in the Dominican Republic was over, Under Secretary Mann sought to rehabilitate the principle of nonintervention, "thought by some to be an obsolete doctrine" but, in his view, a "keystone of the structure of the inter-American system."[74] He repudiated the view of those who would have the United States intervene—"support," he said, was the word most often used—in favor of political parties of the noncommunist Left, a thesis which "overlooks the fact that countries want to solve their internal political problems in their own way." This explained why, he said, in the case of the Dominican Republic, the United States had refrained during the first days of violence from "supporting" any faction in the conflict, had worked for a cease-fire, and had offered her good offices "rather than . . . proposing political solutions with a 'made in U.S.A.' label on them."[75] Mann's

[73] Wolfgang Friedmann has observed that this sort of American defense comes close to the attempts of Nazi and communist lawyers to justify intervention in terms of a legal order of the future. "United States Policy and the Crisis of International Law," *American Journal of International Law*, Vol. 59, No. 4, 1965, p. 869. At greater length, Thomas M. Franck and Edward Weisband have pointed out the resemblance between the justifications urged by the United States for her interventions in Latin America, and those of the Soviet Union in Eastern Europe. They observe further the similarity of the criticisms directed by each at the other's intervention, so that doctrine becomes interchangeable in what the authors call the "echo phenomenon." *Word Politics: Verbal Strategy among the Superpowers*, New York, 1971. For a discussion of "verbal strategy" see below, Chapter Nine, section II. For a discussion of spheres of influence and their relation to a principle of nonintervention, see below, Chapter Eight, section III, and Chapter Nine, section VI.

[74] In "The Dominican Crisis: Correcting Some Misconceptions," address of October 12, 1965, *DSB*, Vol. LIII, No. 1376, November 8, 1965, pp. 730–738, from which the quotations following are taken.

[75] This assertion of American neutrality was used also by Meeker. If it was true of the "first days of violence," which seems doubtful, it was certainly not true as the intervention continued, for the U. S. had ruled out one faction as communist dominated, and was involved in the "unfinished business . . . of constituting among the Dominicans and by the Dominicans a broadly based provisional government," Rusk, news conference, May 26,

other defense of the doctrine of nonintervention was that action to frustrate the intervention of a communist state was "not so much a question of intervention as it is of whether weak and fragile states should be helped to maintain their independence." The argument seemed to be that the United States had not violated the rule of nonintervention, first, because she had not intervened in the sense of taking sides in the conflict, and second, if it was intervention, then it took place to uphold and not to deny independence.

Clearly, the doctrine of nonintervention had come a long way since the Buenos Aires Conference in 1936. The principle of absolute nonintervention, proclaimed in that year, had developed with the principle of collective responsibility for hemispheric security. During the war, this negative aspect of the doctrine of continental solidarity, negative in the sense that it sought to exclude extrahemispheric threats, so predominated over the rule of nonintervention that the question of the desirability of intervention for democracy was raised, intervention on behalf of ideological unity—continental solidarity in its positive aspect. A common outlook, it was thought, contributed more to good neighborliness than mere noninterference. This doctrine did not prevail. At Bogotá nonintervention was acknowledged to be the rule, democracy the aspiration.[76] If this revealed a reluctance on the part of the American states to commit themselves on what was to be included in the American system, they were not so reluctant to agree on what was to be excluded from it. At Rio the upholding of the Monroe Doctrine was made a multilateral responsibility and as the United States later expressed it, collective intervention was the corollary of nonintervention. It was in the interpretation of this doctrine that the new challenge to nonintervention as a hemispheric principle was to take place. Collective response was a mutually tolerable doctrine so long as the states which had devised the doctrine agreed on the need for its application. To the United States, a superpower doing ideological battle with an extra-

---

1965, *DSB*, Vol. LII, No. 1355, June 14, 1965, pp. 938–947. "By the Dominicans," Rusk said, but it was the United States' unfinished business. On Mann's penchant for constructing the straw man of United States intervention on behalf of left-wing parties in order to destroy it, see Draper, *The Dominican Revolt*, pp. 8–19.

[76] On the legal priority of the rule of nonintervention over intervention for democracy, see Thomas and Thomas, *Non-Intervention*, pp. 362–368.

hemispheric rival, the perception of the need for a response was different from that of the Latin Americans.

From the viewpoint of the United States, the appearance of the rival ideology in the American hemisphere was the intrusion of the rival power in an area to which it did not belong.[77] Communism in Latin America was not an indigenous growth but an outside intervention. Just as the Monroe Doctrine had preached the exclusion of the old European system, so now it was reaffirmed against the alien system of communism. Such a broad apprehension of extrahemispheric intervention suggested an equally broad doctrine of counterintervention to meet it. Guatemala, Cuba, and the Dominican Republic witnessed the application of this doctrine, the response of the United States to a threat perceived to be external. This perception was not always shared by all American states, and the doctrine of collective response suffered accordingly. Worse, action taken, in the view of the United States, to uphold the rule of nonintervention was seen elsewhere in the Americas as its violation. The intrusion of the Cold War into inter-American relations raised once more the dilemmas of the first imperial age of the United States.

III

The Eisenhower Doctrine, proclaimed in a special message to Congress in January 1957, applied Truman's general commitment to the defense of free peoples specifically to the Middle East. Eisenhower proposed that the United States should assist any nation or group of nations "in the development of economic strength dedicated to the maintenance of national independence," undertake programs of military assistance and cooperation with any nation or group of nations which desired such aid, and include in such assistance "the employment of the armed forces of the

[77] See, e.g., Lodge's remarks to the United Nations Security Council during the Guatemalan crisis, June 20, 1954: "Why does the representative of the Soviet Union, whose country is thousands and thousands of miles away from here, undertake to veto a move like that? [the move for OAS rather than UN jurisdiction in the crisis] . . . how can this action of his possibly fail to make unbiased observers throughout the world come to the conclusion that the Soviet Union has designs on the American hemisphere . . . I say to you, representative of the Soviet Union, stay out of this hemisphere. . . ." Quoted in *Intervention of International Communism in Guatemala*, p. 17.

United States to secure and protect the territorial integrity and political independence of such nations, requesting such aid, against overt armed aggression from any nation controlled by International Communism."[78] Eisenhower explained the reason for putting these proposals to Congress to be the deterrent they would provide against communist aggression. "If power-hungry Communists," he said, "should either falsely or correctly estimate that the Middle East is inadequately defended, they might be tempted to use open measures of armed attack. If so, that would start a chain of circumstances which would almost surely involve the United States in military action."[79] Thus the United States proclaimed her military commitment to the balance of power in the Middle East.

In July 1958 President Chamoun of the Lebanon, who had previously endorsed the Eisenhower Doctrine, called upon the United States to honor her commitments under it by landing American troops. Civil strife, grounded in the imbalance between social structure and political institutions, and sparked by the President's attempt to arrange for himself an unconstitutional second term of office, had broken out in the Lebanon.[80] Chamoun's complaint was not only that the rebels were receiving ideological comfort from outside the Lebanon but also that Nasser was aiding them with men, arms, and money.[81] In May his foreign minister had informed the Americans, the French, and the British that military assistance would be expected if required, and later that month the Lebanon took the matter to the United Nations.[82] The response of the Security Council was to dispatch a United Nations Observation Group "to arrest infiltration and arms smuggling" between Syria and the Lebanon.[83] Any hopes for the success of this operation were destroyed by the overthrow of the pro-Western regime in Iraq on July 14, Chamoun's appeal for troops on the same day, and the American military intervention on the day fol-

[78] *DSB*, Vol. xxxvi, No. 917, January 21, 1957, p. 86.

[79] *Ibid.*, p. 87.

[80] See Halpern, "The Morality and Politics of Intervention," in Falk, *Vietnam War and International Law*, pp. 40–45.

[81] *Ibid.*, p. 47, and R. F. Wall, "The Middle East," in G. Barraclough, *Survey of International Affairs 1956–1958*, London, 1962, p. 369.

[82] *Ibid.*, pp. 369 and 371. The American reply to the Lebanese pointed out that the United States was already supplying them with small arms and antiriot weapons. At the same time, though the United States disclaimed any connection with the Lebanese problem, the American amphibious force in the Mediterranean was temporarily doubled. *Ibid.*, pp. 369–370.

[83] *Ibid.*, p. 371.

lowing. The coup in Iraq carried the United States over the brink to which she had been brought by the situation in the Lebanon. The intervention demonstrated American fidelity to that part of the Eisenhower Doctrine which promised assistance to those who requested it. More difficult was the demonstration that it had taken place against overt armed aggression from any nation controlled by international communism.

In the weeks before the landing of American troops, Dulles had gone some way toward accommodating the difficulties presented by these latter two requirements by extending the Eisenhower Doctrine beyond them. He made this possible by choosing to emphasize aspects of the Congressional Resolution on the Middle East—the resolution resulting from Eisenhower's proposals—other than the one requiring that any American response be limited to countering the overt armed aggression of a country controlled by international communism. At a news conference on May 20, Dulles said that he considered such an attack unlikely "under the present state of affairs," but this did not mean that nothing could be done.[84] He referred to a provision in the Middle East resolution saying that "the independence of these countries is vital to peace and the national interest of the United States," which, he argued, was "a mandate to do something if we think that peace and our vital interests are endangered from any quarter." Having asserted such a broad mandate for an American response, Dulles, in subsequent news conferences, discovered another line of argument which did not require its invocation. On June 17 Dulles argued that "even though the disturbance assumes, in part at least, the character of a civil disturbance, it is covered by the United Nations resolution of 1949 on indirect aggression"— which had denounced external fomentation of civil strife.[85] Two weeks later, Dulles completed the circle back to one of the main pillars of the Eisenhower Doctrine by treating indirect aggression as functionally equivalent to armed attack, thereby legitimizing

[84] *DSB*, Vol. xxxviii, No. 989, June 9, 1958, pp. 942–950, from which the quotations following are taken.

[85] *DSB*, Vol. xxxix, No. 993, July 7, 1958, p. 8. At his May 20 news conference, Dulles had asserted the interference of outside powers in Lebanon and called the government of Lebanon as witness for the defense of this assertion, even calling it "the best judge of this matter," *DSB*, Vol. xxxviii, No. 989, June 9, 1958, p. 946. At his June 10 news conference, Dulles had "irrefutable evidence" of UAR intervention in the Lebanon, *DSB*, Vol. xxxviii, No. 992, June 30, 1958, p. 1089.

action in collective self-defense under Article 51 of the Charter of the United Nations. "Now we do not think," he said, "that the words 'armed attack' preclude treating as such an armed revolution which is fomented from abroad."[86]

After the American intervention, Eisenhower's defense of it rehearsed much of the Dullesian argumentation of the previous weeks without spelling out the Dulles line on armed attack and indirect aggression. United States forces had been ordered to the Lebanon, said Eisenhower, "to protect American lives and by their presence there to encourage the Lebanese government in defense of Lebanese sovereignty and integrity."[87] Eisenhower added one significant argument, avoided by Dulles, which very nearly took the case for the defense back to the "international communist" aspect of the Eisenhower Doctrine. It stopped short of naming the enemy and concentrated instead on his methods. "What we now see in the Middle East," Eisenhower said, "is the same pattern of conquest with which we became familiar during the period of 1945 to 1950."[88] He cited the communist activity in Greece, Czechoslovakia, China, Korea, and Indochina as examples of this pattern of conquest—the taking over of a nation by means of indirect aggression—and added mysteriously, "Lebanon was selected to become a victim." At the United Nations, the United States put the case equally strongly. "If the United Nations cannot deal with indirect aggression," said Ambassador Lodge, "the United Nations will break up . . . if the United Nations does not meet this challenge, it will invite subversion all over the world."[89] The purpose of the presence of United States troops, in Lodge's submission, was to stabilize the situation "until such time as the United Nations could take the steps necessary to protect the independence and political integrity of Lebanon."[90]

Arguably, the dropping of anticommunism per se as a ground for American intervention was a doctrinal advance for the United

[86] News conference of July 1, *DSB*, Vol. xxxix, No. 995, July 21, 1958, p. 105.

[87] Statement of July 15, *DSB*, Vol. xxxix, No. 997, August 4, 1958, pp. 181–182.

[88] Radio-television statement of July 15, *ibid.*, pp. 183–186, from which the quotations following are taken.

[89] Third statement of July 16 to the United Nations Security Council, *ibid.*, p. 195.

[90] In address by Lodge, September 28, 1958, *DSB*, Vol. xxxix, No. 1004, September 22, 1958, pp. 448–451.

States beyond a hitherto greater concern with communism than with aggression.[91] But emphasis on the need for counterintervention against indirect aggression was another hornets' nest. The Dulles equation of indirect aggression with armed attack stressed external participation in a civil war rather than its internal sources and dimensions. This involved him in a factual and in a legal controversy: a factual one about the extent of outside participation, a legal one about the sort of response allowable in the light of the answer to the factual question.[92] Eisenhower deepened the controversy by placing the pattern of indirect aggression alongside the pattern of communist conquest. In the Lebanon the practical consequences of American doctrine were not disastrous. The shortcomings of a doctrine which saw no difference between indirect aggression and armed attack, justifying in consequence American counterintervention, were to be revealed in Indochina, where the rationale of preventing indirect aggression and that of stopping communism were joined.

IV

From the outset, the United States considered her involvement in Indochina to be a response to communist aggression. Though the Americans were troubled at the prospect of helping a colonial power to put down a struggle for independence, this was not considered to be the most appropriate interpretation of the conflict in Indochina. Beginning in 1950, American aid to the French was based on the view that the real issue there was "whether the peoples of that land will be permitted to work out their future as they see fit or whether they will be subjected to a Communist reign of terror and be absorbed by force into the new colonialism of a Soviet Communist empire."[93] The conflict was not primarily

[91] Halpern notes that some observers, at the time of the enunciation of the Eisenhower Doctrine, hoped that the United States would take a stand against aggression by any nation in the Middle East and not just those under the control of international communism. *The Politics of Social Change in the Middle East and North Africa*, Princeton, N.J., 1963, p. 386.

[92] On the legal aspect, see Quincy Wright, "United States Intervention in the Lebanon," *American Journal of International Law*, Vol. 53, No. 1, 1959, pp. 112–125.

[93] In address by Assistant Secretary Rusk, November 5, 1951, *DSB*, Vol. xxv, No. 647, November 19, 1951, pp. 821–825.

between French imperialists and Vietnamese nationalists, but between international communism and the free world. The Eisenhower Administration continued the support for the French begun under Truman and, in discussions with France, recognized that "Communist aggressive moves in the Far East obviously are parts of the same pattern."[94] Dulles saw the conflict in Indochina as the southern end of a single Chinese-communist aggressive front which extended to Korea in the north, a front in the attempted communist conquest of freedom.[95] In the following year, when the French were desperately holding the southern front against the Vietminh at Dien Bien Phu, Dulles' Under Secretary Smith referred to the battle as a "modern Thermopylae."[96] Expressed perhaps less apocalyptically and with varying emphasis, this interpretation of the real issue in Indochina as being an international one, not domestic, of global, not local, significance, about the cause of freedom everywhere, not just in Vietnam, informed the reactions of all subsequent administrations to events in Indochina.

Though the mantle of resistance to communist aggression was spread over all the postwar American administrations, their thoughts on the nature of that aggression varied according to what was actually happening in Indochina and according to the way the American response to those happenings was rationalized. Aggression was a word frequently used but loosely defined. It tended to be identified with the mere existence of communism, and in Vietnam, as in Latin America, that existence was not considered to be separable from the parent movement.[97] Spelling out the problem in Indochina after the defeat of the French at Dien Bien Phu, Dulles made the concept of aggression more intelligible. He said that the situation there was not that of "open military aggres-

[94] In the text of United States and French discussions, March 28, 1953, *DSB*, Vol. xxviii, No. 719, April 6, 1953, pp. 441–442.

[95] In address by Dulles, September 2, 1953, *DSB*, Vol. xxix, No. 742, September 14, 1953, pp. 339–342.

[96] In television interview, April 11, 1954, *DSB*, Vol. xxx, No. 773, April 19, 1954, pp. 589–590.

[97] See, e.g., Secretary Acheson's press conference statement, June 18, 1952: "The Communists have made a most determined effort in Indo-China," *DSB*, Vol. xxvi, No. 679, June 30, 1952, pp. 1009–1010. In an address of May 7, 1954, Dulles referred to the conflict in Indochina as a "civil war . . . taken over by international communism for its own purposes," *DSB*, Vol. xxx, No. 777, May 17, 1954, pp. 739–744.

sion by the Chinese Communist regime" but of Chinese fomentation of disturbances in the area.[98] This problem of indirect aggression was not solved for the Americans by the 1954 Geneva Accords formally ending the First Indochina War; it was merely rearranged. The temporary "regrouping zones" for the combatants, agreed upon at Geneva—the Vietminh to the north of the seventeenth parallel, the French Union forces to the south—solidified into *de facto* separate states. It was partly this development, offending as it did against the Geneva expectations, that returned Vietnamese politics to their violent pre-Geneva patterns. A marked increase in the level of communist insurgency toward the end of the decade in South Vietnam forced on the new Kennedy Administration another assessment of the nature of the conflict there.

An assessment by the State Department in Kennedy's first year of office placed the basic pattern of Vietcong activity in South Vietnam in the methodological tradition of communist attempts at takeover established in Malaya, Greece, the Philippines, Cuba, and Laos.[99] It saw the conflict as an attempt by the Vietcong to take over the government of the South supported by an "elaborate organization" in the North. The problem for Kennedy, as it had been for Dulles, was seen to be one of indirect aggression, but the political geography of Vietnam having changed since Geneva, the principal guilt was North Vietnam's not China's.[100] But in Kennedy's view the indirectness of the aggression did not make it any the less aggressive either in objective or in method.[101] He rejected the communist label "wars of national liberation" as a description of the sort of conflict taking place in Laos and Vietnam, because these were "free countries living under their own

[98] In address of June 11, 1954. Excerpt in the United States Senate Committee on Foreign Relations, *Background Information Relating to Southeast Asia and Vietnam*, 3d rev. ed., Washington, D.C., 1967, pp. 48–50.

[99] *A Threat to the Peace: North Viet-Nam's Effort to Conquer South Viet-Nam*, Department of State Publication, 7308. Excerpt cited in Marcus G. Raskin and Bernard Fall, eds., *The Viet-Nam Reader*, New York, 1967, pp. 123–125.

[100] This did not mean that Kennedy perceived the problem as a discrete Vietnamese one. He took careful note of Khrushchev's speech of January 1961 announcing Soviet support for wars of national liberation and directed that all members of his administration read it and "consider what it portended," see Roger Hilsman, *To Move a Nation*, New York, 1967, p. 414.

[101] See his address to the United Nations General Assembly, September 25, 1961, *DSB*, Vol. XLV, No. 1164, October 16, 1961, pp. 619–625, from which the quotations following are taken.

governments." He did not see that such wars were less aggressive because men were "knifed in their homes and not shot in the fields of battle."

As the war continued and escalated, the United States representation of its nature changed in one fundamental respect. A State Department White Paper, *Aggression from the North*, released in February 1965, denied categorically that the war in Vietnam was "a spontaneous and local rebellion against the established government" and affirmed, equally categorically, that "a Communist government has set out deliberately to conquer a sovereign people in a neighboring state."[102] Differences were now found where in 1961 there were similarities between the war in Vietnam and the conflicts in Greece, Malaya, and the Philippines. But it was in the total refusal to admit a domestic dimension to the war in Vietnam that the Johnson Administration departed radically from its predecessors. Though both Johnson and Rusk endeavored to bevel the sharp edges of the change in emphasis by stressing continuity and by making the new revelation retroactive—there all the time but previously unnoticed—the American image of the war was now one of "armed attack" by one state on another and not of external interference in civil strife.

As the United States image of aggression in Indochina developed, so her response to it hardened. The failure of American aid to alleviate the waning fortunes of the French in the First Indochina War brought the United States to the verge of active intervention with air and sea forces.[103] But the enthusiasm of Dulles and the Chairman of the Joint Chiefs of Staff, Admiral Radford, for intervention was tempered by the insistence of congressional leaders that any such action be taken in alliance and not unilaterally.[104] Consequently, Dulles looked for allies who would issue, before the scheduled Geneva Conference, "a solemn declaration of their readiness to take concerted action under Article 51 of the United Nations Charter against continued interference by China

[102] Department of State Publication, 7839, p. 1.

[103] The visit to Washington in March 1954 of the French Chief of Staff, General Ely, to warn the United States that unless she intervened Indochina would be lost, must have evoked memories in Washington of the British handing-over of the Greek and Turkish problem in 1947. Unlike 1947, a doctrine was not produced for South East Asia.

[104] Chalmers M. Roberts, "The Day We Didn't Go to War," in Raskin and Fall, p. 59.

in the Indochina war."[105] The search foundered in London. Dulles preferred to demonstrate strength rather than negotiate from weakness; Eden preferred to rescue by negotiation whatever was possible from a weak situation rather than risk world war in a dubious military exercise. The Geneva Conference met, was accompanied by "distant thunder" from the United States about American and French military action in Indochina, and produced an armistice in Cambodia, Laos, and Vietnam.[106] The American anxiety to establish collective responsibility for the defense of the area was satisfied at Manila, after the Geneva Conference, with the signature of the South East Asia Collective Defense Treaty. Article 4 outlined the action to be taken should aggression by means of armed attack occur in the treaty area, and the consultation which was to take place if the sovereignty and political independence of any party in the treaty area were threatened in any way other than by armed attack.[107] A protocol to the treaty designated Cambodia, Laos and "the free territory under the jurisdiction of the State of Vietnam" for the purposes of Article 4. Thus Dulles had his collective warning against aggression, direct or indirect, in Indochina. A month later, Eisenhower wrote his now-famous letter to

[105] Sir Anthony Eden, *Full Circle*, London, 1960, p. 92.

[106] *Ibid.*, pp. 107–140. See also David Lancaster, "Power Politics at the Geneva Conference 1954," in Marvin E. Gettleman, ed., *Vietnam*, Harmondsworth, 1966, pp. 125–144. The United States did not sign the Geneva Accords. She took note of them and declared that she would "refrain from the threat or use of force to disturb them."

[107] Article 4 of the SEATO treaty reads: "1. Each Party recognizes that aggression by means of armed attack in the treaty area against any of the Parties or against any State or territory which the Parties by unanimous agreement may hereafter designate, would endanger its own peace and safety, and agrees that it will in that event act to meet the common danger in accordance with its constitutional processes. Measures taken under this paragraph shall be immediately reported to the Security Council of the United Nations. 2. If, in the opinion of any of the Parties, the inviolability or the integrity of the territory or the sovereignty or political independence of any Party in the treaty area or of any other State or territory to which the provisions of paragraph 1 of this Article from time to time apply is threatened in any way other than by armed attack or is affected or threatened by any fact or situation which might endanger the peace of the area, the Parties shall consult immediately in order to agree on the measures which should be taken for the common defense. 3. It is understood that no action on the territory of any State designated by unanimous agreement under paragraph 1 of this Article or on any territory so designated shall be taken except at the invitation or with the consent of the government concerned.

Ngo Dinh Diem offering American aid to the "Government of Vietnam."[108]

During Kennedy's Presidency, the number of American military advisers in South Vietnam, under a program begun by Eisenhower in 1955, increased from fewer than a thousand at the end of 1960 to more than sixteen thousand at the end of 1963.[109] For the Kennedy Administration, the problem in Vietnam was one of finding an answer to "subterranean" war, the guerrilla warfare on which the Communists were interpreted to be relying.[110] As Secretary of Defense McNamara expressed it in 1964, the problem was to "cope with Communist 'wars of liberation' as we have coped successfully with Communist aggression at other levels."[111] The administration sought a "strategic concept" which would allow them to cope, and one result of the search was the professional counterinsurgency capability of the Special Forces.[112] Kennedy looked for greater efficiency in closing the guerrilla war gap and increased significantly the number of American advisers in Vietnam, but he stopped short of involving troops in a combat role. This did not happen until 1965 when Johnson's decision to commit such troops, and to bomb the North, transformed the limited commitment of his predecessors to the war in the South into open war between the United States and North Vietnam.[113]

In explanation and justification of her involvement in Vietnam, the United States presented three sorts of arguments—strategic and political, ideological and moral, and legal.[114] Indochina was strategically important because it was said to be the "key to all of Southeast Asia."[115] South East Asia was strategically significant because its "location across east-west air and sea lanes flanks

[108] Text in Gettleman, pp. 214–215.

[109] The exact figures—773 and 16,500—are quoted from the Congressional Record in Draper, *Abuse of Power*, New York, 1967, p. 52.

[110] See Hilsman, pp. 413–416 and Arthur M. Schlesinger, Jr., *A Thousand Days*, London, 1965, p. 471.

[111] In address of March 26, 1964, *DSB*, Vol. L, No. 1294, April 13, 1964, pp. 562–570.

[112] See Hilsman, pp. 424–427.

[113] See Draper, *Abuse of Power*, pp. 62–63.

[114] The arguments are separated for the purposes of analysis. In reality it is not possible to separate them since, for example, American fidelity to a rule of law and willingness to uphold it may be a demonstration of political will as well as one of moral principle.

[115] In address by Assistant Secretary Allison, July 1, 1952, *DSB*, Vol. XXVII, No. 682, July 21, 1952, pp. 97–103.

the Indian subcontinent on one side and Australia, New Zealand, and the Philippines on the other and dominates the gateway between the Pacific and Indian Oceans."[116] The security of the United States would be seriously threatened should the area fall into communist hands.[117] This perceived connection between American security and that of Indochina was strengthened by the domino theory and its variants, which posited the automatic collapse of the remaining states of South East Asia should Vietnam fall to communism.[118] As McNamara put the American position, "to defend Southeast Asia, we must meet the challenge in South Viet-Nam."[119]

By meeting the challenge, the United States was not only defending South East Asia, but also upholding the cause of freedom everywhere. In 1954 Dulles thought "the imposition on Southeast Asia of the political system of Communist Russia and its Chinese Communist ally" would be a grave threat to the "whole free community."[120] For Johnson in 1964, Vietnam was not "just a jungle war, but a struggle for freedom on every front of human activity."[121] Even after the 1968 ceiling was placed on the United States commitment and Nixon's subsequent determination to with-

[116] McNamara's March 26, 1964 address, p. 565.

[117] *Ibid.*

[118] This at any rate was how the author of the theory expressed the "falling domino" theory: "You have a row of dominoes set up, you knock over the first one, and what will happen to the last one is the certainty that it will go over very quickly." News conference of April 7, 1954, *The Public Papers of the Presidents of the United States, Dwight D. Eisenhower, 1954*, Washington, D.C., 1960, p. 383. Two days earlier, Dulles had put the matter in terms of communist intentions: "The large purpose is not only to take over Indo-China but to dominate all of Southeast Asia. The struggle thus carries a grave threat not only to Viet-Nam, Laos, and Cambodia, but also to such friendly neighboring countries as Malaya, Thailand, Indonesia, the Philippines, Australia and New Zealand." Address to House Foreign Affairs Committee, April 5, 1954, *DSB*, Vol. xxx, No. 773, April 19, 1954, pp. 579–582. In 1963 Kennedy declared his belief in the domino theory in terms of the opportunities presented to China if South Vietnam went, in television interview September 9, *DSB*, Vol. xlix, No. 1266, September 30, 1963, pp. 499–500. In a statement of June 2, 1964, Johnson declared the issue in Vietnam to be the "future of Southeast Asia as a whole," *DSB*, Vol. l, No. 1303, June 15, 1964, p. 953.

[119] In March 26, 1964 address, p. 565.

[120] In address of March 29, 1954, *DSB*, Vol. xxx, No. 772, April 12, 1954, pp. 539–542.

[121] Statement of June 2, 1964, *DSB*, Vol. l, No. 1303, June 15, 1964, p. 953.

draw American troops, this universalism persisted. In 1969 Nixon was anxious to avoid the first defeat in American history which, he thought, would result in "a collapse in confidence in American leadership not only in Asia but throughout the world."[122]

In Vietnam the United States was committed to peace as well as to freedom, and the way to peace lay in the defeat of aggression. In 1954 Dulles would not buy peace at the price of surrender.[123] Ten years later, Johnson described America's efforts "in Viet-Nam, in Cyprus, and in every continent" as being directed toward a world order of peaceful procedures rather than forceful settlement.[124] In 1969 Nixon argued that the abandonment of the South Vietnamese people would jeopardize more than lives in South Vietnam, "it would threaten our longer term hopes for peace in the world."[125] Thus the defense of South Vietnam was a demonstration of the American commitment to a peaceful world order, a "concrete demonstration that aggression across international frontiers or demarcation lines is no longer an acceptable means of political change."[126]

[122] Address of November 3, 1969, *DSB*, Vol. LXI, No. 1587, November 24, 1969, pp. 437–443.

[123] In address by Dulles, June 11, 1954. Excerpt in *Background Information*, pp. 48–50. Both Eisenhower and Dulles used analogies from the 1930's in support of the call for united action to check communist expansion in Indochina. Eisenhower wrote to Churchill, April 4, 1954: ". . . we failed to halt Hirohito, Mussolini and Hitler by not acting in unity and in time. That marked the beginning of many years of stark tragedy and desperate peril. May it not be that our nations have learned something from that lesson?" *Mandate for Change*, p. 347. Eden reports that during his talks with Dulles a week later, he was not convinced by the assertion of Dulles' that "the situation in Indo-China was analogous to the Japanese invasion of Manchuria in 1931 and to Hitler's reoccupation of the Rhineland," *Full Circle*, p. 97. On the persistence of this sort of comparison in official American thinking, and in particular Rusk's view, see Schlesinger, *The Bitter Heritage*, London, 1967, pp. 75 and 92–101.

[124] In address of August 12, 1964; excerpt in *Background Information*, pp. 129–130.

[125] In address of May 14, 1969, *DSB*, Vol. LX, No. 1562, June 2, 1969, pp. 457–461. This remained an important theme for Nixon. In 1972, he informed the American people in a television and radio address that they wanted ". . . honor and not defeat. You want a genuine peace, not a peace that is merely a prelude to another war." Address of May 8, *DSB*, Vol. LXVI, No. 1718, May 29, 1972.

[126] In address by Johnson, March 15, 1967, *DSB*, Vol. LVI, No. 1449, April 3, 1967, pp. 534–539.

Apart from this general objection to aggression, the United States was concerned to provide an emphatic answer to the particular form it was taking in Indochina. As General Maxwell Taylor testified before the Senate Committee on Foreign Relations in 1966, "we intend to show that the 'war of liberation,' far from being cheap, safe, and disavowable, is costly, dangerous, and doomed to failure. We must destroy the myth of its invincibility in order to protect the independence of many weak nations which are vulnerable targets for subversive aggression—to use the proper term for the 'war of liberation.' "[127] The United States agreed with General Giap that Vietnam was a test case for wars of national liberation and she was determined to meet the test.[128] The test had to be met in order to deny the "wave of the future" in South East Asia to China and the Communists.[129] It had to be met because "[i]f guerrilla warfare succeeds in Asia, it can succeed in Africa. It can succeed in Latin America. It can succeed anywhere in the world."[130]

To these strategic and political arguments the United States added ideological and moral ones that were held with a tenacity which did much to explain the more elaborate but less fundamental, political and strategic doctrine. Opposition to aggression, the stronger as it was communist aggression, has been noted above as a principle guiding all postwar American administrations. At its most general level, fidelity to this principle stemmed from moral precepts—it did not arise from mere irritation with a disagreeable and alien system of rule. The moral precepts were two and both were illustrated during Eisenhower's presidency. The first held that social relations between individuals should be so arranged as to protect the freedom of the individual, a freedom vaguely defined but thought not to be protected by the communist system. Hence, in 1954, Eisenhower's fear that a partition of Vietnam "would probably lead to Communist enslavement of millions," and the failure of the United States to sign the Geneva

[127] In statement of February 17, 1966, *DSB*, Vol. LIV, No. 1393, March 7, 1966, pp. 356–362.

[128] See; e.g., address by Rusk of April 23, 1965; excerpt in *Background Information*, pp. 156–160.

[129] Kennedy in television interview of September 9, 1963, *DSB*, Vol. XLIX, No. 1266, September 30, 1963, pp. 499–500.

[130] Johnson in address of July 23, 1966; excerpt in *DSB*, Vol. LV, No. 1416, August 15, 1966, pp. 226–228.

Accords which partitioned Vietnam.[131] The second moral precept transposed the first to the relations between states; it held that those relations ought not to interfere with the independence of states and that aggression was just such an interference. Hence, the reiteration by the United States at the final session of the Geneva Conference, of her "traditional position that peoples are entitled to determine their own future."[132] Hence, also, Eisenhower's explanation of the refusal of the United States to respond unilaterally to French pleas for help in Indochina as "our tradition of anticolonialism."[133] On this aspect of the principle of self-determination Eisenhower declared that "[n]ever, throughout the long and sometimes frustrating search for an effective means of defeating the Communist struggle for power in Indochina, did we lose sight of the importance of America's moral position."[134]

As the American involvement in Vietnam continued and deepened, the involvement itself became a moral argument for its continuation. Especially under the Johnson Administration, the involvement became a commitment which it was the duty of the United States to honor.[135] Eisenhower's letter of 1954 offering aid to Diem became the first point in the establishment of a moral obligation to assist South Vietnam. The need to demonstrate that "America keeps her word" became a prominent justification of United States intervention.[136] Explaining, in 1965, why the United States was in Vietnam, Johnson said:

> We are there because we have a promise to keep. Since 1954 every American President has offered support to the people of South Viet-Nam. We have helped to build, and we have helped to defend. Thus, over many years, we have made a national pledge to help South Viet-Nam defend its independence. And

[131] Eisenhower, *Mandate for Change*, pp. 357 and 370–371.

[132] In statement by Under Secretary Bedell Smith at the concluding session of the Geneva Conference, July 21, 1954, in *Background Information*, p. 83.

[133] Eisenhower, p. 373.

[134] *Ibid.*, p. 374.

[135] See Don R. and Arthur Larson, "What Is Our "Commitment" in Viet-Nam?" in Raskin and Fall, *Viet-Nam Reader*, pp. 99–108, for the emergence of the words "commitment," "obligation," and "pledge" to describe the United States relation to Vietnam during the Johnson years.

[136] See Johnson's statement of June 2, 1964, *DSB*, Vol. L, No. 1303, June 15, 1964, p. 953.

I intend to keep that promise. To dishonor that pledge, to abandon this small and brave nation to its enemies, and to the terror that must follow, would be an unforgivable wrong.[137]

In 1969 Nixon echoed the Johnson view. "A great nation," he said, "cannot renege on its pledges. A great nation must be worthy of trust."[138] This conversion of a policy choice into a moral obligation had a similar effect to the interpretation of the Vietnam war of national liberation as a test case; it made the ending of American involvement increasingly difficult.

It was during Johnson's presidency also that the United States addressed herself in circumstances of mounting domestic criticism to an explicitly legal defense of her involvement in Vietnam.[139] The defense relied on the assertion that an armed attack had been inflicted on South Vietnam by North Vietnam. Though it was not clear when exactly North Vietnamese aggression had grown into armed attack, there was "no doubt that it had occurred before February 1965." An armed attack having been asserted if not established, the United States invoked the right, recognized in traditional international law and in Article 51 of the United Nations Charter, to individual and collective self-defense against it. This right was held to exist whether or not South Vietnam was a member of the United Nations, it being an inherent right not conferred by the Charter, and it was held to exist whether or not South Vietnam was an independent sovereign state since there was "no warrant for the suggestion that one zone of a temporarily

[137] In address of April 17, 1965, *Background Information*, pp. 148–153. The commitment itself became an important political, as well as a moral, argument for continuing the war. In John T. McNaughton's view, it became the overriding reason for such continuation—"to preserve our reputation as a guarantor, and thus to preserve our effectiveness in the rest of the world." This, he argued, was much more compelling than helping a friend, or stopping communism, or proving that wars of national liberation did not work. Excerpts from memorandum "Some Paragraphs on Vietnam," January 19, 1966, cited in N. Sheehan, et. al., *The Pentagon Papers*, New York, 1971, p. 492.

[138] In address of May 14, 1969, *DSB*, Vol. LX, No. 1562, June 2, 1969, pp. 457–461.

[139] Meeker, "The Legality of United States Participation in the Defense of Viet-Nam," rept. in Falk, *Vietnam War and International Law*, pp. 583–603, from which the quotations following are taken. This document arose from criticism and led to further controversy. My concern here is to report American doctrine. Some of the controversies will be looked at in Chapter Eight, section III, and Chapter Nine, section VI.

divided state . . . can be legally overrun by armed forces from the other zone." The United States had fulfilled her obligations to the United Nations by reporting to the Security Council on measures taken "in countering the Communist aggression in Viet-Nam" and by submitting the Vietnam question for its consideration in 1966; but the Council had "not seen fit to act."

In Vietnam, the United States was meeting commitments beyond those to the United Nations. By her signature of the South East Asia Collective Defense Treaty the United States was interpreted as having undertaken an international obligation to defend South Vietnam. An armed attack had taken place on a state covered by the protocol to the treaty, and the United States was acting under Article 4(1) "to meet the common danger in accordance with its constitutional processes." In addition to her obligation to the South East Asia Collective Defense Treaty the United States had given other undertakings against any renewal of communist aggression and several assurances of support to the government of South Vietnam.

By reference to the United Nations Charter and to the South East Asia Collective Defense Treaty, the United States asserted a right to act to uphold international law—her references to the Geneva Accords justified its apparent breach. From the very beginning, the United States argued, the North Vietnamese had violated the Accords, and increasing American aid to the South was justified by "the international law principle that a material breach of an agreement by one party entitles the other at least to withhold compliance with an equivalent, corresponding, or related provision until the defaulting party is prepared to honor its obligations." The failure of the South Vietnamese to consult with the North regarding the general elections agreed upon at Geneva was justified on the ground that South Vietnam did not sign the Accords and that conditions in the North were such "as to make impossible any free and meaningful expression of popular will."

The final part of the legal defense asserted presidential authority to commit American troops to Vietnam under the domestic law of the United States. Such action was within the constitutional power of the president; it was his responsibility to decide whether an armed attack had taken place and his responsibility to determine the measures to be taken in reply. In addition, the Joint Resolution of Congress of August 10, 1964, requested by Johnson on the occasion of naval engagements in the Tonkin Gulf which

223

were represented as "further deliberate attacks" by the North Vietnamese regime "against U. S. naval vessels operating in international waters," was taken as authority for the dramatic increase in American involvement during the following year.[140] "The Congress," the defense argued, "has acted in unmistakable fashion to approve and authorize United States actions in Viet-Nam."

The crucial point on which the legal defense relied was the perception of the conflict in Vietnam as an international, not a civil, war, and the related perception that armed attack had taken place, not merely indirect aggression. In December 1966, the Legal Adviser returned to this crucial question.[141] He observed that "some commentators" on Vietnam had set up three categories of situations in their legal analysis of the problem. He thought the first category—"wholly indigenous rebellion"—to be wholly inaccurate. He accepted that the second category—"large-scale intervention from outside short of armed attack"—was probably accurate "for quite some period of time." He considered the third category—"armed attack, in which one country employs its regular military forces to gain control of another country"—to be wholly accurate since the end of 1964. He seemed to concede, though tentatively, that direct action against the intervening power was unlawful in a category two situation, but argued that when an armed attack had taken place "legitimate defense includes military

[140] For Johnson's representation of the Tonkin Gulf incident, see his message to Congress of August 5, 1964, *Background Information*, pp. 120–122. The Congressional Resolution which resulted read in part: ". . . the Congress approves and supports the determination of the President, as Commander in Chief, to take all necessary measures to repel any armed attack against the forces of the United States and to prevent further aggression. . . .

"Consonant with the Constitution of the United States and the Charter of the United Nations and in accordance with its obligations under the South East Asia Collective Defense Treaty, the United States is . . . prepared, as the President determines, to take all necessary steps, including the use of armed force, to assist any member or protocol state of the South East Asia Collective Defense Treaty requesting assistance in defense of its freedom." Text of the resolution in *DSB*, Vol. LI, No. 1313, August 26, 1964, p. 268.

[141] In address by Meeker of December 13, 1966, *DSB*, Vol. LVI, No. 1437, January 9, 1967, pp. 54–63, from which the argument following is taken. The section of Meeker's address looked at here seems to refer to the legal analysis contained in R. A. Falk, "International Law and the United States Role in the Vietnam War," *Yale Law Journal*, Vol. 75, No. 7, June 1966, pp. 1122–1160.

action against the aggressor." Thus the bombing of the North was regarded as legitimate, and the domestic dimension of the war was legally ignored since late 1964.

The principle of nonintervention as such was not mentioned in the legal defense of American involvement in Vietnam whether to extol its virtues or to deny its relevance. American intervention in Asia, unlike her intervention in Latin America, did not have to come to terms with a deep-rooted doctrine of nonintervention. Moreover, as Nixon put it in 1969, "we no longer have the choice of not intervening . . . the urgent question today is what to do now that we are there."[142] The choice had been made long before. In 1954 the doctrine of nonintervention, in its Cobdenite sense, had been found inferior to the competing imperative of restraining communist aggression, and since that time the question was not again asked in the stark terms of intervention or nonintervention. Yet, if the doctrine of nonintervention is understood in Mill's sense, the whole of the history of American intervention in Vietnam can be read as the history of counterintervention to uphold the principle of nonintervention, the invocation of self-defense against armed attack, the commitment to the South East Asia Collective Defense Treaty and the rest being but the elaboration of this primary obligation.

If counterintervention were the rationale, it might have been expected that the American combat commitment would come to an end when intervention from the North had been effectively neutralized. And it was the appearance, at least, of such an achievement, that the United States attempted to portray in the Cease-Fire Agreement signed in Paris on January 27, 1973. Thus, in the agreement, the South Vietnamese people's right to self-determination is held to be sacred, inalienable, and requiring the respect of all countries, and foreign countries are not to "impose any political tendency or personality on the South Vietnamese people."[143] If

[142] In address of May 14, 1969, *DSB*, Vol. LX, No. 1562, June 2, 1969, pp. 457–461.

[143] Chap. IV, Articles 9(a) and 9(c) of the Agreement as reported in *The New York Times*, January 25, 1973. These provisions have to be read, however, in the context of Article I of Chap. I, which declares that "[t]he United States and all other countries respect the independence, sovereignty, unity and territorial integrity of Vietnam as recognized by the 1954 Geneva Agreements on Vietnam," and of Article 4 of Chap. II, which baldly announces that "[t]he United States will not continue its military involvement or intervene in the internal affairs of South Vietnam."

this use of the formula of self-determination arguably was dictated by the need for a certain ambiguity that a declaration of the sovereignty of South Vietnam would not provide,[144] there is one sense in which the agreement presses beyond any idea of simply restoring South Vietnamese sovereignty. In requiring that "[t]he South Vietnamese people shall decide for themselves the political future of South Vietnam through genuinely free and democratic general elections under international supervision," Article 9(b) of Chapter IV seems to suggest that the conflict had a positive aspect—war for democracy—besides the negative aspect of war against intervention.

If the Cobdenite doctrine of nonintervention was overruled early in the piece, the doctrine of counterintervention to uphold the principle of nonintervention offered little more for the guidance of policy beyond pointing out that a supposedly foreign intrusion had to be neutralized. In practice, a third sense of the doctrine of nonintervention imposed itself on American policy-makers—in requiring a calculation of what latitude the South Vietnamese government was to have in the everyday conduct of its affairs. For though the United States had intervened or counterintervened, she had not taken over the government of the country, and thus the question of how much of an independent voice the Saigon regime was to have in South Vietnamese affairs was of crucial importance. Sometimes, this dimension of the doctrine of nonintervention meant simply that the United States had an excuse for choosing not to exercise an unfavorable option in Saigon politics.[145] The same dimension of the doctrine was also available, to Saigon politicians when the United States was thought to have trespassed on matters internal to South Vietnam.[146] But apart from such use

[144] Dr. Kissinger's news briefing of January 24, 1973, seems to bear out this point. Kissinger drew attention to Articles 14, 18(e), and 20 of the Agreement, which "have specific references to the sovereignty of South Vietnam," as if to buttress a position known to be weak—the references to sovereignty in the places mentioned being *en passant*, and apparently not deserving of an article to themselves like the right to self-determination. For the text of the briefing see *The New York Times*, January 25, 1973.

[145] Thus Chester L. Cooper recounts how he fended off a Vietnamese request, on New Year's Eve 1964, that General Khanh be dropped, by declaring that "the United States Government did not wish to intervene in the internal politics of Saigon even if it had the knowledge and ability to do so." *The Lost Crusade*, New York, 1970, p. 252.

[146] Thus, when the United States was anxious to acquire information about the potential for success of a general's plot against Diem in 1963,

as a tactical device, this version of the doctrine of nonintervention stood as a permanent reminder of the problem of deciding to what extent policy in Vietnam could be determined in Washington, of how far the Saigon regime was to be left alone to do as it would within its own "proper" domain.[147]

There is a fourth sense in which the rule of nonintervention seemed to have meaning in official American doctrine with regard to Vietnam. Rather like Kennedy and Cuba in 1961, it drew a line around the limits of the American commitment. Kennedy's disillusionment with Diem led him to say on September 2, 1963: "I don't think that unless a greater effort is made by the Government [of South Vietnam] to win popular support that the war can be won out there. In the final analysis, it is their war. They are the ones who have to win it or lose it. We can help them, we can give them equipment, we can send our men out there as advisers, but they have to win it—the people of Viet–Nam—against the Communists."[148] In 1968, when Johnson announced the limited but unconditional cessation of the bombing of the North, he returned to this theme by remarking that, "[o]ur presence there has always rested on this basic belief: The main burden of preserving their freedom must be carried out by them—by the South Vietnamese themselves."[149] Under the Nixon Administration, these earlier utterings solidified into a Nixon Doctrine. Though not always stated with the utmost clarity, the doctrine suggested that in future wars of the Vietnam type, the United States would expect the states in which they occurred to bear the main burden of their own defense, and would limit her support to military and economic assistance if such were requested.[150] This expectation of in-

General Tran Van Don, for fear of an American leak, "made it clear many times that this is a South Vietnamese affair." Cablegram from Ambassador Lodge to McGeorge Bundy, October 30, 1963, cited in Sheehan, *The Pentagon Papers*, p. 226.

[147] For awareness of this problem, if also for different reactions to it, see cablegram from Ambassador Durbrow to Secretary of State Herter, September 16, 1960, cited in Sheehan, pp. 115–118; cablegram from McGeorge Bundy to Lodge, October 30, 1963, cited in Sheehan, pp. 230–231.

[148] In television interview, *DSB*, Vol. XLIX, No. 1266, September 30, 1963, pp. 498–499.

[149] In address of March 31, 1968, *DSB*, Vol. LVIII, No. 1503, April 15, 1968, pp. 481–486.

[150] As Nixon described his Doctrine in an address of November 3, 1969, it had three elements: "First, the United States will keep all of its treaty commitments. Second, we shall provide a shield if a nuclear power threatens

creased local responsibility, sketching an American foreign policy for the future, was also applied to Vietnam in the present. "Vietnamization"—the respectable term for American withdrawal—had an interesting history during 1970 and early 1971. In the early summer of 1970, American and South Vietnamese troops were used in an attack on Vietcong base areas in Cambodia, thereby allowing, in the United States view, the withdrawal to go ahead as planned. In February 1971 a similar operation in Laos took place without American ground forces, the American participation being limited to logistics and air support.[151] The importance attributed to not committing combat troops was reminiscent of the days before Johnson.

The Nixon Doctrine of partial disengagement, casting doubt on the inevitability of United States intervention wherever the old line of containment was breached or threatened, was framed with regard to relations with small powers, but allowed, or was concurrent with, a normative reconciliation at the level of superpower relations. Thus the United States could agree with the People's Republic of China that regardless of their social systems, they should conduct their relations "on the principles of respect for the sovereignty and territorial integrity of all states, non-aggression against other states, non-interference in the internal affairs of other states, equality and mutual benefit, and peaceful coexistence."[152] Similarly, at Moscow in May 1972, the United States and the Soviet Union agreed to "proceed from the common determination that in the nuclear age there is no alternative to conducting their

---

the freedom of a nation allied with us or of a nation whose survival we consider vital to our security. Third, in cases involving other types of aggression, we shall furnish military and economic assistance when requested in accordance with our treaty commitments. But we shall look to the nation directly threatened to assume the primary responsibility of providing the manpower for its defense." *DSB*, Vol. LXI, No. 1587, November 24, 1969, p. 440.

[151] At a news conference on July 30, 1970, Nixon had stated that air power would be used in Laos to interdict the flow of enemy supplies down the Ho Chi Minh trail, but that there was "no intention of using ground forces." *DSB*, Vol. LXIII, No. 1625, August 10, 1970, p. 164. For a strong statement of the limits of the United States commitment, again in terms of when and where ground forces were not to be used, see Nixon's news conference, February 17, 1971, *DSB*, Vol. LXIV, No. 1654, March 8, 1971, p. 281.

[152] Text of communiqué, Shanghai, February 27, 1972, in *DSB*, Vol. LXVI, No. 1708, March 20, 1972, pp. 735–738.

mutual relations on the basis of peaceful coexistence." Ideology was no bar to the bilateral development of normal relations on this basis, and, moreover, the two powers looked beyond their mutual relations in reassurance and warning that they would neither make nor recognize claims to special rights or advantages in world affairs, since they recognized the sovereign equality of all states.[153] Nonintervention seemed thus a principle of *détente* as well as of disengagement, and also a norm whose proclamation acknowledged the existence of a link between them. In Vietnam the realization that there were limits to intervention demonstrated some awareness that the conflicts of others were not necessarily within the power of the United States to resolve, that the military solution of counterforce was not always applicable, and that there were areas in the lives of other states beyond American control. The 1973 Cease-Fire Agreement, a witness to this realization, was also a derivative of and a contribution to a more relaxed relationship between the United States and the two great Communist powers.

V

Truman's proud declaration, in the spring of 1947, that it must be the policy of the United States to support free peoples resisting attempted subjugation by armed minorities or by outside pressures did not ossify in the tradition of statements made to justify a particular act of foreign policy, but developed and became the theme, even the cliché, of American foreign policy. The doctrine came of age when, shortly after taking office as secretary of defense, and playing an important part in reversing the direction of American policy in Vietnam, Clark Clifford restated the Truman vision and applied it to Asia. Of the American involvement in Vietnam, he said:

> We are assisting that brave and beleaguered country to fight aggression, under the S.E.A.T.O. Treaty—and for the same reason that we extended our aid to Greece and Turkey over 20 years ago. This is in the tradition of the Truman doctrine, which announced 20 years ago that we would help defend the liberty of peoples who wished to defend themselves. . . . The America that brought N.A.T.O. into being is the same America support-

---

[153] Text of Basic Principles, May 29, 1972, *DSB*, Vol. LXVI, No. 1722, June 26, 1972, pp. 898–899.

ing freedom in Asia today—and for the Asians, not for the Americans.[154]

Following the Truman theme meant forcible counterintervention in the last resort if freedom were thought to be under a threat irremediable by other means. But the use of force did not always seem to be a last resort. Though the commitment of American troops, or the clandestine support for armed exile bands, was always motivated and explained by the need for a response to communist aggression, or to aggression from which only the communists could benefit, its timing or execution frequently laid the United States open to the charge that she was violating rather than upholding the principle of nonintervention; that, of the intervening powers, she was the "more guilty." Thus preventive intervention against the spread of communism in Latin America left the burden of proof of the existence of Communists on the United States, which led to charades like the hunt for Communists in the Dominican Republic, and presented the United States as the imperial power she so fervently declared that she was not. The manner of American counterintervention in Vietnam, the eventual Americanization of the war, seemed to make nonsense of the claim that the United States was protecting independence, not destroying it. Vietnam demonstrated the limits of the Truman theme: that overprotection of freedom might mean its extinction if indeed freedom was there to be protected in the first place. It demonstrated that there was perhaps a kernel of good sense in the Cobdenite doctrine of nonintervention despite the inescapable logic of Mill's position.

The responsibilities of world power, the pressures of the Cold War, led to an American frustration with the law which had always been the doctrinal prop of the United States in international relations. Sometimes this took the form of irritation with the traditional rules of international law. Assistant Secretary Cleveland made a picturesque assault on these in 1961:

> So long as we think of relations between nations, we are schooling ourselves to deal with the War of Jenkins's Ear. . . . In the 18th and even the 19th century we could describe a country as

[154] In address of April 22, 1968, *DSB*, Vol. LVIII, No. 1507, May 13, 1968, pp. 605–607. The restatement of the old carried the germ of the new—the emphasis on self-help.

either friendly or an enemy. . . . We had trouble with governments from time to time but the definitions held. How do we describe Cuba, Laos and the Congo today? By our relations with the embodiment of the nation's sovereignty? Of course not. These countries are the marchlands of mutual intervention. We have friends and we have enemies in each. Yet when we seek to aid the one or oppose the other, we too often find ourselves caught in a conceptual traffic jam created by our inherited concepts of international law, while Communist guerrillas rush past us in the fast outside lane. . . . Perhaps they [international organizations] alone offer breakthrough possibilities in rethinking the old doctrine of non-intervention in the domestic affairs of other nations. This doctrine has been the self-denying ordinance under which the democracies have labored throughout the 20th century, an unenforced international Sullivan Law that disarms the housholder but never bothers the burglar.[155]

Meeker's defense of American intervention in the Dominican Republic in terms of the creation of new law was a less persuasive development of Cleveland's sort of argument. Rusk was perplexed in a different way: not with the unreasonable restraints of traditional international law in a revolutionary age, but with an equally revealing concern that the United States was being pilloried for upholding the law, for too rigid an insistence on legal methods in international relations. "Current United States policy," he said in 1965, "arouses the criticism that it is at once too legal and too tough. . . . Today, criticism of American attachment to the role of law is that it leads not to softness but severity. . . . We are criticized for acting as if the Charter of the United Nations means what it says . . . for taking collective security too seriously."[156] Thus exasperation with the traditional doctrine of nonintervention, which the United States herself had played an important part in contributing to the body of rules guiding international relations, was coupled with a feeling of hurt innocence at criticism of an America that was upholding the rule in spite of herself. The comfortable nineteenth-

[155] In address of May 7, 1961, *DSB*, Vol. XLIV, No. 1145, June 5, 1961, pp. 858–862.

[156] In address of April 23, 1965, *DSB*, Vol. LII, No. 1350, May 10, 1965, pp. 694–701. Rusk, in fact, took comfort from this criticism, interpreting it as a sign of American strength, "a tribute to a blending of political purpose with legal ethic."

231

century doctrine of nonintervention according to an anarchical American view of international society, became distinctly uncomfortable in the age of American world power and concern for a managed world order. The Nixon Doctrine, while not a doctrine of nonintervention, is perhaps a recognition that to abanon nonintervention is as uncomfortable as to adhere to it.

SEVEN

DOCTRINES OF NONINTERVENTION
AT THE UNITED NATIONS

Whether as a rule which had to be taken into account in the framing of foreign policy, as a malleable political slogan which was thought to advance the purposes of foreign policy, as a statement of a preferred pattern of conduct in international relations, or, as is most likely, a mixture of each, nonintervention was an important doctrine for both the United States and the Soviet Union. If the debates in the General Assembly of the United Nations and the resolutions passed by that body are any guide, it was no less important for the remainder of the states of the international community. But if a consensus existed about the importance of the principle of nonintervention, there was less agreement beyond generalities about its definition and range of application, about the sorts of behavior it proscribed.

This chapter will examine the history of the principle of nonintervention at the United Nations from its place, if any, in the Charter, to its acceptance by the General Assembly in 1970 as one of seven principles of international law concerning friendly relations and cooperation among states. From an analysis of the place of the rule in the Charter, the chapter will go on to highlight the issues in the political and legal debate on nonintervention in the General Assembly. It will next examine the case of *apartheid* in South Africa as the perhaps notorious example of the limits of the nonintervention principle, or indeed of its erosion. Finally, an attempt will be made to discern any patterns in the views expressed by states about the principle and to assess the legal status and political significance of the Assembly's espousal of the principle. But the primary focus of attention will be on states' doctrines of nonintervention at the United Nations and not on the United Nations' doctrine. It will be on the United Nations as a forum and not as an actor. In addition, the application of the principle of nonintervention to the United Nations as an independent political force in international politics, as for example to its role in the Congo, will not be considered here except as it emerges from the views of individual states.

233

I

Nowhere in the Charter is the principle of nonintervention explicitly laid down as a rule governing the relations between the members of the United Nations. The closest the Charter comes to embracing such a rule is in Article 2, which sets out the principles that are to guide the actions of the organization and its members. Article 2(4) requires all members to "refrain in their international relations from the threat or use of force against the territorial integrity or political independence of any state, or in any other manner inconsistent with the Purposes of the United Nations." Territorial integrity and political independence were protected by disallowing the use of force against them. They were further protected by the phrase "in their international relations," which precluded the use of force between states but not within them, upholding thereby state sovereignty as a principle of domestic order.[1] But despite its prohibition of the use of force in international relations, Article 2(4) is not quite a principle of nonintervention. Territorial integrity and political independence can be impaired by actions not directly involving the threat or use of force.[2] Further, territorial integrity—preserved so long as none of the territory of the state is taken from it—is not the same thing as territorial inviolability—"the right of a state to exercise exclusive jurisdiction within its own territory."[3] It was in the gray areas beyond the use of force and beyond the concept of territorial integrity that much of the United Nations debate about intervention was to center. Indeed, for many of the members of the United Nations, intervention was to become a word used to describe the sorts of behavior not covered by Article 2(4) and hence nonintervention a rule not to be found there.

Article 2(7) of the Charter declares that "nothing contained in the present Charter shall authorize the United Nations to intervene in matters which are essentially within the domestic jurisdiction of any state or shall require the Members to submit such

[1] See L. M. Goodrich and E. Hambro, who argue that the principle "does not prevent a state from using force within its metropolitan area . . . nor . . . in suppressing a colonial disorder." *Charter of the United Nations*, 2d ed., London, 1949, p. 103.

[2] Goodrich and Hambro argue that the obligation of the paragraph is not directed against "economic and psychological methods" of coercion, *ibid.*, p. 104.

[3] These definitions are in *ibid.*, p. 105.

matters to settlement under the present Charter; but this principle shall not prejudice the application of enforcement measures under Chapter VII." Here is a principle of nonintervention, but it was to apply to relations between the United Nations as an organization and its several members, and not to relations between the members themselves.[4] Ostensibly, an analysis of Article 2(7) raises questions similar to those involved in an analysis of the principle of nonintervention as it applies to the relations between states. Light might be shed on the principle in both these aspects by an examination of the definition of intervention and of the scope of domestic jurisdiction. But the two are not identical. It may be that the concept of intervention, as it applies to the United Nations, refers to a different range of activity from its application in interstate relations. Whether, for example, General Assembly resolutions amount to intervention is not a question relevant to the examination of intervention between states. Again, it might be that intervention by the United Nations, being the action of the international community, will not carry the same legal or moral opprobrium as the unilateral intervention of a state in another's affairs.[5] Similarly, the frontier drawn around the principle of domestic jurisdiction may be pushed back further when considered in relation to the activity of the United Nations than it is when considered in the context of the relations between states. These considerations apart, the principle of nonintervention as laid down in Article 2(7), fits into a solid tradition of thought about the purpose of the principle in international relations. It echoes Canning's suspicion of the "European Areopagus," it seeks to preserve the sovereignty of the state against the emergence of a superstate, even if the latter be a benign United Nations and not a malevolent Holy Alliance.[6]

[4] See Kelsen, *The Law of the United Nations*, p. 770. This interpretation of the principle was a matter of some controversy in the General Assembly, where some states argued that the restriction on the competence of the United Nations applied a fortiori to its members. See the following sections.

[5] Rajan makes a similar point in *United Nations and Domestic Jurisdiction*, p. 93, n. 1.

[6] For some writers this is a matter for regret. Alf Ross argues that the "idea behind Article 2(7) is an interest in preserving international law at its present stage and opposing a further development of it through the efforts of the United Nations to regulate those things which are now abandoned, in anarchistic fashion, to the struggle for political power.

"It is not difficult to determine which group of states is interested in

If the principle of nonintervention between states is nowhere explicit in the Charter, it is, in the statement of Principles, everywhere implicit. Article 2(1) bases the organization on the "principle of the sovereign equality of all its Members." Article 2(3) demands the peaceful settlement of international disputes, and Article 2(4) requires states to refrain in their international relations from the threat or use of force. This concern with the "international," not with the "domestic," was emphasized by Dulles at the San Francisco Conference. Dulles thought the domestic jurisdiction principle necessary to the delineation of the function of the United Nations as an "organization which deals essentially with the governments of member-states, and through international relations," and not one "which is going to penetrate directly into the domestic life and the social economy of each one of the member-states."[7] Evatt, the leader of the Australian delegation at San Francisco, in proposing that the exception to the principle of domestic jurisdiction be limited to "the application of enforcement measures," argued that it was desirable to give states that were not members of the Security Council some of the protection against interference in domestic affairs which the permanent members enjoyed under the Security Council voting procedure.[8]

The Charter, then, was primarily concerned with building an order between states not within them, with eliminating international war not civil conflict.[9] Its concern with human rights and fundamental freedoms, values whose defense would require an intrusion into a traditionally domestic matter, was more aspiration than legislation. It appears in the statement of the Purposes of the United Nations, and not of its Principles. In the subsequent history of the United Nations, written against the background of the popular doctrine that the distinction between domestic and international politics was subject to increasing erosion, two apparently

---

this. The major powers alone can reap benefit from asserting the sovereignty principle and lawlessness at the expense of the competence of the United Nations to adjust disputes and a further development of international law. From a legal point of view, Article 2(7) is *the quintessence of the tendency of the sovereignty dogma to resist progress." Constitution of the United Nations*, Copenhagen, 1950, p. 129 (Ross' emphasis).

[7] Quoted in Rajan, p. 56.

[8] See Goodrich, "The United Nations and Domestic Jurisdiction," *International Organization*, Vol. III, 1949, pp. 18–19.

[9] See Linda B. Miller, *World Order and Local Disorder*, Princeton, N.J., 1967, pp. 21–22.

contradictory developments took place. On the one hand, a movement led by the communist states and taken up with enthusiasm by the new states, perceiving a world visited frequently by interventionary politics, sought to close a gap in the Charter by making the implicit principle of nonintervention explicit. On the other hand, the same movement placed limits on the rule. A new legitimacy developed, proclaiming nonintervention but insisting first on an end to colonialism in all its manifestations. The sections following will examine the working out of these doctrines at the United Nations.

II

In 1949 with the Essentials of Peace Resolution of the General Assembly and again in 1950 with the Peace Through Deeds Resolution, the implicit noninterventionism of the Charter began to be made explicit in the practice of the United Nations.[10] The Essentials of Peace Resolution called upon every nation to *"refrain from any threats or acts, direct or indirect, aimed at impairing the freedom, independence or integrity of any State, or at fomenting civil strife and subverting the will of the people in any State."* The Peace Through Deeds Resolution condemned the "intervention of a State in the internal affairs of another State for the purpose of changing its legally established government by the threat or use of force," and went on to solemnly reaffirm that "whatever the weapons used, any aggression, whether committed openly, or by fomenting civil strife in the interests of a foreign Power, or otherwise, is the gravest of all crimes against peace and security throughout the world." Both resolutions were passed at the end of debates on an item, included in the agenda of the General Assembly by the Soviet Union, which would have had the Assembly declare against the preparation and threat of a new war and for the strengthening of peace. The Soviet draft resolutions, principally vehicles for the criticism of the West, were opposed by Western drafts, eventually to be accepted by the Assembly which made more general statements about the requirements of peace while including a Western version of the objection to intervention. Neither of the resolutions was a conscious exercise in Charter "gap-filling." Both were concerned to restate Charter principles

[10] General Assembly Resolutions 290(IV) of December 1, 1949, and 380(V) and 381(V) of November 17, 1950.

and to point them in the direction of that intervention which threatened to undermine them.

In 1957 a Soviet initiative to have the Assembly consider a Declaration Concerning the Peaceful Coexistence of States was more successful than its earlier declamations against Western preparation for war because the resolution adopted after debate in the Assembly was not unlike the Soviet draft which was not pressed to a vote. The draft resolution adopted by the Assembly was sponsored jointly by India, Sweden, and Yugoslavia. It realized the need to develop peaceful and tolerant relations among states, in conformity with the Charter, "based on mutual respect and benefit, non-aggression, respect for each other's sovereignty, equality and territorial integrity and non-intervention in one another's internal affairs, and to fulfil the purposes and the principles of the Charter."[11] Thus the *Pancha Shila* entered the vocabulary of the United Nations, but the resolution did not make it clear whether the entry restated Charter principles or added to them.[12] It had it both ways; it called upon states "to develop co-operative relations and settle disputes by peaceful means as enjoined in the Charter of the United Nations and as set forth in the present resolution."

In 1965, again at the request of the Soviet Union, the question of "[t]he Inadmissibility of Intervention in the Domestic Affairs of States and the Protection of their Independence and Sovereignty" was considered by the General Assembly. Once more, a Soviet draft resolution on the matter was not adopted by the Assembly, but many of its ideas were incorporated in the draft declaration which was adopted, a draft sponsored by 57 powers, mainly from Asia, Africa, and Latin America.[13] It's preambular paragraphs expressed the Assembly's concern at the threat to universal peace

[11] From General Assembly Resolution 1236(xii) of December 14, 1957.

[12] "Filling gaps" or "adding to" or "going beyond" the Charter are expressions used loosely here to describe Assembly resolutions which recommend that states behave in ways not strictly demanded of them in the Charter. Whether such resolutions impose obligations on states, whether the Assembly is the proper place for Charter revision, or whether its resolutions add anything to general international law are matters of legal controversy which will be touched on in the course of this chapter, and returned to in its conclusion.

[13] For the text of the declaration, Resolution 2131(xx) of December 21, 1965, see Appendix a. Only Cyprus, Trinidad and Tobago, and Yugoslavia of the sponsors did not fit the Asia-Africa-Latin America category geographically. It was a "Third World" draft. On the use of this term see section iii of this chapter.

due to intervention; equated armed intervention with aggression; considered that direct intervention, subversion, and all other forms of indirect intervention constituted a violation of the Charter of the United Nations; and recognized that full observance of the principle of nonintervention was "essential to the fulfilment of the purposes and principles of the United Nations." The preamble added doctrinal support to these assertions of the importance of the principle, and the gravity of its violation, by reaffirming the principle as it appeared in the charters of the Organization of American States, the League of Arab States, and the Organization of African Unity, and as it was affirmed by various international conferences—of American states and of the Third World. The particular importance of the principle to countries which had "freed themselves from colonialism" was emphasized, and, straying from the path marked out by the traditional doctrine of nonintervention, the preamble stressed the place of the principle of self-determination in the constitution of the United Nations and in subsequent General Assembly doctrine.

The first operative paragraph of the declaration borrowed, with minor changes, the statement of the principle of nonintervention from the most ambitious source—Article 15 of the Charter of the Organization of American States. The second operative paragraph borrowed again from that Charter to disallow economic and political methods of coercion. Not content with these broad prohibitions the same paragraph went on to declare that "no State shall organize, assist, foment, finance, incite or tolerate subversive, terrorist or armed activities directed towards the violent overthrow of the regime of another State, or interfere in civil strife in another State." Another paragraph included the "use of force to deprive people of their national identity" in the activities proscribed by the principle of nonintervention. The sixth operative paragraph stated that "all States shall respect the right of self-determination and independence of peoples and nations, to be freely exercised without any foreign pressure, and with absolute respect for human rights and fundamental freedoms. Consequently, all States shall contribute to the complete elimination of racial discrimination and colonialism in all its forms and manifestations." Clearly, this declaration went well beyond not only the obligations of the Charter, but also beyond the most comprehensive of the traditional doctrines of nonintervention. And in going beyond them, it could be held to be, by its insistence on the principle of self-determination and "absolute respect" for human rights, radically interventionary.

In 1966, again on the initiative of the Soviet Union, the Assembly considered the "Status of the Implementation of the Declaration on the Inadmissibility of Intervention in the Domestic Affairs of States and the Protection of their Independence and Sovereignty." The resolution resulting from the debate on the item reaffirmed all the principles and rules embodied in the declaration of the previous year.[14] Further, the Assembly deemed it "to be its bounden duty" to urge the immediate cessation of intervention, whatever its form, to condemn it as a basic source of danger to the cause of world peace, and to call upon all states to carry out their obligations under the Charter and the provisions of the declaration. It seemed that the declaration was becoming as important to the Assembly as the Universal Declaration of Human Rights and the Declaration on the Granting of Independence to Colonial Countries and Peoples.

During its twenty-fifth session, the General Assembly adopted a Declaration on Principles of International Law concerning Friendly Relations and Co-operation among States in Accordance with the Charter of the United Nations.[15] Consideration of the item leading to the declaration had its origin in a twelve-nation proposal in 1961 that the Assembly should consider "principles of international law relating to peaceful co-existence of States." Amended to consideration of "friendly relations and cooperation among States," the item was placed on the provisional agenda of the next Assembly.[16] After discussion in the Assembly's Sixth Committee in 1962, a resolution was passed charting a rudimentary course to be taken in the consideration of the principles of international law.[17] It isolated seven principles of international law concerning friendly relations and cooperation among states, principles embodied in the Charter of the United Nations, which was their "fundamental statement." The third such principle was "the duty not to intervene in matters within the domestic jurisdiction of any State, in accordance with the Charter."[18] During the next

[14] General Assembly Resolution 2225(xxi) of December 19, 1966.

[15] General Assembly Resolution 2625(xxv) of October 24, 1970.

[16] General Assembly Resolution 1686(xvi) of December 18, 1961.

[17] General Assembly Resolution 1815(xvii) of December 18, 1962.

[18] The remaining six principles listed in the resolution were: the principle that states shall refrain in their international relations from the threat or

eight years, the seven principles were considered and their content debated in the Sixth Committee, and in a Special Committee established by a decision of the Assembly in 1963.[19]

The formulation of the principle of nonintervention as a legal principle commanding general agreement was a daunting task, seemingly beyond the resources of either committee. The first three meetings of the Special Committee produced no such consensus, but at the 1970 session of the Committee, an agreed formulation emerged as part of a general draft of all seven principles, and with minor changes this draft was adopted in the Assembly's declaration of October 1970.[20] The principle of nonintervention as formulated in this declaration was not greatly different from the 1965 Declaration on the Inadmissibility of Intervention. The influence of inter-American Law was just as noticeable, the wording altered only marginally, and the paragraphs dropped were those which has strayed from simply stating the rule of nonintervention.[21] Thus the Assembly placed its imprimatur on the non-

---

use of force against the territorial integrity or political independence of any state, or in any other manner inconsistent with the purposes of the United Nations; the principle that states shall settle their international disputes by peaceful means in such a manner that international peace and security and justice are not endangered; the duty of states to cooperate with one another in accordance with the Charter; the principle of equal rights and self-determination of peoples; the principle of sovereign equality of states; the principle that states shall fulfill in good faith the obligations assumed by them in accordance with the Charter.

[19] The Special Committee met six times between 1964 and 1970. On the pressures leading to the establishment of the committee see Edward Mc-Whinney, "The New Countries and the 'New' International Law; the United Nations Special Conference on Friendly Relations and Co-operation Among States," *American Journal of International Law*, Vol. 60, No. 1, 1966, p. 3.

[20] The problem of formulating the principle of non-intervention was addressed at the first three meetings of the Special Committee and at the last. According to the official reports, the committee did not have time to discuss the principle at its 1968 session, and no reference was made to it, except to summarize past discussions, at the 1969 session. See *Reports of the Special Committee on Principles of International Law concerning Friendly Relations and Co-operation among States*, 1968, U. N. Doc. A/7326, p. 69, para. 204, and 1969, U. N. Doc. A/7619, p. 7, para. 15.

[21] For the text of the principle as it appeared in the declaration see Appendix b. Where the 1965 declaration had condemned "armed intervention and all other forms of interference again the personality of the State or against its political, economic and cultural elements," the 1970 declaration instead found them "in violation of international law." The paragraph of

intervention principle as a legal as well as a political principle, but it remained coy about the status of the declaration. At the outset, the Assembly had been conscious of "the significance of the emergence of many new States and of the contribution which they are in a position to make to the progressive development and codification of international law," but had looked to the Charter for the fundamental statement of the principles of international law concerning friendly relations and cooperation.[22] Similarly at the end, the Assembly was deeply convinced that the adoption of the declaration constituted a "landmark in the development of international law and of relations among States," but it also emphasized the "paramount importance of the Charter of the United Nations for the maintenance of international peace and security and for the development of friendly relations and co-operation among States."[23] Though the Assembly's principle of nonintervention had gone beyond the Charter, the Charter was still relied upon as the source of its legitimation.

III

If voting in the General Assembly on the question of the principle of nonintervention can be taken as an indication of agreement in that body on its definition and interpretation, then the question must be considered distinctly uncontroversial. The 1965 Declaration on Nonintervention was passed with but one abstention and with one state refusing to vote. The United Kingdom thought the matter required a more thorough and more expert study. Malta alone announced that the emperor was naked. Even these doubts were apparently removed by 1970, when the Assembly adopted the Declaration on Principles of International Law without a vote.[24]

---

the 1965 declaration offering an opinion on the importance of observing the nonintervention principle for the maintenance of international peace was not included in the 1970 declaration, nor was the paragraph calling for respect for the right of self-determination.

[22] See General Assembly Resolution 1815(XVII) of December 18, 1962.

[23] Preamble to General Assembly Resolution 2625(XXV).

[24] Other votes on matters related to the principle of nonintervention were opposed by a few only. The Essentials of Peace Resolution was passed by 50 votes to 5 with 1 abstention, the Peace Through Deeds Resolution by 53 to 5 with 1 abstention, Resolution 1236(XII) on Peaceful Coexistence by 77 to 0 with 1 abstention, Resolution 222(XXI) on the Status of the Declaration on Nonintervention by 114 to 0 with 2 abstentions.

And yet, the debate in the Assembly revealed the scope and content of the principle of nonintervention to be a fiercely contentious issue. The simple explanation of the apparent discrepancy is that even unanimous voting is no indicator of consensus, that General Assembly resolutions on the matter were so vaguely worded as to allow each state to vote for its conception of their meaning without violating its principles or its interests. If this answer encompassed the whole truth, then the mere existence of consensus in the General Assembly would attest to very little except to the status of the institution as a political curiosity.[25] This question will be looked at in the concluding section of the chapter. The present purpose is to go beyond the resolutions to the views expressed by states in Assembly debates on the principle of nonintervention. A brief statement of the points at issue in the debates will introduce an examination of the doctrines of states considered in three broad categories: those of the communist states, of the states of the Third World and Latin America, and of the Western states.[26]

The one thing about the principle of nonintervention which was not at issue was its perceived importance. It was commonly regarded as the "corner-stone of the United Nations system."[27] The one issue common to all states, and taken up by most, was that which attributed responsibility for violation of the rule to others. The principle was part of the doctrinal armory of all states available for deployment against malefactors outside their own frontiers. Beyond the permanent presence of such political rhetoric

[25] The question of the nature of the consensus in the General Assembly is all the more important in strictly legal matters in view of the argument put by some powers that without consensus "legal" principles were not properly legal.

[26] The categories of communist states and Western states seem to speak for themselves. Broadly, the Third World is used here to describe those states which fit neither of the first two categories—they are non-European, noncommunist and poor. See J.D.B. Miller, *The Politics of the Third World*, London, 1966, pp. x–xiv, and the argument advanced there for supposing the Third World to be "more than a journalist's tag." Yugoslavia will be considered a Third World state here because of an attitude to the principle of nonintervention that placed her more comfortably in that class than among the communist states. Latin America, because of its special doctrinal contribution to nonintervention will be taken as a special group within the Third World (or perhaps a Fourth World, see *ibid.*, p. xi).

[27] See, e.g., *Report of the Special Committee on Principles of International Law concerning Friendly Relations and Co-operation Among States*, 1964, U. N. Doc. A/5746, p. 115, para. 211.

in the Assembly, there was stubstantial disagreement about the scope and content of the principle of nonintervention. The first conflict was about the status of the principle, about whether it was to be considered in its 1965 guise an expression of a legal obligation or a mere political aspiration. Some states thought that the declaration defined a general principle of law, but did not object to "expanding the area of agreement" reflected in that document; others thought the declaration was not intended as a legal document.[28] Related to this question were the controversies about whether it was the job of the Assembly to make new law or to elaborate and clarify the old, and whether the Charter was sacrosanct as the comprehensive statement of principles of international conduct or just a skeleton to which the flesh had to be added.

There were also differences about the legal basis of the principle.[29] Most states thought the principle to be implicit in the Charter. Several thought that Article 2(7) should extend a fortiori to members in their relations with each other, and considered also that the rule was a corollary to Article 2(4). On the other hand, one representative argued that Article 2(7) applied only to intervention by the United Nations and that by the maxim *expressio unius est exclusio alterius* it could not be extended to states. It argued further that the prohibition of the use of force or its threat in Article 2(4) could not be "stretched to encompass all sorts of extraneous standards of conduct."[30]

Problems about definition began with conflicting views on the desirability of spelling out the activities considered to constitute intervention.[31] Some states favored a categorical statement pro-

[28] See *Report of the Special Committee*, 1966, U. N. Doc. A/6230, p. 67, paras. 295–297. Still other states sought to prevent any further consideration of the principle, believing its 1965 statement to be adequate, see P.H. Houben, "Principles of International Law Concerning Friendly Relations and Co-operation Among States," *American Journal of International Law*, Vol. 61, No. 3, 1967, p. 716.

[29] See *Report of the Special Committee*, 1964, pp. 116–117, paras. 216–219, from which the following summary is taken.

[30] *Ibid.*, para. 219, and see Luke T. Lee, "The Mexico City Conference of the United Nations Special Committee on Principles of International Law Concerning Friendly Relations and Co-operation Among States," *International and Comparative Law Quarterly*, Vol. 14, Pt. 4, October 1965, pp. 1304–1305.

[31] See *Report of the Special Committee*, 1964, pp. 121–122, 125 and 128, paras. 230–231, 240–241, and 249, from which the summary following is taken.

hibiting intervention, and a list of the main types of actions which constituted it. Others took the view, reminiscent of the argument against defining aggression, that an extensive definition of intervention would stultify the growth of international cooperation while a restrictive one would leave states without protection against real dangers, and argued from this the unwisdom of an attempt by the Special Committee to define intervention. The coercive nature of an act of interference was argued, apparently uncontroversially, to be the characteristic which made that act "intervention," but problems arose again when some states wanted to make a distinction between "lawful" and "unlawful" coercion. This distinction was opposed on the ground that it was an attempt to justify the one category of "so-called" lawful intervention. When the debate moved on to the values protected by the principle of nonintervention, some states argued that, particularly for the benefit of small states, both internal and external affairs should be so protected. Others, doubtful of the meaning of "external affairs," preferred the formula "matters within the domestic jurisdiction," though the latter was itself a subject for debate.[32] This issue was rehearsed when some representatives favored the limitation of the scope of the principle to allow the "generally recognized freedom of States to seek to influence the policies and actions of other States in accordance with international law and settled international practice."[33] Others feared that such a provision would legitimize intervention and argued that if international law "referred only to ordinary diplomatic and consular activities, there was no need for the provision."[34] Another proposed limitation to the scope of the principle, to allow support for a victim of intervention by whatever means permissible under international law, and in accordance with the Charter, was called a dangerous departure from the Charter and from international law in general, even "tantamount to an attempt to legitimize preventive war."[35] Thus Mill's doctrine of nonintervention was asserted in the Special Committee and countered with an extreme statement of Cobden's doctrine.

The sorts of political entities entitled to the protection of the rule were also debated. Some states wanted to extend its protection

[32] See *Reports of the Special Committee*, 1964, p. 120, paras. 228–229 and pp. 123–124, para. 235; 1966, p. 68, paras. 306–307; 1967, U. N. Doc. A/6799, p. 51, paras. 343–347.

[33] *Report of the Special Committee*, 1966, p. 73, paras. 330–331.

[34] *Ibid.*, p. 73, para. 332.   [35] *Ibid.*, p. 72, para. 326.

to such groups as peoples and nations struggling against "the colonial yoke"—to make it a duty following from their interpretation of the right to self-determination.[36] To these arguments that the principle "had acquired a new and universally valid dimension" and that the concept of a "people" was now recognized to be of legal importance, the reply was that the principle dealt only with the duty not to intervene in the domestic affairs of states.[37] Nor did the argument stop there. Some states wanted to go beyond the affording of the protection of the rule to "oppressed peoples" living under "foreign domination," to legitimize intervention on their behalf, and to assert such assistance as a duty.[38] This position was opposed by other representatives who argued that it would sanction intervention whenever a state considered that elements within another state were under foreign domination.[39]

Despite the argument of some states against any attempt by the Special Committee to define the activities constituting intervention, it spent much of the time devoted to the consideration of the principle of nonintervention on just such an exercise. The long list of "acts prohibited under the principle of non-intervention" considered by the Special Committee was composed of three basic elements.[40] The first of these consisted not of the sorts of acts prohibited by the principle, but of the aspects of the sovereignty of states against which such acts, however defined, were directed. Many states favored such an exhaustive account of the sacred aspects of sovereignty which were to remain untouched by intervention, and the list included acts against the political, economic, or social system of a state, its personality and sovereign equality, the promulgation or execution of its laws, the disposal of its natural wealth and resources, and the national identity of a people.[41] Those who opposed these elaborations of the concept of sovereignty thought terms like the "personality" of the state

[36] *Ibid.*, p. 70, para. 313; *Report of the Special Committee*, 1964, p. 130, paras. 257–258.

[37] *Report of the Special Committee*, 1966, p. 71, para. 322 and p. 70, paras. 313–314.

[38] *Ibid.*, p. 71, para. 322. [39] *Ibid.*, para. 323.

[40] The *Report of the Special Committee*, 1964, included "Acts Prohibited" as a heading for much of the discussion. The 1966 *Report* had no such category but discussed the issues contained in it. The 1967 *Report* had the same discussion under the heading "Content of the Principle."

[41] Equally sacrosanct, as seen above, were both the "internal and external affairs" of states, and the right of peoples to self-determination.

and the "national identity" of a people to be dubious legally, and that the expansion of the forbidden area to matters like the disposal of natural wealth and resources tended to obstruct natural and useful relations between states.[42]

The second element in the list was composed directly of the acts considered to be prohibited by the principle of nonintervention. Among these acts were coercive measures of a political or economic nature used to obtain advantages of any kind, the threat to sever diplomatic relations, and generally the use of duress by one state to gain advantages over another. Armed intervention was disapproved of whether it took the form of the organization and training of armed forces for the purpose of incursion into other states, subversive and terrorist activities or interference in civil strife in another state, or the provision of arms and materials in support of a rebellion within another state. Though all representatives objected to coercion, and this was the common thread running through the various views on the actions the principle disallowed, some representatives pointed out the difficulty of distinguishing between "impermissible coercion and legitimate persuasion."[43]

The third element in the list inverted the first. It was composed of prohibitions which would restrict rights traditionally regarded as being within the sovereign power of states rather than expanding them. Thus some representatives wanted to prohibit the imposition on a state of concessions of privileges to foreigners which went beyond the rights granted to nationals under the municipal law. In the same category fell the objection of some representatives to the use of duress to obtain or maintain territorial agreements or special advantages of any kind, and the objection to the recognition of territorial acquisitions or special advantages obtained by duress. These matters, which raised the thorny questions of *pacta sunt servanda* and *rebus sic stantibus*, were little discussed.

Clearly, the debate in the Special Committee brought practicing international lawyers no nearer to a consensus on such central questions as the definition of intervention, and the scope and content of the principle proscribing it, than the debate among their academic counterparts. But apart from being jurists, the members of the Special Committee were also, and more importantly, repre-

[42] See *Reports of the Special Committee*, 1966, p. 68, para. 305; 1964, p. 138, para. 280.

[43] *Report of the Special Committee*, 1967, p. 52, para. 353.

sentatives of states on whose attitudes to the principle the next section of the chapter will concentrate.

IV

That the principle of nonintervention was discussed so extensively at the United Nations was in large part due to the persistence of the Soviet Union and of the communist states in general. For those states, it seemed to be a useful peg on which to hang criticism of the Western states and above all of the United States. In 1957 the Assembly discussed a complaint by the Soviet Union of intervention by the United States "in the domestic affairs of Albania, Bulgaria, Czechoslovakia, Hungary, Poland, Romania and the USSR." The Soviet delegate to the Special Political Committee thought such intervention was not a matter of chance, it was "part and parcel of United States foreign policy, the object of which was to subject the world to United States leadership, and thus, in effect, to secure the domination of the monopolies."[44] This was a few months after Hungary. The purpose of the complaint seemed to be partly to provide a smokescreen for the Soviet intervention, and partly to justify it.[45] In 1965 there were no such recent embarrassments for the Soviet Union, and it was the year of American escalation in Vietnam and intervention in the Dominican Republic. Introducing the motion on the Inadmissibility of Intervention in the General Assembly, the Soviet Union pronounced the matter urgent because of "the increasingly grave turn of world events" resulting from "certain Western powers . . . intervening by force in the domestic affairs of States" and for proof the Soviet Union looked to Vietnam, the Congo and the Dominican Republic.[46] Czechoslovakia deplored the fact that the policy of

[44] General Assembly, *Official Records* (hereafter GAOR), 11th sess., Special Political Committee, 36th mtg., February 25, 1957, p. 161.

[45] The Czechoslovakian delegate declared that the "entire Hungarian counterrevolution had been based on a plan drawn up by the United States Intelligence Service," GAOR, 11th sess., Special Political Committee, 37th mtg., February 25, 1957, p. 168. However, the Soviet Union did not want the justification tested at the United Nations, invoking Article 2(7) against its discussion as a "gross interference in the domestic affairs of Hungary." See *Year Book of the United Nations*, 1956, pp. 66 and 69–70.

[46] GAOR, 20th sess., 1st Committee, 1395th mtg., December 3, 1965, pp. 243–244.

intervention had been raised by the United States Government to "the status of an actual political doctrine."[47] When the question was raised again at the next Assembly, the Soviet Union generalized its criticism of the Western powers. Not only was the United States disregarding the Declaration on Nonintervention in Vietnam, Laos, Cambodia, Korea, the Dominican Republic, and Cuba, but together with Germany and the United Kingdom, she was doing the same in Africa.[48] In 1968 the Soviet Union decided that the lack of progress in codifying the principles of peaceful coexistence was due to the negative attitude of the states with misgivings about the Declaration on Nonintervention, misgivings which reflected their overall policies. The answer, the Soviet Union thought, was that those states should halt all interference in the internal affairs of other states.[49]

As well as having a function as an instrument for criticizing the West, the Soviet espousal of the principle of nonintervention was also thrust forward as a sort of doctrinal bauble with which to attract the new states of Africa and Asia. During the 1965 debate on the Inadmissibility of Intervention, the Soviet Union drew attention to the plight of the Asian, African, and Latin American states as the victims of Western intervention; deferred to the principle of nonintervention as expressed by Third World conferences such as those at Bandung, Belgrade, and Cairo; and projected herself, through her sponsorship of the principle, as the protector of the "vital interests of small countries which were not in a position to defend their rights and independence against imperialist interference."[50] Soviet sponsorship of the principle distinguished her from the powers which had been seeking to "impede the advance of history by aggressive acts and open intervention in the domestic affairs of States and peoples fighting against colonial domination, for their national liberation and for their independent sovereign

[47] GAOR, 20th sess., 6th Committee, 871st mtg., November 8, 1965, pp. 191–192.

[48] The "political blackmail," "diktat," and "economic pressure exerted in the interest of the imperialist monopolies" of the United States and her allies were also criticized as methods of intervention. GAOR, 21st sess., 1st Committee, 1473d mtg., December 5, 1966, pp. 287–288.

[49] GAOR, 23d sess., 6th Committee, 1092nd mtg., December 11, 1968, p. 3.

[50] GAOR, 20th sess., 1st Committee, 1395th mtg., December 3, 1965, p. 245.

existence."[51] Thus criticism of the West and support for those it oppressed were joined.

Though the legal discussion of the principle of nonintervention in the General Assembly took place under an item entitled "principles of international law concerning friendly relations and cooperation among states," the communist states preferred to refer to them as principles of peaceful coexistence. The principle of peaceful coexistence was thought to have "permeated contemporary international law," the United Nations was a reflection of its existence, and its rejection would mean a "denial of the purposes and principles" of that Organization.[52] Its fundamental tenet, on which the "very existence of contemporary international law" was supposed to depend, was the peaceful coexistence of states with different political and social systems.[53] Hence the principle of nonintervention, which represented a "legal safeguard against encroachments aimed at imposing a change in the social system."[54]

Beyond this general affirmation of the importance of peaceful coexistence, the communist states seemed to conceive of three categories of international law relevant to the Assembly's deliberations: the principles confirmed in the Charter of the United Nations, those which had been proclaimed "in virtue of the Charter," and those "now being worked out in the United Nations with the participation of the new States."[55] The nonintervention principle seemed to fit into each of these categories. It was a principle ex-

[51] See the summary of the USSR's explanatory memorandum of September 24, 1965, accompanying the request that the "Inadmissibility of Intervention" be placed on the agenda of the Assembly, in *Year Book of the United Nations*, 1965, pp. 87–88.

[52] Statement by Czechoslovakian representative, GA*OR*, 17th sess., 6th Committee, 753d mtg., November 5, 1962, p. 96.

[53] Statement by Soviet delegate, GA*OR*, 17th sess., 6th Committee, 754th mtg., November 6, 1962, p. 104.

[54] Statement by Soviet representative, GA*OR*, 18th sess., 6th Committee, 802d mtg., October 29, 1963, p. 111. The USSR argued that the principle had fulfilled this function since the time of its first formulation "by the French bourgeoisie during their revolution, as a defence against the absolutist feudal state." This aspect of the principle, as a protector of ideology, was contained in a Czechoslovakian draft proposal on the formulation of the principle submitted to the 1964 Special Committee. The same proposal contained a paragraph directed unmistakably at the Hallstein Doctrine, by which West Germany withheld recognition from states recognizing East Germany. For the text of the proposal see Appendix c.

[55] Statement of Soviet representative, GA*OR*, 17th sess., 6th Committee, 754th mtg., November 6, 1962, p. 105.

tant since the French Revolution, confirmed in the Charter through Article 2(7).[56] It was a principle proclaimed in virtue of the Charter. The 1965 Declaration on Nonintervention was supported by the Soviet Union in part because it "gave more concrete form" to the principles of the Charter.[57] And it was a principle worked out with the participation of new states. The communist states explicitly extended "the inalienable right" to freedom, independence and defense of sovereignty to every people as well as to every sovereign state.[58]

The principles of peaceful coexistence as proclaimed in contemporary communist legal doctrine were borrowed from the Third World.[59] From that world, Asian states in particular claimed a long pedigree for the *Pancha Shila*. Afghanistan considered the principle of coexistence to be founded on "historic Asian principles."[60] To its venerable age, some added a mystical quality as when Laos affirmed that "the very essence of the Buddhist religion was embodied in the *Pancha Shila*," and India declared that one of its component principles, that of nonintervention, was "an article of faith for the non-aligned countries."[61] More prosaically, the United Arab Republic thought that the "principle of nonintervention had evolved from the historical experience of many small States."[62] But whatever the thoughts about its origin, and whether or not it was considered to be part of the peaceful coexistence package, the particular importance of the nonintervention principle to the small and weak states of the Third World was averred almost without exception, and its consecration in an Assembly

[56] See statement of Czechoslovakian representative, GAOR, 18th sess., 6th Committee, 802d mtg., October 29, 1963, p. 107, and of Romanian representative, 20th sess., 1st Committee, 1403d mtg., December 8, 1965, p. 301.

[57] Statement of Soviet representative, GAOR, 20th sess., 1st Committee, 1395th mtg., December 3, 1965, p. 246.

[58] See, e.g., summary of Soviet draft declaration on the "Inadmissibility of Intervention," *Year Book of the United Nations*, 1965, p. 88.

[59] See above, Chapter Five, section VI.

[60] GAOR, 17th sess., 6th Committee, 762d mtg., November 19, 1962, p. 142. See also the Saudi Arabian statement that the principles underlying the concept of peaceful coexistence were "deeply rooted in Arab thinking, traditions and culture." GAOR, 12th sess., 1st Committee, 936th mtg., December 13, 1957, p. 410.

[61] GAOR, 12th sess., 1st Committee, 939th mtg., December 14, 1957, p. 438, and 20th sess., 1st Committee, 1403d mtg., December 8, 1965, p. 302.

[62] GAOR, 20th sess., 1st Committee, 1403d mtg., December 8, 1965, p. 299.

declaration was hailed as an "historic moment" in the annals of the United Nations.[63]

The Third World was not unique in finding more difficulty defining intervention than in affirming the importance of preventing it. Some states dwelt upon the problem of giving precise meaning to terms like "intervention" and "domestic jurisdiction" about whose definition they were dissatisfied.[64] Most attempted definitions resulted in a list of unfriendly acts which were considered to constitute intervention in which any inadequacy or oversight was covered by an absolute statement of the principle of nonintervention, prohibiting intervention by a state or group of states "directly or indirectly, for any reason whatsoever, in the internal or external affairs of any other State."[65] Among the states of the Third World, above all, support was to be found for an expansive definition of sovereignty, an elaborate recording of the acts constituting intervention, and at the same time a restriction of the claims to sovereignty of the states with the power to intervene. Frequently, the list of unfriendly acts was composed with an eye more to the behavior of a neighbor than to the elaboration of a legal principle, as when the Laotian representative "appreciated the Soviet Union's initiative" on nonintervention in 1965, "coming as it did at a time when Laos was being invaded by North Vietnam."[66] Similarly, though this time with a perspective beyond his own frontiers, the Tanzanian representative translated the "real issues" from principles into practice, listing as such the Vietnam War, provocations by Portugal, aggression against the Arab countries, economic and political pressures on small states, and "the machinations of the imperialist Powers to overthrow the Governments of independent African and Asian countries that dared to oppose the interest of

[63] See statement of representative of Afghanistan, GAOR, 20th sess., 1408th plenary mtg., December 21, 1965, p. 15.

[64] See statement by Ceylonese representative, GAOR, 18th sess., 6th Committee, 805th mtg., November 5, 1963, pp. 127–128, and of the Tunisian representative, GAOR, 18th sess., 6th Committee, 822d mtg., November 29, 1963, p. 233.

[65] From the proposal on the formulation of the principle submitted by Ghana, India, and Yugoslavia to the 1964 Special Committee; text in Appendix d.

[66] GAOR, 20th sess., 1st Committee, 1399th mtg., December 7, 1965, p. 269. In the same way, the behavior of each other was uppermost in the minds of the representatives of Israel and the Arab states when the nonintervention principle was being discussed.

the monopolies."[67] This last was a general grievance among the states of the Third World. Though seldom put with the rhetoric of the Guinean delegate, who spoke of "the imperialist counter-offensive against the formerly enslaved countries" by "unrepent-ant colonialists," and the "remote control of people's minds," the concern with economic and social, as well as political intervention, was common to all the states of the Third World.[68] The adoption of the principle of nonintervention was to put an end to these manifestations of imperialism, colonialism, and neocolonialism.[69]

Though these extensive claims about the content of the principle were made principally with a mind to the behavior of the Western powers, there was a broad strand of Third World doctrine which sought to direct the principle against great powers as such and not just those of a particular political color. Thus the United Arab Republic thought that "in the final analysis, non-intervention was for the great Powers a duty, and for the small Powers a right and an immunity."[70] The Philippines thought the whole purpose of the principle was "to protect the weak from the depredations of the strong."[71] Liberia wished to carry the immunity a stage further —to shut out the ideological quarrel between the great powers which tended to spill over into the Third World, and Tunisia "re-fused to regard peaceful coexistence in terms of ideological blocs, for that would inevitably destroy the personality of small states."[72] The principle of nonintervention had been a positive factor in

[67] GAOR, 21st sess., 1st Committee, 1480th mtg., December 9, 1966, p. 332. The representative of Mali linked practice with principle by citing the action of the United States and her allies in Vietnam as an example of the "deceitful pretext" of counterintervention by which imperialist powers sought to maintain their influence in some parts of the world, GAOR, 21st sess., 1st Committee, 1480th mtg., December 9, 1966, p. 332.

[68] GAOR, 21st sess., 1st Committee, 1478th mtg., December 8, 1966, pp. 321–322. The distinction between political, and social and economic intervention was made by the representative of Ceylon, GAOR, 18th sess., 6th Committee, 805th mtg., November 5, 1963, pp. 127–128.

[69] See statement of the representative of the UAR, GAOR, 20th sess., 1st Committee, 1403d mtg., December 8, 1965, p. 299; of Liberian repre-sentative, GAOR, 21st sess., 1st Committee, 1480th mtg., December 9, 1966, p. 331; and of the Kenyan representative, ibid., p. 335.

[70] GAOR, 20th sess., 1st Committee, 1403d mtg., December 8, 1965, p. 299.

[71] Ibid., p. 303.

[72] See GAOR, 20th sess., 1st Committee, 1401st mtg., December 8, 1965, p. 288, and 17th sess., 6th Committee, 754th mtg., November 6, 1962, p. 102.

developing the policy of nonalignment and it followed from that policy.[73] It was a standard of conduct among the states of the Third World which they sought to apply to the powers outside it.[74]

Most states of the Third World asserted the emphatic existence of the nonintervention principle in the Charter of the United Nations, though there were differences as to its exact location in that document.[75] But it was also held to be part of new law adapted to a changed international order to meet "the needs of the majority of nations."[76] According to the representative of Afghanistan, the sources of the novelty were two: first, the vastly increased membership of the United Nations since its foundation had rendered the Charter insufficient as a reflection of the views of the majority of states and, second, the role of the nonaligned states in world affairs added support for the principles of coexistence.[77] For India, the status of the 1965 Declaration on Nonintervention as a legal and not merely a political principle was a consequence of "the modern dimensions of international law." The declarations of Latin American conferences, those of Bandung and Belgrade, and

[73] See statement of the UAR representative, GAOR, 20th sess., 6th Committee, 875th mtg., November 15, 1965, p. 207, and of the representative of Burundi, GAOR, 20th sess., 1st Committee, 1406th mtg., December 10, 1965, p. 327.

[74] See statement of the representative of Nepal, GAOR, 21st sess., 1st Committee, 1477th mtg., December 8, 1966, and of the Indonesian representative, GAOR, 12th sess., 1st Committee, 939th mtg., December 14, 1957, p. 439.

[75] See, e.g., Yugoslavia's assertion that the rule had been "consecrated" in Article 2(4) and (7) of the Charter, GAOR, 17th sess., 6th Committee, 753d mtg., November 5, 1962, p. 98. Dahomey, among many other states, thought that Article 2(7) applied a fortiori to states, GAOR, 20th sess., 6th Committee, 885th mtg., November 30, 1965, p. 268. Both the UAR and Cyprus drew a distinction between Article 2(7) and the interstate principle of nonintervention and asserted the wider scope of the latter, GAOR, 18th sess., 6th Committee, 811th mtg., November 14, 1963, p. 164, and 822d mtg., November 29, 1963, p. 230. Interpreting Article 2(4), Tanzania included economic pressure in the definition of the term "force," GAOR, 23d sess., 6th Committee, 1093d mtg., December 12, 1968, p. 6. Thailand was one of the few states of the Third World entertaining any doubts about the principle, considering it "more of a doctrine than an established principle of international law," GAOR, 17th sess., 6th Committee, 763d mtg., November 20, 1962, p. 152.

[76] Statement of Malaysian representative, GAOR, 22d sess., 6th Committee, 1000th mtg., November 17, 1967, p. 243.

[77] GAOR, 17th sess., 6th Committee, 762d mtg., November 19, 1962, p. 143.

the Charter of the Organization of African Unity constituted "some of the positive legal and juridical bases of the Declaration."[78] A third newness was the attachment of Third World states to the concept of "people" as one having legal meaning. The principle of nonintervention was thought to be a "natural extension of the principle of self-determination" and did not apply to aid given to peoples under colonial domination on behalf of the latter principle.[79]

The views of Latin American states on the principle of nonintervention were close to but marginally more conservative than the mainstream of Third World doctrine. Less radical in their protestations than such states as Guinea or Kenya, they clung no less tenaciously to the 1965 Declaration of Nonintervention as an affirmation of legal as well as political principle. Nor was this surprising, for the declaration was, in large part, the adoption by the international community of an inter-American principle which was "a way of life" for the peoples of Latin America.[80]

It was the presence, in the late nineteenth and in the twentieth centuries, of a colossus to the North which had concentrated the Latin American mind on an absolute prohibition of intervention. By a longer tradition, which the Latin American countries shared with the United States, such a prohibition was to apply to states and their ideologies which were alien to the hemisphere. The contemporary threat to the hemisphere was posed by communism and all its works.[81] Latin American states favored a definition of

[78] GAOR, 21st sess., 1st Committee, 1481st mtg., December 10, 1966, p. 345. See also statement of Zambian representative, GAOR, 22d sess., 6th Committee, 1003d mtg., November 20, 1967, p. 270. When the draft declaration on principles of international law was nearing adoption in 1970, India urged that the words "in accordance with the Charter of the United Nations" not be included in the title on the ground that they might have a limiting effect, GAOR, 25th sess., 6th Committee, 1183d mtg., September 28, 1970, p. 4 in provisional records.

[79] See statement of the UAR representative, GAOR, 20th sess., 6th Committee, 875th mtg., November 15, 1965, p. 207, and of Kenyan representative, GAOR, 22d sess., 6th Committee, 997th mtg., November 14, 1967, p. 218.

[80] See statement of Colombian representative, GAOR, 21st sess., 1st Committee, 1476th mtg., December 7, 1966, p. 305.

[81] See, e.g., the Brazilian reaction to the First Solidarity Conference of the Peoples of Africa, Asia, and Latin America which was thought to have called for revolution and thus to have threatened interference in the internal affairs of states. Brazil was suspicious of the "so-called national

intervention which took account of unfriendly acts originating within and outside the hemisphere.[82] The Mexican representative recognized the difficulty of defining intervention, but argued that this difficulty should not be invoked "to invalidate the principle that certain types of pressure or coercive action were unquestionably illegal and constituted forms of intervention."[83] Mexico thought that the United Nations should explicitly prohibit these forms of intervention and in support of this view she offered a special reason. An apparent lacuna in Article 2(4) of the Charter arguably allowed the use of force when it was not directed against the territorial integrity or political independence of any state. To close this possible loophole, Mexico advocated a legal proclamation of the principle of nonintervention in the form used by the Organization of American States.[84]

The Latin American states were not reluctant to see gaps in the Charter filled, the less so as the filling came from their own law. The Chilean representative regarded the 1970 Declaration on Principles of International Law as "the most serious attempt made yet to produce a set of international legal principles" and looked forward to a "world based on the principles of natural law."[85] But the enthusiasm for new law between states was not matched, as it frequently was in the Third World, by an equal anxiety to extend the franchise of international law to entities other than states. Though the Peruvian representative welcomed some of the "important" ideas which had emanated from the Afro-Asian states,

---

liberation movement" and concerned about the expansion of the sphere of action of communism. GAOR, 21st sess., 1st Committee, 1473d mtg., December 5, 1966, p. 290. Colombia saw in revolutionary and guerrilla warfare "a real conspiracy against the principle and practice of non-intervention," GAOR, 20th sess., 1st Committee, 1395th mtg., December 3, 1965, p. 247.

[82] See, e.g., the Mexican proposal on the formulation of the principle submitted to the 1964 Special Committee; text in Appendix e. An exception was Cuba: she wanted to point the principle in just one of those directions, GAOR, 22d sess., 6th Committee, 995th mtg., November 10, 1967, p. 206.

[83] GAOR, 20th sess., 6th Committee, 886th mtg., December 1, 1965, p. 278.

[84] GAOR, 18th sess., 6th Committee, 806th mtg., November 6, 1963, p. 134.

[85] GAOR, 25th sess., 6th Committee, 1178th mtg., September 23, 1970, p. 5 in provisional records. See also statement of the representative of Ecuador, GAOR, 23d sess., 6th Committee, 1096th mtg., December 13, 1968, p. 2.

such as their objection to the use of force to deprive peoples of their national identity, and the principle of self-determination, it was noticeable that he referred to the latter as "the right of every state to choose its political, economic, social and cultural systems without interference" and not of every people.[86] On this aspect of new law, the Latin American states were closer to the West than either the communist states or the Third World.

The Western powers spent much of their time, during Assembly consideration of the principle of nonintervention, reacting to the initiative of others, replying to their criticisms, and stating a preferred view on matters of law. In 1957 the United States considered "the various false and sensational accusations" leveled against her by the Soviet Union, to be part of a propaganda offensive to "divert world attention from its own programme."[87] When the Soviet Union launched the Assembly into consideration of nonintervention in 1965, the United States thought it was to "serve as a pretext for a violent attack on the Western States."[88] The United Kingdom found the principles of peaceful coexistence "unexceptionable," and all of them contained in the Charter, but was convinced that they "meant something quite different to the Soviet Union from its own understanding of the words."[89] France stated a general Western view when she felt that "merely to recall the general principles of peaceful coexistence could not influence the actions of Member States very greatly" and that it would be more useful to attempt to define the means of arriving at the goal of "genuine peaceful coexistence."[90]

There were concerns which the Western powers shared with those who would write extensive lists of the acts prohibited by the rule of nonintervention—such as the desire to outlaw subversive activities of any sort, and to protect the inalienable right of a state to choose its own political, economic, social and cultural system without interference by another state. But it was precisely

[86] GAOR, 21st sess., 1st Committee, 1473d mtg., December 5, 1966, p. 289.

[87] GAOR, 11th sess., Special Political Committee, 36th mtg., February 25, 1957, p. 164.

[88] GAOR, 20th sess., 1st Committee, 1396th mtg., December 3, 1965, p. 251.

[89] GAOR, 12th sess., 1st Committee, 938th mtg., December 13, 1957, p. 424.

[90] GAOR, 13th sess., Special Political Committee, 118th mtg., December 3, 1958, p. 143.

in the exceptions to the rule allowed by those who otherwise favored an elaborate prohibition of intervention that the Western powers saw the most danger to the international order. The asserted legitimacy of intervention on behalf of peoples living under foreign domination, the justice proclaimed for the war of national liberation, seemed to the West to exclude the characteristically modern use of force in international relations from legal control. Thus the Australian representative thought that "the danger of world conflict now arose more from forms of intervention short of open warfare, such as propaganda, subversion and terrorism."[91] The United States representative considered "the aim of subversion and infiltration, which were the chief modern forms of intervention," to be "not essentially different from the aim of aggression throughout history," namely, "the overthrow of a lawful and established Government in order to set the stage for some form of external authority, overt or otherwise."[92]

Thus a perception on the part of the Western powers of the dangers of defining intervention if that exercise did not fill all the possible gaps was added to an appreciation of the intrinsic problems involved in discovering the meaning of "intervention" and "domestic jurisdiction."[93] Further, the United Kingdom was concerned that a consideration of the scope of "intervention" should recognize that it was "inevitable and desirable" that states should seek to influence each other's policies and actions.[94] Making the same point, the United States argued that many acts by states had consequences in the internal affairs of other states but that they should not thereby be considered interventionary.[95] A third Western concern, in this context, was that any prohibition of intervention should not prevent a state which was the victim of subversive activities from gaining help against such "indirect aggression."[96]

[91] GAOR, 20th sess., 1st Committee, 1399th mtg., December 7, 1965, p. 270.

[92] GAOR, 21st sess., 1st Committee, 1479th mtg., December 9, 1966, p. 329.

[93] See the British proposal on the formulation of the principle of nonintervention submitted to the 1964 Special Committee; text in Appendix f.

[94] See British proposal, Appendix f.

[95] GAOR, 18th sess., 6th Committee, 825th mtg., December 3, 1963, p. 250.

[96] See statement of British representative, GAOR, 18th sess., 6th Committee, 822d mtg., November 29, 1963, p. 235. See also British proposal to the 1964 Special Committee, and the joint proposal on the formulation

Awareness of the pitfalls involved in definition made the Western powers hesitant about going beyond the Charter, and in the case of the United States in 1964, reluctant to admit the presence of the nonintervention principle in the Charter.[97] The defense of the less extreme of these positions seemed to be that too broad a prohibition of intervention would inhibit the exercise of the right to self-defense at the same time as restricting the "natural" interplay of international relations.

The doubts which the Western powers entertained about the "new law" championed by the communist states and by the Third World were rooted in a distinction they made between legal principles on the one hand and political and moral principles on the other. Two sorts of reasons supported the distinction. The first was that lists of generalities were not law and could not become such before being pursued into detail so that their application to particular circumstances was clear and their interpretation unambiguous.[98] The 1965 Declaration on Nonintervention, in particular, was thought not to be a juridically sound text, for the production of which a "more competent" body than the General Assembly, such as the Special Committee, was suggested.[99] Furthermore, a consensus of all the members of the Assembly was held to be important on matters of this sort, for only then could a resolution command general respect.[100] The second reason supporting the distinction between politics and law was more fundamental. The

---

of the principle submitted to the 1966 Special Committee by Australia, Canada, France, Italy, the United Kingdom, and the United States; texts in Appendixes f and g.

[97] See Houben, "Principles of International Law," *American Journal of International Law*, Vol. 61, No. 3, 1967, p. 716.

[98] See statement of the British representative, GAOR, 17th sess., 6th Committee, 761st mtg., November 16, 1962, p. 136, and of Belgian representative, GAOR, 21st sess., 1st Committee, 1480th mtg., December 9, 1966, p. 333.

[99] See statement of Italian representative, GAOR, 21st sess., 1st Committee, 1480th mtg., December 9, 1966, pp. 334–335, of the representative of the Netherlands, GAOR, 22d sess., 6th Committee, 1000th mtg., November 17, 1967, p. 243, and of Canadian representative, GAOR, 20th sess., 1st Committee, 1404th mtg., December 9, 1965, p. 308.

[100] See statement of the British representative, GAOR, 20th sess., 1st Committee, 1398th mtg., December 6, 1965, p. 261. The American representative recognized that "the results of consensus might seem somewhat mild," GAOR, 23d sess., 6th Committee, 1091st mtg., December 10, 1968, p. 4.

Australian representative argued that the adoption of a resolution by the General Assembly "was not, under the Charter, a method of making international law" and that resolutions might serve as a foundation for rules of international law "only in so far as they reflected the general practice of States."[101] The French representative took this argument further. The creation of new law, he said, "presupposed a political choice concerning orientation and methods of improvement" of existing law, and that was a power the Assembly did not have.[102] In other words, because the Assembly was not an international legislature, its acts were not law for the international community.

Perhaps protected by these statements of Australia and France, the Western powers felt able to accept the 1970 Declaration on Principles of International Law as a "tribute to the spirit and aim of consensus," but not without making certain understandings clear.[103] For Italy, the declaration contained an implied reference to all the reports of the Special Committee since 1964, as "so to speak, *travaux préparatoires*" of the declaration.[104] The Dutch thought it could not be interpreted as "a carefully drafted legal document would be interpreted."[105] The United Kingdom maintained her position on the inevitability and desirability of influence between states, though the text of the principle referred to intervention in internal or external affairs.[106] Toward the beginning of the eight years over which the Assembly's consideration of principles of international law concerning friendly relations and cooperation among states was spread, the French representative had looked with disfavor on "the method of stating subsidiary principles or corollaries to the principles of the Charter" because

[101] See *GAOR*, 17th sess., 6th Committee, 758th mtg., November 13, 1962, p. 120, and 23d sess., 6th Committee, 1095th mtg., December 13, 1968, pp. 1–2.

[102] *GAOR*, 22d sess., 6th Committee, 995th mtg., November 10, 1967, p. 207.

[103] The remarks about consensus were those of the British representative, *Report of the Special Committee*, 1970, p. 111, para. 223.

[104] *Ibid.*, p. 85, para. 135.

[105] *Ibid.*, p. 95, para. 164.

[106] The United Kingdom was also careful about the principle of self-determination, claiming that Article 2(4) of the Charter applied between states and not, "truly interpreted," to situations affecting dependent peoples. As against an extreme interpretation of the right of self-determination, she also asserted a right to limited police action to maintain law and order in dependent territories. *Ibid.*, pp. 111–114, paras. 228–234.

the method would weaken the Charter.[107] At the end of the Assembly's consideration of the item, the West had not moved far from this position. "The Special Committee had not been charged with the revision of the Charter," said the United States in 1970, "but only with the spelling out, carefully and fairly, of what had already been agreed by Governments."[108]

V

In the Assembly's discussion of the principle of nonintervention, the states of the communist world and of the Third World had taken the initiative, holding high the standard of nonintervention, while the Western powers beat a cautious retreat before them, refusing, however, to surrender points of vital interest. On the question of *apartheid* in South Africa, the communist states and the Third World took up the cause with equal enthusiasm, but on this issue it was the Western powers proclaiming the virtues of nonintervention and the radical view asserting that here was an exception to the rule—a higher imperative. The exception claimed was to the principle of nonintervention as expressed in Article 2(7) of the Charter which excluded the United Nations from matters within the domestic jurisdiction of states. The claim asserted the right of the United Nations, as the representative of international society, to overrule the plea of domestic jurisdiction if standards of conduct within states fell below standards asserted to have been agreed between them.[109] The counterclaim asserted the opposite:

[107] GAOR, 18th sess., 6th Committee, 810th mtg., November 13, 1963, p. 159. France thought that the Charter would be weakened "especially when the statements referred to transitory or changing situations and, above all, to political or ideological notions foreign to international law," *ibid.*, pp. 159–160.

[108] *Report of the Special Committee*, 1970, p. 119, para. 254.

[109] This claim relied upon the following articles of the Charter: Article 1(2) and Article 1(3) stating the purposes of the United Nations—"[t]o develop friendly relations among nations based on respect for the principle of equal rights and self-determination of peoples, and to take other appropriate measures to strengthen universal peace," and "[t]o achieve international co-operation in solving international problems of an economic, social, cultural, or humanitarian character, and in promoting and encouraging respect for human rights and for fundamental freedoms for all without distinction as to race, sex, language, or religion"; Article 13(1b) authorizing the Assembly to initiate studies and make recommendations for the purpose of "promoting international co-operation in the economic,

261

the domestic jurisdiction clause was prior to any claim, on the part of international society, to competence in the matter of conduct within states. Thus the debate about South Africa raised, once more, two familiar themes in international relations. The first was the debate between those who would intervene on behalf of justice and those who would refrain from intervention in the interests of order.[110] The second and related theme was the concern of some to conserve the sovereignty of states against the threatened intrusions of a superstate.[111]

The practice of the United Nations on the South African issue ran against the argument for an extreme interpretation of Article 2(7), and as the issue recurred at each Assembly, so the frontiers of domestic jurisdiction receded. In the early years of the Assembly's consideration of the question of race conflict in South Africa, the resolutions it adopted were comparatively bland.[112] In 1952,

---

social, cultural, educational, and health fields, and assisting in the realization of human rights and fundamental freedoms for all without distinction as to race, sex, language, or religion"; Article 55(c) authorizing the United Nations to promote "universal respect for, and observance of, human rights and fundamental freedoms for all without distinction as to race, sex, language, or religion"; and Article 56—"[a]ll Members shall pledge themselves to take joint and separate action in co-operation with the Organization for the achievement of the purposes set forth in Article 55."

[110] In fact, the debate was and is more complex than this simple dichotomy would suggest as we shall see later in the chapter; see also Chapters Eight and Nine below.

[111] These themes inevitably arise in any discussion of the principle of nonintervention. The particular reason for selecting the issue of *apartheid* in South Africa to illustrate the contemporary debate on the principle is that it raises the question of intervention in internal affairs in its "pure" form. The issue is almost uncluttered with argument about aggression across international frontiers and consequent claims to the right of self-defense or counterintervention. Though many states asserted that the South African situation was a threat to international peace and security, they could not base this assertion on evidence of international aggression but had to show that a situation within a state was a danger to international peace, which required evidence of a quite different sort. Nor was the issue one of colonialism—in the proper sense of control of a country by a metropolitan power which is not of that country—even if South Africa was widely regarded as an "internal colonialist" because of her policy of *apartheid*. See Alan James, *The Politics of Peace-Keeping*, London, 1969, p. 254.

[112] The question was first placed on the agenda of the Assembly for its 7th session in 1952 at the request of thirteen Arab-Asian states. The Assembly had been considering the question of the treatment of people of Indian origin in South Africa since its first session in 1946.

while setting up a commission to study the question, the Assembly did not single out South Africa as the malefactor, but merely addressed a call to all states to bring their policies into conformity with their obligations.[113] In 1954 South Africa was singled out and "invited" to reconsider her position in the light of the "high principles" of the Charter.[114] In 1955 she was "called upon" to observe her obligations and by 1957 the Assembly was deploring her failure to do so.[115] After the Sharpeville shootings in 1960 and with the increasing pressure for action from the African states in particular, the concern of the United Nations became more intense. The Security Council recognized that the situation in South Africa was one that had led to international friction and "if continued might endanger international peace and security."[116] In the following year, the Assembly requested, with only Portugal dissenting, all states to consider such separate and collective action as was open to them in comformity with the Charter of the United Nations, to bring about the abandonment of racial policies in South Africa.[117] This was followed up in 1962 by a much less popular request that states take particular measures against South Africa, including breaking off diplomatic relations and restraining trade, and a further request to the Security Council to impose sanctions and to consider the expulsion of South Africa from the United Nations.[118] In 1963 the Security Council responded to the extent of solemnly calling upon all states "to cease forthwith the sale and shipment of arms, ammunition of all types and military vehicles to South Africa."[119] Now, Assembly resolutions were no

[113] General Assembly Resolution 616A and B(VII) of December 5, 1952. A was passed by 35 votes to 1 with 23 abstentions, and B by 24 to 1 with 34 abstentions.

[114] General Assembly Resolution 820(IX) of December 14, 1954, adopted by 40 votes to 10 with 10 abstentions.

[115] General Assembly Resolution 917(X) of December 6, 1955, adopted by 41 votes to 6 with 8 abstentions, and 1016(XI) of January 30, 1957, adopted by 56 votes to 5 with 12 abstentions.

[116] Security Council Resolution S/4300 of April 1, 1960, adopted by 9 votes to 0 with 2 abstentions.

[117] General Assembly Resolution 1598(XV) of April 13, 1961.

[118] General Assembly Resolution 1761(XVII) of November 6, 1962, adopted by 67 votes to 16 with 23 abstentions.

[119] Security Council Resolution S/5386 of August 7, 1963, adopted with only Britain and France abstaining. A resolution which called less stridently for the cessation of "the sale and shipment of equipment and materials for the manufacture and maintenance of arms and ammunition in South

longer the restrained requests of the previous decade. The South African situation was declared to be a threat to international peace and security, demanding action under Chapter VII of the Charter, since universally applied economic sanctions were the only means to a peaceful solution.[120] The legitimacy of the struggle of "the oppressed peoples of South Africa for the exercise of their inalienable right of self-determination" was recognized, and all states and organizations were urged to give greater moral, material, and political assistance to the "South African liberation movement."[121] The Assembly also turned an accusing eye in the direction of those states which were encouraging South Africa, urging them to desist from collaboration with the regime.[122] In 1971 the NATO powers were condemned for contributing "to the creation in Southern Africa of a military-industrial complex aimed at suppressing the struggle of peoples for their self-determination and at interfering in the affairs of the independent African states."[123]

But beyond the adoption of resounding resolutions, the setting-up of a trust fund to assist the victims of *apartheid*, and the establishment of a precarious arms embargo, the United Nations took little action against South Africa. The great powers not being unanimously agreed on the existence of a threat to international peace and security, the Security Council could not authorize action under Chapter VII of the Charter.

Of the great powers, it was the Soviet Union that asserted the existence of such a threat. In general, however, where the communist states had led the nonintervention movement, they were content to follow the lead of the Third World on the South African

---

Africa" was carried unanimously. Resolution S/5471 of December 4, 1963. In 1970 a detailed resolution aiming to strengthen the arms embargo against South Africa was adopted by the Secretary Council with France, the United Kingdom and the United States abstaining. Resolution 282(1970) of July 23, 1970.

[120] See, e.g., General Assembly Resolution 2054(xx) of December 15, 1965, adopted by 80 votes to 2 with 16 abstentions. This view was asserted the more strongly as South Africa was accused of military intervention and assistance to the "racist minority regime in Southern Rhodesia," General Assembly Resolution 2396(xxiii) of December 2, 1968, adopted by 85 votes to 2 with 14 abstentions.

[121] Resolution 2396(xxiii).

[122] Resolution 2396(xxiii), and General Assembly Resolution 2506(xxiv) of November 21, 1969, adopted by 101 votes to 2 with 6 abstentions.

[123] General Assembly Resolution 2787(xxvi) of December 6, 1971, adopted by 76 votes to 10 with 33 abstentions.

issue. That the issue was an international one, not of purely domestic concern, was never doubted by the communist states, the Polish representative arguing that a United Nations duty to settle the matter was "manifest in Articles 55, 56 and 1 of the Charter."[124] He thought South Africa's plea of domestic jurisdiction to be an attempt to transform general discussion into a debate on competence and declared that the question was "not whether the United Nations had the right to discuss the problem but whether it could possibly keep silent about it."[125]

To their interpretations of the Charter, the communist states added political reasons for the impossibility of silence on the South African issue. Bulgaria thought that South Africa had to be compelled to reappraise its policy of *apartheid* because "there was an imminent danger that the race conflict would soon become acute, thus threatening world peace and security."[126] Poland thought the international significance of the issue lay in the fact that racialism was "a venomous and contagious disease," whose gains or losses anywhere affected all humanity.[127] And the Romanian representative invoked an analogy from the 1930's. Spotting an "inner link" between official racial policy and aggressive designs, he declared that the United Nations "must not misinterpret the principle of non-intervention as the League of Nations had."[128] The representative of the Soviet Union saw the matter in moral terms which, at the same time, demonstrated his oneness with the underdeveloped world. He thought the South African policy of racial discrimination to be "an insult to the non-white peoples of

[124] *GAOR*, 10th sess., Ad Hoc Political Committee, 11th mtg., November 7, 1955, p. 37. The Soviet representative argued that "to question the international nature of the issue, as the United States representative had done, was tantamount to supporting and defending the policy of discrimination against the non-white population." *GAOR*, 8th sess., Ad Hoc Political Committee, 41st mtg., December 4, 1953, p. 216.

[125] *GAOR*, 8th sess., Ad Hoc Political Committee, 37th mtg., December 1, 1953, p. 192, and 13th sess., Special Political Committee, 88th mtg., October 14, 1958, p. 16.

[126] *GAOR*, 11th sess., Special Political Committee, 12th mtg., January 14, 1957, p. 51.

[127] *GAOR*, 13th sess., Special Political Committee, 88th mtg., October 14, 1958, p. 17.

[128] *GAOR*, 13th sess., Special Political Committee, 90th mtg., October 16, 1958, p. 25, and 14th sess., Special Political Committee, 145th mtg., November 6, 1959, p. 91.

Asia, Africa and South America," and that the Security Council had a duty to hear their voice.[129]

As to what to do about South Africa, the communist states listened to the voice of the Third World. The Soviet Union supported the imposition of a boycott, the severance of diplomatic relations, the discontinuance of communication, and she later took up the cry for sanctions and the expulsion of South Africa from the United Nations.[130] Confident that strong measures—the translation of words into action—would bring about the desired effect in South Africa, and irritated by the view that the voice of world conscience would achieve the same end, the communist states also developed a theory to explain the persistence of *apartheid* in the face of United Nations opposition. In the words of the Czechoslovakian representative, "the South African regime would have found it impossible to maintain that policy had it not been for the economic, political, and military support of certain imperialist Powers."[131] This theory, which tarred the West with the racialist brush, was also popular among the states of the Third World.

The states of the Third World could not possibly allow a South African claim to domestic jurisdiction, because her actions were contrary to their view of the fundamental purposes and principles of the Charter. It was absurd to speak of United Nations intervention in a matter essentially within South Africa's domestic jurisdiction, because, as the Indian representative put it, "the question of human rights and fundamental freedoms, having passed into the international domain, was a matter of international concern."[132] With less support in legal doctrine, the Iranian representative asserted "an inherent power in the General Assembly, as the most representative organ of the international community, to impose its

[129] GAOR, 8th sess., Ad Hoc Political Committee, 41st mtg., December 4, 1953, p. 216, and Security Council Official Records, 15th year, 851st mtg., March 30, 1960, p. 4.

[130] GAOR, 15th sess., Special Political Committee, 240th mtg., April 4, 1961, p. 65, and 17th sess., Special Political Committee, 329th mtg., October 11, 1962, p. 14.

[131] GAOR, 20th sess., Special Political Committee, 475th mtg., December 2, 1965, p. 3.

[132] GAOR, 7th sess., Ad Hoc Political Committee, 18th mtg., November 17, 1952, pp. 96–97. The Iranian representative argued that "even if the questions referred to in Article 55 [of the Charter] fell within the domestic jurisdiction of States, Article 56 obliged the States to allow the United Nations to intervene," GAOR, 7th sess., Ad Hoc Political Committee, 18th mtg., November 17, 1952, p. 102.

will."[133] But what made the matter incontestably one of international concern was the threat it presented to international peace and security, in support of which view, three sorts of evidence were offered. First, it was simply asserted that the situation in South Africa was such that sooner or later it was bound to threaten the world with a new conflict unless the United Nations stepped in.[134] In the second place, peace, particularly racial peace, and freedom, were held to be indivisible; if they were compromised in South Africa then they would be compromised everywhere.[135] The Indian representative feared the spreading of the doctrine and practice of *apartheid* beyond the borders of South Africa, and the representative of Ghana saw the creation of race hatred as a cause of war.[136] Moreover, the Tanzanian representative thought the solution to the race conflict in South Africa "would determine the course of race relations in the future."[137] The third sort of evidence of the danger in *apartheid* for international peace was the claim of the Kenyan representative that the "white supremacists of South Africa had sent armed gangsters as far as the borders of the Sudan, Uganda, Rwanda, Burundi, the United Republic of Tanzania, Zambia and the Congo" as part of "a colonial design on Africa."[138]

[133] *GAOR*, 12th sess., Special Political Committee, 50th mtg., October 21, 1957, p. 43.

[134] See statement of the Indian representative, *GAOR*, 7th sess., Ad Hoc Political Committee, 13th mtg., November 12, 1952, pp. 67–68. It was not always clear whether the states of the Third World saw international conflict arising from the situation in South Africa, or whether they asserted a duty to intervene to avert an internal race conflict whatever the international aspects of that conflict. See statement of the representative of Pakistan, *GAOR*, 7th sess., Ad Hoc Political Committee, 15th mtg., November 13, 1952, p. 77, and of the representative of Burundi, *GAOR*, 22d sess., Special Political Committee, 558th mtg., November 2, 1967, p. 35.

[135] See statement of Yugoslav representative, *GAOR*, 7th sess., Ad Hoc Political Committee, 18th mtg., November 17, 1952, p. 100; of the representative of Syria, *GAOR*, 10th sess., Ad Hoc Political Committee, 5th mtg., October 26, 1955, pp. 12–13; of the representative of Ghana, Security Council, *Official Records* (hereafter *SCOR*), 15th year, 853d mtg., March 31, 1960, pp. 2–3, and of the representative of Togo, *GAOR*, 17th sess., Special Political Committee, 339th mtg., October 30, 1962, p. 67.

[136] *GAOR*, 10th sess., Ad Hoc Political Committee, 12th mtg., November 9, 1955, p. 43, and *SCOR*, 15th year, 853d mtg., March 31, 1960, pp. 2–3. See also statement of Zambian representative, *GAOR*, 24th sess., Special Political Committee, 647th mtg., October 24, 1969, p. 19.

[137] *Ibid.*, p. 23.

[138] *GAOR*, 22d sess., Special Political Committee, 562d mtg., November 8, 1967, p. 62.

Variously interpreted as originating with or produced by it, as operating with its philosophy or being its modern manifestation, *apartheid* was generally despised in the Third World as a species of colonialism.[139] Its elimination was considered to be a moral duty above the law. The Pakistan representative thought the issue was "in essence a purely moral one."[140] The Egyptian representative declared that "human solidarity could not be confined within national boundaries."[141] And the representative of Saudi Arabia dismissed the South African plea of domestic jurisdiction with an assertion that "the exigencies of moral law could not be sacrificed to legal questions."[142]

A moral problem, moral pressure was not thought sufficient to solve it.[143] The call for sanctions originated in the Third World and became more strident as the Western powers were slow to respond. For Ghana, the answer was "to ostracize South Africa from the community of civilized nations," and for many Third World states the West was the obstacle in the way of a solution.[144] To the representative of Uganda "it really appeared that, for the Western states, a threat to peace and security meant a threat against their own interests and those of the white population."[145] As the issue remained unresolved, the call for action escalated. Algeria declared that "the people of South Africa had no choice but to re-

[139] See statement of the UAR representative, GAOR, 14th sess., Special Political Committee, 140th mtg., October 30, 1959, p. 69; of the Pakistan representative, SCOR, 15th year, 852d mtg., March 30, 1960, p. 31; of the Indonesian representative, GAOR, 16th sess., Special Political Committee, 282d mtg., November 8, 1961, p. 113, and of Morocco, GAOR, 21st sess., Special Political Committee, 532d mtg., December 5, 1966, p. 197.

[140] GAOR, 10th sess., Ad Hoc Political Committee, 9th mtg., November 3, 1955, p. 27.

[141] GAOR, 10th sess., Ad Hoc Political Committee, 7th mtg., November 1, 1955, p. 17.

[142] GAOR, 7th sess., Ad Hoc Political Committee, 18th mtg., November 17, 1952, pp. 95–96.

[143] See statement of Iraq representative, GAOR, 15th sess., Special Political Committee, 239th mtg., April 3, 1961, p. 57.

[144] GAOR, 16th sess., Special Political Committee, 269th mtg., October 25, 1961, p. 47. The Philippines was one of the few Third World states to have doubts about sanctions, see GAOR, 11th sess., Special Political Committee, 11th mtg., January 11, 1957, p. 49.

[145] GAOR, 22d sess., Special Political Committee, 557th mtg., November 1, 1967, p. 30.

sort to armed struggle."[146] The Zambian representative urged the United Nations to "support the South African freedom-fighters and find ways of inducing the masses inside South Africa to fight for their freedom."[147] In the context of *apartheid*, the principle of nonintervention had become a totally discredited doctrine, Guinea accusing France of invoking the principle "to justify its support for the racist and fascist minority regime in South Africa."[148]

Generally more cautious than the states of the Third World, the Latin American states were no less convinced that the question of *apartheid* was a matter of international, and not purely domestic, concern.[149] The representative of Ecuador argued that by their signature of the Charter states had accepted a limitation on their freedom of action in the area of human rights and that sovereignty could not be invoked to undermine this established order.[150] He also maintained that the question of "intervention" did not arise because that was "a technical term which referred to interference in the affairs of a State and the use of force to that end; it did not have the broad meaning ascribed to it by South Africa.[151] The representative of Argentina disposed of the South African claim to domestic jurisdiction in more radical manner, declaring

[146] *GAOR*, 24th sess., Special Political Committee, 648th mtg., October 27, 1969, p. 25.

[147] *GAOR*, 24th sess., Special Political Committee, 647th mtg., October 24, 1969, p. 19.

[148] *GAOR*, 20th sess., Special Political Committee, 469th mtg., November 29, 1965, p. 4. The Liberian representative had already deplored the attitude of certain delegations which persistently sought shelter behind the "legal fiction" of noninterference in domestic affairs of states. See *Year Book of the United Nations*, 1960, p. 150.

[149] At first, Peru was an exception, asserting in 1955 that South Africa was protected by the principle of nonintervention. By 1957 her view had changed, and in 1959 her representative argued that the general principles of the Charter "by their very nature, prevailed over the narrow concept of national competence." See *GAOR*, 10th sess., Ad Hoc Political Committee, 11th mtg., November 7, 1955, p. 39, and 14th sess., Special Political Committee, 143d mtg., November 4, 1959, p. 54.

[150] *GAOR*, 17th sess., Special Political Committee, 339th mtg., October 30, 1962, p. 66. See also statement of the representative of Costa Rica, *GAOR*, 12th sess., Special Political Committee, 54th mtg., October 29, 1957, p. 57.

[151] *GAOR*, 10th sess., Ad Hoc Political Committee, 7th mtg., November 1, 1955, pp. 19–20.

it to be inadmissible "where the majority of the people did not exercise sovereign rights."[152] The Guatemalan representative went beyond law and the interpretation of the Charter to find a justification for United Nations competence in the matter in "the moral right conferred on the Organization by a feeling of human solidarity with the non-white population of South Africa."[153]

Though most Latin American states sooner or later were persuaded of the existence in the policy of *apartheid* of a threat to the peace, it took longer to convince them of the need for sanctions. In 1961 the Chilean representative "was opposed to any measure which would lead South Africa to withdraw from the Organization, since that country would then be free to intensify its policy of racial discrimination and would be beyond the reach of any moderating influence."[154] He was against sanctions on the ground that "an attack from outside always strengthened national unity within a country," and the Argentinian representative was against them because they "would lead to hardship for the very people whom the United Nations wished to help."[155] By 1965 many of the Latin American states were responding in kind to the cries of the Third World for sanctions against South Africa.[156] Doubt lingered, however. In 1967 the Mexican representative could still make a plea for the complexity of the issue and the need for its careful study.[157] As to the principle of nonintervention, he regarded it as "significant that the representatives of States which had contributed to the reinforcement of that principle should now

[152] GAOR, 8th sess., Ad Hoc Political Committee, 40th mtg., December 4, 1953, p. 210.

[153] GAOR, 16th sess., Special Political Committee, 276th mtg., November 2, 1961, p. 85.

[154] GAOR, 16th sess., Special Political Committee, 281st mtg., November 7, 1961, p. 109.

[155] Ibid., p. 109, and GAOR, 16th sess., Special Political Committee, 282d mtg., November 8, 1961, p. 111.

[156] See, e.g., statement of Colombian representative, GAOR, 20th sess., Special Political Committee, 473d mtg., December 1, 1965, p. 6; of Guatemalan representative, 20th sess., Special Political Committee, 480th mtg., December 6, 1965, p. 3; of the Chilean representative, 20th sess., Special Political Committee, 481st mtg., December 7, 1965, p. 1, and of the representative of Ecuador, 22d sess., Special Political Committee, 559th mtg., November 3, 1967, p. 41.

[157] GAOR, 22d sess., Special Political Committee, 562d mtg., November 8, 1967, pp. 64–65.

disagree with the South African attitude" to it.[158] But in making an exception in the case of *apartheid*, the Latin American states were very anxious to find doctrinal support in the Charter.

The South African interpretation of the Charter was very different. With Evatt at San Francisco, she thought that Article 2(7) was to the smaller powers what the veto was to the great, and that the use of the word "essentially" rather than "solely" broadened rather than diminished its scope.[159] In support of a broad definition of intervention extending to discussion and consideration of the question of *apartheid*, she offered the view that if it were restricted to the meaning of "dictatorial interference" it would not apply to a measure taken by the General Assembly, which had only the power to recommend. In denying the competence of the United Nations, the South African representative drew attention to the matters to which the racial conflict related. From legislation on land tenure to combat services in the armed forces, he argued "they covered the whole field of domestic administration in a modern state." To allow the United Nations to intervene in such matters, he continued, "was tantamount to denying the principle and attributes of national sovereignty," and it would "signal the end of the United Nations as an organization of sovereign states." Without the protection of Article 2(7), South Africa later argued that she would not have become a member of the Organization.[160]

There was some sympathy elsewhere in the Western world for South Africa's extreme interpretation of Article 2(7). The United Kingdom, France, and Australia shared the view that the United Nations was not a superstate with all-embracing powers, and that the discussion of the question of race conflict in South Africa was beyond the Organization's competence.[161] The French representa-

[158] *GAOR*, 8th sess., Ad Hoc Political Committee, 19th mtg., October 26, 1953, p. 91.

[159] *GAOR*, 7th sess., Ad Hoc Political Committee, 13th mtg., November 12, 1952, p. 66, and 8th sess., Ad Hoc Political Committee, 32d mtg., November 23, 1953, p. 156, from which the quotations following are taken.

[160] *GAOR*, 16th sess., 1014th Plenary mtg., September 25, 1961, p. 70.

[161] See *GAOR*, 7th sess., Ad Hoc Political Committee, 20th mtg., November 19, 1952, p. 76; 8th sess., Ad Hoc Political Committee, 20th mtg., October 27, 1953, p. 98; 8th sess., Ad Hoc Political Committee, 38th mtg., December 2, 1953, p. 197; 9th sess., Ad Hoc Political Committee, 47th mtg., December 8, 1954, p. 232, and 10th sess., Ad Hoc Political Committee, 5th mtg., October 26, 1955, p. 13.

tive thought that the stipulation in Article 2(7) that "nothing contained in the present Charter shall authorize the United Nations to intervene," clearly defended domestic jurisdiction from the other articles of the Charter, and he declared that France "did not assume the right to set itself up as a judge and condemn the internal policy of a foreign government."[162] The line taken by the United States, Canada and the Scandinavian countries was less insistent on the sanctity of domestic jurisdiction. The Norwegian representative thought that "leaving all legal aspects aside, the repercussions which . . . the *apartheid* policy . . . had had on world public opinion and on the relations between States had put the matter outside the realm of purely domestic problems."[163] The United States representative thought that discussion did not contravene Article 2(7) and that the United Nations had an obligation "to be concerned with national policies in so far as they affect the world community."[164]

In 1961 the United Kingdom defected to this more moderate school of Western thought and justified the change with an ingenious argument. A year earlier, after the Sharpeville shootings, the Italian representative had argued that "the special political purport of the recent tragic developments . . . appear[s] to justify, within limits some kind of exceptional procedures" on the part of the Security Council.[165] The representative of the United Kingdom embroidered this argument. "While the importance attached by the United Kingdom to Article 2, paragraph 7, of the Charter remained undiminished," he declared, "it regarded *apartheid* as being now so exceptional as to be *sui generis*."[166] It was unique in that it involved "the deliberate adoption, retention and development of policies based entirely on racial discrimination" and the problem was now thought to cause "grave international repercussions."[167] But while the Western states were now prepared to con-

[162] *GAOR*, 8th sess., Ad Hoc Political Committee, 38th mtg., December 2, 1953, p. 197; and 14th sess., Special Political Committee, 146th mtg., November 6, 1959, p. 93.

[163] *GAOR*, 7th sess., Ad Hoc Political Committee, 13th mtg., November 12, 1952, pp. 69–70.

[164] *GAOR*, 7th sess., Ad Hoc Political Committee, 17th mtg., November 15, 1952, p. 90, and *SCOR*, 15th year, 851st mtg., March 30, 1960, p. 4.

[165] *Ibid.*

[166] See *GAOR*, 15th sess., Special Political Committee, 242d mtg., April 5, 1961, p. 77.

[167] *Ibid.*

cede that the situation in South Africa was leading to "international friction," or that its continuance was "likely to endanger international peace and security," they did not concede that it was a threat to the peace within the meaning of Chapter VII of the Charter.[168]

Western suggestions about solutions to the problem of *apartheid* reflected views held about interpretation of the Charter and about the limits of United Nations activity. In 1953 France thought that the United Nations could address recommendations to the community of states as a whole, but that improper interference began when a state was designated by name.[169] In 1955 the Swedish representative did not object to the naming of names, but thought that the United Nations had no right to recommend a state to take specific action: "The General Assembly could only point the road without issuing directives."[170] But as the anti-*apartheid* movement in the Assembly swept past these restrictions, the West was forced to address it at a new level—that of stating the case against sanctions. Thus Italy thought that "excessively drastic action" would harm the interests of the African peoples whom the United Nations wished to help.[171] The representative of the United Kingdom argued that the further isolation of South Africa would reduce the possibility of exercising influence for the better, and that the imposition of sanctions might be the final step towards destroying liberal opinion there.[172] And the Canadian representative thought that "perhaps the best argument" against sanctions was that they would "run counter to the principle established by the Charter that sanctions were intended solely for the purpose of preventing or putting an end to international hostilities."[173] The West had

[168] See statement of the British representative, SCOR, 18th year, 1054th mtg., August 6, 1963, pp. 18–20, and of the representative of the United States, SCOR, 18th year, 1052d mtg., August 2, 1963, p. 14.

[169] GAOR, 8th sess., Ad Hoc Political Committee, 38th mtg., December 2, 1953, p. 197.

[170] GAOR, 10th sess., Ad Hoc Political Committee, 5th mtg., October 26, 1955, p. 11. See also statement of Canadian representative, GAOR, 15th sess., Special Political Committee, 243d mtg., April 5, 1961, p. 79.

[171] GAOR, 16th sess., Special Political Committee, 272d mtg., October 30, 1961, p. 63.

[172] GAOR, 16th sess., Special Political Committee, 274th mtg., October 31, 1961, p. 69, and 17th sess., Special Political Committee, 339th mtg., October 30, 1962, p. 66.

[173] GAOR, 15th sess., Special Political Committee, 243d mtg., April 5, 1961, p. 79.

273

always preferred to rely on the force of conscience and world public opinion.[174] France, observing that *apartheid* sprang from an idea, looked for the triumph over it of another idea supported by the United Nations—the idea of the equality of races.[175] Italy looked for a morally effective means to solve a problem which was essentially moral.[176] This did not salvage the principle of nonintervention to the satisfaction of South Africa, because the West had admitted the problem of *apartheid* to be one of international concern. But in holding out against the call for action under Chapter VII of the Charter, the West attempted to preserve the substance of domestic jurisdiction.

VI

The development of the United Nations doctrine of nonintervention witnessed the entrance of new states into an international community whose rules were not fashioned with their interests in mind. Among their principal foreign policy concerns was the protection of their newly won independence against the encroachment of outsiders and the proclamation of their solidarity against colonialism and racialism—the relics of an order made redundant by their arrival. Faithful to these concerns, the new states insisted on a near-absolute principle of nonintervention but made an exception in the case of peoples struggling for their independence against the persistence of the old order. Just as the Soviet Union looked to a higher law of socialist internationalism and as the United States came close to asserting a duty above the law during the Dominican intervention, so the new states affirmed the transcendent legitimacy of the struggle against colonialism. While the communist states swam with the tide of this new legitimacy, the West seemed taken aback by the doctrinal onslaught, consenting, for the sake of its political posture in the Third World, to disagreeable declarations and resolutions.

Revealed most clearly in the extreme positions in the debate about *apartheid* taken up by South Africa (insisting on domestic

[174] Statement of the representative of the United States, GAOR, 7th sess., Ad Hoc Political Committee, 17th mtg., November 15, 1952, p. 91.

[175] GAOR, 16th sess., Special Political Committee, 277th mtg., November 2, 1961, p. 89.

[176] GAOR, 24th sess., Special Political Committee, 654th mtg., November 4, 1969, p. 66.

jurisdiction even to the extent of precluding discussion) and by the militant black African states (demanding active United Nations intervention on behalf of the black population of South Africa) but discernible also in the general positions adopted by the West as against the communist states and the Third World were two different conceptions of the nature of the international order established by the United Nations. South Africa, asserting the primacy of domestic jurisdiction and of the principle of nonintervention and emphasizing the character of the United Nations as an international body concerned with peace and security between states, warned of the collapse of the organization as one between sovereign states, if it interfered in matters within them.[177] The militant Africans, on the other hand, emphasized respect for human rights and fundamental freedoms as the essential purpose of the United Nations. In this regard, conduct within states was a crucial concern of the Organization on which peace between states depended.[178] On this view, the United Nations would be "digging its own grave" if it tolerated the abuse of human rights within states—if it failed to intervene.[179] Thus the controversy about the principle of nonintervention and about the legitimate exceptions to the rule went beyond the debate about the proper limits of United Nations activity to conflicting theories of the requirements for peace and of the relation between domestic and international politics.

The development of a United Nations doctrine of nonintervention was not, however, a mere political game in which the stronger or the more persuasive interest prevailed, and in the course of which different opinions about the fundamentals of international order were canvassed. The General Assembly was also recording the practice of states, and while it was not empowered to legislate for the international community, it was at least providing some evidence by reference to which claims could be asserted in international law.[180] Given that Assembly resolutions are legally sig-

[177] *GAOR*, 8th sess., Ad Hoc Political Committee, 32d mtg., November 23, 1953, p. 156.

[178] See, e.g., statement of the representative of Sierra Leone, *SCOR*, 19th year, 1130th mtg., April 12, 1964, p. 12.

[179] See, e.g., statement of Tunisian representative, *GAOR*, 16th sess., Special Political Committee, 273d mtg., October 30, 1961, p. 67.

[180] This is a matter of some controversy which is beyond the scope of this work. See Rosalyn Higgins, *The Development of International Law through the Political Organs of the United Nations*, London, 1963, and "The United Nations and Law-Making: the Political Organs," *Proceedings*

nificant as well as politically interesting, it remains to discover the contribution to law made by the 1965 Declaration on Nonintervention and the 1970 Declaration on Principles of International Law. Both borrow from the inter-American doctrine of nonintervention and both assert a near-absolute prohibition of intervention. But the term "intervention" is no nearer to a consensual definition, and the sorts of actions which escape the net of the principle of nonintervention remain a matter for the unilateral interpretation of states. Nor is the principle, in the form it takes in the 1970 Declaration, a discrete injunction readily distinguishable from the other principles proclaimed there, from the prohibition of the threat or use of force to the principle of equal rights and self-determination of peoples, the first of which seemed to absorb much of the content of the nonintervention principle and the second to constitute an exception to it. In the context of the 1970 Declaration, the principle of nonintervention seemed to function as a sort of "back-stop" principle proscribing all those unfriendly acts not explicitly dealt with under other headings. In general, the principle of nonintervention at the United Nations was rather like Brierly's domestic jurisdiction—a "fetish about which . . . little seems to be generally known except its extreme sanctity."[181]

The practice of the United Nations as an actor in world politics, rather than as a forum for them, was perhaps a surer guide to the boundaries of domestic jurisdiction and of the nonintervention principle. In one sense, a decision by the United Nations that a matter was within its jurisdiction, and not an essentially domestic matter, ruled out the question of intervention and nonintervention, for it would be absurd to speak of United Nations "intervention" in a matter within its own jurisdiction. Yet the question of intervention and nonintervention reappears in an inquiry into just how far the writ of the United Nations runs. Thus the practice of the United Nations might be said to show that the discussion of the

---

of the American Society of International Law, April 1970, rept. in American Journal of International Law, Vol. 64, No. 4, 1970; Falk, "On the Quasi-Legislative Competence of the General Assembly," American Journal of International Law, Vol. 60, No. 4, 1966, and N. G. Onuf, "Professor Falk on the Quasi-Legislative Competence of the General Assembly," American Journal of International Law, Vol. 64, No. 2, 1970.

[181] "Matters of Domestic Jurisdiction," British Yearbook of International Law, Vol. VI, 1925, p. 8.

question of race conflict in South Africa and the issuing of recommendations thereon do not constitute intervention in her internal affairs, but the line was drawn at mandatory sanctions under Chapter VII of the Charter. The drawing of that line has left South Africa with what might be called *de facto* domestic jurisdiction, but in the light of United Nations practice on human rights, any claim to exclude outside authority can, perhaps, no longer be asserted as of right.[182] More generally, the practice of states and their votes at the United Nations seem to have sanctioned a right of self-determination—at least as it applies to emancipation from colonial rule.[183] In the matter of human rights and of the right to self-determination, in this limited sense, it seems that an extreme claim to domestic jurisdiction, of the sort made by South Africa, is no longer admissible. But neither the white South African, nor the black African, prophecy of doom for the United Nations has yet come to pass. What has happened to the nonintervention principle as it applies between the United Nations and its members is that it now stands legal guard over a narrower right of domestic jurisdiction.

[182] Higgins, *The Development of International Law through the Political Organs*, pp. 120–123. But see further below Chapter Eight, section II, and Chapter Nine, section III.

[183] *Ibid.*, pp. 99–102. See further below Chapter Nine, section VI.

PART FOUR

International Society and the Principle of Nonintervention

EIGHT

THE CONTEMPORARY INTERNATIONAL LAW
OF NONINTERVENTION

The history of the principle of nonintervention at the United Nations revealed it to be a norm which most states, at least in their public utterances, held to be fundamental to harmonious international relations. But the deliberations and resolutions of the United Nations testified more to the perceived importance of the rule than to its content and scope. This chapter will attempt to fix the position of the principle of nonintervention, if indeed it has one, in the body of rules making up current international law. The chapter will have three sections. The first will examine the inheritance of traditional international law on the principle, the extent of its prohibition of intervention and the exceptions to the rule it allowed. The second will look at the recent changes in the structure of international society and in theories advanced about its nature that have led many international lawyers to cast doubt upon the relevance of the nonintervention principle and upon the values of sovereignty and domestic jurisdiction which it existed to protect. In the light of argument noted in this part, the third section will go on to discuss the place of the principle in contemporary international law.

I

The inheritance of traditional international law has not provided the subject with an agreed body of doctrine on the question of intervention. Indeed, one writer doubted the possibility of subjecting intervention to legal control. Sir William Harcourt, writing during the American Civil War, thought intervention to be a "question rather of policy than of law."[1] "It is above and beyond the domain of law," he went on, "and when wisely and equitably handled by those who have the power to give effect to it, may be the highest policy of justice and humanity."[2] Although it was first a question

[1] *Letters by Historicus on Some Questions of International Law*, London, 1863, p. 14.
[2] *Ibid.*, p. 41.

of policy and not of law, Harcourt held at the same time that the essence of intervention was illegality, and success its justification. This being the case, there was nothing worse than an intervention that failed: "Of all things, at once the most unjustifiable and the most impolitic is an unsuccessful intervention."[3] While Harcourt did not wish to abandon the question altogether to politics the efficacy of intervention was the fundamental criterion, not its lawfulness. Lorimer, the rogue Naturalist of the nineteenth century, took exception to this doctrine, arguing that it degraded jurisprudence "by supposing it to depend on *lower* principles than those which govern politics."[4] Lorimer thought the question of intervention fell "within the scope of the science of jurisprudence" and criticized Harcourt's position for its haziness as to the relation between ethics and jurisprudence.[5] Lawrence, while he did not address himself directly to the Harcourt heresy, provided a less obscure answer to it than Lorimer. Thinking state practice to be a useless guide to legal rules about intervention, he argued that the alternative source was inference from first principles.[6] By looking to principles which no one doubted—the right of independence or the duty of self-preservation—for legal guidance, Lawrence was able to escape the positivists' difficulty of deciding on the rule when an appeal to the practice of states was unprofitable.[7]

While recognizing the difficulties involved in formulating rules about intervention, most writers on international law did not surrender completely to politics as Harcourt came close to doing. Wolff in the eighteenth century, and Bernard in the nineteenth, solved the problem by prohibiting intervention altogether, allowing no legal justification for breach of the principle of nonintervention.[8] Other writers espoused such a principle but so limited its

[3] *Ibid.*

[4] *Institutes of the Law of Nations*, 2 vols., London, 1884, Vol. II, p. 44. (Lorimer's emphasis).

[5] *Ibid.*, pp. 44–49.

[6] *Principles of International Law*, p. 121. See also above, Chapter Two, pp. 36–37.

[7] Lawrence did not state this doctrine quite as clearly as is suggested here, for he went on to agree with Harcourt that in most cases intervention was a question of policy and that only in exceptional cases was it a matter of legal right. *Principles of International Law*, p. 121. Inference from first principles it seems did not necessarily bring the question of intervention into the province of the law.

[8] See above, Chapter Two, pp. 26–28 and 37–39. For other writers who

scope by allowing the doctrine of necessity to override it as to approach a position nearly opposite to that of Wolff and Bernard.[9] Between these two positions, Winfield traced a middle course. Since state independence was the foundation of modern international law, he argued, nonintervention was the rule and intervention the exception.[10] What follows will examine the arguments most commonly urged in justification of the exception.

Grotius did not allow subject peoples to fight for their liberty against the oppressor, requiring them, in the interests of order, to be satisfied with their lot.[11] But he did allow others to take up arms on their behalf, to exercise "the right vested in human society."[12] This, in Lauterpacht's words, was the "first authoritative statement of the principle of humanitarian intervention."[13] The subsequent career of this principle was unpromising until it received some recognition in the positive international law of the twentieth century. That Grotius could espouse such a doctrine was made possible by his conception of an international society made up of individuals as well as of states. Individuals were members of international society not only in the ultimate sense of their being the representatives of states but also directly as recipients of rights and bearers of obligations in that society.[14] This was not a position which the Positivists of the nineteenth century could accept, conceiving, as they did, of an international society made up exclusively of states. To intervene on humanitarian grounds on behalf of individuals was to meddle in a matter with which international relations were not concerned.[15] It might be morally right but it was

---

favored an absolute ban on intervention, see Fenwick, "Intervention: Individual and Collective," *American Journal of International Law*, Vol. 39, No. 4, 1945, p. 646, n. 5.

[9] See, e.g., Wheaton, *Elements of International Law*, Pt. II, Chap. I, section 72.

[10] "History of Intervention in International Law," *British Yearbook of International Law*, Vol. III, 1922–1923, p. 139.

[11] *De Jure Belli ac Pacis*, Bk. II, Chap. XXII, section XI.

[12] *Ibid.*, Bk. II, Chap. XXV, section VIII.

[13] "The Grotian Tradition in International Law," *British Yearbook of International Law*, Vol. XXIII, 1946, p. 46.

[14] *Ibid.*, p. 27.

[15] See Hall, *Treatise on International Law*, p. 342. On the differences between Grotius and Oppenheim on the question of humanitarian intervention see Bull, "The Grotian Conception of International Society," in Butterfield and Wight, *Diplomatic Investigations*, pp. 63–64.

beyond the domain of law.[16] Moreover, the moral claim was itself dubious because it was so prone to abuse by selfish ambition.[17]

The question of humanitarian intervention was frequently raised in consideration of the proper conduct for outside states when a state was torn by civil war. Grotian doctrine allowed intervention on the just side in such a war. States were entitled to undertake war to enforce the rights of others as well as their own, and the others included the wronged subjects of a ruler.[18] Similarly, Vattel thought that "if a prince, by violating the fundamental laws, gives his subjects a lawful cause for resisting him; if, by his insupportable tyranny, he brings on a national revolt against him, any foreign power may rightfully give assistance to an oppressed people who ask for its aid."[19] But this was not an immediate right. Vattel thought that in a situation of civil war it was not the part of foreign nations to decide between citizens who had taken up arms, nor between the sovereign and his subjects.[20] Only when the interposition of good offices, an act required by the natural law, had failed, were nations entitled to "decide for themselves the merits of the case, and assist the party which seems to have justice on its side."[21]

The positivist international lawyers could not follow Vattel into a decision on the merits of a case, for this, in Hall's view, was beyond the legal range of vision—it had nothing to do with the relations between states.[22] In the eyes of the law, the excesses of a revolution and the tyranny of a sovereign were strictly equivalent.[23] Neither the view that favored intervention at the request of an

---

[16] Lawrence, p. 128. E. C. Stowell on the other hand, found support in the practice of states and in legal doctrine for his contention that humanitarian intervention could be defined as "the reliance upon force for the justifiable purpose of protecting the inhabitants of another state from treatment which is so arbitrary and persistently abusive as to exceed the limits of that authority within which the sovereign is presumed to act with reason or justice." *Intervention in International Law*, Washington, D.C., 1921, p. 53.

[17] Hall, p. 343; Phillimore, *Commentaries on International Law*, Vol. I, Pt. IV, Chap. I, section CCCC.

[18] *De Jure Belli ac Pacis*, Bk. II, Chap. XXV, section VIII.

[19] *The Law of Nations*, Bk. II, Chap. IV, section 56.

[20] *Ibid.*, Bk. III, Chap. XVIII, section 296.

[21] *Ibid.*

[22] Hall, p. 347. [23] *Ibid.*, p. 343.

established government, nor that which allowed support for the just party found the approval of Lawrence, who thought that either would prejudice the freedom of the people of a state to settle their own affairs in their own way.[24] Fidelity to this doctrine required that respect be shown to the independence of states by the refusal of invitations to intervene whether they were issued by incumbents or insurgents. But if the Positivists had any bias in this respect, it was toward the established government. The bias was due to the argument that a lawful sovereign authority should not lose its membership in the international club and the advantages deriving from it merely because it was being challenged at home, unless and until the challenge was such as to replace the authority or to establish a separate one.[25]

This last consideration, introducing as it does the factor of time, reveals the difficulties involved in the insistent noninterventionism of Lawrence, Bernard, and Stowell. If the purpose of such a doctrine is to isolate domestic conflict from the purview of international law, then it fails when a rebellion forces itself upon the notice of international society by successfully establishing a new entity.[26] The solution of this problem for international society, and in particular for those of its members whose interests were most directly affected by any civil war, lay in that device of traditional international law which allocated rights and duties to outside states and to the warring factions according to a status assigned to the

[24] Lawrence, pp. 131–132. For similar views see Bernard, *On the Principle of Non Intervention*, pp. 15–16 and 20–23; Stowell, pp. 330–331.

[25] See H. Lauterpacht, *Recognition in International Law*, Cambridge, 1948, pp. 230–233. See also for a view which finds the authorities less clear on this matter, I. Brownlie, *International Law and the Use of Force by States*, Oxford, 1963, pp. 321–327.

[26] Moreover, if a further purpose of the doctrine is to allow domestic events to run their course free from outside interference then absolute noninterventionism might achieve this only by depriving the established government of that international support which was regarded hitherto as altogether normal, and thus helping the insurgents by default. It may be for this reason that Wheaton speaks of outside states remaining indifferent spectators by "still continuing to treat the ancient government as sovereign, and the government *de facto* as a society entitled to the rights of war against its enemy," *Elements of International Law*, Pt. I, Chap. II, section 23, p. 29. This confused statement of the recognition of belligerency doctrine nevertheless indicates Wheaton's awareness that strict noninterventionism might not achieve its desired goal of international impartiality towards conflict within states.

civil conflict.[27] Thus Lauterpacht speaks of four conditions which, if they prevail in a situation of civil war, impose a duty of recognition of belligerency on outside states:

> . . . first, there must exist within the State an armed conflict of a general (as distinguished from a purely local) character; secondly, the insurgents must occupy and administer a substantial portion of national territory; thirdly, they must conduct the hostilities in accordance with the rules of war and through organized armed forces acting under a responsible authority; fourthly, there must exist circumstances which make it necessary for outside States to define their attitude by means of recognition of belligerency.[28]

The recognition of belligerency in turn imposes a duty of neutrality on outside states: they are bound to treat the parties to a civil conflict equally.[29] Recognition of belligerency deprives the incumbent of its status as sole international actor for the disputed territory and admits the insurgent into membership, though not full membership, in the international club.[30] Traditional international law also recognized a status of insurgency, "an intermediate stage between a state of tranquillity and a state of civil war."[31] The rights and duties involved in the allocation of the status of insurgency were unclear. Indeed, Lauterpacht took this to be one of its defining characteristics: "belligerency is a relation giving rise to definite rights and obligations, while insurgency is not."[32] At the least it was "in essence a domestic proclamation, drawing the attention of the public to a state of fact in a foreign State which calls for special caution."[33] At the most it was a "catch-all designation" that encompassed the practice of states which had conferred rights and imposed duties on rebellious factions without recognizing them as belligerents.[34] But while the condition of insurgency lasts, the presumption for international society is in favor of the established

[27] See Falk, "The International Law of Internal War: Problems and Prospects," in *Legal Order in a Violent World*, pp. 117–127.

[28] Lauterpacht, p. 176, and see the authorities he cites at pp. 240–243, as recognizing an international duty of recognition of belligerency.

[29] Thomas and Thomas, *Non-Intervention*, p. 219.

[30] *Ibid.*

[31] T.-C. Chen, *The International Law of Recognition,* ed. L. C. Green, London, 1951, p. 398.

[32] Lauterpacht, p. 270.   [33] Chen, p. 400.

[34] Falk, p. 119; see also Lauterpacht, pp. 270–278.

government.[35] This doctrine applied the more forcibly to a third category of internal conflict recognized in traditional international law—that of rebellion, a state of unrest which had not reached the proportions of an insurgency—of which the society of states was to take no formal notice.[36]

The problem of civil war, then, raised many more issues for traditional international law than just the disputed question of humanitarian intervention. In order to accommodate the interests of states affected by civil war in another state and those of successful insurrectionists, the law admitted entities other than fully sovereign states into its purview. The international order was to be preserved in the first instance by allowing governments a free hand in keeping order within states. When that policy failed, the order was to be preserved by treating disputants as separate states.[37]

If there was some doubt in traditional international law as to the rights and duties it accorded individuals and groups within states, there was no doubt at all about the right of states to self-defense. For Grotius, the right had its origin in "the fact that nature commits to each his own protection."[38] The contribution of the naturalist writers to the international law of self-defense lay in their conception of the right as one being called into play when an international wrong had been done, when "a breach of a legal duty owed to the state acting in self-defence" had occurred.[39] In the nineteenth century, there was a tendency to break away from this restricted interpretation of the right of self-defense illustrated by the expansion of the concept to include that of self-preservation.[40] Lawrence thought that the right of self-preservation was even more sacred than the duty of respecting the independence of

[35] *Ibid.*, p. 233. See also Thomas and Thomas, who state the case for the incumbent more strongly than does Lauterpacht, *Non-Intervention*, p. 217.

[36] Falk, pp. 118–119; Thomas and Thomas, p. 216.

[37] But as Falk points out, this "functional role attributed to the distinctions between rebellion, insurgency and belligerency is more an invention of commentators than a description of state behavior," "International Law of Internal War," p. 124.

[38] *De Jure Belli ac Pacis*, Bk. II, Chap. I, section III.

[39] D. W. Bowett, *Self-Defence in International Law*, Manchester, 1958, p. 9. Bowett bases his own account of the law of self-defense on this doctrine, arguing that the right exists to protect "certain essential legal rights" of states, *ibid.*, p. 20.

[40] Brierly, *Law of Nations*, p. 404.

others, and Hall went as far as to say "in the last resort almost the whole of the duties of states are subordinated to the right of self-preservation."[41] This doctrine of self-preservation has since been criticized on two main grounds. In the first place, it was thought to destroy the imperative character of the law by making the obligation to obey it merely conditional.[42] Second, the doctrine was objected to on the ground that it was unmeaning legally; it belonged to the realm of policy and ideology not of law, providing an excuse for all manner of international lawlessness but no legal justification.[43]

So long as the right of self-defense, or indeed of self-preservation, was invoked to justify the defense of the sovereignty of the state against outside attack, and the remedy was applied within the claimant's territorial jurisdiction, then there was little controversy in traditional international law as to the existence of the right.[44] The matter of intervention in self-defense was more problematical. It raised the question of the extent to which the right of one state to self-defense held sway over the right of another to independence. Two examples, the one concerning protective intervention, the other concerning preventive intervention, will illustrate the difficulties of deciding upon the relation between these rights. A right of states well established by their practice is that of intervention to protect the lives and property of their citizens. In the absence of agreement among states as to the standards of conduct required of their subjects, which might have given the society of states a right of intervention on this ground, the positivist international lawyers based the protective right on that of the state to self-preservation.[45] The violation of the rights of individuals was a violation

[41] Lawrence, p. 125; Hall, p. 322. See also Winfield, "The Grounds of Intervention in International Law," *British Yearbook of International Law*, Vol. v, 1924, p. 151.

[42] Brierly, p. 404. J. Westlake speaks of the function of the law as being to tame such a primitive instinct, *Chapters on the Principles of International Law*, Cambridge, 1894, p. 112.

[43] Brierly, p. 404; Bowett, p. 10.

[44] So little in fact, that as Bowett points out, there was some doubt about the relevance of the rule in this instance, it being covered by the right to territorial sovereignty. *Self-Defence in International Law*, p. 22.

[45] See *ibid.*, p. 92. He cites Hall and Westlake to this effect, the latter with the proviso that an action of a trivial nature does not infringe the right, due to the maxim *de minimis non curat lex*. Thomas and Thomas do not deal with the right as one of self-defense, but as one which concerns an international standard of justice, *Non-Intervention*, pp. 303–309.

of the rights of the state of which they were nationals.[46] The difficulty with this doctrine lies in fixing the point at which the danger to nationals arising from any situation in another state justifies intervention on their behalf. On the question of preventive intervention or anticipatory self-defense, the doctrine of contagion espoused by the Holy Alliance as an explanation for and justification of intervention on behalf of legitimate governments, was not sanctioned in the writings of many international lawyers. Westlake stated the case against the doctrine in two ways. First, international society was not one for the "mutual insurance of established governments."[47] In the second place, Canning's doctrine requiring proof that principles were to be propagated across frontiers by the sword before intervention could take place against them was accepted as conclusive.[48] But though in this case Westlake found in favor of the right of independence and against that of self-defense, the general problem of the boundary between them remained. The *Caroline* case, the "*locus classicus* of the right of self-defence," provided some guidance.[49] On preventive intervention, a "necessity of self-defence" had to be shown, "instant, overwhelming, leaving no choice of means, and no moment for deliberation."[50] On protective intervention, "the act, justified by the necessity of self-defence, must be limited by that necessity and kept clearly within it."[51] The guidance here lay in the plea for restraint and for the careful measuring of relative rights; there was no account of the circumstances which might give rise to the "necessity of self-defence."[52] The variety of these, and the peculiar

[46] The "rights of individuals" here means their rights as citizens of states, not of the world.

[47] Westlake, p. 124.   [48] *Ibid.*, p. 126.

[49] Bowett, p. 58. The *Caroline* incident took place in 1837 during an insurrection in Canada in which American citizens were involved. The steamer *Caroline*, an American vessel, was occupied in reinforcing the American force. On December 29, a British force entered American territory, seized and destroyed the offending vessel, and was responsible for the death of two American citizens. Battle was joined diplomatically after 1840 when a British subject who had taken part in the raid was arrested in the United States.

[50] From Note of United States Secretary of State Webster to Lord Ashburton, July 27, 1842, cited in Bowett, p. 59.

[51] *Ibid.*, p. 59.

[52] Perhaps this is what Brownlie means when he describes the *Caroline* formula as "primarily verbal," *International Law and the Use of Force*, p. 260.

289

urgency with which states must necessarily choose to act in preventive self-defense, makes the matter easier to adjudicate after the event than to lay down precise rules for in advance.[53]

Intervention in the interests of the balance of power was sometimes included in treatises on international law as an act deriving its legitimacy from the right of self-defense.[54] More often it was included under the wider doctrine of self-preservation.[55] Vattel, though his view amounted to the assertion of a right to self-preservation, did not rely on that right, or on that of self-defense, to establish the justice of intervention for the balance of power. He conceived of Europe as a political system whose members were independent, but were bound together by a common interest in "the maintenance of order and the preservation of liberty."[56] This common interest had given rise to the balance of power, "an arrangement of affairs so that no State shall be in a position to have absolute mastery and dominate over the others."[57] Nations were always justified in not allowing a powerful sovereign to increase his power by force of arms, and if the formidable prince betrayed his plans by preparations then other nations had the right to check him.[58] Lawrence made this doctrine of Vattel's legally respectable by vesting the right of intervention for the balance of power not in the interests of the members of an international system, but in their rights as members of international society. Membership of that society implied duties among which was abstention "from con-

[53] While Stowell recognizes this he tries to lay down some rules relating to preventive intervention, *Intervention in International Law*, pp. 355–390.

[54] See Phillimore, *Commentaries on International Law*, Pt. IV, Chap. I, section CCCCII.

[55] See Thomas and Thomas, p. 82. These authors point out, however, that the notion of intervention for the balance of power formed no part of the legal or political doctrine of the Americas. Westlake denied that intervention for the balance of power was part of the right of self-preservation if it meant action against the internal acquisition of power by another state, when that state had shown no sign of an intention to use it. *Chapters on the Principles of International Law*, pp. 121–123.

[56] Vattel, *Law of Nations*, Bk. III, Chap. III, section 47.

[57] *Ibid.*

[58] *Ibid.*, section 49. Thus Vattel allowed preventive intervention on grounds other than those of the right to self-defense. He also seemed to come close to the doctrine of which Westlake disapproved—allowing intervention in internal affairs to prevent a prince becoming too powerful, *ibid.*

duct that endangers the vital interests of the society as a whole."[59] Action against a member who violated this duty was a service to international society.[60] Though they might have accepted Lawrence's notion of rights being vested in international society, other writers doubted whether the right to intervene for the balance of power could be numbered among them. Oppenheim thought of intervention on this ground as an action which could not be considered illegal, though it did not take place by right. It took place, when necessity demanded, "in default of right."[61] Winfield thought that it was preferable to "regard the balance of power as a principle of international policy, not of international law."[62]

Though it might not have won general acceptance in support of a right of intervention for the balance of power, the argument of Vattel and the more sophisticated one of Lawrence raised the question of the legitimacy of a right on the part of international society to combat the illegal intervention of one of its members. Taken literally, the exercise of such a right would constitute an exception to the principle of nonintervention, since it would interfere in the internal affairs of a state. But such an interpretation is absurd, for the purpose of the right of counterintervention is to uphold the rule of nonintervention and not to subordinate it to a higher imperative.[63] Thus Creasy thought that intervention became "lawful and proper, and sometimes even quite necessary, when its purpose is to prevent or to repel the wrongful intervention of others."[64] Similarly, Hall argued that a grave infraction was com-

---

[59] Lawrence, pp. 130–131. Lawrence called this the "new theory" of the balance of power. He rejected the "older theory," "the assumption that the division of territory and authority among the chief states of Europe at any given time was the right and proper division, and must be maintained at all costs," *ibid.*, p. 129.

[60] *Ibid.*, p. 131.

[61] Oppenheim, *International Law*, Vol. I, pp. 311–312.

[62] Winfield, "Grounds of Intervention," p. 152.

[63] In the same sense that the execution of a convicted murderer is literally an exception to the general rule against killing in domestic society, but its purpose is to support that rule. Whether it achieves that purpose in the broad sense of providing an example to others is not relevant to its categorization as law enforcement and not law-breaking.

[64] Sir Edward Creasy, *First Platform of International Law*, London, 1876, p. 295. There is a logical difficulty here in the notion of "preventive counterintervention," involving, in effect, the same problems as the notion of preventive self-defense.

mitted when the independence of a state was improperly interfered with, and that in consequence "another state is at liberty to intervene in order to undo the effects of illegal intervention."[65] The more cautious statement of this doctrine was that a state directly affected by an illegal intervention might intervene to remedy it but that a general threat to the "peace and order of the international community" must exist before states not directly concerned could intervene.[66]

The question of intervention to enforce nonintervention raises the more general one of the legitimacy of intervention to uphold the law. In a decentralized system, the right of self-help—not only in the particular interests of states but also in the general interests of the society formed between them—is the principal source of law enforcement.[67] Thus Hall argued that "[i]nternational law being unprovided with the support of an organised authority, the work of police must be done by such members of the community of nations as are able to perform it."[68] The contrary view asserted that for a state not directly injured by a delinquency to intervene against it, would be to set itself up in judgment over the actions of others, infringing thereby the principle of equality of states.[69] Thomas and Thomas assert a *via media* akin to their doctrine of counterintervention. A general right to remedy a violation of the law exists if the violation is so serious as to threaten the peace and order of the community of nations.[70]

Some jurists dealt with the question of the propriety of intervention on the latter ground alone—the right of collective intervention, not to undo a legal wrong, but to maintain the peace and order of the society at large. This was the doctrine under which

[65] Hall, p. 342. [66] Thomas and Thomas, p. 405.

[67] Though as Rosalyn Higgins points out, this is not the only important source of sanctions in international law, another being reciprocity—the restraint provided by the knowledge of states that a "breach of the law would incur a reciprocal response," *The Development of International Law Through the Political Organs of the United Nations*, p. 8.

[68] Hall, p. 66. See also Oppenheim, Vol. I, p. 276. Both these authorities seemed to conceive of such a right in the context of *serious* violations of *fundamental* rules.

[69] See Thomas and Thomas, who cite Accioly to this effect, *Non-Intervention*, p. 88. As these writers go on to point out, the difficulty with this doctrine is that it would deny the possibility of deciding on the illegality of any action in international relations, because judgment itself is ruled out by the principle of equality. *Ibid.*, pp. 88–89.

[70] *Ibid.*, p. 91.

the great powers presided over the separation of Belgium from the Netherlands in 1831: "Chaque Nation a ses droits particuliers; mais l'Europe aussi a son droit; c'est l'ordre social qui le lui a donné."[71] Though Lawrence conceded that intervention carried on by the great powers of Europe was more likely to be just and beneficial than intervention by one power alone, Hall denied that the body of states had any right of control arising from their being bound together by a social tie, because the nature of that bond was so rudimentary.[72] Justification for such action was moral, not legal; it relied entirely on the benefit it secured.[73] Collective intervention did not become legal merely because it was collective.[74]

Despite the variety, even the confusion, of justifications urged by statesmen and jurists in support of intervention—and this has been a summary of the more important ones—the weight of opinion was that they constituted exceptions to the principle of nonintervention, that they did not preponderate to the extent of converting that principle from the rule to the exception.[75] One apparent curiosity in the inheritance of traditional international law is that it provided a doctrine of nonintervention, but none outlawing war. After Grotius and the Naturalists, for whom the distinction between intervention and war was either unmade or unimportant, the Positivists proscribed the lesser act but allowed the greater. Perhaps this demonstrated a "realistic" awareness on their part of the limited function of law in restraining the actions of states. But whatever the motive, they conceived of two branches of international law—the one applying to peace between states, the other to war. The nonintervention principle applied in the regime of peace. In the regime of war, the law made no such demand of states, seeking to regulate only the conduct of war and not its incidence, for the right to undertake war remained a sovereign prerogative.[76]

[71] In protocol of a conference of February 19, 1931, *British and Foreign State Papers*, Vol. xviii, *1830–1831*, London, 1833, p. 781.

[72] Lawrence, *Principles of International Law*, p. 134; Hall, pp. 347–348.

[73] *Ibid.*, pp. 348–349.

[74] See Winfield, "Grounds of Intervention," p. 162; Thomas and Thomas, pp. 98–100.

[75] Winfield has an exhaustive list of the various grounds urged in justification for intervention, "Grounds of Intervention," p. 150.

[76] See on the place of war in positivist as opposed to naturalist thought, Bull, "The Grotian Conception of International Society," in Butterfield and Wight, pp. 54–57.

II

For the positivist jurists of the nineteenth century, international law was a body of norms that applied only between states. Only states were admitted to international society and international society extended only as far as the Europe of civilized states. The domain of international law is no longer so limited. With the transformation of colonies into independent states, the law of European states has become the law of all states. From its *ad hoc* organization in the nineteenth century, international society has developed to the extent of receiving a formal and permanent monument to its existence in the establishment of the League of Nations and after it the United Nations. The emergence of these institutions has unsettled the nineteenth-century conception of international law as exclusively a law of states, and this in turn has unsettled the traditional doctrine of state sovereignty. The limited function of the United Nations as an actor in the international system, and the references in the Charter of the Organization to human rights and fundamental freedoms raise the question for states of their sharing membership in the international society with individuals as well as with international organizations. If this entails any derogation from the sovereignty of states, it is compounded with the denial in the Charter as well as the Covenant of rights formerly associated with sovereignty, foremost among which was the right to go to war.

These developments in the direction of a universal international law have led one writer to see in them "the common law of mankind in an early stage of its development."[77] Only if it is so regarded, according to Jenks, can "contemporary international law . . . be intelligently expounded and rationally developed."[78] The law governing the mutual relations, "and in particular delimiting the jurisdiction," of states forms in Jenks' view only one of the major divisions of contemporary international law, and he argues that the development of the substance of that law in the twentieth century renders any account of the law based on this traditional formula inadequate.[79] The formula preferred is that of the common law of mankind:

. . . the law of an organized world community, constituted on the basis of States but discharging its community functions in-

[77] C. Wilfred Jenks, *The Common Law of Mankind*, London, 1958, p. xi.
[78] *Ibid.*, p. 1.   [79] *Ibid.*, pp. 1–2 and 7–8.

creasingly through a complex of international and regional institutions, guaranteeing rights to, and placing obligations upon, the individual citizen, and confronted with a wide range of economic, social, and technological problems calling for uniform regulation on an international basis which represents a growing proportion of the subject-matter of the law.[80]

The exposition of this law is the task which Jenks sets himself. He refers to the challenge issued by Sir Alfred Zimmern, who, writing in 1934, had unfavorably compared international law with that model of law provided by the Greek *polis*.[81] Law for the Greek, said Zimmern, was the "formulation of the will of the community . . . an external manifestation of its continuing life."[82] It was obeyed because men associated themselves with the object of the lawmaker—the promotion of the purpose of the community and through it their own lives.[83] The problem, it appears, is to establish an association on the part of individuals with an international community. But Jenks seems to hold that the problem lies not in the building of such a community, but in the scholarly appreciation by jurists of that law which, in practice, already bears witness to the community's existence.[84]

The concern here is not with the needs of the science of international law, but with the truth of the assertion that there is such a thing as even a rudimentary common law of mankind. It is not proposed to examine Jenks' contention that the contemporary international system presents a challenge to legal science similar to that which confronted Grotius in the seventeenth century;[85] it is rather to ask whether the contemporary international society resembles more closely the Grotian conception of a universal society or the Positivists' conception of a primitive society of states combining for minimum purposes, for on such an analysis hangs

[80] *Ibid.*, p. 8.

[81] *Ibid.*, p. 10, and see Sir A. Zimmern, "International Law and Social Consciousness," *Transactions of the Grotius Society*, Vol. 20, 1934, pp. 27–28.

[82] *Ibid.*   [83] *Ibid.*

[84] Jenks, p. 16. For criticism of Jenks' work on the two main grounds that it not infrequently mistakes what is desired for what is, and that it supposes that what is required for the realization of the common law of mankind is a mere intellectual and not a political revolution, see Stone, "A Common Law for Mankind?" *International Studies* (New Delhi), Vol. I, *1959–1960*, pp. 414–442.

[85] Jenks, *A New World of Law?* London, 1969, p. 18.

the place of the principle of nonintervention in contemporary international law. In particular, those who would assert the continued relevance of the nonintervention principle have to meet three sorts of argument. In the first place, a principle which draws attention to and requires respect for the principle of state sovereignty has to confront the doctrine that the reserved domain of sovereignty is contracting as the law binding states expands. Though the destination of the process is not precisely spelled out, this doctrine seems to have as its end product, a situation in which the principle of nonintervention has nothing left to protect. Second, the argument has to be met that the emergence of international organizations had diminished the scope of the principle and that they are progressively assuming functions formerly performed by the state. In the third place, the notion that the admission of individuals to international society, through the concern of the law for human rights, is withering away the sovereign state, requires examination.

The doctrine of "relative sovereignty," the view that the sovereignty of the state is limited by rules of international law binding upon it, that sovereignty exists "within the law," has been called the "dominant doctrine" among the publicists of the twentieth century.[86] At first sight is a simple truth, without which international law would be no more than an empty phrase; its demonstration raises questions about the basis of obligation in international law and about the relationship between municipal and international law that have been the perennial preoccupation of legal science.[87] In the accommodation of the doctrine of state sovereignty to the affirmation of the existence of international law, theories have been advanced which range from Austin's denial of international law as not emanating from the command of the sovereign and the neo-Hegelian doctrines that allow international law only as the result of the self-limitation of sovereign will, through Oppenheim's conception of international law as a law between states not above them, to the Kelsenite assertion of the primacy of international law and the denial of state sovereignty. The examination of these theories is not relevant to the discussion here which will rely upon the "dominant doctrine" of sovereignty restrained by law. The

[86] Marek St. Korowicz, "Writings of Twentieth Century Publicists," in Arthur Larson et al., *Sovereignty Within the Law*, New York, 1965, pp. 414–415.

[87] See Brierly, *The Basis of Obligation in International Law*, ed. H. Lauterpacht and C.H.M. Waldock, Oxford, 1958, pp. 1–67.

nonintervention principle serves a double purpose in relation to the principle of state sovereignty. It expresses the idea that states are to be immune from interference by other states, and it stands at the frontier between international law and domestic law—where international law respects sovereignty, but conceives it as "that competence which remains to States after due account is taken of their obligation under international law."[88]

If the former purpose is a noncontroverted part of the international law of sovereign states, it is the latter purpose which is of crucial significance to the present task—the examination of "the primary preoccupation of progressive thought in the field of international law since 1919," which has been "to subdue the claims of sovereignty in the interests of the rule of law"[89] and the implied rider that the more sovereignty is so limited the better.[90] What follows will review whether the primary preoccupation has been rewarded with the actual retreat of the claims of sovereignty in the law agreed between states and in their practice.

In traditional writing on international law and relations, a familiar distinction is that between sovereignty in its external and in its internal aspects. The principal legal limitation on sovereignty in its external aspect since 1919 has been the limitation imposed on the right of states to go to war. The Covenant of the League of Nations has been described as creative of a "presumption against the legality of war as a means of self-help."[91] It imposed an obligation upon states to settle their disputes by peaceful means,[92] and the members of the League undertook to "respect and preserve as against external aggression the territorial integrity and existing political independence of all Members of the League."[93] But by Article 15(7) of the Covenant, the members reserved to themselves "the right to take such action as they shall consider necessary for the maintenance of right and justice." Moreover, the obligation to settle disputes peacefully did not extend beyond the compulsory period of delay laid down in the Covenant.[94] The Paris Pact of 1928 seemed, less equivocally, to take war from within the sovereign right of the state. The parties to it

[88] Myres S. McDougal in International Law Association, Report of the 20th Conference, 1959, quoted in Korowicz, p. 427.
[89] Jenks, *Common Law of Mankind*, p. 123.
[90] F. J. Berber, "German Law," in Larson et al., p. 92.
[91] Brownlie, p. 56. [92] Articles 12, 13 and 15.
[93] Article 10. [94] Article 12.

renounced war as "an instrument of national policy" and agreed that the solution of conflict should never be sought by other than peaceful means. But this was not a blanket prohibition of war. All states reserved the right of self-defense, and the United States and the United Kingdom, in particular, entered extensive reservations to this effect. The prohibition of war as an instrument of national policy also left untouched the doctrine of war as a sanction—as an instrument of international policy; and the unfortunate wording of the prohibition left in doubt the legitimacy of that traditional technical category of international law—the use of force short of war.[95]

From the perspective of restraining the use of force in international relations, the Charter of the United Nations seemed to have improved on the Paris Pact which had been considered in turn superior to the Covenant. Article 2(4) of the Charter proscribed not war but the use or threat of force against the territorial integrity or political independence of any state, or in any other manner inconsistent with the purposes of the United Nations. Force, it appears, in the post-Charter legal order, is legitimate only in self-defense under Article 51 of the Charter, or as a collective measure in response to the authorization of the competent organs of the United Nations under Chapter VII of the Charter. But again this restrictive view overlooks the possibility of the use of force which is not directed against the territorial integrity or political independence of any state, and is consistent with the purposes of the United Nations.[96] Clearly, the nineteenth-century doctrine that placed war within the sovereign prerogative of states and attempted to restrain by law only its prosecution is no longer applicable. However, it is doubtful whether the progressive doctrine

[95] For an account of the various interpretations of the Pact, and for a view favoring a restrictive interpretation of it, see Brownlie, pp. 74–92. For a "realist" inclination, taking account of the exceptions to the Pact's restraint on the use of force rather than minimizing them, see Stone, *Legal Controls of International Conflict*, 2d imp., rev., New York, 1959, p. 300.

[96] Stone argues that there is no reason why the extreme view of the prohibition of force in Article 2(4) should be the only possible exegesis of that article, or even the most likely. He points out, in this respect, that it would be a strange interpretation that allowed the violation of such principles and purposes of the Charter as the requirements of justice, the respect for the obligations of treaties and international law, and of sovereign equality, without forceful recourse. *Aggression and World Order*, p. 97.

of the twentieth century that war, except when conducted in self-defense or as a collective sanction, is unlawful, can be said to have fully replaced it.

As to sovereignty in its internal aspect, the concept written into the Covenant and the Charter under the title of the domestic jurisdiction of states, the progressive doctrine teaches that its erosion by international law is to be welcomed, or more strongly that the erosion is necessary to the establishment of a sound international legal order. The difficulties of defining domestic jurisdiction, whether to point out its general features or to enumerate those matters contained in the concept, are notorious, and the desirability of such an exercise has been called frequently into question.[97] For the present purpose it is sufficient to conceive, with Brierly, of domestic jurisdiction as consisting of those matters or disputes to which no rule of international law is applicable.[98] An example used by Jenks, purporting to demonstrate the progressive thesis of the increasing range of applicability of rules of international law, is the acceptance of the principle of full employment. In virtue of Article 55 of the Charter and of many other international instruments since the foundation of the United Nations, he argues that the question of full employment seems no longer a matter of domestic jurisdiction.[99] He goes on to assert that while the Charter does not commit states "to a particular philosophy of the relationship between the Government and the individual," which remains a matter essentially within domestic jurisdiction, "the obligation to promote and maintain full employment is a legal obligation from which legal consequences can be drawn," and that it is in this sense no longer a matter of domestic jurisdiction.[100] Among the consequences, says Jenks, is the obligation of consultation on matters of economic policy that are of international concern.[101] So far as it goes, there can be no objection to Jenks' assertion of a duty of full employment and his citation of positive support for it in the agreements of states. Again from the perspective of the formal limitation of state sovereignty by international law it goes beyond nineteenth-century doctrine, but there are immense practical dif-

[97] See, e.g., M. S. Rajan, "The Question of Defining 'Domestic Jurisdiction'," *International Studies* (New Delhi), Vol. I, *1959–1960*, pp. 248–279.
[98] "Matters of Domestic Jurisdiction," in *Basis of Obligation in International Law*, p. 84.
[99] Jenks, *Common Law of Mankind*, p. 283.
[100] *Ibid.*, p. 287.   [101] *Ibid.*, pp. 287–290.

ficulties with the doctrine, which will be examined after a third sort of doctrinal assault on the concept of sovereignty has been introduced.

Assault is the wrong word. Rather, the progressive doctrine sees the law between states as members of international society being added to and outnumbered by the law of an international community whose subject-matter

> increasingly includes cross-frontier relationships of individuals, organisations, and corporate bodies which call for appropriate legal regulation on an international basis, problems of economic and technological interdependence requiring the regulation on the basis of common rules of matters which do not *per se* involve inter-State relations in any real sense, and rights designed to provide the individual, and in some cases organisations, with a measure of protection against the individual member States of the international community.[102]

According to this view, the sovereignty of the state is not being eroded directly, but is being built over by a network of relationships that require legal control such that the law of the international community "has long since ceased to be merely, and is rapidly ceasing to be primarily, a law between States."[103] As Jessup puts this thesis, it is to question "the line between the international and the national . . . as a basis for legal classification" and to replace it with a conception of "transnational law" which would "deal out jurisdiction in the manner most conducive to the needs and convenience of all members of the international community," rather than rely on old dogmas like territoriality, sovereignty, and nationality.[104] Again, the supposed growth of transnational law and relations in the twentieth century is not here in question. What is in dispute

---

[102] *Ibid.*, p. 17.

[103] *Ibid.*, p. 17. Among the subjects making up his presentation of the contemporary international law of peace, apart from law between states, Jenks includes:—the law governing the structure and law-making processes of the international community, human rights protected by international guarantees, property rights of a distinctively international character, common rules established by international agreement which apply to public services, corporations and individuals rather than to States, international rules governing the conflict of laws, and various categories within these headings. *Ibid.*, pp. 59–60.

[104] Philip C. Jessup, *Transnational Law*, New Haven, 1956, pp. 70–71 and 103.

is whether the mere "outnumbering" of the law between states can be said to have led to a decline in the importance of the state in the international political order.

The difficulty with these examples of the doctrine that sovereignty is and should be bending increasingly before international law is not that they posit norms of international conduct which are not matched by the practice of states, for it is of the nature of rules that they would establish a standard from which some deviation is expected. It is that the gap between norm and practice is too wide. To take undue comfort from the outlawry of war is to fail to confront the familiar account of the weakness of international law in its lack of an impartial authority to judge a breach of the law and of centralized means of law enforcement. States judge and states enforce. International law is not ignored but is severally interpreted by each of the units to which it applies. Article 2(4) is a clear prohibition of the threat or use of force only if the limits of territorial integrity and political independence are indisputably clear in a particular case. Where they are not, and this has been characteristically the case in the postwar world of disputed frontiers and of internal war, states have been able to make diverse and plausible claims that they were upholding the values of territorial integrity and political independence rather than denying them. Partly because of the same lack of clarity in the distribution of territorial integrity and political independence (and partly as a consequence of a decentralized international system), Article 51 of the Charter, allowing individual and collective self-defense against armed attack has been converted from an exception intended to be "not much larger than a needle's eye," into a "loophole through which armies have passed."[105] The withdrawal of the right to make war from the category of sovereign rights of the state has had the practical effect of enlarging the category of exceptions to the withdrawal.

The problems involved in Jenks' espousal of the view that the principle of full employment is no longer a matter within the domestic jurisdiction of states can be illustrated in terms of the deference he continues to show to the principle of domestic jurisdiction by distinguishing an obligation of full employment that leaves untouched the philosophy of the relationship between the

[105] Hoffmann, "International Law and the Control of Force," in Deutsch and Hoffmann, eds., *The Relevance of International Law*, p. 29.

301

government and the individual. The principle of full employment is a modern political principle which, inescapably, is bound up with principles of government, and its acceptance by international law is the endorsement of a "particular philosophy." But the assertion of an international legal duty makes no contribution to the problem of how to govern so as to bring about full employment. It is a worthy aspiration to which most governments are committed along with many other, often contradictory, goals, but its achievement is not dependent on international law but on governance. And this is the cardinal difficulty with the celebration of the decline of domestic jurisdiction—not only in the matter of full employment but also in all areas of political decision—that it takes little account of the effectiveness of the new international compared to the old domestic jurisdiction. A doctrinal solution might be found in a preference for monistic theories asserting the primacy of international law over domestic law, rather than dualistic theories asserting the independence of the two systems of law. A more practical solution might lie in an expanded role for domestic courts in the international legal order.[106] In practice, and here and now, matters like that of full employment, which undoubtedly have international repercussions and are of international concern, are aims which the individual looks to his government to satisfy. Automatic applause for the erosion of domestic jurisdiction, and the more · the better, overlooks the possible ineffectiveness or irrelevance of the formal transfer of jurisdiction, and might even prejudice the establishment of a sound legal order between states—making weak law weaker by loading it with responsibilities it is not strong enough to bear.[107]

As to the outnumbering of the law of sovereign states by the transnational law of the international community, though there is, perhaps, less distance here between doctrine and practice,[108] it cannot be taken as an unerring signal of the eclipse of sovereignty. For, as Raymond Aron has pointed out, the interstate order re-

[106] See generally, Falk, *The Role of Domestic Courts in the International Legal Order*, Syracuse, 1964.

[107] Perhaps this is what George A. Finch means by the "menace of internationalism," in "The American Society of International Law, 1906–1956," *American Journal of International Law*, Vol. 50, No. 2, 1956, pp. 311–312.

[108] For a fuller treatment of transnationalism, see below, Chapter Nine, section v.

mains relatively autonomous.[109] The building of bridges across international frontiers, which might very well be necessary to the ultimate construction of an international community, is not remotely sufficient to it.[110] The expansion of transnational communication in the twentieth century has not rewarded progressive thought with a simultaneous expansion in the solidarity of states and the consequent promotion of peace.[111] The principle of nonintervention is a rule which applies in the relatively autonomous order of states. As a testament to their minimal solidarity, to an agreement that the society of states is not competent, because of its rudimentary nature, to assume authority on matters within states, the doctrine of nonintervention might be closer to reality than the progressive doctrines that would unseat it.

If there are serious difficulties with the doctrine that sees sovereignty tamed increasingly by international law, regards the process as inexorable,[112] and celebrates its working out, what can be said of the view that sees international organizations as assuming those fragments of authority which international law has wrested from the sovereignty of states? In the nineteenth century, Hall and Lawrence had been doubtful about dignifying collective intervention for the peace and order of Europe with the stamp of legality. No such doubts are entertained by contemporary jurists. The Covenant of the League of Nations and the Charter of the United Nations formally endowed the proper organs of international organization with the authority to intervene on behalf of the peace of nations. The province of the United Nations was the maintenance of peace and security in respect of which states had no plea of domestic jurisdiction. The progressive view sees this formal advance into a regime of collective security, of social rather than individual responsibility for order, reflected in the practice of states. Thus Jenks takes Manchuria, Ethiopia, and Korea as "successive landmarks in the development of international organisation."[113] In the Man-

[109] *Peace and War*, London, 1966, p. 105.

[110] *Ibid.*

[111] For a criticism of this aspect of progressive thought on the particular ground that the growth of physical communication does not necessarily mean a growth in "human communication," see Stone, *Legal Controls of International Conflict*, pp. xli–liii.

[112] Larson, "International Organizations and Conventions," in Larson et al., *Sovereignty within the Law*, p. 365.

[113] Jenks, *Common Law of Mankind*, p. 192.

churian case, the international community placed on record its condemnation of aggression by a great power. In the Ethiopian case, economic coercion was attempted. And in Korea, the United Nations Security Council, adapting itself to the realities of the Cold War, asked the United States to direct the forces cooperating in restraint of aggression—a "significant, and one may hope a decisive, stage in the evolution of collective security."[114] The clear long-term trend, in Jenks' view is in favor of collective security, every failure being "followed by a more insistent attempt to succeed."[115]

To take the Manchurian and Ethiopian cases as evidence for the want of solidarity in the international community is perhaps more accurate than to see them as landmarks in its development. Korea is a happier example in the sense that the limited military action undertaken under the flag of the United Nations did at least achieve the objective of keeping South Korea independent of the North. But whether it can be taken as evidence of the reality of an embryonic collective security is more doubtful. The unanimity required in the Security Council to launch the enterprise was provided by the fortuitous absence of the Soviet Union—solidarity by default. The United Nations action was undertaken by a Western coalition—partial solidarity. And it was undertaken against a small power—the perennial solidarity of the strong against the weak. Walter Schiffer has pointed to the central weakness of the progressive confidence in collective security in its assumption of the indivisibility of peace and of the equal interest of all peoples in the maintenance of the general peace.[116] The doctrine of collective security presupposes a solidarity in the international community which, if it existed, would make an organization to enforce peace unnecessary.[117] Where states remain politically divided and are free to make up their own minds about the existence of threats to their security, the prospect of an international authority taking over the states' responsibility for international order remains distant.

Primarily an organization whose function was to maintain peace between states, the United Nations included, among the purposes stated in its Charter, the promotion of values within them such as respect for human rights and fundamental freedoms. With regard

[114] *Ibid.*, p. 194. [115] *Ibid.*, p. 196.
[116] *The Legal Community of Mankind*, New York, 1954, p. 202.
[117] *Ibid.*, p. 199.

to the latter, progressive thought envisages an extension of the competence of the United Nations to the domestic order of states affirming the legitimacy of and advocating, in the words of one writer, "legislative intervention by the United Nations in the internal affairs of states."[118] Falk would authorize intervention by the United Nations whenever civil strife threatened world peace or whenever gross abuses of fundamental human rights took place.[119] When internal conflict threatens to provoke the cold-war pattern of intervention and counterintervention, Falk argues, United Nations action is legitimate both as a means of eliminating the risks of involvement by nuclear nations and as a way of realizing the "fundamental preferences of the international community" like the liquidation of colonialism and institutional racism.[120]

The primary difficulty with this doctrine is, as Falk himself recognizes, that the possibility of legislative intervention by the United Nations exists only in circumstances of almost universal consensus.[121] Moreover, the existence of such a consensus, as for example against *apartheid,* does not indicate a consensus on the sort of action to be taken against it. Falk recognizes a distinction between a Western preference for persuasive interference and a preference on the part of revolutionary and excolonial nations for coercive interference, but minimizes the difference between them.[122] It is perhaps in the difference between them, between the reluctance to allow authority to a "superstate" on the one hand and a willingness to coerce South Africa in fulfillment of a competing conception of international order on the other that the lack of solidarity in the international community is still demonstrated, even on a matter about the undesirability of which nearly all states ostensibly agree. In a modern context and with regard to a very different segment of the political spectrum, it is the difference between Castlereagh's refusal to act on abstract and speculative principles of precaution and the intervention of the Holy Allies against the contagion of revolution, though both were agreed about the undesirability of revolution. Outside matters of near consensus, themselves doubtful as platforms for action, the conception of United

---

[118] Falk, *Legal Order in a Violent World*, pp. 336–353.

[119] *Ibid.*, p. 344. Falk is careful to point out that "authorization is concerned with the empowering of the United Nations to act, not with action itself," since considerations of prudence might rule out intervention in a particular case.

[120] *Ibid.*, pp. 346–347.　　　　　　　　[121] *Ibid.*, pp. 349–351.

[122] *Ibid.*, p. 348.

Nations intervention as a substitute for the rivalries of the Cold War is but the latest manifestation of that pattern of progressive thought which supposed that law would be observed and reasonable conduct would prevail if only power politics did not intervene.[123]

A less ambitious form of the notion of transfer of sovereignty is that which sees the emergence of regional organizations taking over some of the functions formerly allotted to the competence of states. The European Communities are the obvious example. There is no reason to doubt that such a transfer has taken place in the Europe of the Six, and will take place in the Europe of the Nine, in the area of economics and trade, where the establishment of a common market has led to the removal of commercial and tariff matters from the exclusive competence of the states. But matters of defense and foreign policy, the traditional bastions of state sovereignty, remain within the competence of the parts of an economic community, the history of which does not seem to have followed the inexorable functionalist logic of the increasing erosion of sovereignty as one area of integration "spills over" into another.[124] Again, Aron's distinction between transnational communication and the relative autonomy of the political order is relevant. He calls it the "great illusion of our times . . . that economic and technological interdependence among the various factions of humanity has definitively devalued the fact of 'political sovereignties,' the existence of distinct states which wish to be autonomous."[125] Moreover, whether the pattern of integration advocated or pursued is functional or federal, if its end product is not the destruction of the state but its expansion from nation to region, then the progressive desire to tame the beast of sovereignty merely serves to convert it into a monster.

If the principle of nonintervention is to be held to have continuing relevance in contemporary international law, a third sort of argument which has to be met is that which sees in recent developments in the law the admission of the individual to membership in international society as a direct bearer of rights and duties

[123] For the evolution of this pattern of thought, see generally W. Schiffer, *The Legal Community of Mankind.*

[124] For a critique of this logic and for an account of the survival of the nation-state in Europe, see Stanley Hoffmann, "Obstinate or Obsolete? The Fate of the Nation-State and the Case of Western Europe," *Daedalus*, Vol. 95, No. 3, Summer 1966, pp. 862–915.

[125] *Peace and War*, p. 748.

without the go-between of the state.[126] As Lauterpacht puts this argument: ". . . in so far as international law as embodied in the Charter [of the UN] and elsewhere recognises fundamental rights of the individual independent of the law of the State, to that extent it constitutes the individual a subject of the law of nations."[127] He goes on to assert that it is in the Charter of the United Nations "that the individual human being first appears as entitled to fundamental human rights and freedoms," that it is a legal duty of states to respect and observe them, and that this duty exists in spite of the difficulty of enforcement and the lack of clarity and precision in the definition of human rights.[128]

The elevation of the individual to formal parity with states in the international club involves two sorts of difficulty in practice— the related problems of the solidarity of the international community and of the possibility of enforcing the law. In the first place, it is doubtful whether international society can be said to make up what Julius Stone has called a "justice constituency" in which, among other things, individual human beings can express their felt needs or demands.[129] Indeed, in an international environment which opposes "the nationalization of truth and justice"[130] to such a postulated constituency, the individual tends to look for a just share or reward or compensation for injury within the frontiers of the state of which he is a citizen, and would not expect to find justice in any constituency beyond them.[131] Hence the lack of

[126] Recent developments such as the references to human rights in the German-Polish Upper Silesian Convention, the International Military Tribunal at Nuremberg, the United Nations Charter, and the Universal Declaration of Human Rights. For a concise summary see Korowicz, "The Problem of the International Personality of Individuals," *American Journal of International Law*, Vol. 50, No. 3, 1956, pp. 545–558.

[127] *International Law and Human Rights*, London, 1950, p. 4.

[128] *Ibid.*, pp. 33 and 147–154.

[129] "Approaches to the Notion of International Justice," in Falk and Cyril E. Black, eds., *The Future of the International Legal Order*, Vol. 1, *Trends and Patterns*, Princeton, N.J., 1969, pp. 425–426.

[130] *Ibid.*, p. 428.

[131] The exception here, providing some grounds for confidence in at least an emergent European "justice constituency," is the European Convention on Human Rights, by which the parties declared their "common heritage of political traditions, ideals, freedom and the rule of law," and resolved to "take the first steps for the collective enforcement of certain of the rights stated in the Universal Declaration." Article 25 of the Convention embodied the right of individual petition, "provided that the High

clarity of definition of human rights in the Charter is but the tip of an iceberg, the submerged parts of which testify to a lack of consensus in international society about what human rights are, how they are to be protected, and what priority within the state and the international order that protection shall enjoy. It is due to this lack of consensus that Lauterpacht's rationale for humanitarian intervention that "ultimately, peace is more endangered by tyrannical contempt for human rights than by attempts to assert, through intervention, the sanctity of human personality"[132] is open to question. In an ultimate sense, it may very well be that peace and the protection of human rights are related, and the debates in the United Nations show how widespread are the doctrines of peace and freedom indivisible. But the weakness of the rationale for humanitarian intervention lies in the assumption that states are able to operate or to cooperate to uphold human rights with a surgical precision having no side-effects and no ulterior motives.[133]

The second difficulty with the admission of the individual to international society can be illustrated by reference to Lauterpacht's interpretation of the relationship between the assertion of human rights in the Charter and Article 2(7) reserving domestic jurisdiction. He opts for a compromise between them. The "intervention" disallowed by Article 2(7) Lauterpacht takes to be a ban on "dictatorial interference in the sense of action amounting to a denial of the independence of the State."[134] This interpretation of the term, he argues, provides a guide to the permissible limits of the action of United Nations organs in the field of the encouragement and promotion of human rights.[135] They may discuss matters in that field, initiate studies of them, and make general or specific recommendations with respect to them.[136] What is ruled out by Article 2(7) is "direct legislative interference by the United Na-

---

Contracting Party against which the complaint has been lodged has declared that it recognises the competence of the Commission to receive such petitions." Eleven of the seventeen parties have recognized that competence. On this article, and on European practice generally, see J.E.S. Fawcett, *The Application of the European Convention on Human Rights*, Oxford, 1969.

[132] Lauterpacht, *International Law and Human Rights*, p. 32.

[133] But for an examination of the question whether genocide is a justifiable ground for humanitarian intervention despite these observations, see below, Chapter Nine, section III.

[134] Lauterpacht, *International Law and Human Rights*, p. 167.

[135] *Ibid.*, pp. 168–169.   [136] *Ibid.*

tions—*i.e.* an attempt to impose upon States rules of conduct as a matter of legal right."[137] Here is the deference to domestic jurisdiction. And yet Lauterpacht also asserts that the observance of human rights and freedoms has become an international obligation not essentially within the domestic jurisdiction of states. In view of this, why is there the continuing deference to domestic jurisdiction by disallowing dictatorial interference and shackling the authority of the United Nations? The answer is provided by the Charter. In order to unshackle the authority of the United Nations, it would have to be shown that a breach of human rights constituted a threat to the peace under Chapter VII of the Charter. There is no quarrel here with Lauterpacht's interpretation of the Charter; if it is illogical it reflects the document it interprets. It does show, however, the centrality of the problem of enforcement.

On this problem, Lauterpacht recognizes that "in so far as the availability of a remedy is the hallmark of a legal right, they [fundamental human rights] are imperfect legal rights."[138] But he adds that, as a rule, there is "no compulsory jurisdiction in the matter of the fulfillment of international duties" and that even if the United Nations had no power of enforcement at all, "the legal duty itself would still remain in full vigour."[139] Certainly, it seems pedantic to cavil at the particular legal obligation to respect human rights by reference to a notorious weakness of international law in general. But the pedantry is justified for two reasons. In the first place, the gap between the possibility of a state enforcing its legal rights, or carrying out its duties, and the desirability of such from the point of view of legal order is less wide than is the case with an individual, for the simple reason that while the former might have the power (if not the will) to do so, the latter never has (his will does not matter). Second, the Charter system's overriding concern for peace and its endowing of the Security Council with certain rights in respect of its maintenance attests to the minimal, if too optimistic at that, ambitions of the drafters. To a greater extent, the adding of a "maximalist" concern for the welfare of the individual within the state was the imposition of a responsibility which the international society was not mature enough to administer. With Emerson, Lauterpacht expressed the hope that "man shall treat with man as a sovereign state with a

[137] *Ibid.*, p. 171.   [138] *Ibid.*, p. 34.
[139] *Ibid.*, pp. 34 and 166–167.

sovereign state."[140] Surely, he would not have conceived of the model for those relations as the Hobbesian state of nature—a condition against which there is no guarantee if men are released from their obligations as members of states.

The doctrines of sovereignty increasingly retreating before the law, of international authority increasingly substituting for national authority, and of the sovereignty of the individual, exhibit weaknesses which can be summarized in two tendencies typifying each of them. First, they tend to assume the demise of state sovereignty in a century that has witnessed an explosive growth in the number of sovereign states and in the functions which they fulfill.[141] In the second place, they tend to applaud the eclipse of sovereignty which they suppose to be taking place as an unqualified good, which exposes them to the danger of overlooking the function of the principle of sovereignty as an ordering device within and hence among states.[142] It may be that the values to which the principle of nonintervention draws attention and which it legally protects are more tenacious and less uncivilized than progressive thought has allowed for.

III

If the principle of nonintervention retains a place in contemporary international law, it is not, if it ever has been, as a clear injunction against a particular act. The values it draws attention to and protects are those included under the rubric of the principle of state sovereignty, such as the rights of a state to territorial integrity and political independence. Standing guard over such imprecisely defined rights and requiring respect for them in a sort of legal shorthand, the principle appeals more perhaps to governments than it does to jurists. As a slogan of protest and legitimation, it recommends itself to governments as a serviceable tool of international politics. As a part of legal science, because of its very generality and imprecision, it has less to recommend it either as a

[140] *Ibid.*, p. 70.

[141] See Hinsley, *Sovereignty*, p. 226. If this observation begs the question of an explosive growth in the number of functions which the state is not able to fulfill, this is examined below in Chapter Nine, section v.

[142] On the connection between order within and order among states see below, Chapter Nine, section i.

tool for the juristic evaluation of the policies of states or for the building of a system of international law. Furthermore, as a piece of legal shorthand, implying as it does a clear distinction between an order between states with which international law is concerned and an order within them which is not to be interfered with, it perhaps oversimplifies. As McDougal puts the case against such oversimplification,

> the interrelation of international law and national law is most realistically viewed . . . in terms of the interpenetration of multiple processes of authoritative decision of varying territorial compass. The rules commonly referred to as international law are but perspectives of authority—perspectives about who should decide what, with respect to whom, for the promotion of what policies, by what methods—which are constantly being created, terminated, and recreated by established decision-makers located at many different positions in the structures of authority of both states and international governmental organizations.[143]

Again from the perspective of legal science and of the legal evaluation of state policy, the conception of the principle of nonintervention lying at the frontier between international and domestic jurisdiction, however true at a sufficiently general level of abstraction, is perhaps too general to be helpful.

If the principle of nonintervention can be said to be unsatisfactory on these grounds as a general principle, what can be said of it as a legal barrier to intervention in its technical meaning of "dictatorial interference" as one form of "force short of war in international relations?" There is a twofold difficulty with this supposedly technical and consensual definition of intervention.[144] On the one hand, the conception of intervention as force short of war in international relations, if it purports to depict a relationship of violence between states whose scale and scope is more restricted than that commonly associated with war, then the Vietnam War, a war of intervention, is the most recent example of the frailty of

[143] "The Impact of International Law upon National Law: A Policy-Oriented Perspective," in Myres S. McDougal and Associates, *Studies in World Public Order*, New Haven, Conn., 1960, p. 229.

[144] The supposition is Lauterpacht's in *International Law and Human Rights*, pp. 167–168.

the distinction between war and intervention.[145] If, on the other hand, the term intervention is restrictively understood as interference by use or threat of force, then it fails to capture those forms of coercion, such as subversion and the dissemination of hostile propaganda, which need not rely upon force.[146] Because of the difficulties of distinguishing between a state of war and a state of peace, and, a fortiori, a third state which hovers uneasily between them, McDougal and Feliciano suggest a concept of "coercion" as a factual and seamless process described in terms of "certain participants applying to each other coercion of alternately accelerating and decelerating intensity, for a whole spectrum of objectives, by methods which include the employment of all available instruments of policy, and under all the continually changing conditions of a world arena."[147]

Following this lead, another writer thinks not of intervention but of "minor international coercion."[148] In such a framework, a principle of nonintervention seems to have no place, except again as a general notion declaring a presumption against the legitimacy of coercion across international frontiers. Moreover, the place of the principle of nonintervention as a specific injunction might seem superfluous in practice. In order to determine the legitimacy of a particular act of intervention, the question to be asked is not whether it violated the principle of nonintervention, but whether rules existed which might justify the act in that particular case.

---

[145] See on the frailty of this distinction, F. Grob, *The Relativity of War and Peace*, New Haven, Conn., 1949, pp. 224–237. Grob does, however, detect a "calculated *political* and *legal* design" in the use of the term "intervention" by Presidents Taft and Wilson. Politically, it was supposed to signal America's lack of land-hunger, her concern only for American lives and property and for the independence and stability of the states in the Panama Canal area as a bulwark against extra-hemispheric interference. The internal legal design was to avoid excessive executive assumption of the war-making power formally vested in Congress. *Ibid.*, pp. 231–237.

[146] Falk, "United States Practice and the Doctrine of Non-intervention in the Internal Affairs of Sovereign States," in *Legal Order in a Violent World*, p. 160.

[147] "International Coercion and World Public Order: The General Principles of the Law of War," in McDougal and Associates, p. 247.

[148] W. T. Burke, "The Legal Regulation of Minor International Coercion: A Framework of Inquiry," in R. J. Stanger, ed., *Essays on Intervention*, Columbus, Ohio, 1964, pp. 87–125.

These considerations together seem to relegate the principle to an unhelpful generality.

Despite them, the nonintervention principle lives on in contemporary international law as a rule which states have bound themselves to observe in various international instruments, as a slogan lodged in the minds and frequenting the sayings of statesmen, and as a doctrine which has received the imprimatur of the United Nations. In the writings of jurists, it has a central place in the discussion of the international law of internal war, and it persists as a *de facto* principle discerned by some writers as a rule of "inter-bloc" rather than interstate law.

The frequent appearance of the principle in international instruments has already been noticed.[149] So also has its partly implicit, partly explicit position in the Charter of the United Nations.[150] This latter position is not denied by either side in the debate between the "restrictionists," who think of the legitimacy of the use of force in the post-Charter legal order in terms of the three categories of collective United Nations sanctions, delicts, and actions in self-defense,[151] and the "realists" who would admit the possibility of a nondelictual use of force which is neither collective sanction nor self-defense.[152] The difference between these two schools of thought with reference to the principle of nonintervention can be illustrated by reference to the *Corfu Channel* case. Britain claimed that a minesweeping operation carried out in Albanian territorial waters after two British vessels had been mined, could be justified as intervention for the purpose of "safeguarding evidence necessary for the purposes of justice," as intervention to abate an international "nuisance," and on the grounds of "self-protection or self-help." The International Court of Justice in rejecting the British claim, held that it could "only regard the alleged right of intervention as the manifestation of a policy of force, such as has in the past given rise to most serious abuses and such as cannot, whatever be the present defects in international organization, find a place in international law."[153]

[149] For contemporary appearances, see above, Chapters Five, Six, and Seven.

[150] See above, Chapter Seven, section I.

[151] See Bowett, *Self-Defence in International Law*, p. 12.

[152] See Stone, *Aggression and World Order*, pp. 92–103.

[153] I.C.J. Reports, 1949, cited in Bowett, p. 14.

The Court could not accept the particular plea of self-protection or self-help because "[b]etween independent states, respect for territorial sovereignty is an essential foundation of international relations."[154] Here, it seemed, was confirmation of the restrictionist view of the right to use force. The right of one state to intervene was not superior to the right of another to territorial sovereignty, and for the protection of the latter the Court seemed to rely upon the outlawry of individual use of force. But the realist view does not necessarily have less regard for territorial sovereignty. It recognizes the frequency with which the practice of states has placed it under threat and allows its vindication by individual resort to force—force for right not force as a "policy." Both views can be said to endorse the principle of nonintervention. One interprets it as ruling out the use of force even in the absence of a collective response ("whatever be the present defects in international organization"), but the other would allow individual intervention to uphold the law precisely because of the defects in international organization.[155] Whether contemporary international law imposes an absolute duty of nonintervention (intervention here in the sense of the threat or use of force) on individual states remains a disputed question. The use of the language of intervention and nonintervention in the context of the legitimacy of the use of force is a matter of convenience—it summarizes a complex debate.

The speeches of statesmen and a number of resolutions adopted by the General Assembly constitute a second area occupied by the principle of nonintervention in contemporary international politics. Homage paid to the principle in the former has carried over into its more formal acknowledgment in the latter. This widespread deference can be said to demonstrate the common concern of all states for the values embodied in the principle of state sovereignty for which the principle of nonintervention requires respect. But each state tends to expound a doctrine of nonintervention which is framed with reference to those particular forces in world politics which seem to present an actual or potential challenge to its own sovereignty or, more broadly, to the maintenance or propagation of its conception of international order. Ubiquitous declaratory deference to the principle then obscures sometimes

154 *Ibid.*, p. 14.
155 And thus the positions of both Cobden and Mill survive in contemporary international law.

fundamental differences between states as to the values protected by it and the the sorts of actions it proscribes. In this respect, the differences between Western, Communist, and Third World doctrine have already been described.[156] That one of the few points of similarity between these doctrines might be that they share the same title as principles of nonintervention does not justify the dismissal of the principle as a mere political slogan, having a propaganda function as a weapon of diplomacy, lightly used and just as easily discarded. For it is no surprise that the scope and content of the principle should vary according to the conception of international order, however well articulated, of which it is a part. The different interpretations of the principle, however, do point up the problems for an international law which would transcend the peculiarities in the doctrines of particular states and apply equally to them all. In particular, the debate at the United Nations about the principle of nonintervention and generally about the principles which were to guide friendly relations and cooperation among states, threw two such problems into relief. In the first place, a Western preference for a pragmatic, problem-by-problem approach to international law, wary of precise definition and suspicious of abstract doctrine was opposed to a marked Third World (and Latin American) preference for a detailed spelling-out of the actions ruled out by the principle of nonintervention, and by a preference among the communist states for a general endorsement of the five principles of peaceful coexistence.[157] Second, Western reluctance to leave the doctrinal umbrella of the Charter and doubt as to the legal status of General Assembly resolutions confronted Third World enthusiasm for such resolutions as representative of a new international law which the newly independent states had helped to fashion, and the communist states joined in this development demonstrating their support for it by extending the new law to peoples as well as to states. Though differences were apparent when doctrine was pursued into detail, the general and abstract

[156] See above, Chapter Seven, sections IV and V.

[157] See Edward McWhinney, *"Peaceful Coexistence" and Soviet-Western International Law*, Leyden, 1964, pp. 86–90; "Friendly Relations and Co-operation Among States (Coexistence) and the Principle of Non-Intervention," in M. K. Nawaz, et al., *The Legal Principles Governing Friendly Relations and Co-operation among States*, Leyden, 1966, pp. 69–97; *International Law and World Revolution*, Leyden, 1967, pp. 69–82.

character of the formal proclamations of nonintervention by the United Nations allowed each state to adhere to them without violating its preferred interpretation.

A third area occupied by the principle of nonintervention in contemporary international law is that beyond the specific range of the injunctions of the Charter. In particular, this is an occupation or partly so of two areas. First, Article 2(4) refers only to the threat or use of force against territorial integrity or political independence. This formulation neglects the possibility of these values being threatened by activities other than the use or threat of force, such as subversion or the dissemination of hostile propaganda, and the principle of nonintervention has been invoked as a legal safeguard against such threats.[158]

The principle has, in the second place, been called in to supplement the Charter in the area of internal war—the typically modern instrument of change in international society.[159] But the circumstances of its invocation are more complex than is the case with the simple extension of Article 2(4). Traditional international law relied on noninterventionist norms in regard to internal war. It was a domestic affair which international law formally ignored. When a successful rebellion forced itself upon the notice of the law, it attempted to preserve a neutralist stance serving the purposes of nonintervention by allowing the working out of domestic affairs without external influence. Thus a government was not to be discriminated against by international society when facing a mere rebellion, but neither was a rebellion to be discriminated against if it matured through insurgency to belligerency. When the internal war arrived at the latter status, international law was to secure a noninterventionary effect by requiring equal treatment for

[158] Bowett, in arguing that the duty of nonintervention is a broader duty than that imposed upon states by Article 2(4), correlates the right of political independence with the duty of nonintervention and shows how the former can be impaired (and the latter breached) by actions other than the use of force or its threat. He does add, however, that the extent of the right of political independence and the duty to respect it are unclear. *Self-Defence in International Law*, pp. 44–50.

[159] On the difficulties involved in thinking about internal war, and on the problem it presents to world order, see generally, H. Eckstein, ed., *Internal War*, New York, 1964; Rosenau, ed., *International Aspects of Civil Strife*, Princeton, N.J., 1964; W. H. Smith, "Intervention in Civil Strife and International Order," unpublished Ph.D. dissertation, Australian National University, Canberra, 1970.

each belligerent. The difficulty with this model was that it assumed that internal war could somehow remain internal, that a convulsion could take place within a state in isolation from international society, and that all that society would and could do was to award the prize of membership in it to the victor. Where, as in the contemporary world, international politics take place within as well as between states, with rival states seeking to award the prize of membership on grounds quite other than success in an internal war, sparking off thereby the cycle of intervention and counter-intervention, the old model, if it ever was in working order, seems so no longer.

The Charter did not produce a new model. It assumed a tolerably clear distinction between matters domestic and matters international. It sought to restrict and regulate conflict between states not within them. Its inflexibility in this respect is illustrated in Article 51 which imagined war as the massive use of force across international frontiers and made no reference to action other than "armed attack." Any form of conduct whose intensity or extent can be said to be less than armed attack, no matter how much it might impair the sovereignty of its victim, does not formally trigger the right of self-defense. The Charter does disallow the use or threat of force in Article 2(4) but permits no individual recourse where it is below the threshold of armed attack. In the post-Charter world, whether or not the wording of the Charter is responsible, revisionist states or groups within them have typically depended on methods short of overt and blatant armed attack to implement change in the international system. On the other hand, the *status quo* powers have been encouraged to upgrade any hostile threat or use of force into armed attack, reading into Article 51 the prohibition contained in Article 2(4) in order to legitimize action in individual or collective self-defense. Where these related developments coincide in a situation of internal war, they illustrate the breakdown of the traditional dichotomy between domestic and international affairs. One solution to the problem this presents to the law might be simply to import the norms about international conflict into the domestic arena. Another might be to rely on traditional noninterventionist norms. A third might consist in meeting the new complexity in international relations with a more sophisticated legal response. It is in this third area that the principle of nonintervention features as a general summary of the presumption in favor of nonparticipation—as a "nonintervention

317

standard" in the international law of internal war. It appears also in the interpretations of Mill and of Cobden as a prescription *de lege ferenda* in respect of certain categories of internal conflict. The issue of how to cope with the difficulties presented by internal war has been joined as a by-product of the scholarly debate on the legality of American participation in the Vietnam War.

In order to clarify the debate about the Vietnam War and to guide thought about the problem of internal war in general, Falk has distinguished between three types of violent conflict and between the corresponding remedies available to states when they occur.[160] Type I conflict involves the direct and massive use of military force across international frontiers for which the appropriate remedy is either the use of force in self-defense or the organization of collective action on a regional or global basis. Type II conflict comprises substantial military participation by one or more foreign states in a struggle for control within a state. After the exhaustion of procedures for peaceful settlement and machinery for collective security, the proper response to this situation, is the taking of military counteraction confined to the internal arena. Type III conflict consists of internal struggle for the control of a national society, a circumstance in which it is inappropriate for any outside state to use military power to influence the outcome.[161]

Looking at the Vietnam War in terms of these categories, Falk identifies the conflict as an example of Type III but goes on to argue that it was converted to Type II primarily through the participation of the United States.[162] The government of the United States, not without some scholarly support from academic international lawyers, saw the Vietnam War as Type I conflict with

[160] "International Law and the United States Role in the Viet Nam War," in Falk, *Vietnam War and International Law*, pp. 366–367, from which the summary following is taken. Falk points out that his "types" are analytical rather than empirical in character and that in the real world a particular occasion of violence is likely to be a mixture of types, classification depending on the nature of the mixture. *Ibid.*, p. 366, n. 16.

[161] In a subsequent elaboration, Falk adds a fourth category of conflict which exists "whenever a competent international organization of global (IVa) or regional (IVb) dimensions authorizes the use of force." "International Law and the United States Role in Viet Nam: A Response to Professor Moore," in *Vietnam War and International Law*, pp. 456–457.

[162] "International Law and the U.S. Role in the Viet Nam War," pp. 368–373; "A Response to Professor Moore," pp. 459–470.

aggression coming from the North.[163] The assessment of the Vietnam conflict in terms of Falk's categories depends partly upon interpretation of the facts. But it also depends upon the normative construction to be put upon the facts from the point of view of world order.[164] Assuming that the choice of category has been made, and the crucial issue in making it is the decision whether infiltration of men and arms across a civil war cease-fire line intended to be temporary but made less so by events is to be considered an armed attack, what are the legal consequences of the choice? If Hanoi's participation in the war in the South is regarded as tantamount to armed attack (Type I) across an international frontier, then the norms which are to apply are those of international conflict. Article 51 is preferred to any admission of the civil strife aspects of the war. If, on the other hand, Hanoi's participation in the war in the South is regarded either as involvement in a civil war between North and South (Type III) or as intervention in a civil war in the South (Type II), then the norms which are to apply cannot be found in Article 51 of the Charter, and the only guidance provided by the Charter is a general presumption against intervention and the use of force, and for collective action in the event of its breach.

Taking the aspects of this debate which are of general significance in evaluating the principle of nonintervention beyond the Vietnam context, Falk's conception of Type II and Type III conflict represents a plea for maintaining a distinction between internal and international war as a device for the limitation of conflict, and a plea also for the clarification of the rules which are to apply to intervention in civil strife. In the event of Type III conflict, a principle of nonintervention is to apply, not merely as a general Charter assumption but as a rule relevant to a specific situation. It requires an outside state to refrain from intervention in an internal war provided all other states have done so—it seeks to hold the

[163] For the United States government position see above Chapter Six, section IV. For scholarly support for that position see Moore, "International Law and the United States Role in Viet Nam: A Reply," in Falk, *Vietnam War and International Law*, pp. 401–444, and "The Lawfulness of Military Assistance to the Republic of Viet-Nam," in *ibid.*, pp. 237–270.

[164] This order aspect will be examined in greater detail below, Chapter Nine, section VI. Here the purpose is merely to locate the areas occupied by the principle in contemporary international law, and for this purpose a factual inquiry into the Vietnam conflict is superfluous.

ring around civil strife. Falk's Type II conflict readmits intervention as a technical term describing a form of coercion short of armed attack, and having an explicitly normative connotation in the sense that it allows a forcible remedial response provided it is confined to the internal arena—it seeks to restore the ring around internal conflict. But in allowing intervention to uphold the principle of nonintervention, Type II rules out a punitive attack on the other intervening state or states, for such would require not only a finding that an armed attack had taken place but also that the response was necessary to effective self-defense. If this technical interpretation of Type II were accepted, it would rule out, for example, the propriety of a United States claim that her participation in the Vietnam War was counterintervention to uphold the principle of nonintervention, because by bombing the North she exceeded the legitimate response.

The use of the concepts of intervention and counterintervention in this way to identify and to allow for phenomena below the threshold of armed attack still leaves the difficulty of defining intervention, of deciding, for example, on when a Type III conflict exists. Are economic and military aid to an incumbent government to be considered "intervention" justifying offsetting aid to the insurgent? Responding to this problem, Farer has suggested a "prohibition on tactical support" which would exclude foreign troops from active involvement in an internal war zone.[165] An outside state could give aid to either incumbent or insurgent, but this should stop short of sending personnel for actual combat. This proposal does not abandon that frontier between internal and international war which the traditional norm of nonintervention was intended to police; it simply moves the transgression of the rule from the vague area between diplomatic pressure and dictatorial interference to the more readily identifiable area between aid and commitment of combat troops. As such, it is not an attempt to meet the new complexity in the international relations of internal war with a new complex of norms, an exercise which Farer deprecates,[166] but an attempt to cut through the complexity with a simple

[165] Tom J. Farer, "Intervention in Civil Wars: A Modest Proposal," in Falk, *Vietnam War and International Law*, pp. 518–522, and "Harnessing Rogue Elephants: A Short Discourse on Intervention in Civil Strife," in Falk, ed., *The Vietnam War and International Law*, Vol. 2, Princeton, N.J., 1969, pp. 1111–1116.

[166] "Harnessing Rogue Elephants," p. 1105.

rule which, despite its lack of sophistication, has the primary virtue, in Farer's view, of holding out the prospect of observance.[167]

If opposition to the Vietnam War has been productive of thought about the international law of internal war below the threshold of armed attack, it is not the case that the more sophisticated defense of American participation in the Vietnam War has been content to rely simply on the rationale of self-defense against armed attack in its analysis of internal war. Indeed, it is a defender of the legality of American intervention in that war, John Norton Moore, who has produced the most elaborate contemporary account of that part of international law that would control foreign intervention in internal conflict.[168] The principle of nonintervention, or "nonintervention standards," is a summary term used by Moore for the whole of the international law of internal war, and nonparticipation in internal war is at the same time the preferred situation against which Moore measures claims that would override it.[169] For the measurement of claims, Moore has three criteria summarily representing, in his view, the basic community policies at stake in intervention: self-determination, the preservation of minimum human rights, and the maintenance of minimum public order.[170] Consideration of these policies underlies Moore's subsequent account of the international law of internal war—of what nonintervention standards are and what they ought to be.

In this analysis, the traditional questions relating to civil war reappear—the legitimacy of humanitarian intervention, the distinction between insurgency and belligerency, the decision as to the point at which an insurgency has succeeded sufficiently as to impose on outside powers a duty of neutrality—but they are asked against the background of a framework which is sensitive to different types of internal war, recognizing that some types might pose a greater threat to international order than others. Thus Moore

[167] In this regard, we have noticed above that strand of United States doctrine that would stop short of committing ground troops to conflicts within foreign states, and Farer argues that such a norm "does appear to codify Soviet and Chinese practice." "Intervention in Civil Wars," p. 520.

[168] Moore, "The Control of Foreign Intervention in Internal Conflict," in *Law and the Indo-China War*, pp. 115–286. Moore's account implicitly and explicitly rejects Farer's desire to cut through the complexity and establish a single, unequivocal rule of nonintervention. For argument explicitly rejecting the Farer view see *ibid.*, pp. 258–267.

[169] *Ibid.*, pp. 163, 251–252, 268, and 276.

[170] *Ibid.*, pp. 163–173.

distinguishes six types of internal war according to the objectives of the conflict: Type I in which conflict is nonauthority-oriented; Type II, anticolonial war; Type III, wars of secession; Type IV, indigenous conflict for the control of internal authority structures; Type V, external imposition of authority structures; and Type VI, Cold-War divided nation conflicts.[171] Moore goes on to develop and to analyze the legitimacy of twenty-one claims that can be, or have been, held to justify intervention in internal conflict.[172]

Although in the case of Cold-War divided nation conflicts a claim relating to intervention for minimum order, and, at the other end of the spectrum, a claim of humanitarian grounds for intervention in nonauthority-oriented conflicts might be found for different reasons more pressing than a plea for nonintervention, an imperative of nonparticipation informs Moore's analysis of each of the claims he examines.[173] Similarly, in dealing with the customary international law of nonintervention, he finds more to be said in favor of a "neutral non-intervention standard," which holds that it is unlawful to aid either faction in an internal struggle for control of authority structures once the outcome is uncertain, than of what he calls "the traditional standard," which allowed discrimination in favor of the incumbent until the stage of belligerency was reached.[174] And it is a modified neutral nonintervention standard that Moore adopts as his preferred norm, holding, at the same

[171] *Ibid.*, p. 175.

[172] *Ibid.*, pp. 176–225.

[173] Though this presumption of outside nonparticipation in internal conflict does not arise in virtue of the principle of self-determination. On the contrary, it arises principally from the "difficulty of determining genuine self-determination, with a resulting preference for allowing indigenous conflict to run its course." *Ibid.*, p. 277. This seems to be a respect for the principle of independence, or for something more vague like a domestic balance of forces, rather than for one of Moore's basic community policies—that of self-determination. For a discussion of the competing claims of self-determination and of state sovereignty or independence see below, Chapter Nine, section VI.

[174] Moore holds the view that the neutral nonintervention standard "provides probably the most useful normative base of any generally accepted standard." He holds this view in spite of observing that such a standard is not clear as to when aid to incumbents must be frozen at preinsurgency levels, that it might obscure the legitimacy of counterintervention, and that it fails to take into account the full range of interventionary claims. *Ibid.*, pp. 254–258. Moore himself attempts to spell out the conditions in which an insurgency imposes a duty of neutrality on outside powers in *ibid.*, p. 251.

time, that a case can be made for the view that such a standard *is* the present international law of nonintervention.[175] The modifications that Moore requires are three: that the norm should admit the legitimacy of preinsurgency assistance to a widely recognized government; that it must allow counterintervention on behalf of a widely recognized government; and that it must sometimes permit "non-partisan participation for the purpose of restoring orderly processes of self-determination."[176] If these modifications have a familiar ring, it is in the perception that internal wars are not all of a piece, and that various types of conflict having different consequences for the international society might require legal standards which are sensitive to such differences, that the specifically modern contribution to the international law of nonintervention lies.[177]

If these areas of internal war beyond the reach of the Charter, over which the principle of nonintervention has been stretched thinly, are precisely the areas into which international politics have probed the most deeply, setting legal doctrine and state practice apart from each other, there is a final area in which the principle can be described as a ground rule reflecting state practice rather

[175] In summarizing his normative suggestions, Moore seems to identify "is" with "ought" in saying that "a good case can be made that these recommendations summarize the present international law of non-intervention in internal conflicts as well as present community consensus permits." *Ibid.*, p. 280.

[176] *Ibid.*, p. 276.

[177] Though this recognition does not solve the crucial problem of classifying a particular conflict. Thus disagreement about the Vietnam War, we have seen, can be said to stem from the defense placing it in Moore's Type VI, and the prosecution placing it in Moore's Type IV (or in Falk's Types I and III respectively). At the same time as the spelling-out of different types of internal conflict has been going on, the traditional exercise of examining various justifications for outside participation in internal war has been continued and elaborated. Thus Rosalyn Higgins, while taking account of various types of civil conflict and of the community policies relevant to the justifications for participation in them gives a central place in her survey of the international law of internal war to the guidance which that law provides on claims made with regard to four aspects of civil strife: claims concerning the existence of a civil war, claims concerning the conduct of an internal war, claims concerning participation in internal war, and claims by factions concerning relations with third states. "Internal War and International Law," in Black and Falk, eds., *The Future of the International Legal Order*, Vol. III, *Conflict Management*, pp. 81–121. As an attempt to come to grips with the actual international law of internal war, this paper is a useful complement to the work of Falk and Moore.

than being set over against it. But here it operates as a principle of interbloc rather than interstate law.[178] Where the predominance of the United States in the American hemisphere and that of the Soviet Union in Eastern Europe is recognized, and the recognition demonstrated by the restraint of each from intervention in the sphere of influence of the other, it is possible to discern an interbloc principle of nonintervention as a ground rule of relations between the superpowers. Neither the Soviet assertion of her predominance in Hungary and in Czechoslovakia, nor the American assertion of her predominance in Guatemala, Cuba, and in the Dominican Republic was actively challenged by the rival power.[179] Eastern European and Latin American states have no access to counterintervention from outside their blocs to uphold the principle of nonintervention within them because of the superimposition of prior interbloc norms on interstate norms.[180]

Outside the spheres of influence of the superpowers, the ground rules are less clear. The tacit agreement between the United States and the Soviet Union not to confront each other in those areas where their respective preponderance has been established provides no guidance beyond those areas where competitive interference, the attempt to establish preponderance, has typified postwar international politics. Thus the United States participation in the Vietnam War might be represented as an attempt to preempt the establishment of a Chinese sphere of influence in South East

---

[178] See McWhinney, *"Peaceful Coexistence,"* pp. 92–94. There is a precedent for this development in the assertion by the United States of the Monroe Doctrine as an interhemispheric principle precluding European intervention in the Americas and American intervention in Europe. See above, Chapter Four, section III.

[179] "Cuba" here means the Bay of Pigs adventure of 1961. The Cuba crisis of 1962 can be regarded as the demonstration of the ground rule by the willingness of the United States to defend it rather than its invalidation by a Soviet challenge. See McWhinney, p. 94.

[180] This has not meant the extinction of the principle of nonintervention within the blocs, though it has rendered it more fragile and more prone to being overridden by higher imperatives. It certainly has not discouraged the assertion of the rule by Latin American states and by Eastern European states as an intrabloc as well as an interbloc norm. See R. Rosenstock, "The Declaration of Principles of International Law Concerning Friendly Relations: A Survey," *American Journal of International Law*, Vol. 65, No. 5, 1971, p. 726. See also above, Chapters Five, Six, and Seven. For further discussion of interbloc nonintervention, see below, Chapter Nine, section VI.

Asia.[181] In the Afro-Asian world, outside the spheres of influence, established or inchoate, of the superpowers, Falk suggests a rule of mutual nonintervention allowing the interstate order to prevail without the attempted superimposition of bloc norms by the superpowers.[182] In terms of Falk's categories of conflict, this norm would disallow the conversion of Type III conflict into any other category except Type IV which would authorize intervention by a regional or global organization.[183] A rule of nonintervention in this area, however, commands less support in the practice of states than is the case with the interbloc norm of nonintervention.

IV

International law as inherited from the nineteenth century conceived of the principle of nonintervention as a general rule which was cut across by more pressing imperatives justifying its breach in particular cases. The Charter of the United Nations seemed to abandon the specific notions of nonintervention and sometimes justifiable intervention by speaking instead in the language of the legitimacy of the use of force. And yet the principle has survived this transformation. It survives in the form of a general assumption about the nature of international society which the Positivists of the nineteenth century received from the Naturalists and handed on to the twentieth century. The assumption takes two forms: first that the world is a world of states accepting no authority above them except that of international law—nonintervention as the rejection of a superstate; and second that in a world of sovereign states there must be a rule recognizing and requiring respect for the allocation of authority among them—nonintervention as a necessary rule in an interstate order. The post-Charter legal order has not significantly shaken either of these assumptions, though it has gathered adherents to the view that it carries the germ of a different and better world order. The principle has certainly survived as a favorite phrase of statesmen, and the United Nations General Assembly has endorsed it as a fundamental principle of international law, although the canvas of the principle tends to be filled in according to states' particular leanings about what is desirable and what is not in international politics. Nailing down the

[181] See Falk, "A Response to Professor Moore," p. 497, n. 131.
[182] *Ibid.*, pp. 498–499.   [183] *Ibid.*, p. 499.

specific areas of application of the principle, some international lawyers and much state practice acknowledge its particular if shadowy existence beyond the margins of Article 2(4), its relevance and effectiveness are debated in the context of internal war, and it exists as a quasi-legal norm of international politics conducted between blocs.

NINE

NONINTERVENTION AND
INTERNATIONAL ORDER

The foregoing chapters have been mainly concerned with doctrines of nonintervention held by individual states or by groups of states, though the theme of a principle of nonintervention as a legal rule applying to all states, independent of the peculiarities of national interpretation, has been traced through them. It remains to invert this procedure: to consider the principle in terms of the function it fulfills in the international system, the contribution (if any) it makes to international order, rather than the part it plays in the foreign policy of states. Clearly, the two procedures are not mutually exclusive. The part the principle plays in the foreign policy of a great power may determine its function in the international system to the extent that the fiat of that power prevails, but the focus of this chapter will be on the international system and not on the states which make it up. To establish this focus the chapter will first introduce a notion of international order. It will go on to examine the sense or senses in which the principle may be said to be functional to that order and whether the concept of "function" sheds any light on how the principle contributes to international order. The third section of the chapter will place the principle of nonintervention alongside some other imperatives or ground rules of international relations that are normally associated with the maintenance of order in international society in order to discover or suggest the extent to which the principle may be said to cohere with them in a harmonious system. The fourth and fifth sections of the chapter will rehearse the principal challenges presented to the sovereign-state order by contemporary international politics, and if these challenges render the position of the nonintervention principle uncomfortable and confused the sixth section will explore a place for the principle in conceptions of international order, or if "international" is an inappropriate adjective, world order, other than the one which informs this work. Finally, the threads of the various approaches (political and legal, historical and functional, state-centered and system-centered) will be drawn together in a summary of the places inhabited, some would say infested, by the principle of nonintervention in thought about international relations, of the purposes its espousal has served, and in a conclusion as to its effectiveness as a rule which would restrain the entities to which it applies: a conclusion, in particular, as to whether international society has moved beyond the era in which its writ could possibly run.

I

Order, in an elementary sense, denotes "regular, methodical or harmonious arrangement in the position of the things contained in any space or area, or composing any group or body."[1] But harmony is a more exacting condition than the others implying more than mere regularity. It requires not only that the arrangement of things be regular or methodical but also that they should form together an agreeable whole. The conductor of an orchestra expects his players to keep time and to be the masters of their instruments, but he expects too that the sounds they make should combine in a pleasing way—to produce symphony and not cacophony. To achieve the purpose of harmony, to provide for that particular end, the things contained in any space or area, group or body, must occupy their "proper place" and perform their "proper functions"—order in a less elementary sense than just regularity. The task in regard to order in social life is to discover in what this proper disposition consists, by what principle the propriety is to be judged, or, in other words, the discovery of the purposes for the achievement of which the pattern of social relations is arranged.

Regularity and method may be discerned in social life if it is conducted according to rules. Order in this elementary sense may be said to exist if the relations between men or groups are not simply fortuitous but show a degree of conformity to common standards of conduct. But to define order in social life as conformity to rules fails to capture fully the purposive connotation of order, the goals which the rules are designed to achieve, except to the extent that rules are obeyed for their own sake, their mere

---

[1] *Oxford English Dictionary.* The phrases in quotation marks in this paragraph are taken from this dictionary. As to the conception of order to be developed here, I owe its main outline to ideas obtained from Professor Hedley Bull, though he might not fully recognize the form which they now take.

existence compelling their observance. No need here to speculate on the reasons impelling men to gather together in society, but it is possible to isolate three purposes whose achievement, in some degree, seems necessary if not sufficient to the existence of social life.[2] In the first place, life itself must be secure against violence. Second, there must be confidence among the members of a society that contracts made between them will be honored. And in the third place, there must be some arrangement for the existing distribution of property, public or private, to endure and not to be subject to plunder or forcible annexation. None of these requirements for social life is absolute in the sense that each must be perfectly observed all the time before it is possible to say that order prevails in society. Indeed, they may at times, even frequently, conflict with one another—the life of one man being found inferior to the defense of the property of another, or the concern of one man for his life being superior to the expectation of another that he carry out a promise made to him. Other values which men hold dear, such as the yearning for ideological oneness, may override any of these values in a particular case. But without some degree of respect for them, life in society, cooperation among its members, and the development of industry in it hardly seem possible. This is a static conception of order. It may be that flexibility (the maintenance, for example, of stability of possession over time by making provision for it to change hands peacefully) and legitimacy (the securing of assent to social arrangements once made) are also important to continuing order.[3] But these dynamic requirements can apply only once the conditions for static order have been to some extent satisfied.

If order in any society is dependent upon the realization of these primary goals, it might be said that order in the relations between states does not exist, that the pattern of relations formed between them does not justify the attachment of the label "society."[4] The

---

[2] In the same way, Hoffmann relates that the Bellagio Conference on Conditions of World Order, which met in June 1965, chose at Raymond Aron's suggestion, to think of order as the "minimum conditions for existence" or the "minimum conditions for *co*existence." See Hoffmann, ed., *Conditions of World Order*, Boston, 1968, p. 2.

[3] Thus Hoffmann has it that order is achieved in any political system if the three requirements of security, satisfaction, and flexibility are met, "International Systems and International Law," in *The State of War*, New York, 1965, p. 97.

[4] Or it might be said that it is possible to speak of order in international

account of the elements of order, or of the reasons for disorder, among states traditionally begins where the account of order within states finishes; the consequence of order within states is taken to be anarchy between them. Whether the international anarchy is more bearable as compared to anarchy between men, as in Hobbes's account, or less so, as Rousseau suggested, order among states is a precarious condition.[5] Expectations about the lives of individual men in the arena of international relations are not that they will find protection there, but that they will be laid down there in the service of some higher imperative. Contracts, the sanctity of promises in international relations, are but words unless swords are drawn to enforce them. And possession, in the international state of nature, is stable only so long as considerations of power do not intervene to unsettle it, a stability obtaining only under constant threat of disruption.

If, however, the account of the elements of order between states begins not where the order established within them finishes but includes these islands of order as an integral part of the conception of international order, then that account emerges somewhat from the classical gloom which accompanies it. The goals of the security of human life, of the sanctity of contracts, and of the stability of possession of property are not pursued directly by men in international society. They are not the immediate tasks of that society, but are matters which are principally delegated to the responsibility of individual states. Men look to their states for the realization of these primary goals, and the intervention of the state as the provider of order in domestic society renders the task of a rudimentary international order to that extent less demanding. Such a rudimentary order can be said to exist in international relations if states accept rules which acknowledge the delegation of authority among them. In this respect, a principle of nonintervention is fundamental. If international society is accurately described as being split up into islands of order, the distribution of which is determined by the principle of state sovereignty, then it is the function of the rule of nonintervention to draw attention to that distribution and require respect for it. It is a first principle, an elementary rule of orderly

relations if order is defined in a less demanding sense than that used here. See generally Georg Schwarzenberger, *International Law and Order*, London, 1971.

[5] On the differences between Hobbes and Rousseau in this respect, see Hoffmann, "Rousseau on War and Peace," in *The State of War*, pp. 60–70.

international relations because its observation would demonstrate the recognition by states of the existence of others and the legitimacy of their separateness in a society bound together only by mutual acknowledgment of the autonomy of its parts. It is fundamental to order in a society without government because it stands guard over the established enclaves of order. So long as international society is primarily composed of sovereign states, observance of a general rule of nonintervention can be regarded as a minimum condition for their orderly coexistence.

The principle of state sovereignty can be said to serve the purpose of stabilizing possession in international relations, just as rules about property do within the state. The principle of nonintervention placed at the frontiers of state sovereignty fulfills an analogous function to that of a "No Trespassing" sign standing at the perimeter of a piece of property held under domestic law. The analogy is imperfect. The decline of the theory of the patrimonial state led to a distinction between the *imperium* of the right of sovereignty and the *dominium* of the right of property, the former conveying the idea of supreme authority over territory, but not of ownership of it as in the latter.[6] If *imperium* is in this sense a more restricted right than *dominium*, the right of sale or gift being less generally associated with sovereignty than it is with property, there are other senses in which sovereignty is a more pervasive and complex right than property. Whereas property rights over a piece of land imply no rights over people except in strict relation to that land, the right of territorial sovereignty is a right directly over people, albeit people within a given territory. Further, the owner of a piece of land draws attention to his rights in just one dimension by the erection of his "No Trespassing" sign. The sovereign state, on the other hand, draws attention to its rights not only in the dimension of territorial integrity but also in the less clearly defined dimension of political independence. The rule of nonintervention is not just a reminder about the distribution of property in international life. Despite these important differences, the primary functions of the rights of property and sovereignty and of the duties not to trespass or intervene are similar. They distinguish between "*mine* and *thine*" in social life and require respect for the distinction. "The

[6] Though in Soviet law the two notions are joined in the sense that the state exercises simultaneously (with the abolition of private property) both *dominium* and *imperium* over its territory. See T. A. Taracouzio, *The Soviet Union and International Law*, New York, 1935, pp. 49–53.

331

reaction against patrimonial ideas," wrote Lauterpacht, "cannot obliterate the fact that the two notions are essentially analogous on account of the exclusiveness of enjoyment and disposition which is in law the main formal characteristic of both private property and territorial sovereignty."[7]

If the sovereign state is the principal guarantor of the values of the security of life, the sanctity of contracts, and the stability of possession, and if the analogy between sovereignty and property is at all accurate, it can be said that of the three goals of order, it is the stability of possession which is fundamental to international life, prior in that environment to the other two. It is then possible to put a different construction on the dismal account of the international anarchy. If the laying down of life in international politics takes place for the defense of order within the state, or for the defense of a system of states based on the minimal uniting principle that the order within them is not to be interfered with, or if covenants are broken for the same purpose, then the international anarchy is not as desperate as it first appears because it witnesses the laying down of life to protect life. The unhappy events which accompany anarchy between states might at least serve a recognizable purpose and are not necessarily futile sacrifices to an insatiable and unreasonable god of conflict.

It is clearly not the case that observance of a principle of nonintervention would exhaust the requirements for international order. That could only hold true in an international environment that was not only anarchical but also populated by states that were totally isolated from each other, so that international relations became an agreement not to relate as well as not to intervene. Where this isolation does not obtain but where various degrees of separateness and independence do, the requirements for order are more complex, and indeed the closest approximation to order between states might require the ending of international relations—the imposition of a government over states just as it has required the institution of government within them. Beyond isolation, where nonintervention is a rule perfectly observed, and short of world government in which a rule of nonintervention has no place, minimum order among states depends upon their recognition that their interests are generally served by mutual toleration—toleration not only of the existence of each other but also of diverse behavior

[7] Lauterpacht, *Private Law Sources and Analogies of International Law*, London, 1927, pp. 95–96.

within them, so long as it presents no international threat. In this respect, the rule of nonintervention is not only a protector of the right of sovereignty, it also points out the limits of that right. Unlike the right of self-preservation which is a state-centered imperative tending to swallow up international law, the rule of nonintervention has its origin in the society of states. It arises from their coexistence and provides for their continued coexistence.

Whether the practice of states meets these minimum requirements of order is a question on which this chapter will conclude. Meanwhile, this analysis of order does at least demonstrate that while the international anarchy suggests a generally gloomy outlook for world order, it is not possible on that account to say that no element of order is to be discovered in international relations.

II

The function of the nonintervention principle, we have argued, is to draw attention to and require respect for the principle of state sovereignty. But what does "function" mean and how does it illustrate the part played by the principle in international society, the contribution it makes to international order? The notion of "function" as the use or purpose of anything has been used in this work to analyze the place of the principle in the foreign policies of states, to identify the various ways in which the principle furthered the objectives of diplomacy—by rationalizing policy, by legitimizing it at home and abroad, by criticizing the actions of others, and by informing others of the sticking-places of the proclaiming state. The dismissal of these functions as mere words, we have seen, is a failure to realize that Castlereagh's feeling unable to applaud in church was as important for the future of Europe as Metternich's insistence on preaching the sermon.[8] And in a contemporary study of infractions of the principle of nonintervention by great powers within their blocs, two writers have drawn attention to the functions of principles, of "verbal strategy," in the process of international politics.[9] Pointing to a false dichotomy between words and acts in international politics, words being a kind of action, they have sought to demonstrate that the intervention of one superpower in the internal affairs of a state within its sphere of influence, and

[8] See above, Chapter Four, section II(i).

[9] Franck and Weisband, *Word Politics: Verbal Strategy among the Superpowers.*

doctrine developed for the defense of such action, have provided a license authorizing similar behavior by the other superpower within its sphere.[10] Thus the Brezhnev Doctrine, formulated with respect to Czechoslovakia in 1968, is not merely similar to, but is an acceptance of an offer made in regard to superpower behavior, by the Johnson Doctrine formulated in relation to the Dominican Republic in 1965.[11] This reciprocal behavior, in the instruction of which doctrines from Truman's to Brezhnev's have had a function, suggests a rule of prudence that nothing be said in a crisis which can be applied at another time in a way which is against the interests of the proclaiming state. It suggests also, more generally, an awareness that the future international system is being shaped by reactions to the crises of the present.[12]

If principles can be said thus to have a function not merely in the legitimation of action in international relations, but in the precipitation of such action, some international lawyers have been concerned to point out the functions of international law in general in more than just the one dimension of restraint of state action. It has been said to afford "a framework, a pattern, a fabric for international society, grown out of relations between nations in a real world and ordering these relations in turn."[13] It has been described as an "institutional device for communicating to the policy-makers of various states a consensus on the nature of the international system," and as preparing the conceptual ground for building world order "by shaping attitudes about the nature and promise of international political reality."[14] One of its major contributions in conflict situations has been regarded as the provision of a "regular and highly articulated procedure for the assertion and refutation of national claims," enabling "precise communication to take place in a horizontal authority structure."[15] It might be said then that the principle of nonintervention functions so as to communi-

[10] *Ibid.*, particularly Chap. 7.

[11] *Ibid.*, Chaps. 3, 5, 6, and pp. 128–129.

[12] *Ibid.*, pp. 126–136. Apart from observing the importance of verbal strategy, Franck and Weisband direct their argument at changing it—as a first step in the dismantling of spheres of influence. See below, section vi.

[13] L. Henkin, *How Nations Behave*, London, 1968, p. 7.

[14] W. D. Coplin, "International Law and Assumptions about the State System," *World Politics*, Vol. xvii, No. 4, July 1965, pp. 617 and 634. See also the same author's *The Functions of International Law*, Chicago, 1966.

[15] Falk, "The Regulation of International Conflict by Means of Law," in *Legal Order in a Violent World*, p. 67.

cate ideas about the structure of the international system, about the continuing importance of the values of sovereignty and, in some interpretations, of self-determination. By the exchange of information and the entry into debate about the principle of nonintervention, states might be made aware of each other's attitudes, and restrained by them, at least to the extent that knowledge of another's position makes one wary of it. But though communication in terms of international law might serve an important political function at the same time as demonstrating that states regard international law as something whose language has to be talked, this communication function does not substitute for the function of legal restraint, and to place too much stress on it might be to inspire unwarranted confidence in this regard.[16] The different interpretations of the principle of nonintervention from state to state and from bloc to bloc, particularly the fundamental differences about the exceptions allowable to the rule, render expectations about states' general allegiance to *a* principle of nonintervention uncertain when generality is pursued into detail.

If the concept of function is taken beyond its everyday meaning of use or purpose to the "special kind of activity proper to anything—the mode of action by which it fulfils its purpose, especially as contrasted to structure,"[17] a link can be discerned between it and the concept of order. Order, it was suggested in the previous section, is a pattern or whole in which the parts fit into their proper place. The parts might now be said to be "functional" to that pattern or whole if they not only fit into their proper place but also operate properly so as to maintain the whole—to fulfill that purpose. The discussion of social institutions in terms of the part they play in the society as a whole is the method which distinguishes the "functionalist" approach in social science. The question here is the extent to which thought about the "function" of the principle of nonintervention, in this technical sense of the term, can help to explain its place in international society.

The sort of explanation that functionalism offers for any social item is a teleological one. It places the whole of society before a part within it, and would explain the latter in terms of a need of the former to which it is a response. It is then the sort of explanation which neglects the immediate cause of a social institution in

---

[16] Hoffmann, "International Law and the Control of Force," in Deutsch and Hoffmann, *The Relevance of International Law*, p. 24.

[17] *Oxford English Dictionary*.

favor of its final cause—the purpose it can be said to serve—leading some to doubt whether functionalist theory can be held to explain anything at all.[18] But so long as this purposiveness involved in the concept of function is made explicit and the consequent limitations to its explanatory power recognized, it might be of some value. It might serve, as an introductory and general apprehension of the social universe, to place social items on a teleological map. If we look first at domestic society, H.L.A. Hart has demonstrated that much of the teleological point of view survives in some of the ways in which we think and speak of human beings.[19] It is latent, Hart says, in our identification of certain things as human needs which it is good to satisfy. Food and rest are needs of this sort, the fulfillment of which is not a mere convention or human prescription. When we say that it is the function of the heart to circulate the blood, we imply that there is something good and natural about it. What makes sense of this mode of thought, Hart argues, is the tacit assumption that the proper end of human activity is survival, resting on the simple contingent fact that most men, most of the time wish to continue existence. Survival is a goal because men desire it and it is the general wish to live that gives meaning to terms like need and function.

It is then possible for Hart to show that so long as certain simple truisms about human nature and the world in which men live hold good, there are certain rules of conduct which any social organization must contain if it is to be viable. These truisms he calls the "minimum content of Natural Law," and he isolates five of them.[20] First, because of human vulnerability, for social life to be possible there must be some rules restricting the use of violence in killing or inflicting bodily harm. In the second place, the approximate equality of men, no one man being sufficiently powerful to subdue others for any length of time, makes necessary a system of mutual forbearance and compromise to prevent the war of all against all. Third, this system of mutual forbearance is made both necessary

[18] For an examination of this doubt, among others, see R. J. Vincent, "The Functions of Functionalism in International Relations," *Year Book of World Affairs*, Vol. 27, 1973, pp. 332–344.

[19] *The Concept of Law*, p. 186. The summary following is of pp. 186–195 of this book.

[20] Hart acknowledges Hobbes, *Leviathan*, Chaps. 14 and 15, and Hume, *Treatise on Human Nature*, Bk. III, Pt. 2, especially sections 2 and 4–7, as the bases for his empirical version of natural law.

and possible through man's limited altruism. If men were angels, rules to guide their relations would be superfluous. If they were devils, life according to a code of rules would be impossible. Because they are neither, but somewhere in between, rules to govern their conduct are required and general adherence to them is possible. Fourth, limited resources make necessary some minimal form of the institution of property in order that resources may be won from the environment.[21] Finally, man's limited understanding and strength of will mean that sanctions are required as a guarantee that those who would voluntarily obey the law shall not be sacrificed to those who would not.

Survival then is a goal or purpose which requires that men adhere to certain fundamental rules if they are to live together in society. If these rules are conceived of as cultural items whose function it is to contribute to the survival of the society of which they are part, this is the core of the functionalists' thesis reduced, in Hart's analysis, to formal statements or truisms. Survival is the ultimate purpose, but if the survival of men in society is generally provided for by the state, what can be said of the survival of states in international society? What can be said of a functionalist formulation of the principle of nonintervention that might describe it as a social item whose function is the contribution it makes to the survival of the sovereign state system of which it is a part? In the section defining order, it was suggested that rules about state sovereignty and nonintervention could be considered primary or fundamental to international order because it was within the territory of the state that order among individual men was achieved and that the minimum requirement for order among states was the preservation of order within them. But the simple truisms that apply to individuals and indicate those rules which must apply if society is to be formed between them do not hold good for states. In particular, sovereign states do not share with men the attribute

[21] Hart adds here that the division of labor which all but the smallest groups must develop in order to obtain adequate supplies, brings with it the need for dynamic rules allowing individuals to create obligations and vary their incidence. He goes on to identify minimum forms of protection for persons, property, and promises as indispensable features of municipal law. *Concept of Law*, pp. 192–193. This is similar to the notion of minimum order outlined in the first section of this chapter which encompassed the conditions logically necessary for social life, but Hart has added the simple statements about the nature of men which explain why they can be considered such.

of approximate equality. The rule of nonintervention is a rule of mutual forbearance; it requires that states shall respect each other's sovereignty, that they shall treat each other in this respect as equals. But where this formal equality does not reflect the facts of international life, it remains a question whether an international order based upon the fiction of state equality is not a very tenuous one. International order could be conceived of in circumstances of actual inequality between states in two ways. It could be imagined firstly if states would, like

> The heavens themselves, the planets, and this centre,
> Observe degree, priority and place,
> Insisture, course, proportion, season, form,
> Office, and custom, in all line of order. . . .[22]

But if states would not accept Ulysses' warnings about "neglection of degree," the cruder ordering device is the principle that might is right, "a system in which the weak submitted to the strong on the best terms they could make and lived under their 'protection.' "[23] Neither of these systems need necessarily eclipse the principle of state sovereignty as a guarantor of internal order. Indeed the former might establish sovereigns in a rigid hierarchy that would include a principle of nonintervention between its levels subject to a rule of intervention should one of them fail to observe degree, priority, and place. And ordering according to the principle that might is right need not generally disrespect the order of sovereign states except to determine the outcome in a conflict between weak and strong. But in either case the sovereignty of the weak is held as it were under license from the strong; the mutual forbearance of nonintervention might prevail, but it is not a forbearance dictated by reason in the same elementary sense as requires tolerance between individuals. It is still possible to declare that order between states is dependent upon mutual recognition of order within them, but no "minimum content of Natural Law" can be invoked to establish its necessity.

Herein lies the difficulty of applying the functionalists' thesis to international relations. The truism that among men some minimal form of the institution of property is required before they can live together in society is more difficult to establish of states in inter-

[22] From Ulysses' speech in Shakespeare's *Troilus and Cressida*, Act I, Scene iii.
[23] Hart, p. 194.

338

national society. Whereas men are permanent and irreducible units, the basic atoms of social life, states as the inventions of men have no such natural existence. There is no reason to suppose that men must always choose to live together in states, and no warrant for the claim that there is some natural law suggesting the necessary conditions of existence for international society. All that can be asserted is that the state is, in contemporary international politics, the "owner" of property and that while international society is populated mainly by sovereign states, observation in some degree of the principle of nonintervention is a necessary condition for their survival. If this explains the place of the principle by reference to the purpose it serves, it is also tautological since respect for sovereignty excludes intervention by definition, and to say that the principle of nonintervention contributes to the survival of sovereign states is merely to repeat the definition without shedding any light on the real world. It does not, for example, show how allegiance to or violation of the rule might contribute to system-maintenance in a particular circumstance. The simple statement that adherence to the rule serves the purpose of protecting sovereignty gives no guidance as to right conduct for states, from the point of view of system-maintenance, when one of their number has broken the rule. Should it be counterintervention or nonintervention?

Another difficulty involved in talking functionalists' language about the principle of nonintervention contributing to the survival of the system of which it is a part is the identification of the system. It is possible to say that the nonintervention principle is functional to the sovereign-state system, but important ingredients of the international system may be found elsewhere than in the account of its parts as sovereign. Distribution of power among the parts may be more significant to the system than their formal sovereignty. And if the power of states is taken as the vantage point from which the international system is viewed, if what is considered is not the "sovereign-state" system but the "balance of power" system or the "loose bipolar" system, then a very different account of the function of the principle of nonintervention might emerge. So the simple formula which renders the principle functional to the system will not do unless the system is clearly identified.[24]

Examination of the notion of function, then, will not greatly advance the discussion of the relationship between the principle

[24] See Vincent, "The Functions of Functionalism," section IV.

of nonintervention and international order, except perhaps to show what cannot be borrowed from the discussion of order between individuals. The next section will examine how well the principle of nonintervention relates with other rules of the interstate order which have been regarded as indispensable to its working. And from this look into the individual mechanisms of the international system, the chapter will go on to look at the system itself—at the challenges which contemporary international politics present to the order of sovereign states.

III

It has been said earlier in the chapter that adherence to the principle of nonintervention would exhaust the requirements for order between states only if they were totally isolated from each other.[25] Where this is not the case, where there are international relations, the rule must share the field with competing imperatives of order, or at least with imperatives that are not necessarily in harmony with it. To illustrate the place of the principle in this more complex environment, this section will examine its relation to three distinct doctrines for which there is a tradition of championship as imperatives of order between states but which have stopped short of advocating the overthrow of the states system and its replacement by some superior order. The principle will be placed first alongside the doctrine which teaches that order between states is to be maintained by the preservation of legitimate governments within them. In the second place, it will be examined in relation to the doctrine which holds that international order is best provided for by the maintenance of a balance of power between states. Third, the principle will be measured against the doctrine that the achievement of justice within the state might have, in any instance, a claim prior to order among them, a doctrine the extreme form of which holds that the realization of domestic justice is the only guarantee of international order.[26]

[25] See above, section I.

[26] Holbraad, in his *The Concert of Europe*, has distinguished these three broad traditions of thought about the functions of the Concert of Europe in German and British international theory, labelling them the conservative group of ideas, the balance of power group, and the progressive group. They will be taken here as general ideas about how order is to be maintained in international society and not specifically related to the Concert.

Ordering the relations between states according to the principle of nonintervention supposes that the character of the order established within them is not the proper concern of states in their international relations. Order between states is dependent upon order within them, but not upon a particular kind of order. It is a conservative principle, but it seeks to conserve sovereign states not sovereigns. It is Castlereagh's theory of foreign policy not Metternich's. Castlereagh held that it was sufficient for European order to uphold the territorial settlement of 1815, and he adhered to a principle of nonintervention which allowed an exception to be made only when that settlement was under threat.[27] Metternich found Castlereagh's doctrine necessary but not sufficient to a European order, and to fill the more exacting bill of sufficiency the dynastic arrangements legitimized by the Congress of Vienna had to be preserved. Metternich's scheme for European order was social as well as political. Revolution within a state challenged not merely the local regime but the social order of Europe, the disease of revolution spreading both by contagion and by the deliberate injection of conspirators. Rather than wait for revolution to manifest itself internationally in aggression, the powers of Europe had a right of intervention to stamp out the social threat at its source. Metternich acknowledged the distribution of territorial sovereigns but added to this conception of an international political order a transnational or Europe-wide conception of social order—the European civilization of which the great powers were the custodians.

This solidarist notion of international order stands opposed to the pluralist notion in which the doctrine of nonintervention has meaning. In a world of Metternich's designing, the only functions remaining to a doctrine of nonintervention would seem to be either as a principle gracing an international order within which the objective of sustaining the legitimacy of thrones had been fully realized or as a protest uttered against an international order which presumed too greatly on the independence of states. In so far as the American interventions of the postwar world, however well or ill-disguised as counterinterventions to uphold the principle of nonintervention, have been motivated by the desire to protect "legitimate" democratic governments within states or simply to

[27] See above, Chapter Four, section III.

maintain established governments of whatever noncommunist color against the threat of revolution, they have followed in the tradition of Metternich rather than of Castlereagh.[28] And the doctrine of nonintervention has been available to the critics of American foreign policy, among whom it has perhaps sat more comfortably than in the version appearing in the formal justifications of the United States.

If the balance of power is thought of as Castlereagh understood it, as the principle by which the great powers would join together against any state which actively set out to disturb the established distribution of territorial sovereignties, then it need not be an imperative demanding a different pattern of conduct from that required by the principle of nonintervention. Both are designed to protect the independence of states, and action taken in accordance with the doctrine that counterintervention is legitimate to uphold the principle of nonintervention might coincide in a particular case with action taken to redress a balance of power identified with the territorial status quo. Moreover, ordering according to the principle of balance, moving now beyond Castlereagh's territorial conception of it, might supplement the principle of nonintervention precisely where it has its most conspicuous weakness as a rule of order in its fictional assumption of the equality of states. If the balance of power is thought of not as an equal distribution of power among the states of the international system but as an approximate equilibrium of power in the system as a whole, the working of such a system might provide for the independence of the small "unequal" states in three ways. First, the independence of small states might be preserved in an equilibrium system by the attention of the great to the demands of balance. Any one great power might be deterred from encroaching on the independence of small states from fear that by thus upsetting the overall balance it would unite a coalition against it. Or, in the second place, such

---

[28] The American doctrine of nonintervention has never in fact conformed to that clinical neutrality between competing political principles that is suggested for the principle here. In that part of American doctrine which excluded European states from meddling in the American hemisphere was contained also the idea of excluding the *monarchical system* of the European powers. See above, Chapter Four, section III. If Britain came closer to this clinical neutrality, at least in the time of Castlereagh and Canning, it has been seen how this reflected her interests as the great power isolated from the social upheavals of Europe. See above, Chapter Four, sections IIi and IIii.

342

a balance of power system might allow for the independence of small states by giving them a vital role in its working. For in any instance it might be a small state which holds the balance or maintains it by opting for one coalition rather than another.[29] Third, if balance is maintained by shifting alliances, then the internal order of states need not be touched by the vicissitudes of international politics.[30]

But the move away from Castlereagh's principle of balance to a conception of balance as overall equilibrium in the system, as a move from a static balance based on the *status quo* to a dynamic balance taking account of changes in power relations and adjusting to meet them, from concern with the independence of the several parts of the system to the maintenance of the system as a whole, means also a move away from the principle of nonintervention as a rule conserving the established territorial order. Order is still an order of sovereign states but one in which an equilibrium of power in the system, the arrangement of which is primarily the responsibility of the great powers, takes priority over the concern for the sovereignty of each member of the system. It was at the shrine of balance that Poland was notoriously sacrificed. Martin Wight has distinguished one of nine distinct meanings of the "balance of power" as "the principle of equal aggrandizement of the Great Powers at the expense of the weak."[31] So the mere fact that both the principle of nonintervention and the principle of balance of power can be said to serve the same ultimate purpose of preserving the independence and integrity of states cannot be taken as a sign of their necessary compatibility in a particular case.[32] The two may be said to coexist with greater harmony than do the principle

[29] See H. Butterfield, "The Balance of Power," in Butterfield and Wight, *Diplomatic Investigations*, pp. 142–143.

[30] Independence, then, in three distinct senses: independence in the first case because it is convenient to the great powers—independence by accident of the system; independence in the second case for the foreign policy of small states—independence by design of the system; and independence in the third case in the internal affairs of states—independence outside the system.

[31] "The Balance of Power," in Butterfield and Wight, pp. 151 and 156–157.

[32] This discussion of the relationship between the two principles has assumed a multiple balance. What happens to the principle of nonintervention when the international system can be described in terms of a balance of two will be examined in the next section.

343

of nonintervention and that of intervention for dynastic legitimacy. But just as one of the functions for the doctrine of nonintervention to be salvaged from a world of the latter design was that of a protest against it, so Cobden's doctrine of nonintervention was opposed to the notion of balance of power as one of England's "stock pretences" paraded as an excuse for interfering in the affairs of others, when her real motive was lust for conquest.[33]

A state adhering to an absolute principle of nonintervention must tolerate injustice, such as the abuse of human rights, within another state because to interfere against it would be to violate the principle of state sovereignty; the values associated with statehood would be deemed superior to the plea for humanitarian intervention. By the same token, however, adherence to the rule of nonintervention would allow a just and successful rebellion against a tyrannical prince to run its course. It might be said then that the principle is neither just nor unjust, that the morality of adhering to it can only be judged by reference to the circumstances of a particular case. But this is misleading if it suggests that no general moral judgment can be made about the principle of nonintervention. For the principle, in requiring mutual toleration by states of what happens in their domestic affairs, in so placing order between states before justice for individuals within them, allows states to avoid the responsibility of making a decision as to whether an act or institution within any of them is just or unjust.[34] It provides the state also with a convenient legal excuse for ignoring considerations of justice for individuals within other states. A general moral judgment then, might be that the principle of nonintervention is an amoral rule—that it might serve a moral purpose only accidentally and not by design.

Nor does this conclusion provide a final judgment on the morality of the principle of nonintervention. It is worth remembering that those who first expounded the doctrine of nonintervention thought of it as primarily a principle of justice either arising from or being part of the doctrine of the fundamental rights of states. The rights of states to equality, liberty and independence, and thus the duty of nonintervention were the expression in international life of the natural rights and duties of individual men.[35] Though it

[33] See above, Chapter Three, p. 49.

[34] Indeed, in its absolute form, the principle of nonintervention *requires* a state to abstain from sitting in judgment over the internal affairs of others.

[35] See above, Chapter Two, pp. 26–31 and 39–43.

is not generally possible to identify morality between individuals with morality between states,[36] one useful analogy between them might illustrate the moral content of the principle of nonintervention. Just as the moral criterion of respect for persons as having ends of their own, and not just as objects of the will of others, suggests a rule that the pursuit of those ends is not to be interfered with so long as it does not itself interfere with the equal rights of others, so a similar rule might be applied to states as "associations of individuals with their own common interests and aspirations, expressed within a common tradition."[37] And in international relations there are three reasons for supposing the rule of nonintervention to be superior in a moral scale to any principle of intervention. In the first place, there is no guarantee of the impartiality of the state which intervenes in the internal affairs of another. More likely, it intervenes for some interest of its own, the target state being the object of its will, rather than the arena for the realization of some moral good.[38] Second, even if it were possible to guarantee the impartiality of the intervening state, intervention might be unwelcome simply because it stemmed from abroad, because it was foreign to whatever common culture united the citizens of the target state. The moral purpose of the intervening state obedient to the values of its own culture might appear to the target as "moralism" in foreign policy—the attempted imposition of alien values.[39] It was one of Cobden's favorite shafts against England's foreign policy to satirize its arrogant enforcement of "the behests of the Almighty in every part of the globe."[40] The third reason for thinking the nonintervention principle superior to any principle of intervention is the lack of a common Almighty, of a coherent and pervasive morality which transcends international frontiers

[36] See Carr, *The Twenty Years' Crisis*, 2d ed., London, 1946, pp. 146–169.

[37] S. I. Benn and R. S. Peters, *Social Principles and the Democratic State*, London, 1959, p. 361. The authors note the similarity between the principle of noninterference in international morality and Mill's "self-protection principle" which he regarded as fundamental to personal liberty.

[38] *Ibid.*, p. 361. There is no reason why the interests of the intervening state and the realization of some moral good should not coincide in a particular case, but there is no guarantee of their coincidence.

[39] *Ibid.*, p. 362. This fact of cultural difference is clearly uppermost in Halpern's mind when he accepts the necessity of intervention but stresses the relevance of knowledge and the efficient use of power to moral intervention. "The Morality and Politics of Intervention," in Falk, *Vietnam War and International Law*, pp. 39–78.

[40] See above, Chapter Three, p. 51.

and which might then inform and justify particular acts of intervention. The argument that the principle of nonintervention is morally destitute because it neglects the claims to just treatment of individuals within states does not then bear examination. True it does rule out the claim of an individual to any recourse beyond the state in favor of the requirements of order between states, but it can be argued that it is by safeguarding that order that the possibility of justice within the state is established.

Though the principle of nonintervention may be shown thus to have a moral content, it is nevertheless opposed by the doctrine that states are bound by higher duties than that of abstaining from interference in each other's affairs. This doctrine may take the form of exceptions asserted to a generally admitted principle of nonintervention as, for example, the view that when a state by its behavior so outrages the conscience of mankind no doctrine can be deployed to defend it against intervention. Thus it might be argued that states had not only a right but a duty to overrule the principle of nonintervention in order to defend the Jews against Nazi persecution, and a parallel is drawn and a similar argument urged in support of intervention against the institution of *apartheid* in present-day South Africa.[41] By urging the legitimacy of certain exceptions to the rule, this doctrine asserts that there are internationally sanctioned minimum standards of human conduct and that the state failing to meet them has no recourse to the principle of nonintervention.

Four doctrines tending to "maximize" these minimum standards of conduct, inverting the order before justice formula of the principle of nonintervention and thus diminishing its scope, have appeared or reappeared in the postwar world. In the first place, the doctrine that respect for human rights and fundamental freedoms was not a mere aspiration of the Charter signatories, but a substantive legal duty imposed upon states would render these matters no longer ones for domestic jurisdiction.[42] Second, the Third World doctrine of self-determination, were it to become the rule, would undermine more drastically the principle of nonintervention by extending the franchise of sovereignty to groups within states, though when the doctrine is used to mean anticolonialism or anti-

[41] For the argument to this effect in the General Assembly of the United Nations, see above, Chapter Seven, section v.

[42] For an examination of this doctrine, see above, Chapter Eight, section II.

racism it accepts the interstate order and merely requires states to avoid undesirable forms of order within them.[43] Third, the affirmation by the communist states of the justice of wars of national liberation, by raising anew the doctrine of the legitimacy of intervention on the just side in a civil war, would prejudice the function of the rule of nonintervention as a device for limiting conflict whatever the merits of the case.[44] By their expectation of a particular order, a "just" order, within states, each of these doctrines resembles Metternich's doctrine of legitimacy; they would subordinate "the inviolability of frontiers . . . to the illimitability of truth."[45]

Whether or not it is a view urged as part of a broader doctrine that order between states is dependent upon the achievement of justice within them, there is a fourth claim, arising in part from the concern with human rights in the Charter of the United Nations, which seems more pressing than these other assertions regarding minimum standards of international conduct. More pressing and yet less grandiose because it makes no claim to a vision of a just order of truth illimitable, the argument for the legitimacy of humanitarian intervention against genocide has found support in recent years in view of the events in Burundi, Nigeria, Sudan, and Bangla Desh. If the goal is one of preventing wholesale slaughter, it may seem but a quibble to object to intervention on the ground of its want of impartiality, or of the impurity of the motives of the intervening state or states. The legal case for humanitarian intervention can be made by drawing attention to those authorities who have pronounced it a right, however vague and amorphous, under international law. It can be strengthened by the argument that the protection of human rights was, with the maintenance of peace, a major purpose of the Charter of the United Nations, and by the "realist" observation that in the absence of collective action authorized by the world body, a humanitarian purpose might be achieved only by allowing unilateral intervention. And the case can be taken further by pointing to the absurd position in which some nineteenth-century Positivists found themselves when, by conceding that humanitarian intervention might sometimes snatch a remedy beyond

[43] See above, Chapter Seven, sections III and IV, and section VI below.

[44] But, on the caution with which the Soviet Union expounded this doctrine, see above, Chapter Five, sections VI and VII.

[45] Wight, "Western Values in International Relations," in Butterfield and Wight, p. 113.

the law, they seemed to deny its legality while recognizing it to be state practice.[46]

It is not necessary to rely upon a "restrictionist" interpretation of the legitimacy of the use of force under the Charter, or upon showing a lack of altruism by states intervening on purportedly humanitarian grounds, in order to point up the practical difficulties—and hence doctrinal doubts—about a principle of humanitarian intervention.[47] But if a right of humanitarian intervention is to be allowed despite the partiality of the intervening state, and notwithstanding its mixture of motives, then the less worthy consequences of that doctrine have to be tolerated along with any good effect that it might achieve. In the case of India's intervention in Pakistan's affairs against the slaughter of Bengalis in what was East Pakistan, this action, while it may be upheld as humanitarian intervention against that slaughter, may also be taken as intervention on behalf of the self-determination of Bangla Desh (a doctrine which, if adopted, might have uncomfortable consequences within the frontiers of India) and even as intervention to hobble the power of a disagreeable neighbor (a doctrine whose legitimacy few international lawyers would concede). In the light of these considerations, that absurd position in which some Positivists found themselves becomes explicable, and it expresses a general dilemma for international law. Between a naturalism careless of state practice and a positivism that would simply render any and all state conduct as the law, international law has to find a middle way. In the present case, it is not yet clear that a middle course of humanitarian

[46] For this position as held, for example, by Harcourt and Lawrence, see above, Chapter Eight, section I. A case for humanitarian intervention relying on these points among others is made by Richard B. Lillich in "Humanitarian Intervention: A Reply to Dr. Brownlie and a Plea for Constructive Alternatives," forthcoming in Moore, ed., *Law and Civil War in the Modern World*, Baltimore, Johns Hopkins Press. Brownlie's paper in the same volume bases the case against humanitarian intervention on a "restrictionist" view of the use of force under the Charter. On "restrictionism" and "realism" see above, Chapter Eight, section III.

[47] For an examination of the practical difficulties with the doctrine that would have individuals subjects of international law see above, Chapter Eight, section II. In fact, those who support a right of humanitarian intervention do themselves seem to require such altruism by imposing a stringent test for the legitimacy of humanitarian intervention. See Lillich, "Humanitarian Intervention," and Moore, "The Control of Foreign Intervention in Internal Conflict," in *Law and the Indo-China War*, pp. 185–186.

intervention has been traced between a virginal doctrine of non-intervention that would allow nothing to be done and a promiscuous doctrine of intervention that would make a trollop of the law. And until that course can with confidence be traced, it is perhaps nonintervention that provides the more dignified principle for international law to sanction. But should any doctrine asserting standards of conduct to be maintained within states capture the field against that of nonintervention, then the function of the latter doctrine would become once more that of a protest against it, though in this case, the standard of nonintervention would be raised in defense of the old order, and not, as with Cobden and the balance of power, in opposition to it.

It can be said then of the relationship between the principle of nonintervention and these other imperatives which have been regarded as indispensable for international order—the doctrine of the legitimacy of thrones, the balance of power, and the view that requires the establishment of domestic justice—that it is characterized as much by discord as by harmony. None of them, however, countenanced the overthrow of the order of states. It will be the task of the next two sections to examine the place of the principle of nonintervention in the contemporary international system, particularly in the light of the political and technological challenges it presents to an order of sovereign states.

IV

Whether or not their realization in the eclipse of state sovereignty could be said to be desirable, those progressive doctrines which saw the sovereignty of states receding before the expansion of international law, or being superseded by the emergence of international organizations, or undermined by the admission of the individual to international society, were found wanting as evidence that the eclipse had taken place or that it was imminent.[48] One of the primary objections to these doctrines was that they set the standard for conduct in international relations impossibly high, that the gap between norm and practice was too wide.[49] In the light of recent developments in the international system—the advent of nuclear weapons, the polarization of power, ideological

[48] See above, Chapter Eight, section II.
[49] See above, Chapter Eight, section II, p. 301.

conflict between the principals in the system, and the combination of these factors in the phenomenon of internal war as an instrument of international change—the same question suggests itself of rules about state sovereignty and nonintervention: whether they are not too widely divorced from international practice to have any relevance as standards of conduct.[50]

The underlying factor accounting for "the peculiar unity, coherence, or compactness of the modern nation-state," providing the factual basis for norms like that of nonintervention, has been identified as its "impermeability," "impenetrability," or simply its "territoriality."[51] The state was the ultimate unit for the protection of those living within its boundaries, surrounded as it was by a "hard shell" defending it against foreign penetration.[52] The basic political unit throughout history, the argument runs, has been that which has been in a position to afford security to human beings; peace within and security from without.[53] Thus the castle or the fortified town of the Middle Ages gave way under the impact of the gunpowder revolution to the modern territorial state with the "hard shell" at its frontiers.[54] Nuclear weapons are the gunpowder of the contemporary international system, and it is their appearance which has signaled, above all other developments, the passing of the age of territoriality and with it the usefulness of all its associated and resultant concepts such as sovereignty, independence, and nonintervention. At any rate, the "chief external function of the modern state seems to have vanished."[55] But unlike the gunpowder revolution, the nuclear revolution has brought with it the potential of universal destruction. The walled city might remain impermeable to the longbow, and the territorial state to weapons using gunpowder, but no conceivable political unit could remain impermeable to weapons of mass destruction.[56] So while it is true that the territorial state is strategically obsolete, the coming of nuclear weapons having penetrated its defensive "hard shell," it is difficult to envisage this penetration spawning some new entity because this too would be vulnerable to a nuclear attack. The observation that the coming of gunpowder foreshadowed the

[50] Not too progressive, but too reactionary.

[51] J. H. Herz, *International Politics in the Atomic Age*, New York, 1959, p. 40.

[52] *Ibid.*   [53] *Ibid.*

[54] *Ibid.*, pp. 13, 43–48, and 51.   [55] *Ibid.*, pp. 22 and 42.

[56] Herz himself makes this point in *ibid.*, p. 13.

emergence of the territorial state, however true, provides no helpful analogy for the nuclear age. The nation-state holds the field as the most sophisticated unit of political organization, and as the primary actor in international politics, in spite of the nuclear revolution.

Moreover, while the superpowers in possession of nuclear weapons outclass the lesser powers to an extent which the great powers of the past might have envied, it is not a negotiable power in the sense that the most impressive weapon of the great powers of the past was. For the superpowers in their relationship of deterrence direct their overwhelming power at each other, and for one of them to make use of nuclear weapons outside that relationship to reap the traditional spoils of power in international relations would be to invite retaliation and mutual destruction. So "under the umbrella of the nuclear stalemate," the old international politics of "sovereign" states continues and even flourishes on the assumption that the *ultima ratio* of nuclear power will not be used, that the nuclear umbrella will not close over them.[57] Permeable though it is, the nation-state survives.

The international politics of the present have been depicted in terms of a "loose bipolar" model of the international system and compared to a "balance of power" model taken to approximate the international politics of the eighteenth and nineteenth centuries.[58] In the balance of power system, nation-states are the members of international society; they provide for the survival of individuals within them, and it is on the survival of nation-states that the account of the behavior of the important participants in the balance of power system model is predicated. In the relations between nation-states, the attention of each to its own security is paramount. Each state must be prepared to move from one alliance to another if such a move conduces to the achievement of that goal. But the pursuit of security has an essential limitation:

[57] Hoffmann, "Obstinate or Obsolete? The Fate of the Nation-State and the Case of Western Europe," in *Conditions of World Order*, p. 114. Herz too recognizes this fact when he speaks of the decline of the impermeable state and not of the state as such, and of a "preatomic, or extraatomic, level of power relations, the level on which powers will go on facing each other as territorial units." *International Politics in the Atomic Age*, pp. 97 and 222. "Sovereign" is in quotation marks in the text to draw attention to independence without impermeability.

[58] M. A. Kaplan and N. deB. Katzenbach, *The Political Foundations of International Law*, New York, 1961, pp. 30–55, from which the summary following is taken.

351

restraint in victory is a characteristic of the system. For each strong nation has an interest in maintaining the existence of other strong nations to ensure future allies against possible disagreements with present ones. For the working of the system, the more strong nations the better, as a guarantee that the actor who sees his interest in the conquest of others shall be outnumbered by nations with an equal interest in seeing it fail in its endeavors.[59]

"Sovereignty" as an enforceable norm reflects the essential needs of the system. Each nation, organized territorially on the basis of existing culture groups, is an independent unit, not subject to conquest or domination, preserving for itself that independent foreign policy necessary to the flexibility of alignment.[60] The formal sovereignty and equality of states posited by the international lawyers are not doctrines set over against the practice of states but are integral features of the system. Noninterference in the internal affairs of another nation characterized the historic balance-of-power system and meets the requirements of the model because to allow interference would be to sacrifice the independence essential to its operation. But equality of rights and freedom from intervention were necessities only for the great nations; a great power could intervene when such action did not threaten the security of other strong nations. In the balance-of-power system, the rule of nonintervention applied among the great powers, but intervention was the rule outside Europe.

The loose bipolar system is composed not only of nation-states but also of two major blocs, a large number of uncommitted nations, and a universal organization like the United Nations. The blocs are more than alliances, having supranational characteristics. The immediate but system-limited interest in its own security displayed by the nation-state in the balance-of-power system is replaced in the loose bipolar system by the pooling of long-term interests in the integrity of the bloc—nation-states do not shift from one alliance to another to preserve the balance but gather for protection around the bloc leaders. If the Western powers had fol-

[59] "In the 'balance-of-power' system a minimum number of five nations probably was necessary for stability." *Ibid.*, p. 51.

[60] Here the authors add that international organization would have hampered this flexibility, and that the ideology of nationalism, and the political and technical difficulties of one state exercising control over another tended to support rather than detract from equilibrium in the system. *Ibid.*, pp. 33–35.

lowed the rules of the balance-of-power system in the years after the Second World War, they would have provided the communist bloc with a decisive gain in influence in international affairs.[61]

Since the members of one bloc have no interest in maintaining the independence of the members of the competing bloc in order to preserve future allies, the motives that existed in the balance-of-power system for limited objectives and noninterference do not obtain; obedience to the rule of nonintervention and reaction to its violation are no longer vital to the system.[62] Not only does the overwhelming power of the bloc leaders make it very difficult for them not to intervene, they also have a positive interest in interference to prevent defections from the bloc. An important factor making for stability in the system is "the integration of the bloc—and not merely the 'sovereign' independence of its members."[63] Moreover, because of the importance of bloc integration, intervention does not occur in the colonial, dependent, or minor areas of the world as it did under the balance-of-power system. In the loose bipolar system, it is more likely to occur in the major allied bloc nations than in the uncommitted nations. Organic forms of union will reduce barriers among bloc members while the new nations will jealously guard their independence of the blocs—a drive to some extent provided for in the system by a tenuous balance between the United States and the Soviet Union in areas beyond the blocs. So where the balance-of-power system had nonintervention among the great powers of Europe, but interference outside the continent, the loose bipolar system has intervention within the blocs, nonintervention between them,[64] and a tenuous nonintervention prevailing outside them.[65]

[61] *Ibid.*, p. 48.

[62] Objectives are not system-limited in the sense that they were in the balance-of-power system. "Rivalry is direct and is limited primarily by the horrors of thermonuclear war." *Ibid.*, p. 51.

[63] Kaplan, "Intervention in Internal War: Some Systemic Sources," in Rosenau, ed., *International Aspects of Civil Strife*, p. 106.

[64] As demonstrated by the case of Hungary, the United States tolerated Soviet intervention there because Hungary's defection from the communist bloc would have constituted a vital threat to the Soviet Union, but failure to exploit the loss was not a serious threat to the United States. Kaplan and Katzenbach, p. 54.

[65] The nonintervention here of the superpowers outside their blocs makes possible a rule of nonintervention between uncommitted states. But the

If the model of loose bipolarity is at all accurate as a representation of the post Second World War international system, the rule of nonintervention as a norm of interstate rather than interbloc relations would seem to have a possible function only in the narrow domain of relations between uncommitted nations, or as a protest made by those states the independence of which has been compromised against their own bloc leaders, or as homage paid by vice to virtue by the superpowers themselves. But the model is not wholly accurate.[66] In the first place, the defections of Yugoslavia and Albania from the Soviet bloc, and Cuba from the Western bloc, are events which fit only uncomfortably into the predictions of the model.[67] True, the American reaction to the Cuban defection and that of the Soviet Union to the *lèse-majesté* of the Yugoslavs might have conformed initially to the requirements of the model. But neither superpower succeeded in disciplining the insubordinate junior; both bowed to the old-fashioned politics of nation-states. True also that only Yugoslavia has managed to survive as a nonaligned nation independent of either bloc, Cuba looking toward the Soviet Union for aid and comfort, and Albania toward China. But the independence of Cuba and of Albania has not been totally extinguished even if it is only the independence of the servant free to change his master.

A second criticism of the model is that it is insensitive to "gradations of dependency" within the blocs.[68] Insensitive in the case of the communist bloc to the extent to which different members can take their own roads to socialism, and in the case of the Western bloc to the extent to which members can lay down the terms on which they will accept the American alliance.[69] If this is again the

---

latter might not be so committed to nonintervention between themselves as they are to the exclusion of outsiders. *Ibid.*, p. 55.

[66] It might be objected here that in questioning the correspondence of a model first published in 1957 (Kaplan, *System and Process in International Politics*, New York), and claiming only to be the counterpart of the politics of that time, to the international politics of the 1970's is to set up a straw man in order to destroy him. But so influential has the loose bipolar model been in thinking about international relations that it remains relevant to deal with it.

[67] Though Kaplan and Katzenbach assert that a nation once having joined the communist bloc would find it very difficult to leave, "the example of Yugoslavia to the contrary notwithstanding." *Political Foundations*, p. 48.

[68] Herz, pp. 128–129.

[69] Herz distinguishes in this respect between a Norway refusing to be

independence of the servant which does not upset the idea of a master-servant relationship, a more significant challenge to the dominance of the superpowers, stifling the logic of bipolarity, might be perceived through the introduction of the nuclear factor into the model. Thus the unrivaled superiority of the superpowers might be impaired by the nonnegotiability of the nuclear weapons which mark their superiority, and at the same time by the acquisition of those emblems of superiority by third powers. The account of the integration of the bloc as opposed to the independence of its members has been compromised in the West by a France suspicious of the bloc rationale, doubting the credibility of the American deterrent, and developing her own nuclear armory. This has not taken France out of the bloc, but it has cast doubt on the model's assumption that states will sacrifice immediate interests for long-term gains, and in this respect the policy of France is more like "balance of power" behavior than "loose bipolar" behavior.

The Sino-Soviet dispute has been more severe on the assumptions of the loose bipolar model. The challenge of China to the leader of the communist bloc has belied the assumption of the integration of the communist world which first inspired "bloc thought," and her emergence as a potential superpower, armed with nuclear weapons, confronts the central assumption of "bipolarity" with the prospect of a third irresistible node of power in the international system. And if such a prospect were to materialize, China gathering a bloc of nations around herself as their protector, it is possible to imagine bloc nonintervention between three superpowers where before it applied between two.

Indeed, so far has the system moved away from the precepts of the loose bipolar model, that President Nixon has felt able to canvass a notion of a "strong, healthy United States, Europe, Soviet Union, China, Japan, each balancing the other, not playing one against the other, an even balance."[70] Though this view of the world can be said to lack substance on the ground that it chooses to neglect disparities of power among the five, it has been argued that where strategic weapons appear to have become a rather less dynamic form of power and the use of conventional military

---

garrisoned by the United States and a Greece opening its territory to American armed forces. *Ibid.*, pp. 131–132.

[70] Interview with *Time* magazine, January 1972, cited in Alastair Buchan, "A World Restored?" *Foreign Affairs*, Vol. 50, No. 4, July 1972, p. 644.

force has been hedged about with limitations, factors other than those concerning the use or threat of force have increased sufficiently in importance to make some sense of a pentagonal relationship.[71] And if these factors—the internal dynamism of the great powers, their national will, diplomatic skill, and their economic power—enter into the conduct of high politics sufficiently to include in it five rather than just two powers, then a balance between them in both Europe and East Asia can be said to rest on renewed "access" across bloc frontiers—the resistance of any claims to exclusive spheres of influence.[72] If this picture is at all accurate, we might envisage an enhancement of the independence of small states through their being allowed a wider range of choice in foreign policy. The relaxing of a strict rule of bloc nonintervention, even to the limited extent of increasing access across bloc boundaries, might improve the prospects for nonintervention within the erstwhile rigid blocs by providing the weak with a choice of benefactors among the strong. Whatever transpires, it can be said that the nation-state has survived even the tightest bipolarity as the "lowest common denominator" in the competition among the great.[73]

A third form of doubt about the feasibility of the principle of nonintervention in contemporary international politics stems from the observation that the superpowers confront each other not merely as powers but as crusaders on behalf of competing ideologies. When President Truman, in his response to the Greek crisis in 1947, set the tone for a generation of American foreign policy by distinguishing between two ways of life and attaching the American reputation to one of them, he ruled out the option of unilateral nonintervention and proclaimed a doctrine of intervention on behalf of "free peoples . . . resisting subjugation."[74] It might be argued that so long as the American response to the Soviet threat was indeed a response to the prior intervention of the Soviet Union, then the ideological motivation for American foreign policy did not impugn the order of sovereign states but was an inducement to support it—counterintervention helping free peoples at the same

71 *Ibid.*, pp. 646–649.
72 *Ibid.*, p. 649. For the notion of "access" Buchan refers to Marshall Shulman, "What Does Security Mean Today?" *Foreign Affairs*, Vol. 49, No. 4, July 1971.
73 Hoffmann, "Obstinate or Obsolite," p. 114.
74 See above, Chapter Six, section I.

time as upholding the principle of nonintervention. But the argument of counterintervention, the claim to be supporting the struggle for national liberation, this time against imperialist intervention, was also a feature of Soviet doctrine.[75] Where the ideological dispute between the principals in the system overlaid state frontiers, painting local conflicts with colors provided by the principals, the crucial distinction in the order of sovereign states between one exclusive competence and the next became blurred. In such a situation, where both sides could make a more or less plausible claim to be counterintervening against the intervention of the other, it seems feeble indeed to place any confidence in the restraining function of the principle of nonintervention. In both American and Soviet foreign policy, the superficial respectability of the claim of counterintervention came to be discredited as but a thin disguise for interference undertaken on other grounds. And even if the claim could be said to be just in a particular case, the other side always had an ideological ground on which to dismiss it.

This does not mean that there are no limits to the ideological conflict and that the principle of nonintervention will always do service as a mere slogan in its fighting. The anxiety of the superpowers not to confront each other directly because of the nuclear danger tends to mute any ideologically motivated extravagance by one power within the bloc of the other.[76] The emergence of China as a potential superpower has complicated the perception of world politics as the implacable hostility of two rival systems by the admission of a variant to the one which was wont to claim the totality of truth. This admission makes possible for each of the superpowers a conception of its interest which is not subsumed in the universality of its ideological mission. To put it another way, the question of intervention or nonintervention need not be couched as in the days of the rivalry of two in terms of "we or they" because each superpower now has two "theys" to consider. Where before the question was posed in the stark terms of not intervening and allowing the aggressor the spoils or intervening and risking escalation, now nonintervention might be a rational policy for any

[75] See above, Chapter Five, section v.

[76] Falk refers to a moral necessity on the part of the United States to meet the double challenge of totalitarian encroachment and nuclear devastation, and seeks a solution to the problem of balancing the two imperatives in *Law, Morality, and War in the Contemporary World*, Princeton, N.J., 1963, pp. 45–65.

357

one power standing off from the rivalry of the other two.[77] This argument cannot be taken far in support of a principle of nonintervention because the rivalry about forms of government within states, a rivalry which conduct according to the principle of nonintervention would rule out, has not disappeared from the system but has merely taken on a more complicated, if less strident, aspect. Outside the blocs, the ideologies of the superpowers are blunted against a doctrine of national self-determination which asserts the values of mostly new statehood against the competing doctrines about how government within the state is to be carried on. And though the uncommitted nations cannot avoid accepting aid from the superpowers or from other members of the competing blocs, they can attempt to arrange the acceptance in such a way as to avoid becoming the prisoner of any one of them. Clearly, the uncommitted nations are not able to insulate themselves from the ideological battles of the committed, but an astute diplomacy might save them from becoming committed themselves.

Though it might be said that the order of sovereign states shows through the fabric of the contemporary political order in a number of places and that the advent of nuclear weapons, the polarization of power in the system, and the clash of hostile ideologies do not always join in an unequivocal repudiation of that order, they do seem to dispatch the principle of nonintervention as a device for the insulation of internal war from the purview of international relations. Thus it has been argued that the superpowers, fearing that a direct confrontation between them could lead to nuclear catastrophe, have been persuaded to seek less risky avenues of competition, and that the chronic instability of many of the vastly increased number of states making up international society provides such an avenue by giving the superpowers the opportunity to compete vicariously—through interfering in the conflicts of others.[78] The account of the polarization of power in the system subordinating the independence of states to bloc integration suggests intervention in internal war, especially when conflict within

[77] Certainly, we have seen, nonintervention has been taken as a formal guide to relations between China and the United States and the Soviet Union and the United States. See above, Chapter Five, section VI, and Chapter Six, section IV.

[78] Morgenthau, "To Intervene or Not to Intervene," *Foreign Affairs*, Vol. 45, No. 3, April 1967, pp. 427–428; Falk, "The Regulation of International Conflict by Means of Law," in *Legal Order in a Violent World*, pp. 68–70.

a bloc-nation portends, if the insurgent should prevail, the departure of that state from the bloc.[79] And an ideological dispute of universal dimensions between the principals in the system suggests that their interests will be tied to the outcome of any particular internal conflict. In such a situation, if any one great power or group of powers is unready or unwilling to interfere in a particular internal war, it runs the risk of leaving the field to the opposition. The nonintervention agreement erected as a façade over the reluctance of the democracies to counter the intervention of Germany and Italy in the Spanish Civil War has stigmatized the principle of nonintervention as a cowardly doctrine, and is also taken as a prewar lesson to the postwar world on the impossibility of nonintervention in a system containing an important aggressor.[80] This lesson is the more compelling if "warfare *between* states now most frequently takes place *within* a single national society."[81]

However, even the widespread participation of outside states does not allow the total disregard for the internal aspects of internal war. The greater caution of the superpowers outside their blocs than within them and the anxiety of the uncommitted powers to remain uncommitted are factors which the authors most critical of the traditional doctrines of state sovereignty and nonintervention concede as having some force in restraining unlimited intervention everywhere.[82] But it is not just upon the accident of great power abstention or on the efficacy of their ideologies against those of the blocs that small states depend for the maintenance of a degree of independence. The circumstances of internal war in which guerrilla bands face nuclear powers and make nonsense of their technical

[79] Kaplan, "Intervention in Internal War," pp. 106–107.

[80] For the description of nonintervention as a "cowardly device," see *New Statesman* editorial, December 18, 1970, p. 822. On the impossibility of nonintervention in world community in which an important aggressor exists, see Falk, "United States Practice and the Doctrine of Non-Intervention in the Internal Affairs of Sovereign States," in *Legal Order in a Violent World*, pp. 162–163 and 167.

[81] Falk, "The International Law of Internal War: Problems and Prospects," in *Legal Order in a Violent World*, p. 132.

[82] Kaplan, "Intervention in Internal War," p. 120. Kaplan argues that, in terms of the loose bipolar model, the uncommitted nations would have an interest in adhering to a rule of nonintervention between themselves in order not to undermine the rule forbidding bloc intervention, but counters this with the observation that in the real world the uncommitted nations have motivations overriding this apparent interest. *Ibid.*, pp. 107–108 and 113–116.

superiority, circumstances in which "the kind of violence that prevails . . . favors the porcupine over the elephant,"[83] render the small less unequal. Where the internal conflicts of the small remain intractable to the ministrations of the strong, the reality of "internalness" or simply "otherness" to which the doctrine of nonintervention draws attention has not altogether disappeared.[84]

To return to Herz's coinage—the "impermeability" of the state as its essential and life-giving characteristic—it is clear that the coming of nuclear weapons has denied the state its strategic impermeability, that the preeminence of the superpowers has compromised the political impermeability of the lesser powers, and that the doctrine *cuius regio eius religio* as a protection against the penetration of hostile ideologies is more applicable to blocs than to states in the contemporary world. In these circumstances, where civil wars are made international, the "spatial approach to international relations" assuming the "hermetic reality of the national unit" which underlay rules like that of nonintervention seems particularly impoverished.[85] If all these factors, together with others which we shall look at in the next section, like the growth of interdependence and of transnational communication, render the sovereign-state obsolete, particularly in the case of the small, economically and defensively unviable, new states, then the assertion of a continued domain for the principle of nonintervention seems a rather obscure piece of romanticism.

But in some respects, what is striking about the contemporary international system is not its revolutionary newness, but the familiarity of the techniques by which states carry on their foreign relations. Certainly, nuclear weapons have no historical counterpart, but if blocs are thought of as "spheres of influence" and the ideological dispute is discussed in terms of the subordination of state frontiers on the one hand to the legitimacy of established governments, and on the other to the legitimacy of revolution

[83] Hoffmann, "Obstinate or Obsolete?" p. 114.

[84] U. Schwartz goes so far as to conclude that "intervention has had its day, that it has ceased to be a rational weapon in the great power's panoply," because of the ineffectiveness of military power against the political power of the nation, and because of the almost universal condemnation of it by public opinion. *Great Power Intervention in the Modern World*, Adelphi Paper No. 55, London, March 1969, p. 41.

[85] Falk, "The International Law of Internal War," p. 140, n. 69.

which knows no frontiers, then the contemporary international system can be said to have its historical antecedents. The plight of the small state in a system where might tends to determine right is not of recent invention. Its foreign policy is largely taken up by the problem of securing the best arrangement from the strong. The interstate order "has always been anarchical and oligarchical,"[86] and the contemporary dyarchy, if it still is such, is a variation on that theme. Moreover, in two respects it is a variation in which the small state is less unequal. In the first place, nuclear weapons are valueless in counterinsurgency warfare, giving the weak the advantage of the inhibitions of the strong, and even sophisticated conventional weapons are blunted against the tactics of the guerrilla. Second, the factual inequality of states is offset by the consecration of the doctrine of the formal equality of states by and at the United Nations.[87] The claims of the superpowers about the proper form of government within states assert universality but do not achieve it. Only the sovereign-state order has received the imprimatur of all the members of international society and of all the aspirant members. Economically and defensively unviable though they may be, it is to this universally recognized legitimacy that the lesser states cling.

Though there are, in the contemporary international system, powerful forces impelling states to find the principle of nonintervention inferior to competing imperatives in a number of situations, that should not be taken to mean that "the present world is not a world in which non-intervention is possible."[88] A policy of nonintervention may be both possible and desirable for a superpower in any particular circumstance. Of many of the postwar American interventions it can be said, with hindsight, that the better policy from the point of view of her interests was the opposite and "impossible" course of nonintervention. As a principle of interstate conduct, the general presumption it creates against the legitimacy of interference by one state in the affairs of another gives legal pause to the great power which has to find good reasons for overriding it. In the rush to work out a new international law

[86] Aron, "The Anarchical Order of Power," in Hoffmann, *Conditions of World Order*, p. 47.

[87] *Ibid.*, pp. 46–47.

[88] Kaplan, *United States Foreign Policy in a Revolutionary Age*, Policy Memorandum No. 25, Princeton, N.J., 1961, p. 43.

to meet the new political facts of the postwar world, it is worth remembering the principles established in an old sovereign-state order, which, if it is obsolescent, is taking a long time dying.

V

Though the particular shape they have taken in the postwar international system might be unique, the questions about the sorts of weapons available to the great powers, about the distribution of power in the international system, about ideological differences, and about the place of war in the system, which were asked in the previous section, might have found a place in any traditional discussion of international relations. The concern of the present section is with recent developments in world society, developments outside the traditional range of political discourse, which seem to present a challenge to the sovereign-state system and rules like that of nonintervention which are part of it.

In Chapter Eight, when we examined those contemporary legal doctrines that have as their object the erosion of the principle of state sovereignty, we saw that a difficulty which attached to them all was their neglect of the remarkable modern growth in the functions which states have taken it upon themselves to fulfill. It remains to ask whether it is not also the case that there has been a remarkable growth of functions which it is beyond the competence of states to fulfill. Two propositions of this kind merit attention: that there has been a multiplication of problems which can be solved neither by the sovereign state, nor within a system of states, and that such problems are already being solved by transnational cooperation that is bypassing the sovereign state. A third proposition, warranting attention here as a derivative of those same technological forces which led to our two earlier propositions, is that which takes account of the resilience of the sovereign state, but observes that, at least the great states, by taking on functions which penetrate into the affairs of lesser powers, behave in such a way as to reduce the relevance of the doctrine of nonintervention. In the light of these propositions, we raise once more the question—is not an insistence upon a principle of nonintervention far removed from the realities of contemporary international life?

It is the supposed ecological crisis that has provided the most notable recent version of the doctrine that there are problems which the sovereign state or the system of states cannot solve.

362

The adherents to this doctrine hold that the combination of potential nuclear disaster with pressure of population growth, depletion of world resources, and accelerating pollution of the environment provide a threat to human life which is global in extent and can be dealt with only by a global response; it is not, they argue, a problem that can be parceled up according to the existing distribution of authority in international relations.[89] As Herz argued in respect of the advent of nuclear weaponry, these problems are held to have rendered the sovereign state as unviable "as medieval castles and walled towns became after the 'gunpowder revolution'."[90]

The ecologists' case rests not only upon showing that there are planetary problems that extend beyond the competence of the sovereign state but also on the demonstration that these problems require a planetary solution beyond mere international cooperation. In constructing such a case, first it might be argued that the technical and organizational complexity of the modern world, making its parts increasingly interrelated and interdependent, creates a problem of management that cannot be accommodated within the borders of any one state.[91] A second argument that might be adduced to demonstrate the need for problem-solving beyond state frontiers, is that of the sheer size of contemporary problems. The more modest form of this argument holds that the scale of modern industry and the pressures of technology impel an increase in the size of the state to enlarge the market—a development undermining any rationale for the survival of small states and making the state an adequate entity only when it is of continental proportions.[92] The less modest form of the argument asserts that the range of problems associated with the maintenance of the global ecosystem is so formidable as to be beyond the competence of even the largest units.[93]

If these arguments by themselves are not convincing as reasons for abandoning the sovereign state, since cooperation between and across states might yet provide an answer to them, there are rather more fundamental arguments which do seem to press beyond any

[89] These four dimensions of the ecological crisis are dealt with in Falk, *This Endangered Planet*, New York, 1971.

[90] Harold and Margaret Sprout, *Toward a Politics of the Planet Earth*, New York, 1971, p. 425.

[91] See *ibid.*, Chap. 17; Falk, *Endangered Planet*, pp. 94–95.

[92] Falk, *Endangered Planet*, p. 228.

[93] *Ibid.*, pp. 228 and 244.

such solution. In the first place, it can be argued that the sovereign state system, with its insistence upon separateness, generates such conflict and competition as to preclude that degree of cooperation and coordination which is required to cope with pressing ecological problems.[94] Moreover, it can be added, this same organization of the world by which any planetary problem is nationally perceived and priorities are arranged according to national and not to world interests prevents even a sufficient awareness of the planetary problem.[95] A third, more subtle argument entitled the "paradox of aggregation" holds that the pursuit of separate interests for purely individual advantage, in a world of scarce resources which cannot indefinitely indulge such individualism, leads ultimately to the downfall of all.[96] Taken together, these arguments might be said to show not only that the state cannot solve the planetary problems which confront it but also that it is a positive barrier in the way of their solution.

There have always been problems that neither the state, nor the state system, has been able to solve, and the failure to find an answer to them has often been blamed on the existence of the states themselves. War is a problem of this kind, for which states are but a partial answer, solving, in some degree, the problem of domestic order at the same time as creating that of order between states. Moreover, the state system, typified by such devices as the balance of power, left the problem of war untouched and deliberately unsolved by placing the independence of states higher than peace between them in the order of priorities. War in this arrangement was part of the functioning of a system rather than a problem to be solved. As a result, those who would end war have often sought that goal by urging an end to the state system that generated it— the solution to the problem requiring the dismantling of the state. The ecological argument follows this logic but urges it in more pressing fashion since, far from being accommodated as part of a functioning system, the factors which are held to have produced an ecological crisis are taken also to foreshadow doom. Where the problem of war might have put in jeopardy the survival of a state, or even a civilization, the ecological crisis is held to threaten survival *tout court*.[97] In the light of this urgency, together with the planetary scope of the problem, it is thought futile to rely upon the

---

[94] *Ibid.*, pp. 38–39.   [95] *Ibid.*, pp. 40–41 and 203.
[96] *Ibid.*, pp. 46–49.   [97] *Ibid.*, p. 10.

sovereign state for a solution, preoccupied as it is with mere day-to-day emergencies.[98]

The ecologists then urge the solution of two problems, not one, and insist that one solution is dependent upon the other. There is not merely an ecological crisis to be solved by whatever institutions are available, but that solution itself depends upon a concurrent solution to the problem of the international anarchy. The whole case relies on the demonstration that nothing less will do, that there are no partial solutions.

Though it is perhaps because of its apocalyptic nature that the argument is an attractive one and merits our attention anyway as a piece of worst-case analysis, states remain obstinately blind to the demonstration of their obsolescence, and blinder still to the view that they are a positive hindrance to the solution of the ecological problem. As we observed in the discussion of the impact of nuclear weapons, the sovereign state holds the field despite the argument that strategically and now functionally it ought not to. And it is the fact of this continued predominance that constitutes the principal argument against the radical solution to the ecological crisis that would do away with the sovereign state. For it is not by virtue of a purely intellectual demonstration that the sovereign state will release its hold over men, and even if it were so it might still be argued that it is better to radicalize and activate the state with regard to environmental problems than to insist on its demise before they can be approached. If a job of conversion is to be done, it might have more prospect of success if it were limited to existing institutions, rather than taking upon itself the redesigning of the world in an ecologists' image.

If states have yet to be persuaded of their obsolescence, there are those who take the view that it is not a question of persuasion but of demonstration of what already exists, and they draw attention to this circumstance by pointing to the dramatic modern growth in "transnational interactions," in "the movement of tangible or intangible items across state boundaries when at least one actor is not an agent of a government or an intergovernmental organization."[99] Whether these interactions take place under the aegis of nongovernmental but formal organizations, such as inter-

[98] *Ibid.*, p. 100.

[99] Joseph S. Nye Jr., and Robert O. Keohane, "Transnational Relations and World Politics: An Introduction," in Keohane and Nye, eds., *Transnational Relations and World Politics*, Cambridge, Mass., 1972, p. xii.

national scientific associations or multinational corporations, or are brought about by growth in tourism or migration, the simplest concept involved in discussion of them is that they have been the subject of widespread and rapid acceleration in the twentieth century.[100]

Beyond taking notice of their supposed growth, exponents of transnational relationships have thought in terms of their effects upon interstate relations, rather than consigning them, as often in the past, to a category composed of events that are regarded as having no effect on international politics.[101] Of greater interest for the present argument, some writers have seen in the growth of transnationalism not just an effect on interstate politics, but "an early phase of transition to some other kind of world order," populated by entities other than (though not necessarily to the exclusion of) states, which enter into political relations with each other.[102] The idea of transition to a new world order is made more precise by the notion that interdependence (on which the building of a community might be said to depend) among a specified set of states increases as transnational processes increase.[103] If the estab-

---

[100] And even this most simple of propositions is a matter of dispute. See for doubts about it, Kenneth N. Waltz, "The Myth of National Interdependence," in Charles P. Kindleberger, ed., *The International Corporation: A Symposium*, Cambridge, Mass., 1970, pp. 205–223; Klaus Knorr, "Transnational Phenomena and the Future of the Nation-State," in A. Lepawsky, E. H. Buehrig, and H. D. Lasswell, eds., *The Search for World Order*, New York, 1971, pp. 401–415, and Robert Gilpin, "The Politics of Transnational Economic Relations," in Keohane and Nye, pp. 48–69.

[101] Keohane and Nye summarize five effects of transnational organizations or interactions on interstate politics: changes in attitude, creation of international pluralism through transnational growth of interest groups, increasing constraints on states through dependence and interdependence, increases in the ability of some states to influence others, and the emergence of autonomous actors whose private foreign policies may affect interstate politics. "Transnational Relations: An Introduction," in *Transnational Relations and World Politics*, p. xvii.

[102] H. and M. Sprout, *Toward a Politics of the Planet Earth*, pp. 61 and 67–70.

[103] Edward L. Morse, "Transnational Economic Processes," in Keohane and Nye, p. 30. One of the difficulties with this proposition lies in the definition of "interdependence." Is it to be taken to mean that actors in different societies *depend* for their survival or livelihood (and not merely for their well-being) on a transnational relationship, or, more loosely, is it to indicate that their activities are mutually contingent. Morse adopts this looser definition in *ibid.*, p. 29.

lishment of interdependence is a step toward it, some writers have argued that a transnational community can be said already to exist in world society. Thus, the Sprouts, while observing that the notion of community in the social sciences has usually entailed a *sense* of community on the part of its members, have pointed out a different conception of ecological community or ecosystem in which the membership is interrelated with its habitat in ways that are judged to be significant for its well-being or survival.[104] In this view, community is a condition of interrelatedness, not a cognition of it.[105] Whether or not this unusual conception of community can be accepted into the vocabulary of political science, there is a body of transnationalist thought that identifies, in the changing world order, a challenge to the sovereign state that will be decided ultimately against it. It is according to this less ambitious conception of transnationalism as an early shot in the battle leading to the demise of the state that the multinational corporation has been regarded as the standard-bearer for functionalist integration theory.[106]

A more ambitious doctrine has the multinational corporation as a direct challenge to the state here and now, and not a gradual eroder of its functions. So large, and with operations that are global in extent, these corporations might be said to have outgrown the regulation of the nation-state. A dramatic demonstration of the size of multinational corporations shows that in 1965, 87 corporations had a sales volume exceeding one billion dollars, a figure matched by central government expenditure in no more than approximately 40 states and by Gross National Product in only 69 states.[107] And the challenge to the state might be more devastating than sheer size would suggest, since a corporation extending across the frontiers of states, obedient to a logic of economic growth that transcends them, might command a loyalty from the individuals within it that raises the prospect of a society built over the state and owing no allegiance to it. If this challenge is again a long-term one, included here because of its totality and not its immediacy, trans-

[104] H. and M. Sprout, p. 19.

[105] *Ibid.*, In the same way, though rather more polemically, Falk speaks of the unity of the world of facts but of fragmentation in the world of authority and power—as though authority and power were not also (social) facts. See *Endangered Planet*, p. 2.

[106] Robert N. Cox, "Labor and Transnational Relations," in Keohane and Nye, pp. 204–234.

[107] G. Modelski, "The Corporation in World Society," *Year Book of World Affairs*, Vol. 22, 1968, p. 68.

national corporations have also been accused of intervening in the internal affairs of states, of involving themselves in the business of bringing down governments, and even of waging war against sovereign states.[108]

The case to be made for the continuing place of the sovereign state, whether the challenge to it is held to be immediate or long-term, might rely upon the assertion of the relative autonomy of the interstate order, and hence its relative resistance, or better, indifference to transnational developments.[109] But it is precisely at this notion of relative autonomy that much of the recent argument about transnationalism has been pointed, and it therefore requires more attention than it has yet been given. In particular, the argument of an autonomous interstate order has been confronted by the attempt to show that economic issues have become the stuff of the high politics of international relations, politics that were accustomed formally to despise them. Thus Edward L. Morse has argued that the development of nuclear technology has made traditional foreign-policy goals like that of territorial accretion so costly, politically as well as economically, that economic matters have become the forum for high politics, and he adds three observations about the increased political importance of economic relations: that in the relations of the states of the North Atlantic area, security and welfare goals have been amalgamated on the theory that collective defense could be reinforced by economic recovery and growth; that in East-West relations, Western trade policies have been formulated according to the notion that foreign economic policy could bring about political liberalization in Eastern Europe; and in the relations between developed and underdeveloped states, economic policies have become relatively more important for the latter as a result of their relative impotence compared to the former.[110]

[108] See the remarks of President Salvador Allende Gossens of Chile before the United Nations General Assembly, charging serious aggression by United States corporations, banking interests, and governmental agencies, reported in *The New York Times*, December 5, 1972.

[109] As we did in part in dealing with the growth of transnational law; see above, Chapter Eight, section II, and Aron, *Peace and War*, pp. 105 and 748.

[110] Morse, "Transnational Economic Processes," pp. 26–27. Morse pays no attention, with regard to his statement about developed-underdeveloped relations, to the tautological observation that relative impotence has always typified the weak when compared with the strong. It is therefore difficult to know what he intends by identifying it as one cause of the heightened

Whether or not these observations about the increasing political content of transnational relations can be said to have disposed of the doctrine of relative autonomy, their introduction raises a more fundamental issue—that of which activity, economics or politics, holds priority in the building and maintenance of a social order. Do economic activities determine the shape of politics, or have transnational activities been able to develop only under the auspices of a great power, so that we may observe, for example, that the recent growth in transnationalism reflects the interests of the United States.[111]

This issue is not one that can be decided here. But we may take notice of its existence by relying not on the presence of an autonomous interstate order but on the absence of an international community for the assertion of continuing functions for the sovereign state and for a principle of nonintervention. In sketching a politics of the planet earth, the Sprouts commended for the attention of political scientists a biological notion of community as a condition of interrelatedness.[112] In another part of the same work, the authors observe, of political culture within the state, that "without substantial consensus of what is desirable and right, and undesirable and wrong, no firm sense of community is likely to exist."[113] Where there is a want of such substantial consensus in international society, where the feeling of community falls far short of what prevails within the state, the principle of nonintervention persists as witness to that lack.

A third standpoint from which the doctrine of nonintervention has come under fire is not one that draws its ammunition from the assertion of the obsolescence of the state; it accepts the state but asserts changes in statecraft. Arnold Wolfers has made a distinction between "possession goals" and "milieu goals" in foreign policy. The former are concerned with the possessions a state holds, the latter with the shaping of conditions beyond the frontiers of

---

significance of economics in international politics. Nor are his first two observations ones that could be made with reference only to the post-World War II world. We might cite Taft's dollar diplomacy as an earlier example of the amalgamation of security and welfare goals, and also as evidence of a belief that economic policy might bring about political change.

[111] For a useful discussion of this issue which is favorable to the primacy of politics, see Gilpin, "The Politics of Transnational Economic Relations," in Keohane and Nye, pp. 48–69.

[112] *Toward a Politics of the Planet Earth*, p. 19, and above p. 367.

[113] *Ibid.*, p. 91.

the state.[114] Where milieu goals encompass such traditional aims as the maintenance of a balance of power between states, there is in them perhaps no permanent challenge to the sort of environment which gave rise to the doctrine of nonintervention.[115] But in the modern age, it has been argued, states have expanded their milieu goals beyond the relations between states to include matters that were regarded formerly as a purely domestic concern. Thus, one writer has argued that whereas the relations of states hitherto were conducted between governments, in this century they are being supplemented increasingly by informal relations, by means of which the agents of one state may pursue their goals by gaining access to, by penetrating within, the borders of another state to affect its people or processes.[116] Access thus gained might have as its object the attack or the support of a regime within a target state, and it need not have either of these objects, but its techniques—guerrilla operations, subversion, the dissemination of hostile propaganda, cultural exchanges, economic, technical, and military aid and assistance—are taken to constitute a revolution in statecraft at least among the leading nations.[117]

The theory and practice of informal access, and particularly of informal attack, is thought to have received its modern impetus from the conspiratorial foreign policies first of Soviet Russia and then of Hitler's Germany during the interwar years.[118] The Cold War is taken as an heir to this style of international politics with communist techniques of informal attack, ranging from the establishment of front organizations within states to the waging of guerrilla warfare, eliciting an American response through informal support—from economic aid to military assistance.[119] Where such penetration of the nation-state has been the characteristic mode of conducting the international politics of the Cold War, particularly since the advent of nuclear weapons has foreclosed the too dangerous option of conventional war, the answer for the United States and for international law is held to lie in the acceptance of, and systematic response to, the reality of "competitive interference."[120]

[114] Arnold Wolfers, *Discord and Collaboration*, Baltimore, 1962, pp. 73–74.

[115] See above, section III.

[116] A. M. Scott, *The Revolution in Statecraft*, New York, 1965, pp. 4–7.

[117] *Ibid.*, pp. v–vi, 3–4, and 7–9.   [118] *Ibid.*, pp. 7 and 30–68.

[119] *Ibid.*, pp. 45–112.

[120] R. W. Cottam, *Competitive Interference and Twentieth Century Diplomacy*, Pittsburgh, 1967, pp. 27, 33, and 218.

A doctrine that would accommodate competitive interference stands clearly opposed to the doctrine of nonintervention.[121] Nonintervention is rejected by it as a relic of a vanished era of impenetrable sovereign states, as an obsolete principle in view of the political, economic, and military realities of the contemporary world.[122] Also the doctrine is a troublesome relic in American foreign policy, for it delayed adjustment to the fact that the United States cannot help but intervene in the affairs of lesser states if she is to aid their development.[123] And the United States has no alternative but to set aside, or at least to modify, the principle of nonintervention, if disaster is to be averted for herself and her dependents.[124] But it is not merely the principle of nonintervention that informal penetration is supposed to have swept away; it is also held to have carried away much of the substance behind the concept of sovereignty, so that few of the proud functions of the state have been left untouched by it.[125] Territorial boundaries diminish in significance as access is had across them, the legitimacy of governments within states is challenged by ideologies careless of the sanctity of frontiers, even the function of defense has been impaired by forms of aggression that are not immediately obvious and that set out to erode a government's monopoly of force from within.[126]

If such radical changes are to be attributed to the phenomenon of informal penetration, inspection of the phenomenon might be approached by way of the reasons which are held to account for its increase. Scott has five of them: the increasingly important role of public opinion in a great many nations; the development of sharp ideological cleavages in international society; the advance in technology particularly of transportation and communications; the emergence of new states; and the advent of nuclear weapons.[127] We have looked already at the impact of nuclear weapons and of ideological division on the state and on the doctrine of noninter-

---

[121] Though the opposition is not as diametrical as the exponents of competitive interference appear to hold. When, for example, Scott argues for a doctrine of "conditional intervention" to replace the ancient American doctrine of nonintervention, he overlooks the extent to which the ancient doctrine had always been conditional and not absolute. See *Revolution in Statecraft*, p. 108.

[122] *Ibid.*, pp. 101 and 107; Cottam, p. 33.

[123] Scott, p. 102.   [124] *Ibid.*, p. 106.   [125] *Ibid.*, p. 172.

[126] *Ibid.*, pp. 168–172.

[127] *Ibid.*, pp. 11–13; Cottam, p. 35.

vention, and it is proposed here to concentrate on the other reasons which are thought to underlie the penetration of the state.

The increasing importance of public opinion is held to have provided a target for outside states which was not available when decision-making was the preserve of the prince, and to have invited informal, rather than formal, access as the only means of penetrating that part of the target.[128] While there are obvious differences between an age of kings and today's popular involvement in politics and while it is true that such differences in domestic arrangements are likely to have international repercussions, the proposition that popular politics have caused a dramatic increase in informal penetration as opposed to merely inviting the attempt at such access is more difficult to defend. Certainly, public opinion may have become an instrument of diplomacy, a device by which leverage may be exercised in foreign policy, and its function in this regard was not unknown to Castlereagh.[129] But leverage is not penetration, and even during a Cold War that witnessed virulent ideological debate in which the principals submitted their ways of life for the attention of public opinion in third states, a nonaligned world managed to avoid surrendering to either house. It may even be the case that, in an age of popular politics, informal access is less, and not more devastating to the sovereign state. For a popular legitimacy as a basis for rule, as opposed to a dynastic one, might provide, in a psychological sense, that "hard-shell" which strategists suppose to have been breached by modern weapons technology. It is possible that the exponents of informal access are mistaking an increase in the technical opportunities for access for the achievement of penetration itself.

Technology—improvements in transportation, and above all in electronic communications—is advanced as a second cause underlying the penetration of the sovereign state.[130] Again there can be no argument about the increasing sophistication of such techniques by the use of which one state may gain access to another, but as Scott himself points out, there is a distinction to be made between technical and substantive accessibility.[131] The sophisticated com-

---

[128] Scott, p. 11.

[129] See above, Chapter Four, section II(i); Cottam, pp. 78–116.

[130] Scott, pp. 10 and 12.

[131] *Ibid.*, pp. 21–22. See also Stone's distinction between physical and human communication in *Legal Controls of International Conflict*, pp. xli–liii, and above, Chapter Eight, section II.

munications techniques, which are supposed to have penetrated the state, are available domestically as well as internationally and transnationally, and it is a perverse point of view which gives attention to the last two while ignoring the first. Nor is it necessary to posit a conspiracy of government against people propagated by subtle use of communications technology in order to point out that in an international society, which still has as its fundamental component the sovereign state, electronic communications are available for use on behalf of the community formed within the state, as well as for use against that community on behalf of some constituency beyond it.

A third reason advanced to explain the increase in informal penetration is that the desire on the part of many new states for rapid economic growth, which they cannot gratify on their own, involves them in penetration by the great powers which assist them.[132] It has always been the case that great powers have been in a position to dominate the weak, and economic superiority is a variant highlighted by a contemporary preoccupation with economic growth. In economic no less than in political matters, some protection for the small might be derived from the existence of more than one great power, so that a measure of independence might be preserved by a shrewd diplomacy. Thus a doctrine of nonintervention has survived, if under constant threat. The supposition that the mere economic superiority of the great over the small has swept the doctrine of nonintervention entirely away[133] assumes not only the primacy of economics over politics, but also that, as it were, economics have commandeered politics—an assumption, we have seen, that is open to doubt.[134] In summary, of each of these notions about the increase of informal access, it might be said that if they were indeed the potent challenge to the sovereign state that they are represented as being, it is a surprise that the sovereign state has survived as long as it has when confronted by them.

Three versions of transnationalist doctrine have been looked at here: the view that there are problems, the range of which is transnational and the solution to which lies only in an end to the sovereign state, the view that there is already a transnational community in existence which has wrested functions from the sovereign state, and the view that states themselves have added transnational goals

[132] Scott, p. 12.
[133] Scott, pp. 102–106.
[134] See above, pp. 368–369.

to their national and international ones in foreign policy. It may well be that it is in the development of transnationalism along any of these avenues that the long-term threat to state sovereignty and the doctrine of nonintervention lies. But we may dissent from the view that they present an immediate threat by making three observations about transnationalism.

In the first place, the dismissal of the sovereign state as a form of "parochial tribalism" sustaining "a fragmented international order more relevant to the seventeenth than to the twentieth century,"[135] implies that an order be established that is better suited to the needs of today. But this supposes that a states system, or an international order, is something that can be built according to some design or in response to some need as a builder realizes the vision of an architect, or as the architect responds to the needs of his patron—rather than being the inheritance of men preoccupied with mere day-to-day survival. Moreover, it is a dismissal that, in its scorn for the sovereign state as a ridiculous anachronism, overlooks the function of maintaining order that the state might be said still to subserve.

Second, the flagship of the doctrine that a transnational challenge to the state exists in the building of interdependence across frontiers—the multinational corporation—might yet be a vessel that is distinctly state-bound rather than international or transnational. It is regarded as foreign outside its home state. For the purposes of international law its most important feature is its nationality defined by the locality of its incorporation. It is largely nationally owned, and it is geographically situated in the advanced industrial countries from which it sprung.[136] The loyalty it commands is less inclusive than that which a state can command, and its persistent "nationality" suggests that while it might be a threat to the independence of the small states which are the theater of its overseas operations, it is a challenge so far contained by its home state. If there is battle between the multinational corporation and the state, it is not self-evident that the former will win.

In the third place, the idea that transnational access and penetration have undermined not the state as such, but merely the *inviolable* or *impermeable* state,[137] is a curious one when pursued to any

[135] H. and M. Sprout, *Toward a Politics of the Planet Earth*, p. 401.
[136] For these points on the "nationality" of the multinational corporation, see Modelski, "The Corporation in World Society," pp. 72–76.
[137] Scott, p. 172.

length. It seeks to retain the state, for it so patently persists, but seemingly to dispense with its sovereignty; and this is the curiosity. For are not its relative immunity to violation (for whatever reasons) and, we may grant, its relative sovereignty—the exclusion, within a certain geographical space and with regard to a particular collection of people, of the authority of any other state; a domain reserved for the working of the laws and customs of a community which is separate from others and acknowledged to be such in the overriding loyalty it wins from its citizens—the continuing essence of the state? Not technically but substantively, the state remains not perhaps relatively inviolable—for inviolability relates to a technical capacity to resist violation which the state clearly lacks with regard, for example, to nuclear weapons—but relatively unviolated. The doctrine of the state no longer inviolable, or the state penetrated, turns out not to have touched the essence of the state as we have conceived it, and it may be that the flowering of such doctrine to accommodate that competitive interference which was supposed to have arisen from conspiratorial international politics will at some future time be regarded as simply a response on the part of some scholars to a Cold War that was not a permanent feature of the international landscape.

It was Richard Cobden who, in advocating nonintervention, made perhaps the strongest case against intervention as a means of conducting foreign policy. At the same time, he was a fervent transnationalist. In the contemporary world, transnationalism itself has been taken as a challenge to the sovereign state, an activity which, above all others, casts doubt upon the continued relevance of the doctrine of nonintervention. However, it is still possible to question any assertion that this new phenomenon has completely disposed of the Cobdenite advocacy of transnationalism *and* nonintervention.

VI

Though it is premature to celebrate the passing of the order of sovereign states, it is possible to speculate about the conditions for a better world order and to advocate policies which might achieve it.[138] Indeed, the assessment of the lawfulness of any important

[138] "Better world order" here meaning an arrangement of international relations which satisfies more than the minimal requirements for order suggested in the first section of this chapter—that states should recognize

and controversial piece of state behavior is not just a matter of measuring it against the existing rules of international law. For in a society in which the behavior of states, and particularly that of the great powers, is quasi-legislative or precedent-setting, the assessment of legality depends also upon the conception of world legal order espoused by the assessor. The close relationship between conceptions of order and assessment of legality is illustrated by the debate about the lawfulness of American participation in the Vietnam War. The intention in the present section is to look first at this debate with this relationship in mind,[139] then at certain proposals for an improved world order which are, in part, the products of the Vietnam debate and which go beyond reliance upon the sovereign state.

The crucial issue dividing those who regarded the American involvement in Vietnam as lawful and those who did not was that of the proper characterization of the conflict as civil or international. One side viewed the war as fundamentally an internal struggle for the control of a national society, at most a civil war with significant outside participation, and found the United States principally responsible for internationalizing the war.[140] The view which supported the American commitment, on the other hand, rejected as oversimplified this emphasis on the internal aspects of the struggle and insisted that the conflict combined with these features of the Cold War "divided nation problem" and of "aggression from the North."[141]

From these different perceptions of the nature of the war and of Hanoi's participation in it, two different accounts of the legitimate response followed. For Moore, an important part of contemporary international law is the prohibition of coercion as "a

---

each other's right to separate existence. "World" rather than "international" order—since the arrangement might envisage a move away from the state as the primary unit of international relations.

[139] I shall refer to the debate carried on between Professors Falk and Moore in the pages of Volume 75 of the *Yale Law Journal*, reprinted in Falk, *Vietnam War and International Law*, pp. 362–508.

[140] Falk, "International Law and the United States Role in the Vietnam War," in *ibid.*, pp. 367 and 368–373; "International Law and the United States Role in Viet Nam: A Response to Professor Moore," in *ibid.*, pp. 459–472.

[141] Moore, "International Law and the United States Role in Viet Nam: A Reply," in *ibid.*, pp. 402–403 and 404.

strategy of major change" in international relations.[142] Its prevention is no less important because it takes place across a *de facto* boundary about whose legitimacy there is some dispute. And where such a boundary or cease-fire line had become, as in the case of the seventeenth parallel in Vietnam, a boundary separating the "major contending public order systems," the label "civil strife" was misleading, and dangerous to long run community interests if it allowed unilateral military coercion to prevail.[143] The view which clinched for this side the legitimacy of American participation in the war held that "coercive threats to fundamental values can be effectuated as realistically by covert invasion and by significant military assistance to insurgents as by armies on the march."[144] Since Hanoi's participation in the war was tantamount to armed attack, the maximum self-defensive response was available to the South and to her allies and this included the bombing of the North.[145]

The other side, unsympathetic to the American commitment and to the arguments presented in its support, was more sensitive to "permissible levels of coercion" in international relations.[146] It drew attention to the stakes of the First Indochina War as a conflict fought for the control of the whole of Vietnam and argued that even granting the *de facto* independence of the two parts of Vietnam after a Geneva settlement which envisaged reunification, the participation of the North in the war in the South could not be regarded as coercion across an international boundary.[147] According to this view, armed intervention is not equivalent to armed attack, a plea of self-defense was therefore impermissible, and the maximum response available to the United States was counterintervention limited to the territory of South Vietnam—ruling out the legitimacy of the bombing of the North.[148]

The different conceptions of world order underlying this debate amount, to put the matter at its simplest, to a disagreement between the view which insists on the right of self-defense against any coercive activity which has an international aspect and which reaches significant proportions, and an alternative view which en-

[142] Moore, "A Reply," p. 404.   [143] *Ibid.*, p. 405.
[144] *Ibid.*, pp. 419–420.   [145] *Ibid.*, p. 418.
[146] Falk, "International Law and the U S Role," p. 364.
[147] *Ibid.*, pp. 368–373 and 375–383; "A Response," pp. 459–470.
[148] "International Law and the U. S. Role," pp. 367 and 376–379; "A Response," pp. 470–494.

tertains more doubts about expanding the right of self-defense. Both sides affirm the need to minimize coercion, but one seeks to combat it when it occurs while the other is both less trustful of a unilateral response and more receptive to any just claims of those who break the peace. Moore asserts that essentially all uses of force other than those pursuant to the right of individual or collective self-defense, or authorized under Charter peace-keeping machinery are unlawful. And where the latter is not effectively available, he sees the right of self-defense as a "major source of control and sanction against aggression."[149] Falk, on the other hand, sees the minimization of violence and the localization of conflict better served by a United States which respects the outcome of what can be counted as internal political struggles.[150] He argues that to regard hostile intervention as armed attack not only tends to escalate any particular conflict but so broadens the notion of armed attack as to allow a plausible invocation of the right of self-defense in any protracted internal war.[151] This comes close, Falk argues, to abolishing the legal significance of the distinction between internal war and international war, thereby weakening the territorial restraint on the scope of conflict and setting at the same time "an unfortunate precedent in international affairs."[152]

If Moore's doctrine of unilateral judgment and enforcement can be said to represent a very rough approximation to legal order in a world in which the interests of states predominate over those of the international community, Falk looks forward to the substitution of community authority for state authority. He argues that "the whole effort of international law in the area of war and peace since the end of World War I has been to deny sovereign states the kind of unilateral discretion to employ force in foreign affairs that the United States has exercised in Viet Nam."[153] And to allow states wide discretion in deciding for themselves, when aggression has taken place and in responding as they think fit, detracts from this design.[154] Falk goes on to argue that the conversion of an internal conflict into an international war, allowing the sort of response made by the United States in the Vietnam War, should take

---

[149] Moore, "A Reply," p. 404.
[150] Falk, "International Law and the U S Role," p. 365.
[151] *Ibid.*, p. 377.
[152] *Ibid.*, pp. 377 and 397–398. The particularly unfortunate precedent Falk sees as the bombing of North Vietnam by the United States.
[153] "A Response," p. 447.   [154] *Ibid.*, pp. 447–454.

place only under community authorization—regional or universal—but at any rate a community wide enough to include "principal divergent elements."[155] It remains to examine the place of the principle of nonintervention in this conception of order which envisages considerable progress beyond the order of sovereign states; but first there are less ambitious proposals for the revision of the latter order which merit attention.

Although this summary might capture its essence, the debate about the Vietnam War in particular and about the relationship between intervention and international order in general is not one that turns simply upon the two possibilities of relying on approximate order in the world as it is, and of looking forward to a future order guaranteed by an organized world community. There are other possibilities, other claims to be taken into account which arc not accommodated within this dichotomy. They suppose the answer, or part of it, to the problem of order to lie beyond the sovereign state, but stop short of requiring its solution by the establishment of a full-blown international community. It is proposed here to measure two doctrines of this sort against the principle of nonintervention: the doctrine of self-determination which, should it become the rule, would make greater demands on the international society than does the principle of state sovereignty; and the idea of interbloc order which would recognize as legitimate the relative dependence of lesser powers within each bloc.

The right of self-determination has been defined as "the freedom of a people to choose their own government and institutions and to control their own resources."[156] The achievement of this freedom, Moore argues, has been taken up as a basic policy by the international community as is demonstrated by that community's condemnation of intervention and of colonialism.[157] If these stand condemned because they are intrusions from outside a community, Moore adds that self-determination might also be denied by "internal coercion"—the government of a tyrannical prince or the seizure of power by a terrorist minority.[158] It is for this reason that he rejects the "simplistic" view of Hall that states should be left alone in all circumstances to work out their own form of gov-

[155] "A Response," p. 492 and n. 119 on that page, and pp. 456–457.
[156] Moore, "The Control of Foreign Intervention in Internal Conflict," in *Law and the Indo-China War*, pp. 163–164.
[157] *Ibid.*, p. 164, and Moore, "A Reply," p. 430.
[158] "Control of Foreign Intervention," pp. 164–165; "A Reply," p. 431.

ernment and sympathizes with the view that intervention might, in some instances, realize the goal of self-determination rather than detract from it.[159] Thus, Moore suggests that one modification of a generally desirable nonintervention standard in regard to internal war should be "non-partisan participation for restoring orderly processes of self-determination."[160]

Clearly, self-determination is a right much more demanding—in the sense of imposing more extensive duties on the members of international society—than that of state sovereignty. The latter right implies a duty of noninterference no matter how tyrannical the form of government within a state. Confronted by the same objectionable government, guilty of "internal coercion," the right of self-determination, as Moore defines it, might be said to imply a duty on the part of outside states to act in such a way as to bring that coercion to an end. One of the cardinal difficulties with the imposition of such an extensive duty is that of definition of the "self" and of how it is to be "determined."[161] If there is a general right of self-determination in international society, does the "self" refer to any self-conscious group which wishes to run its own affairs from a colony which wishes to become independent, through a group that wishes to secede from a state, to a group external to a state which wishes to take over power within it? And if, as is typically the case, the right of a group to self-determination is disputed, on what settled grounds are outside states to base their policy towards it? The notion of determination is as difficult. Does a group establish its right to determine its own affairs by the demonstration that it is a linguistic, racial, or cultural unity? Can its claim to govern itself be granted as a result of a plebiscite, by dint of electoral success, or by international community authorization? Taken separately, these criteria are often inconclusive, and together they frequently contradict each other. It may be that the only sure

159 "A Reply," p. 431.

160 "Control of Foreign Intervention," p. 276.

161 Moore does recognize this difficulty, and deals with precisely these categories in "Control of Foreign Intervention," pp. 166–169. For a devastating criticism of the doctrine of self-determination on grounds of definition among others, see Farer, "Harnessing Rogue Elephants: A Short Discourse on Intervention in Civil Strife," in Falk, *Vietnam War and International Law*, Vol. 2, pp. 1095–1100. See also on the difficulties of determination in self-determination, Alfred Cobban, *The Nation State and National Self-Determination*, New York, 1969, pp. 66–75.

380

ground on which a group can claim a right to govern itself is by spilling its blood—successful prosecution of a war for independence presenting the international community with a *fait accompli*.[162]

Despite these considerations, it is arguable that state practice has at least established a right of self-determination for colonial peoples.[163] Beyond this aspect of the right, on which there can be said to be something very close to a consensus in international society, it is not merely the problem of definition that gives pause to the proclamation of a general right of self-determination—as if earnest intellectual inquiry were all that was required for its establishment. For this lack of clarity in definition is accompanied by, and is partly the result of, the lack of solidarity in the international community. It is not necessary to take the most mistrustful view of the motives of states and groups within them to expect that they will interpret any principle of self-determination according to their own interests and that, for example, any formula envisaging "nonpartisan participation for restoring orderly processes of self-determination" will, in effect, be at the mercy of the self-serving definitions of interested parties. In view of this, international law might be brought less into disrepute if it were to adopt a cautious attitude toward any right of self-determination. It might yet be wiser to rely on the older tradition of regarding nonintervention as the obverse of the principle of state sovereignty rather than attaching it without reservation to a principle of self-determination.

If it is on grounds of order that the principle of state sovereignty is to be preferred to that of self-determination, it is on these same grounds that the principle of state sovereignty might, in certain circumstances, itself give place to a prior imperative. In a world of superpowers armed with nuclear weapons such an imperative is the avoidance of direct conflict between them, and this in turn can be said to require the avoidance of "overlapping pretensions of authority and commitment on the part of principal rival

---

[162] Which returns the discussion to Moore's point of departure: his objection that the version of nonintervention requiring that neither incumbent nor insurgent be aided from outside adopts a "kind of Darwinian definition of self-determination as survival of the fittest within the national boundaries, even if fittest means most adept in the use of force." "A Reply," in Falk, *Vietnam War and International Law*, p. 431.

[163] See Higgins, "Internal War and International Law," in Black and Falk, *The Future of the International Legal Order*, Vol. III, *Conflict Management*, p. 104.

states."[164] This goal might be subserved by the acknowledgment as "legitimate" of that pattern of conduct which has Zone I actors (the United States and the Soviet Union) asserting their authority, when necessary by supervisory intervention, over Zone II actors, those within their exclusive sphere of influence. This "hegemonial jurisdiction" is marked out by the assertion of the will of the Zone I actor within Zone II by military means and with or without an invitation. It is differentiated further by the acceptance in fact, if not in rhetoric, of each Zone I actor's claim by the other. Falk would have the legitimacy—the acceptability as a ground rule —of this pattern of conduct made explicit rather than have it remain tacit and unavowed except by its opponents. In support of this view, he argues that: "One cost of resting world order partially upon patterns of control that cannot be acknowledged by their own creators is to cast the entire enterprise of law and order in world affairs into cynical disrepute, except for marginal issues of world security."[165]

This argument for the priority of interbloc over interstate norms, within specified limits, is a persuasive one. It is in the positivist tradition that the law should take state practice into account rather than setting impotent rules over against it. One objection, however, might be that to acknowledge hegemonial jurisdiction is to make an exaggerated obeisance to state practice which turns out to be untrue to it. By being insensitive both to gradations of dependency within the blocs and to the extent of the independence which Zone II actors still enjoy,[166] it might be too quick an acknowledgment of a supposedly conventional pattern of international politics.[167] A more radical and more optimistic objection to the acceptance of hegemonial jurisdiction holds that it is not inevitable that superpowers should intervene militarily in the affairs of neighboring states, and that a first step in the destruction of the "dual-ghetto" system might be taken by a United States

[164] Falk, "Zone II as a World Order Construct," in Rosenau, Vincent Davis, and Maurice A. East, *The Analysis of International Politics*, New York, 1972, p. 188. The summary following is taken from pp. 187–201 of this volume.

[165] *Ibid.*, p. 192.

[166] An independence which might be enhanced if increased "access" does indeed accompany a return to a five-power balance in the conception of Nixon; see above, section IV.

[167] Falk takes this observation into account in considering the "precedential effect of the Zone I claim for the future of Zone II." *Ibid.*, p. 200.

that sets an example to the Soviet Union by reaffirming her commitment to and then adhering herself to the principles of national sovereignty and territorial inviolability.[168]

The establishment of international authority in a regional or universal organization need not dismiss the principle of nonintervention, but might reinforce it in one sense by providing a community reaction in the event of its serious violation. It would still be a general rule of interstate conduct but with the one significant departure from contemporary patterns of international politics that international organizations would decide on the circumstances of its breach and authorize any response to it. Regional or universal international institutions would be the guarantors of the rule that their members should not interfere in each other's affairs.[169] Pursuing this conception of order further, it is possible to imagine a world federal government which had a rule of nonintervention between its constituents much as the states of Australia respect each other's autonomy today. But in such a socially developed world the function of the principle of nonintervention as a keeper of order in a primitive and rudimentary international society would be fulfilled by federal intervention.

The difficulty with this conception of order is revealed when attention is paid to another meaning traditionally attached to the doctrine of nonintervention. It has been observed above that the principle has a double aspect—nonintervention between the parts of international society and the exclusion of any "superstate" established over those parts.[170] Though Falk is far from advocating the establishment of a superstate, he does stress the need to subordinate national policy to regional and global policy particularly in the peace-keeping area, and generally to downgrade the role of the state in world politics.[171] But the demonstration of the need for a

[168] This is the thesis of Franck and Weisband in their *Word Politics: Verbal Strategy Among the Superpowers*, especially Chap. 8.

[169] Falk observes that "a policy of insulation was the original idea of a policy of nonintervention with respect to foreign civil strife: the role of the United Nations would be to assure mutual compliance with duties to refrain from intervention." "The Regulation of International Conflict by Means of Law," in *Legal Order in a Violent World*, p. 71.

[170] See above, Chapter One, section II; Chapter Seven, section v; Chapter Eight, section IV.

[171] See, e.g., "The Future of World Order: A Comparison of Reformist and Revolutionary Perspectives," in *Legal Order in a Violent World*, pp.

reformed or revolutionized world order cannot by itself bring the change about. Though the intellectual tasks of charting that want of solidarity in international society which renders international law weak law and of framing policies which might build a sense of community in international relations are necessary to the realization of a better world order, they are not nearly sufficient to it.[172] The values associated with statehood which still give meaning to the doctrine of nonintervention as it would exclude any authority above the state militate against that centralization of the control of force in international relations which might better safeguard nonintervention in its other sense—the exclusion of one state from the affairs of another.

If international order were taken to encompass any of the doctrines examined here, it would be an order more inclusive than that in which the Cobdenite doctrine of nonintervention would find a place. And on grounds of approximation to reality, the Cobdenite doctrine of abstention might still be preferred to trusting states clinically to uphold by intervention the principle of nonintervention, to a doctrine of self-determination which appears to make international society the guardian of democratic processes within states, or to a view that would transfer responsibility in matters of war and peace to the organized international community.[173] Even when,

---

32–33; "Some Notes on the Consequences of Revolutionary Activity for the Quality of International Order," in Falk, *The Status of Law in International Society*, Princeton, N.J., 1970, p. 63.

[172] Falk is the first to recognize these points while urging the need for change. See, e.g., "The International Law of Internal War," in *Legal Order in a Violent World*, pp. 114–115; "Gaps and Biases in Contemporary Theories of International Law," in *The Status of Law in International Society*, pp. 22–23; and on the persistence of the Westphalia order of sovereign states, see generally, "The Interplay of Westphalia and Charter conceptions of the International Legal Order," in Falk and Black, *The Future of the International Legal Order*, Vol. I, *Trends and Patterns*, pp. 32–70.

[173] The argument of approximation to reality can, however, be pointed in more than one direction. To return to the debate with which we began this section, Moore can justly claim realism when he relies upon states to maintain approximate order in the world as it is. Falk has an equal claim to realism when he observes that a legal order which depends upon states judging and acting in their own cause is a poor substitute for objective law impartially applied, and that only a transfer of authority to community institutions can come close to this impartial model of law. Falk, indeed, goes further to argue the need for "a new cynicism which turns out to look curiously like idealism," and that "a contemporary Machiavelli, perceiving

as in the case of the interbloc norm of nonintervention, the doctrine of nonintervention as applied to states has a lesser claim to realism, Cobdenism has survived not merely as a reminder of the limits of intervention but as a model to which some would have us return—pointing the way thither by placing confidence in the power of example in international relations.

VII

Those who would deny the possibility of any legal order among states of unequal power existing together in the absence of government, might dismiss the assertion of a principle of nonintervention, or indeed of any legal principle of international conduct, as a mere delusion, existing in the mind of the person who asserts it but bearing no relation to reality. If it were pointed out to the doubter that most states most of the time did in fact behave as if there were a rule of nonintervention prevailing between them, he might ascribe this pattern of behavior to the common prudence of states and not to their feeling legally obliged to refrain from interference. If it were further pointed out to him that the assertion of a principle of nonintervention obliging states to refrain from interference in each other's affairs was made as frequently by statesmen as by wishful commentators, he might declare that it was simply a slogan covering the real motives of states with a spurious legitimacy. But the felt need on the part of statesmen to justify and criticize in legal language attests to the existence of a community, however fragile, beyond the state, and the view which ascribes the actions of states to motives other than that of obedience to law falsely separates the political from the legal. For the predictability and stability provided by common standards, standards which it is the function of international law to codify, are part of the political motive for action in international relations. The question, "What

---

this novel necessity for a community of mankind, might be dismissed by the best minds as recklessly utopian." "The International Law of Internal War," in *Legal Order in a Violent World*, pp. 114–115. A thoroughgoing "realism" would perhaps be skeptical of both Moore's and Falk's position, and also of the preference for Cobdenism in the text. It is possible, however, to make a case for this preference on the ground that by requiring abstention rather than action from the members of international society, it might place the law in a less undignified position than any principle which, in enjoining action by those members, provides more opportunity for abuse by self-serving definition.

is the lawful course of action?" is part of the wider question, "What is our interest?" for any state contemplating an initiative in international relations, even if it is only put in the debased form of "How are we to justify our action?" That the guidance offered by the law might not be accepted in any particular circumstance provides no warrant for the dismissal of international law as a factor in international relations.

If the principle of nonintervention is taken as part of a law which is law, however weak, its impartiality between contending political doctrines might be said to recommend it as a legal norm. By opposing, in circumstances of conflict within a state, a neutral norm of abstention to political partisanship on behalf of one or other of the factions, it satisfies the legal requirement of impartiality. But its very impartiality, together with its generality, has rendered it politically promiscuous—available for use across the spectrum of political positions. In the debate about British foreign policy in the nineteenth century, it found proponents among Whigs, Tories, and Radicals. The advocates of a policy of nonintervention in the days of America's isolation were of a very different political persuasion from those who have advocated such a policy in the days of the *Pax Americana.*

Perhaps from the point of view of maintaining the order of nonintervening sovereign states, it matters little that the doctrine of nonintervention gathers together strange bedfellows. Indeed it is in allowing the coexistence of strange bedfellows in international relations that the principle has its rationale. But this supposes that while the principle is adhered to for very different reasons and by states with radically different systems of government, the sorts of activity it proscribes remain the same. Where the principle is defined differently according to the conception of world order in which it finds a place, its impartiality no longer obtains. Its vaunted impartiality, it might be said, is anyway a quality ascribed to it by British foreign policy in the nineteenth century when, protected by the Royal Navy and confident in her unique institutions, impartiality between contending political and social doctrines was precisely the interest of England—a very partial impartiality. In the Americas, the "impartiality" of the principle of nonintervention was rarely proclaimed as its primary virtue, since the American doctrine excluded the European system of government as well as alien intervention, regarding the former as a species of the latter. In the contemporary international system, the variation in interpretation of the principle of nonintervention with the contending conceptions of world order is particularly striking. The Western powers tend to limit the scope of the principle to the prohibition of the threat or use of force in international relations, include indirect aggression in this prohibition, and assert the legitimacy of a response to it when it occurs. The communist states proclaim the principle as an essential part of peaceful coexistence between states, find the chief threat to its observance in imperialist oppression, and assert the legitimacy of wars of national liberation against it. The states of the Third World assert the principle as an article of faith, erect it over their recently secured independence, find the principal threat to it in the neocolonialism of the Western powers, and declare the legitimacy of the struggle against all manifestations of colonialism and its offspring racialism.

These conceptions of world order are similar in the sense that each is a more or less ambitious vision of a preferred order and not an attempt to describe the elements of order discoverable in the system as it is. For the principle of nonintervention to be an operable rule of conduct between states, it might be argued, the triumph of one of these visions is required. Both Kant and Mazzini appeared to espouse varieties of this doctrine: the principle of nonintervention might be necessary to the maintenance of peace and order among states, but that order requires first that all states should conform to a particular pattern. If the primary requirement for order among states is that republican government be established within them or that nations should everywhere coincide with states, then until these conditions prevail intervention might be legitimate to bring them about. The principle of nonintervention is not here an impartial rule between contending political doctrines. Indeed, adherence to it is made possible only by the adoption of one particular doctrine by all states.

If the vision of world order looks forward not to the establishment of a particular pattern within states but to the establishment of a superior authority over them or even to the total demise of the state, then the function of the principle of nonintervention is reduced *pari passu* with the waning of the institution it is designed to protect. One form of this doctrine relies upon the establishment of the authority of the law over states. It would not dispense with the state but tame its sovereignty by bringing it increasingly within the law. The principle of nonintervention would be part of that law as it required states to refrain from interference in each other's affairs, but it would not be a doctrine available for invocation against the expansion of international law itself, and in this sense it would stand guard over an ever-shrinking domain of domestic jurisdiction. A second form of this doctrine might hold that the achievement of world order requires the establishment of government over states, much as the Hobbesian account of order between individual men. If such a government were federal, a rule of nonintervention might apply between the still existing states, but a local infraction of the rule would bring federal intervention. A third form of this doctrine, looking to the withering away of the state, would admit individual men to a great society of mankind in which the principle of nonintervention would have no place.

In the existing imperfect and fragile order of states as they are and not as some would have them become, there is equal difficulty in relying for the maintenance of international order on the principle of nonintervention in Cobden's and in Mill's interpretation of it. The problem with Cobden's near-absolute doctrine of nonintervention is that it provides no guarantee that those who would voluntarily adhere to the principle will be protected from those who would not. The weakness of Cobden's doctrine is that there is no sanction to deter the rule-breaker. But if Mill compensates for this weakness by affirming the legitimacy of counterintervention to uphold the principle of nonintervention, the difficulty with this doctrine in turn is its assumption that states will disinterestedly uphold the law. Mill himself recognized that counterintervention was not always prudent if always rightful. It could be argued that the history of American foreign policy since the Second World War has been an extended demonstration of the limits and ultimate poverty of Mill's doctrine and of a core of good sense in the Cobden view. If Cobden's anarchical conception is an abdication of responsibility for order in international relations, the Mill view assumes a solidarity in the international community which does not yet exist, for it remains a community in which the responsibility of one great power is the irresponsible pursuit of selfish interest to another.

The nature of the contemporary international system, it can be argued, is such that the questions that Cobden and Mill asked themselves—to intervene or not to intervene, to uphold by intervention the principle of nonintervention or to act according to a narrower conception of interest—are no longer the relevant ones, and that to persist in asking them is to be the prisoner of a nineteenth-century inheritance. The relevant question today, it might be said,

388

is not whether to intervene, but what kind of intervention and how much and how best to control it when it occurs. The baldest form of this view to appear in the postwar world has been that which regards the sovereign state order as no longer supplemented by a balance of power among many, seeing the rules of such an order overridden by the systemic imperatives of an unstable balance of two. Furthermore, when the two are armed with nuclear weapons and oppose each other as the leaders of ideologically hostile camps, the function of the principle of nonintervention seems to be reduced to a more or less feeble protest against inevitable interference. The only area, on this view, in which the principle of nonintervention is honored in fact and not merely in name, is in its application as a ground rule of interbloc and not of interstate relations. The more insidious form of the doctrine that would unseat the principle of nonintervention, a version of it that has reappeared in the post-war world under the title "transnationalism," is that which sees a community being established across frontiers to accompany the society formed between states—eroding thereby the factual basis for nonintervention.

True, a return to that pristine order of sovereign states each observing a rule of nonintervention, if indeed it ever did exist, is not in prospect where international society is populated by international organizations, regional and universal, as well as by states, and where international politics are conducted between blocs of states and also transnationally across state frontiers, as well as simply between states. But the state remains as the fundamental entity of international relations despite the demonstration of its obsolescence. So long as it continues to win the allegiance of men, the doctrine of nonintervention bears a closer relation to reality than the progressive doctrines predicated upon the disappearance of the state, its civilization by law, or the establishment of a super-authority over it. Though it is not possible, with any pretension to total accuracy, to describe international society in terms of those islands of order which were held to provide the primary rationale for a principle of nonintervention, nor is it yet the case that the islands have merged into a solid continent which makes any reference to their separateness altogether anachronistic.

a. *Declaration on Inadmissibility of Intervention in Domestic Affairs of States and Protection of their Independence and Sovereignty.*

General Assembly Resolution 2131 (xx), December 21, 1965.

"The General Assembly,

"Deeply concerned at the gravity of the international situation and the increasing threat to universal peace due to armed intervention and other direct or indirect forms of interference threatening the sovereign personality and the political independence of States,

"Considering that the United Nations, in accordance with their aim to eliminate war, threats to the peace and acts of aggression, created an Organization, based on the sovereign equality of States, whose friendly relations would be based on respect for the principle of equal rights and self-determination of peoples and on the obligation of its Members to refrain from the threat or use of force against the territorial integrity or political independence of any State,

"Recognizing that, in fulfilment of the principle of self-determination, the General Assembly, in the Declaration on the Granting of Independence to Colonial Countries and Peoples contained in Resolution 1514 (xv) of 14 December 1960, stated its conviction that all peoples have an inalienable right to complete freedom, the exercise of their sovereignty and the integrity of their national territory, and that, by virtue of that right, they freely determine their political status and freely pursue their economic, social and cultural development,

"Recalling that in the Universal Declaration of Human Rights the General Assembly proclaimed that recognition of the inherent dignity and of the equal and inalienable rights of all members of the human family is the foundation of freedom, justice and peace in the world, without distinction of any kind,

"*Reaffirming* the principle of non-intervention, proclaimed in the charters of the Organization of American States, the League of Arab States and the Organization of African Unity and affirmed at the conferences held at Montevideo, Buenos Aires, Chapultepec and Bogotá, as well as in the decisions of the Asian-African Conference at Bandung, the First Conference of Heads of State or Government of Non-Aligned Countries at Belgrade, in the Programme for Peace and International Co-operation adopted at the end of the Second Conference of Heads of State or Government of Non-Aligned Countries at Cairo, and in the declaration on subversion at Accra by the Heads of State and Government of the African States,

"*Recognizing* that full observance of the principle of the nonintervention of States in the internal affairs of other States is essential to the fulfillment of the purposes and principles of the United Nations,

"*Considering* that armed intervention is synonymous with aggression and, as such, is contrary to the basic principles on which peaceful international co-operation between States should be built,

"*Considering further* that direct intervention, subversion and all forms of indirect intervention are contrary to these principles and, consequently, constitute a violation of the Charter of the Uniteu Nations,

"*Mindful* that violation of the principle of non-intervention poses a threat to the independence, freedom and normal political, economic, social and cultural development of countries, particularly those which have freed themselves from colonialism, and can pose a serious threat to the maintenance of peace,

"*Fully aware* of the imperative need to create appropriate conditions which would enable all States, and in particular the developing countries, to choose without duress or coercion their own political, economic and social institutions,

"*In the light of the foregoing considerations, solemnly declares*:

"1. No State has the right to intervene, directly or indirectly, for any reason whatever, in the internal or external affairs of any other State. Consequently, armed intervention and all other forms of interference or attempted threats against the personality of the State or against its political, economic and cultural elements, are condemned.

"2. No State may use or encourage the use of economic, political or any other type of measures to coerce another State in order to obtain from it the subordination of the exercise of its sovereign rights or to secure from it advantages of any kind. Also, no State shall organize, assist, foment, finance, incite or tolerate subversive, terrorist or armed activities directed towards the violent overthrow of the régime of another State, or interfere in civil strife in another State.

"3. The use of force to deprive peoples of their national identity constitutes a violation of their inalienable rights and of the principle of non-intervention.

"4. The strict observance of these obligations is an essential condition to ensure that nations live together in peace with one another, since the practice of any form of intervention not only violates the spirit and letter of the Charter of the United Nations but also leads to the creation of situations which threaten international peace and security.

"5. Every State has an inalienable right to choose its political, economic, social and cultural systems, without interference in any form by another State.

"6. All States shall respect the right of self-determination and independence of peoples and nations, to be freely exercised without any foreign pressure, and with absolute respect for human rights and fundamental freedoms. Consequently, all States shall contribute to the complete elimination of racial discrimination and colonialism in all its forms and manifestations.

"7. For the purpose of the present Declaration, the term 'State' covers both individual States and groups of 'States.'

"8. Nothing in this Declaration shall be construed as affecting in any manner the relevant provisions of the Charter of the United Nations relating to the maintenance of international peace and security, in particular those contained in Chapters VI, VII and VIII."

b. *Declaration on Principles of International Law Concerning Friendly Relations and Co-operation Among States in Accordance with the Charter of the United Nations.*

General Assembly Resolution 2625 (xxv), October 24, 1970.

"The principle concerning the duty not to intervene in matters within the domestic jurisdiction of any State, in accordance with the Charter.

"No State or group of States has the right to intervene, directly or indirectly, for any reason whatever, in the internal or external affairs of any other State. Consequently, armed intervention and all other forms of interference or attempted threats against the personality of the State or against its political, economic and cultural elements, are in violation of international law.

"No State may use or encourage the use of economic, political or any other type of measures to coerce another State in order to obtain from it the subordination of the exercise of its sovereign rights and to secure from it advantages of any kind. Also, no State shall organize, assist, foment, finance, incite or tolerate subversive, terrorist or armed activities directed towards the violent overthrow of the régime of another State, or interfere in civil strife in another State.

"The use of force to deprive people of their national identity constitutes a violation of their inalienable rights and of the principle of non-intervention.

"Every State has an inalienable right to choose its political, economic, social and cultural systems, without interference in any form by another State.

Nothing in the foregoing paragraphs shall be construed as affecting the relevant provisions of the Charter relating to the maintenance of international peace and security."

c. *Proposal on Formulation of the Principle of Non-Intervention by Czechoslovakia.* (A/AC.119/L.6 in Report of the Special Committee on Principles of International Law concerning Friendly Relations and Co-operation among States. Doc. No. A/5746, November 16, 1964, para. 203).

"The Principle of Non-Intervention.
"1. States shall refrain from any direct or indirect intervention under any pretext in the internal or external affairs of any other State. In particular, any interference or pressure by one State or a group of States for the purpose of changing the social or political order in another State shall be prohibited.

"2. States shall refrain from any acts, manifestations or attempts aimed at a violation of the territorial integrity or inviolability of any State.

"3. States shall refrain from exerting pressure by any means, including the threat to sever diplomatic relations, in order to compel one State not to recognize another State."

d. *Proposal on Formulation of the Principle of Non-Intervention by Ghana, India and Yugoslavia.* (A/AC.119/L.27 in Report of the 1964 Special Committee, para. 209).

"Principle C: Non-Intervention.

"1. No State or group of States has the right to intervene, directly or indirectly, for any reason whatsoever, in the internal or external affairs of any other State; nor to interfere in the right of any State to choose and develop its own political, economic and social order in the manner most suited to the genius of its own people.

"2. Accordingly no State may use or encourage the use of coercive measures of an economic or political character to force the sovereign will of another State and obtain from it advantages of any kind. In particular States shall not:

(a) organize, assist, foment, incite, or tolerate subversive or terrorist activities against another State or interfere in civil strife in another State;

(b) interfere with or hinder, in any form or manner, the promulgation or execution of laws in regard to matters essentially within the competence of any State;

(c) use duress to obtain or maintain territorial agreements or special advantages of any kind; and

(d) recognize territorial acquisitions or special advantages obtained by duress of any kind by another State."

e. *Proposal on the Formulation of the Principle of Non-intervention by Mexico.* (A/AC.119/L.24. Report of the 1964 Special Committee, para. 208).

"Principle C: The duty not to intervene . . . in accordance with the Charter.

"1. Every State has the duty to refrain from intervening, alone or in concert with other States, directly or indirectly, for any reason whatever, in the internal or external affairs of any other State. The foregoing principle prohibits any form of interference or attempted threat against the personality of the State or against its political, economic and cultural elements.

"2. Consequently, every State has the duty to refrain from any of the acts specified hereunder, as also any other acts which may possibly be characterized as intervention:

"(1). The use or the encouragement of the use of coercive measures of an economic or political nature in order to force the sovereign will of another State and obtain from the latter advantages of any kind;

"(2). Permitting, in the areas subject to its jurisdiction, or promoting or financing anywhere:

(a). The organization or training of land, sea or air armed forces of any type having as their purpose incursions into other States;

(b). Contributing, supplying or providing arms or war materials to be used for promoting or aiding a rebellion or seditious movement in any State, even if the latter's Government is not recognized; and

(c). The organization of subversive or terrorist activities against another State;

"(3). Making the recognition of Governments or the maintenance of diplomatic relations dependent on the receipt of special advantages;

"(4). Preventing or attempting to prevent a State from freely disposing of its natural riches or resources;

"(5). Imposing or attempting to impose on a State a specific form of organization or government;

"(6). Imposing or attempting to impose on a State the concession to foreigners of a privileged situation going beyond the rights, means of redress and safeguards granted under the municipal law to nationals."

f. *Proposal on the Formulation of the Principle of Non-Intervention by the United Kingdom.* (A/AC.119/L.8 in Report of the 1964 Special Committee, para. 205).

"*Statement of Principles.*

"1. Every State has the right to political independence and territorial integrity.

"2. Every State has the duty to respect the rights enjoyed by other States in accordance with international law, and to refrain from intervention in matters within the domestic jurisdiction of any other State.

"*Commentary*

396

"*Non-Intervention.*

"(1). The basic principle in paragraph 1 is reflected in the United Nations Charter, for example, in Article 2, paragraph 4.

"(2). The first part of paragraph 2 expresses the duty of States correlative to the rights enjoyed by them under paragraph 1.

"The second part of paragraph 2, which expresses the classical doctrine of non-intervention to be found in numerous multilateral, regional and bilateral treaties, is a particular application of the first part. The wording does, however, leave certain questions unresolved, as, for example, what is meant by 'intervention' and what is meant by 'matters within the domestic jurisdiction'. In the context of inter-State relations, 'intervention' connotes in general forcible or dictatorial interference.

"(3). In considering the scope of 'intervention', it should be recognized that in an interdependent world, it is inevitable and desirable that States will be concerned with and will seek to influence the actions and policies of other States, and that the objective of international law is not to prevent such activity but rather to ensure that it is compatible with the sovereign equality of States and the self-determination of their peoples.

"(4). It would, therefore, be impossible to give an exhaustive definition of what constitutes 'intervention.' Much of the classic conception of intervention has been absorbed by the prohibition of the threat or use of force against the political independence or territorial integrity of States in accordance with Article 2, paragraph 4 of the Charter. There are, however, other forms of intervention, in particular the use of clandestine activities to encompass the overthrow of the Government of another State, or to secure an alteration in the political and economic structure of that State, which illustrate the danger of attempting an exhaustive definition of what constitutes 'intervention.'

"(5). In the event that a State becomes a victim of unlawful intervention practised or supported by the Government of another State, it has the right to request aid and assistance from third States, which are correspondingly entitled to grant the aid and assistance requested. Such aid and assistance may, if the unlawful intervention has taken the form of subversive activities leading to civil strife in which the dissident elements are receiving external support and encouragement, include armed assistance for the purpose of restoring normal conditions."

g. *Proposal on the Formulation of the Principle of Non-Intervention by Australia, Canada, France, Italy, the United Kingdom
and the United States.* (A/AC.125/L.13 in Report of the
1966 Special Committee on Principles of International Law
concerning Friendly Relations and Co-operation among
States Doc. No. A/6230, June 27, 1966, para. 279).

Doc. No. A/6230, June 27, 1966, para. 279.

"1. Every State has the duty to refrain from intervening, directly or indirectly, in matters within the domestic jurisdiction of
any State. Every State has an inalienable right freely to choose its
political, economic, social or cultural systems, without intervention
by another State, and the right freely to choose the form and degree of its association with other States, subject to its international
obligations.

"2. In accordance with the foregoing principle:

A. Every State shall refrain from the threat or use of force
against the territorial integrity or political independence of
any other State.

B. No State shall take action of such design and effect as
to impair or destroy the political independence or territorial
integrity of another State.

C. Accordingly, no State shall instigate, foment, organize
or otherwise encourage subversive activities directed toward
the violent overthrow of the régime of another State, whether
by invasion, armed attack, infiltration of personnel, terrorism,
clandestine supply of arms, the fomenting of civil strife, or
other forcible means. In particular, States shall not employ
such means to impose or attempt to impose upon another
State a specific form of Government or mode of social organization.

D. The right of States in accordance with international law
to take appropriate measures to defend themselves individual-
ly or collectively against intervention is a fundamental element of the inherent right of self-defence.

"3. Nothing in the foregoing shall be interpreted as derogating
from

A. The generally recognized freedom of States to seek to
influence the policies and actions of other States, in accordance with international law and settled international practice

398

and in a manner compatible with the principle of sovereign equality of States and the duty to co-operate in accordance with the Charter;

B. The relevant provisions of the Charter of the United Nations relating to the maintenance of international peace and security, in particular those contained in Chapters IV through VIII."

This bibliography contains most of the works cited in the text, omitting those that contributed in a minor way only to the development of the argument, and including other sources which were important but general. In the section, "Articles, Essays, and Pamphlets," I have not included material published in works listed in the "Books" section. In the section on "Documents," United States Department of State Bulletins have not been included, nor have United Nations Official Records; both are fully recorded in the text.

BOOKS

Acheson, D. *Present at the Creation: My Years in the State Department*. New York, W. W. Norton, 1969.

Alexander, R. J. *Communism in Latin America*. New Brunswick, N.J., Rutgers University Press, 1957.

Alperovitz, G. *Atomic Diplomacy: Hiroshima and Potsdam*. New York, Simon & Schuster, 1965.

Armstrong, H. F. *Tito and Goliath*. London, Gollancz, 1951.

Aron, R. *Peace and War*. London, Wiedenfeld & Nicolson, 1966.

Baade, H. W. (ed.) *The Soviet Impact on International Law*. Dobbs Ferry, N.Y., Oceana, 1965.

Bagehot, W. *Biographical Studies*. Ed. R. H. Hutton. 2d ed. London, Longmans, 1899.

Bailey, T. A. *A Diplomatic History of the American People*. 5th ed. New York, Appleton-Century-Crofts, 1955.

Ball, G. W. *The Discipline of Power*. Boston, Little Brown, 1968.

Barnet, R. J. *Intervention and Revolution: The United States in the Third World*. New York, World Publishing Company, 1968.

Beesley, A. H. *Life of Danton*. London, Longmans, 1899.

Bell, C. *Negotiation from Strength*. London, Chatto & Windus, 1962.

Beloff, M. *The Foreign Policy of Soviet Russia 1929–1941*. 2 vols. London, Oxford University Press, 1947, 1949.

Beloff, M. *Soviet Policy in the Far East, 1944–1951*. London, Oxford University Press, 1953.

Bemis, S. F. *The Latin American Policy of the United States*. New York, Harcourt Brace, 1943.

———. *John Quincy Adams and the Foundations of American Foreign Policy*. New York, Knopf, 1949.

Benn, S. I., and Peters, R. S. *Social Principles and the Democratic State*. London, Allen & Unwin, 1959.

Berle, A. A. *Latin America: Diplomacy and Reality*. New York, Harper, 1962.

Bernard, M. *On the Principle of Non-Intervention*. Oxford, J. H. & J. Parker, 1860.

Black, C. E. and Falk, R. A., eds. *The Future of the International Legal Order*. Vol. III. *Conflict Management*. Princeton, N.J., Princeton University Press, 1971.

———, and Thornton, T. P., eds. *Communism and Revolution*. Princeton, N.J., Princeton University Press, 1964.

Borkenau, F. *The Communist International*. London, Faber & Faber, 1938.

———. *European Communism*. London, Faber & Faber, 1953.

Boulding, K. E. *The Impact of the Social Sciences*. New Brunswick, N.J., Rutgers University Press, 1966.

Bowett, D. W. *Self-Defence in International Law*. Manchester, Manchester University Press, 1958.

Brierly, J. L. *The Outlook for International Law*. Oxford, Clarendon Press, 1944.

———. *The Basis of Obligation in International Law*. Ed. Sir Hersch Lauterpacht & C.H.M. Waldock. Oxford, Clarendon Press, 1958.

———. *The Law of Nations*. Ed. C.H.M. Waldock. 6th ed. Oxford, Clarendon Press, 1963.

Bright, J., and Thorold Rogers, J. E. *Speeches on Questions of Public Policy by Richard Cobden, M.P.* 2 vols. London, Macmillan, 1870.

Brownlie, I. *International Law and the Use of Force by States*. London, Oxford University Press, 1963.

Brzezinski, Z. K. *The Soviet Bloc*. Rev. and enl. ed. Cambridge, Mass., Harvard University Press, 1967.

Burton, J. W. *International Relations: A General Theory*. Cambridge, Cambridge University Press, 1965.

————. *Systems, States, Diplomacy and Rules*. Cambridge, Cambridge University Press, 1968.

Butterfield, H. and Wight, M., eds. *Diplomatic Investigations*. London, Allen & Unwin, 1966.

Calvocoressi, P. *World Order and New States*. London, Chatto & Windus, 1962.

The Cambridge History of British Foreign Policy, 1783–1919, Ed. A. W. Ward and G. P. Gooch. Vol. ii. Cambridge, Cambridge University Press, 1923.

The Cambridge Modern History, Ed. A. W. Ward, G. W. Prothero, and S. Leathes. Vols. vii, x, and xi. Cambridge, Cambridge University Press, 1904, 1907, 1909.

Carr, E. H. *The Twenty Years' Crisis*. 2d ed. London, Macmillan, 1946.

————. *The Bolshevik Revolution*. 3 vols. Harmondsworth, Penguin Books, 1956.

Cattell, D. T. *Communism and the Spanish Civil War*. Berkeley, Calif., University of California Press, 1956.

————. *Soviet Diplomacy and the Spanish Civil War*. Berkeley, Calif., University of California Press, 1957.

Chamberlin, W. H. *The Russian Revolution 1917–1921*. 2 vols. London, Macmillan, 1935.

Chen, T. C. *The International Law of Recognition*. Ed. L. C. Green. London, Stevens, 1951.

Cobden, R. *The Political Writings of Richard Cobden*. Ed. F. W. Chesson. London, Cassell, 1886.

Cooper, C. L. *The Lost Crusade: America in Vietnam*. New York, Dodd, Mead, 1970.

Coplin, W. D. *The Functions of International Law*. Chicago, Rand McNally, 1966.

Corbett, P. E. *Law and Society in the Relations of States*. New York, Harcourt Brace, 1951.

Cottam, R. W. *Competitive Interference and Twentieth Century Diplomacy*. Pittsburgh, University of Pittsburgh Press, 1967.

Creasy, Sir E. S. *First Platform of International Law*. London, John van Voorst, 1876.

Dallin, D. J. *Soviet Foreign Policy After Stalin*. London, Macmillan, 1960.

Dawson, W. H. *Richard Cobden and Foreign Policy*. London, Allen & Unwin, 1926.

403

Dedijer, V. *Tito Speaks.* London, Wiedenfeld & Nicolson, 1953.

Dennett, T. *Americans in Eastern Asia.* New York, Barnes & Noble, 1941.

Deutsch, K. W., and Hoffmann, S. *The Relevance of International Law.* Cambridge, Mass., Schenkman, 1968.

Dickinson, E. D. *The Equality of States in International Law.* Cambridge, Mass., Harvard University Press, 1920.

Dinerstein, H. S. *Intervention Against Communism.* Baltimore, Johns Hopkins Press, 1967.

———. *Fifty Years of Soviet Foreign Policy.* Baltimore, Johns Hopkins Press, 1968.

Donelan, M. *The Ideas of American Foreign Policy.* London, Chapman & Hall, 1963.

Dozer, D. M. *Are We Good Neighbors?* Gainesville, University of Florida Press, 1959.

Draper, T. *Castro's Revolution: Myths and Realities.* New York, Praeger, 1962.

———. *Castroism: Theory and Practice.* London, Pall Mall, 1965.

———. *Abuse of Power.* New York, Viking Press, 1967.

———. *The Dominican Revolt.* New York, Commentary, 1968.

Eckstein, H., ed. *Internal War.* New York, Free Press of Glencoe, 1964.

Eden, Sir A., Earl of Avon. *The Eden Memoirs: Full Circle,* London, Cassell, 1960.

Eisenhower, D. D. *Mandate for Change, 1953–1956.* New York, Doubleday, 1963.

———. *Waging Peace, 1956–1961.* London, Heinemann, 1966.

d'Entrèves, A. P. *Natural Law.* London, Hutchinson, 1951.

Falk, R. A. *Law, Morality, and War in the Contemporary World.* London, Pall Mall, 1963.

———. *The Role of Domestic Courts in the International Legal Order.* Syracuse, Syracuse University Press, 1964.

———. *Legal Order in a Violent World.* Princeton, N.J., Princeton University Press, 1968.

———, and Black, C. E., eds. *The Future of the International Legal Order.* Vol. I. *Trends and Patterns.* Princeton, N.J., Princeton University Press, 1969.

———. *The Status of Law in International Society.* Princeton, N.J., Princeton University Press, 1970.

————. *This Endangered Planet*. New York, Random House, 1971.

————, ed. *The International Law of Civil War*. Baltimore, Johns Hopkins Press, 1971.

————, ed. *The Vietnam War and International Law*. 3 vols. Princeton, N.J., Princeton University Press, 1968, 1969, 1972.

Fenwick, C. G. *International Law*. 4th ed. New York, Appleton-Century-Crofts, 1965.

Fischer, L. *The Soviets in World Affairs*. 2 vols. London, Cape, 1930.

Fleming, D. F. *The Cold War and its Origins*. 2 vols. London, Allen & Unwin, 1961.

Fried, J.H.E. (rapporteur) *Vietnam and International Law*. Flanders, N.J., O'Hare, 1967.

Franck, T. M., and Weisband, E. *Word Politics: Verbal Strategy Among the Superpowers*. New York, Oxford University Press, 1971.

Friedmann, W. F. *The Changing Structure of International Law*. New York, Columbia University Press, 1964.

Friedrich, C. J. *Inevitable Peace*. Cambridge, Mass., Harvard University Press, 1948.

————, ed. *Revolution*. New York, Atherton Press, 1966.

Fulbright, J. W. *The Arrogance of Power*. London, Cape, 1967.

Gettleman, M. E. *Vietnam: History, Documents and Opinions on a Major World Crisis*. Harmondsworth, Penguin Books, 1966.

Gittings, J. *Survey of the Sino-Soviet Dispute*. London, Oxford University Press, 1968.

Goebel, J. *The Recognition Policy of the United States*. New York, Columbia University Press, 1915.

Goodman, E. R. *The Soviet Design for a World State*. New York, Columbia University Press, 1960.

Goodrich, L. M., and Hambro, E. *Charter of the United Nations*. 2d rev. ed. London, Stevens, 1949.

Graber, D. A. *Crisis Diplomacy*. Washington, D.C., Public Affairs Press, 1959.

Griffin, C. C. *The United States and the Disruption of the Spanish Empire 1810–1822*. New York, Columbia University Press, 1937.

Griffith, W. E. *The Sino-Soviet Rift*. London, Allen & Unwin, 1964.

Grob, F. *The Relativity of War and Peace*. New Haven, Conn., Yale University Press, 1949.

Grotius, H. *De Jure Belli ac Pacis*. 1646 ed. Trans. F. W. Kelsey et al. Carnegie Classics of International Law. New York, Oceana, 1964.

Hall, W. E. *A Treatise on International Law*. Ed. A. Pearce Higgins. 8th ed. Oxford, Clarendon Press, 1924.

Halle, L. J. *American Foreign Policy: Theory and Reality*. London, Allen & Unwin, 1960.

Halpern, M. *The Politics of Social Change in the Middle East and North Africa*. Princeton, N.J., Princeton University Press, 1963.

Harcourt, Sir W. G.G.V.V. *Letters by 'Historicus' on some Questions of International Law*. London, Macmillan, 1863.

Hart, H.L.A. *The Concept of Law*. Oxford, Clarendon Press, 1961.

Henkin, L. *How Nations Behave*. London, Pall Mall, 1968.

Hershey, A. S. *The Essentials of International Public Law and Organization*. New York, Macmillan, 1939.

Herz, J. H. *International Politics in the Atomic Age*. New York, Columbia University Press, 1959.

Higgins, R. *The Development of International Law through the Political Organs of the United Nations*. London, Oxford University Press, 1963.

Hilsman, R. *To Move a Nation*. New York, Doubleday, 1967.

Hinsley, F. H. *Power and the Pursuit of Peace*. Cambridge, Cambridge University Press, 1963.

——. *Sovereignty*. London, Watts, 1966.

Hobbes, T. *Leviathan*. Ed. M. Oakeshott, Oxford, Blackwell, 1946.

Hobson, J. A. *Richard Cobden: The International Man*. London, Unwin, 1919.

Hodges, H. G. *The Doctrine of Intervention*. Princeton, N.J., The Banner Press, 1915.

Hoffmann, S. *The State of War*. New York, Praeger, 1965.

——. *Gulliver's Troubles, or the setting of American Foreign Policy*. New York, McGraw-Hill, 1968.

——, ed. *Conditions of World Order*. Boston, Houghton Mifflin, 1968.

Holbraad, C. *The Concert of Europe: A Study in German and British International Theory 1815–1914*. London, Longmans, 1970.

————, ed. *Super Powers and World Order*. Canberra, Australian National University Press, 1971.

Hoopes, T. *The Limits of Intervention*. New York, David McKay, 1969.

Horowitz, D. *From Yalta to Vietnam*. Harmondsworth, Penguin Books, 1969.

Hudson, G. F., Lowenthal, R., and MacFarquhar, R. *The Sino-Soviet Dispute*. London, The China Quarterly, 1961.

James, A. M. *The Politics of Peace-Keeping*. London, Chatto & Windus, 1969.

Jamgotch, N. *Soviet-East European Dialogue*. Stanford, Calif., Stanford University Press, 1968.

Jenks, C. W. *The Common Law of Mankind*. London, Stevens, 1958.

————. *A New World of Law?* London, Longmans, 1969.

Jessup, P. C. *A Modern Law of Nations*. New York, Macmillan, 1949.

————. *Transnational Law*. New Haven, Conn., Yale University Press, 1956.

Jones, J. M. *The Fifteen Weeks*. New York, Viking Press, 1955.

Jones, R. E. *The Functional Analysis of Politics*. London, Routledge & Kegan Paul, 1967.

Kaplan, M. *System and Process in International Politics*. New York, Wiley, 1957.

————, and Katzenbach, N. deB. *The Political Foundations of International Law*. New York, Wiley, 1961.

Kelsen, H. *The Law of the United Nations*. London, Stevens, 1950.

————. *Principles of International Law*. Ed. R. W. Tucker. 2d ed. New York, Holt, Rinehart & Winston, 1966.

Kennan, G. F. *American Diplomacy, 1900–1950*. New York, Mentor Books, 1952.

————. *Russia and the West Under Lenin and Stalin*. London, Hutchinson, 1961.

Kent, J. *Commentaries on American Law*. 4 vols. 7th ed. New York, Kent, 1851.

Keohane, R. O., and Nye, J. S., eds. *Transnational Relations and World Politics*. Cambridge, Mass., Harvard University Press, 1972.

Kissinger, H. *A World Restored: Metternich, Castlereagh and the Problem of Peace 1812–1822*. London, Wiedenfeld & Nicolson, 1957.

Kolko, G. *The Politics of War: The World and United States Foreign Policy, 1943–1945*. New York, Random House, 1968.

Kooijmans, P. H. *The Doctrine of the Legal Equality of States.* Leyden, A. W. Sythoff, 1964.

Kozhevnikov, F. I., ed. *International Law*. Moscow, Foreign Languages Publishing House, n.d.

Kulski, W. W. *Peaceful Coexistence*. Chicago, H. Regnery, 1959.

Larson, A., and Jenks, C. W., eds. *Sovereignty Within the Law.* New York, Oceana, 1965.

Lauterpacht, H. *Private Law Sources and Analogies in International Law*. London, Longmans, 1927; rept. New York, Archon Books, 1970.

———. *The Function of Law in the International Community.* Oxford, Clarendon Press, 1933.

———. *Recognition in International Law*. Cambridge, Cambridge University Press, 1947.

———. *International Law and Human Rights*. London, Stevens, 1950.

Lawrence, T. J. *Principles of International Law*. Ed. P. H. Winfield, 7th ed. London, Macmillan, 1925.

Lefebvre, G. *The French Revolution: from its Origins to 1793*. Trans. E. M. Evanson. New York, Columbia University Press, 1962.

Lippmann, W. *The Cold War*. New York, Harper, 1947.

Liska, G. *Imperial America: The International Politics of Primacy*. Baltimore, Johns Hopkins Press, 1967.

Loewenstein, K. *Political Reconstruction*. New York, Macmillan, 1946.

Lorimer, J. *The Institutes of the Law of Nations*. 2 vols. Edinburgh, Blackwood, 1884.

Lowenthal, R. *World Communism*. New York, Oxford University Press, 1964.

Mackintosh, J. M. *Strategy and Tactics of Soviet Foreign Policy.* London, Oxford University Press, 1962.

Manning, C.A.W. *The Nature of International Society*. London, Bell, 1962.

Martens, G. F. von. *The Law of Nations*. Trans. Wm. Cobbett, 4th ed. London, Wm. Cobbett, 1829.

Martin, C. E. *The Policy of the United States as Regards Intervention*. New York, Columbia University Press, 1921.

Matthews, H. L. *The Cuban Story*. New York, George Braziller, 1961.

———, ed. *The United States and Latin America*. 2d ed. New York, Prentice-Hall, 1963.

Mattingly, G. *Renaissance Diplomacy*. Harmondsworth, Penguin Books, 1965.

Mazzini, J. *Life and Writings of Joseph Mazzini*. 6 vols. London, Smith, Elder, 1890.

McDougal, M. S., et al. *Studies in World Public Order*. New Haven, Conn., Yale University Press, 1960.

McKenzie, K. E. *Comintern and World Revolution, 1928–1943*. New York, Columbia University Press, 1964.

McWhinney, E. *Law, Foreign Policy and the East-West Détente*. Toronto, Toronto University Press, 1964.

———. *"Peaceful Coexistence" and Soviet-Western International Law*. Leyden, A. W. Sythoff, 1964.

———. *International Law and World Revolution*. Leyden, A. W. Sythoff, 1967.

Merton, R. K. *Social Theory and Social Structure*. Glencoe, Ill. Free Press of Glencoe, 1949.

Mill, J. S. *Dissertations and Discussions: Political, Philosophical, and Historical*. 4 vols. London, Longmans, 1875.

Miller, J.D.B. *The Politics of the Third World*. London, Oxford University Press, 1966.

Miller, L. B. *World Order and Local Disorder: the United Nations and Internal Conflicts*. Princeton, N.J., Princeton University Press, 1967.

Millis, W., ed. *The Forrestal Diaries*. London, Cassell, 1952.

Moore, J. B. *A Digest of International Law*. 8 vols. Washington, D.C., Government Printing Office, 1906.

Moore, J. N. *Law and the Indo-China War*. Princeton, N.J., Princeton University Press, 1972.

———, ed. *Law and Civil War in the Modern World*. Baltimore, Johns Hopkins Press, 1973.

Morgenthau, H. J. *Politics Among Nations*. 4th ed. Knopf, 1967.

Morley, J. *Life of Richard Cobden*. 2 vols. London, Chapman & Hall, 1881.

Nadel, S. F. *The Foundations of Social Anthropology*. London, Cohen & West, 1953.

———. *The Theory of Social Structure*. London, Cohen & West, 1957.

409

Nawaz, M. K., et. al. *The Legal Principles Governing Friendly Relations Among States.* Leyden, A. W. Sijthoff, 1966.

Nevins, A. *The Diary of John Quincy Adams, 1794–1845.* New York, Longmans, 1929.

The New Cambridge Modern History. Vols. VII, IX, and X, Cambridge, Cambridge University Press, 1960, 1965, 1965.

Nollau, G. *International Communism and World Revolution.* London, Hollis & Carter, 1961.

Nussbaum, A. *A Concise History of the Law of Nations.* Rev. ed. New York, Macmillan, 1954.

Oppenheim, L. *International Law: A Treatise.* 2 vols. Ed. H. Lauterpacht. 8th ed. London, Longmans, 1955.

Osgood, R. E., and Tucker, R. W. *Force, Order, and Justice.* Baltimore, Johns Hopkins Press, 1967.

Padelford, N. J. *International Law and Diplomacy in the Spanish Civil Strife.* New York, Macmillan, 1939.

Parsons, T. *The Social System.* London, Tavistock Publications in collaboration with Routledge & Kegan Paul, 1952.

Perkins, D. *Hands Off: A History of the Monroe Doctrine.* Boston, Little Brown, 1948.

Phillimore, R. *Commentaries on International Law.* 4 vols. London, Butterworth, 1871–1874.

Plank, J., ed. *Cuba and the United States.* Washington, D.C., The Brookings Institution, 1967.

Pufendorf, S. *De Jure Naturae et Gentium.* 1688 ed. Trans. C. H. and W. A. Oldfather. Carnegie Classics of International Law. New York, Oceana, 1964.

Radcliffe-Brown, A. R. *Structure and Function in Primitive Society.* London, Cohen & West, 1952.

Rajan, M. S. *United Nations and Domestic Jurisdiction.* Calcutta, Orient Longmans, 1958.

Ramundo, B. A. *Peaceful Coexistence: International Law in the Building of Communism.* Baltimore, Johns Hopkins Press, 1967.

Raskin, M. G., and Fall, B. B., eds. *The Vietnam Reader.* Rev. ed. New York, Vintage Books, 1967.

Robinson, R. *Definition.* Oxford, Clarendon Press, 1950.

Rosenau, J. N., ed. *International Aspects of Civil Strife.* Princeton, N.J., Princeton University Press, 1964.

———, Davis, V., and East, M., eds. *The Analysis of International Politics,* New York, Free Press, 1972.

410

Ross, A. *A Text Book of International Law*. London, Longmans, 1947.

———. *Constitution of the United Nations*. Copenhagen, Ejnar Munksgaard, 1950.

Runciman, W. G. *Social Science and Political Theory*. 2d ed. Cambridge, Cambridge University Press, 1969.

Salvemini, G. *Mazzini*. Trans. I. M. Rawson, London, Cape, 1956.

Schiffer, W. *The Legal Community of Mankind*. New York, Columbia University Press, 1951.

Schlesinger, A. M. *A Thousand Days: John F. Kennedy in the White House*. London, Deutsch, 1965.

———. *The Bitter Heritage: Vietnam and American Democracy 1941–1966*. London, Deutsch, 1967.

Schwarzenberger, G. *Power Politics*. 3d ed. London, Stevens, 1964.

———. *International Law and Order*. London, Stevens, 1971.

Scott, A. M. *The Revolution in Statecraft: Informal Penetration*. New York, Random House, 1965.

Seton-Watson, H. *The East European Revolution*. London, Methuen, 1950.

———. *The Pattern of Communist Revolution*. London, Methuen, 1953.

Seton-Watson, R. W. *Britain in Europe 1789–1914*. Cambridge, Cambridge University Press, 1937.

Sheehan, N., et al. *The Pentagon Papers*. New York, Bantam Books, 1971.

Smith, W. H. *Intervention in Civil Strife and International Order*. Ph.D. dissertation, Australian National University, Canberra, 1970.

Sorensen, T. C. *Kennedy*. London, Pan Books, 1965.

Southgate, D. G. *The Most English Minister*. London, Macmillan, 1966.

Sprout, H. and M. *Toward a Politics of the Planet Earth*. New York, van Nostrand, Reinhold, 1971.

Stanger, R. J., ed. *Essays on Intervention*. Columbus, Ohio State University Press, 1964.

Stankiewicz, W. J., ed. *In Defense of Sovereignty*. New York, Oxford University Press, 1969.

Stapleton, A. G. *Intervention and Non-Intervention: or the Foreign Policy of Great Britain from 1790 to 1865*. London, J. Murray, 1866.

411

Stark, W. *The Fundamental Forms of Social Thought*. London, Routledge & Kegan Paul, 1962.

Stone, J. *Aggression and World Order*. Berkeley, Calif., University of California Press, 1958.

————. *Legal Controls of International Conflict*. 2d imp. rev. New York, Rinehart, 1959.

Stowell, E. C. *Intervention in International Law*. Washington, Byrne, 1921.

Tannenbaum, F. *The American Tradition in Foreign Policy*. Norman, Okla., University of Oklahoma Press, 1955.

Taracouzio, T. A. *The Soviet Union and International Law*. New York, Macmillan, 1935.

Taylor, A.J.P. *The Trouble Makers*. London, Panther Books, 1969.

Temperley, H.W.V. *The Foreign Policy of Canning, 1822–1827*. London, Bell, 1925.

Thomas. A.V.W., and A. J. *Non-Intervention: The Law and its Import in the Americas*. Dallas, Tex., Southern Methodist University Press, 1956.

Thompson, J. M. *The French Revolution*. Oxford, Blackwell, 1947.

Truman, H. S *The Truman Memoirs*. 2 vols. London, Hodder & Stoughton, 1955, 1956.

Ulam, A. B. *Titoism and the Cominform*. Cambridge, Mass., Harvard University Press, 1952.

————. *Expansion and Coexistence: The History of Soviet Foreign Policy 1917–1967*. London, Secker & Warburg, 1968.

Vattel, E. de. *The Law of Nations or the Principles of Natural Law*. 1758 ed. Trans. C. G. Fenwick. Carnegie Classics of International Law. Washington, D.C., Carnegie Institution, 1916.

Visscher, C., de. *Theory and Reality in Public International Law*. Trans. P. E. Corbett, Princeton, N.J., Princeton University Press, 1957.

Warburg, J. P. *The United States in the Post-War World*. London, Gollancz, 1966.

Webster, Sir C. K. *The Foreign Policy of Castlereagh 1815–1822*. London, Bell, 1925.

————. *The Foreign Policy of Castlereagh 1812–1815*. London, Bell, 1931.

————. *The Foreign Policy of Palmerston 1830–1841*. 2 vols. London, Bell, 1951.

Westlake, J. *The Collected Papers of John Westlake on Public International Law*. Ed. L. Oppenheim. Cambridge, Cambridge University Press, 1914.

Wheaton, H. *Elements of International Law*. Ed. R. H. Dana, 1866. Carnegie Classics of International Law. Oxford, Clarendon Press, 1936.

Whitaker, A. P. *The United States and the Independence of Latin America 1800–1830*. New York, Russell & Russell, 1962.

Windsor, P., and Roberts, A. *Czechoslovakia 1968*. London, Chatto & Windus, 1969.

Wise, D., and Ross, T. B. *The Invisible Government*. New York, Random House, 1964.

Wolfers, A. *Discord and Collaboration: Essays on International Politics*. Baltimore, Johns Hopkins Press, 1962.

Wolff, C. *Jus Gentium Methodo Scientifica Pertractatum*. 1764 ed. Trans. J. H. Drake. Carnegie Classics of International Law. New York, Oceana, 1964.

Wood, B. *The Making of the Good Neighbor Policy*. New York, Columbia University Press, 1961.

Woodward, E. L., et al. *Foundations for World Order*. Denver, University of Denver Press, 1949.

Wright, Q. *International Law and the United Nations*. New Delhi, Asia Publishing House, 1960.

———. *The Role of International Law in the Elimination of War*. Manchester, Manchester University Press, 1961.

Zagoria, D. S. *The Sino-Soviet Conflict 1956–1961*. Princeton, N.J., Princeton University Press, 1962.

Zimmerman, W. *Soviet Perspectives on International Relations, 1956–1967*. Princeton, N.J., Princeton University Press, 1969.

ARTICLES, ESSAYS, AND PAMPHLETS

Baker, P. J. "The Doctrine of the Legal Equality of States," *British Yearbook of International Law*, Vol. IV, 1923–1924.

Baratashvili, D. "International Law Principles of Peaceful Coexistence," *International Affairs* (Moscow), February, 1972.

Beloff, M. "The Theory of Soviet Foreign Policy," *Soviet Studies*, Vol. III, No. 4, April 1951.

———. "Reflections on Intervention," *Journal of International Affairs*, Vol. XXII, No. 2, 1968.

Bemis, S. F. "Washington's Farewell Address: A Foreign Policy of Independence," *American Historical Review*, Vol. XXXIX, No. 2, January 1934.

Bonsal, P. W. "Cuba, Castro and the United States," *Foreign Affairs*, Vol. 45, No. 2, January 1967.

Buchan, A. "A World Restored?" *Foreign Affairs*, Vol. 50, No. 4, July 1972.

Bull, H. "Order vs. Justice in International Society," *Political Studies*, Vol. XIX, No. 3, September 1971.

Chakste, M. "Soviet Concepts of the State, International Law and Sovereignty," *American Journal of International Law*, Vol. 43, No. 1, 1949.

Claude, I. M. "The United Nations and the Use of Force," *International Conciliation*, No. 532, March 1961.

Coplin, W. D. "International Law and Assumptions about the State System," *World Politics*, Vol. XVII, No. 4, July 1965.

Croan, M. "Communist International Relations," *Survey*, No. 42, June 1962.

Davis, K. "The Myth of Functional Analysis as a Special Method in Sociology and Anthropology," *American Sociological Review*, Vol. 24, No. 6, December 1959.

Deutscher, I. "The French Revolution and the Russian Revolution: Some Suggestive Analogies," *World Politics*, Vol. IV, No. 3, April 1952.

Dowse, R. E. "A Functionalist's Logic," *World Politics*, Vol. XVIII, No. 4, July 1966.

Farlow, R. L. "Romanian Foreign Policy: A case of Partial Alignment," *Problems of Communism*, Vol. XX, November-December 1971.

Fenwick, C. G. "Intervention: Individual and Collective," *American Journal of International Law*, Vol. 39, No. 4, 1945.

Finch, G. A. "The American Society of International Law 1906–1956," *American Journal of International Law*, Vol. 50, No. 2, 1956.

Fitzmaurice, Sir G. "The Foundations of the Authority of International Law and the Problem of Enforcement," *Modern Law Review*, Vol. 19, No. 1, January 1956.

Franck, T. M. "Who Killed Article 2(4)?" *American Journal of International Law*, Vol. 64, No. 5, October 1970.

Friedmann, W. "United States Policy and the Crisis of International Law," *American Journal of International Law*, Vol. 59, No. 4, 1965.

414

————. "Interventionism, Liberalism and Power Politics: The Unfinished Revolution in International Thinking," *Political Science Quarterly*, Vol. LXXXIII, No. 2, June 1968.

Gafurov, B. "The Soviet Union and the National Liberation Movement," *International Affairs* (Moscow), July 1971.

Garthoff, R. L. "The Tragedy of Hungary," *Problems of Communism*, Vol. VI, No. 1, January-February 1957.

Goodrich, L. M. "The United Nations and Domestic Jurisdiction," *International Organization*, Vol. III, 1949.

Graber, D. A. "The Truman and Eisenhower Doctrines in the Light of the Doctrine of Non-Intervention," *Political Science Quarterly*, Vol. LXXIII, No. 3, September 1958.

Griffiths, F. "Origins of Peaceful Coexistence: A Historical Note," *Survey*, No. 50, January 1964.

Gross, L. "The Peace of Westphalia, 1648-1948," *American Journal of International Law*, Vol. 42, No. 1, 1948.

Hazard, J. N. "The Soviet Union and International Law," *Soviet Studies*, Vol. I, No. 3, January 1950.

————. "Legal Research on Peaceful Coexistence," *American Journal of International Law*, Vol. 51, No. 1, 1957.

————. "Coexistence Codification Reconsidered," *American Journal of International Law*, Vol. 57, No. 1, 1963.

————. "The Sixth Committee and New Law," *American Journal of International Law*, Vol. 57, No. 3, 1963.

Houben, P. H. "Principles of International Law Concerning Friendly Relations and Co-operation Among States," *American Journal of International Law*, Vol. 61, No. 3, 1967.

Hudson, G. F. "Russia and China," *Survey*, No. 42, June 1962.

Hunter, R., and Windsor, P. "Vietnam and United States Policy in Asia," *International Affairs*, Vol. 44, No. 2, April, 1968.

Kaplan, M. *United States Foreign Policy in Revolutionary Age.* Policy Memorandum No. 25, Center of International Studies, Princeton University, 1961.

Keep, J. "Soviet Foreign Policy: Doctrine and Reality," *Survey*, No. 40, January 1962.

Khrushchev, N. S. *Report of the Central Committee of the Communist Party of the Soviet Union to the Twentieth Party Congress.* Moscow, Foreign Languages Publishing House, 1956.

Korovin, E. "Proletarian Internationalism in World Relations," *International Affairs* (Moscow), February 1958.

Korovin, Y. "Sovereignty and Peace," *International Affairs* (Moscow), September 1960.

———. "International Law Today," *International Affairs* (Moscow), July 1961.

Korowicz, M. St. "The Problem of the International Personality of Individuals," *American Journal of International Law*, Vol. 50, No. 3, 1956.

Kristol, I. "American Intellectuals and Foreign Policy," *Foreign Affairs*, Vol. 45, No. 4, July 1967.

Kuzmin, E. "Sovereignty and National Security," *International Affairs* (Moscow), December 1966.

Labedz, L. "Czechoslovakia and After," *Survey*, No. 69, October 1968.

Laqueur, W. "The Schism," *Survey*, No. 42, June 1962.

Lapenna, I. "International Law viewed through Soviet Eyes," *Year Book of World Affairs*, Vol. 15, 1961.

———. "The Legal Aspects and Political Significance of the Soviet Concept of Coexistence," *International and Comparative Law Quarterly*, Vol. 12, pt. 3, 1963.

Lauterpacht, H. "The Grotian Tradition in International Law," *British Yearbook of International Law*, Vol. XXIII, 1946.

Lee, L. T. "The Mexico City Conference of the United Nations Special Committee on Principles of International Law Concerning Friendly Relations and Co-operation Among States," *International and Comparative Law Quarterly*, Vol. 14, pt. 4, October 1965.

Levin, D. "The Non-Interference Principle Today," *International Affairs* (Moscow), November, 1966.

Levitski, B. "Coexistence within the Bloc," *Survey*, No. 42, June 1962.

Lissitzyn, O. J. "International Law in a Divided World," *International Conciliation*, No. 542, March 1963.

Lowenthal, R. "The Sparrow in the Cage," *Problems of Communism*, Vol. XVII, No. 6, November–December 1968.

Malinowski, B. "Culture," in *Encyclopaedia of the Social Sciences*, New York, Macmillan, 1931.

McWhinney, E. "The 'New' Countries and the 'New' International Law: The United Nations' Special Conference on Friendly Relations and Co-operation Among States," *American Journal of International Law*, Vol. 60, No. 1, 1966.

Modelski, G. "The Corporation in World Society," *Year Book of World Affairs*, Vol. 22, 1968.

Morgenthau, H. J. "To Intervene or Not to Intervene," *Foreign Affairs*, Vol. 45, No. 3, April 1967.

Nicholas, H. G. "Vietnam and the Traditions of American Foreign Policy," *International Affairs*, Vol. 44, No. 2, April 1968.

Onuf, N. G. "The Principle of Non-Intervention, the United Nations, and the International System," *International Organization*, Vol. xxv, No. 2, 1971.

Pachter, H. "The Meaning of Peaceful Coexistence," *Problems of Communism*, Vol. x, No. 1, January–February 1961.

Pavlov, O. "Proletarian Internationalism and Defence of Socialist Gains," *International Affairs* (Moscow), October 1968.

Perkins, D. "John Quincy Adams," in Bemis, ed. *The American Secretaries of State and their Diplomacy*, Vol. iv, New York, Pageant Books, 1958.

Piradov, A. "The Principle of Non-Interference in the Modern World," *International Affairs* (Moscow), January 1966.

Plank, J. N. "The Carribbean: Intervention When and How," *Foreign Affairs*, Vol. 44, No. 1, October 1965.

Rajan, M. S. "The Question of Defining Domestic Jurisdiction," *International Studies* (New Delhi), Vol. i, 1959–1960.

Ramundo, B. A. *The (Soviet) Socialist Theory of International Law*. Institute for Sino-Soviet Studies, George Washington University, January 1964.

Richardson, J. L. "Cold War Revisionism: A Critique," *World Politics*, Vol. xxiv, No. 4, July 1972.

Root, E. "The Declaration of the Rights and Duties of Nations Adopted by the American Institute of International Law," *American Journal of International Law*, Vol. 10, No. 2, 1916.

Rosenau, J. N. "Intervention as a Scientific Concept," *Journal of Conflict Resolution*, Vol. xiii, June 1969.

Rosenstock, R. "The Declaration of Principles of International Law Concerning Friendly Relations: A Survey," *American Journal of International Law*, Vol. 65, No. 5, 1971.

Sacksteder, W. "Kant's Analysis of International Relations," *Journal of Philosophy*, Vol. 51, No. 25, 1954.

Sanakoyev, S. "The Basis of the Relations Between the Socialist Countries," *International Affairs* (Moscow), July 1958.

Schwarz, U. *Great Power Intervention in the Modern World*. Adelphi Paper, No. 55, London, Institute for Strategic Studies, March 1969.

Schwarzenberger, G. "Hegemonial Intervention," *Year Book of World Affairs*, Vol. 13, 1959.

Scott, A. M. "Non-Intervention and Conditional Intervention," *Journal of International Affairs*, Vol. xxii, No. 2, 1968.

Starushenko, G. "The National-Liberation Movement and the Struggle for Peace," *International Affairs* (Moscow), October 1963.

Stone, J. "A Common Law for Mankind?" *International Studies* (Delhi), Vol. i, 1959–1960.

Tannenbaum, F. "The United States and Latin America," *Political Science Quarterly*, Vol. lxxvi, No. 2, June 1961.

Taylor, P. B. "The Guatemalan Affair: A Critique of United States Foreign Policy," *American Political Science Review*, Vol. l, No. 3, September 1956.

Trukhanovsky, V. "Proletarian Internationalism and Peaceful Coexistence," *International Affairs* (Moscow), August 1966.

Tunkin, G. "The Soviet Union and International Law," *International Affairs* (Moscow), November 1959.

————. "International Law and Ideological Struggle," *International Affairs* (Moscow), November 1971.

Vasilyev, V. "Peaceful Coexistence: The Basis of International Relations," *International Affairs* (Moscow), March 1968.

Vincent, R. J. "The Functions of Functionalism in International Relations," *Year Book of World Affairs*, Vol. 27, 1973.

Weinberg, A. K. "The Historical Meaning of the American Doctrine of Isolation," *American Political Science Review*, Vol. xxxiv, No. 4, August 1940.

Wight, M. *Power Politics*. London, Royal Institute of International Affairs, 1949.

Winfield, P. H. "The History of Intervention in International Law," *British Yearbook of International Law*, Vol. iii, 1922–1923.

————. "The Grounds of Intervention in International Law," *British Yearbook of International Law*, Vol. v, 1924.

Wright, Q. "Intervention, 1956," *American Journal of International Law*, Vol. 51, No. 2, 1957.

————. "The United States Intervention in the Lebanon," *American Journal of International Law*, Vol. 53, No. 1, 1959.

————. "Subversive Intervention," *American Journal of International Law*, Vol. 54, No. 3, 1960.

Yost, C. W. "World Order and American Responsibility," *Foreign Affairs*, Vol. 47, No. 1, October, 1968.

Young, G. B. "Intervention under the Monroe Doctrine: The Olney

Corollary," *Political Science Quarterly*, Vol. LVII, No. 2, June 1942.

Young, O. R. "Intervention and International Systems," *Journal of International Affairs*, Vol. XXII, No. 2, 1968.

Zimmern, Sir A. "International Law and Social Consciousness," *Transactions of the Grotius Society*, Vol. 20, 1934.

COLLECTIONS OF DOCUMENTS

Anderson, F. M., ed. *The Constitutions and Other Select Documents Illustrative of the History of France 1789–1907.* 2nd edition, New York, Russell & Russell, 1967.

Bass, R., and Marbury, E., eds. *The Soviet-Yugoslav Controversy, 1948–1958: A Documentary Record.* New York, Prospect Books, 1959.

Commager, H. S., ed. *Documents of American History.* 5th ed. New York, Appleton-Century-Crofts, 1949.

Dallin, A., ed. *Diversity in International Communism.* New York, Columbia University Press, 1963.

Degras, J., ed. *Soviet Documents on Foreign Policy.* 3 vols. London, Oxford University Press, 1951, 1952, 1953.

———, ed. *The Communist International, 1919–1943: Documents.* 3 vols. London, Oxford University Press, 1956, 1960, 1965.

Eudin, X. J., and Fisher, H. H., eds. *Soviet Russia and the West, 1920–1927.* Stanford, Calif., Stanford University Press, 1957.

———, and North, R. C., eds. *Soviet Russia and the East, 1920–1927.* Stanford, Calif., Stanford University Press, 1957.

Gantenbein, J. W., ed. *The Evolution of Our Latin American Policy: A Documentary Record.* New York, Columbia University Press, 1950.

The Soviet-Yugoslav Dispute. Royal Institute for International Affairs, London, 1948.

Temperley, H.W.V., and Penson, L. M., eds. *Foundations of British Foreign Policy from Pitt (1782) to Salisbury (1902), or Documents Old and New.* Cambridge, Cambridge University Press, 1938.

Zinner, P. E., ed. *National Communism and Popular Revolt in Eastern Europe.* New York, Columbia University Press, 1956.

communism (*cont.*)
and Americas, 208; and Brezhnev
Doctrine, 177; ideology of, 170;
and intervention, 196n, 199–202,
222n, 342; national, 66, 67;
stages in building of, 162, 174;
and United States, 192, 196n,
199–202, 217, 222n, 223, 225,
230; and Western intervention,
12n. *See also* international communism
communist bloc, 170, 172, 174–175,
353, 354–355; and Czechoslovakia, 176; and Hungary, 170,
176; and "new law," 259; and
new states, 274; and order, 274,
315; and peaceful coexistence,
387; and principle of nonintervention, 248–251, 261, 387; and
South African issue, 261, 264–
266; at United Nations, 243,
248–251, 261, 264–266; and wars
of national liberation, 347
Communist Information Bureau
(Cominform), 162, 163–164
Communist International (Comintern), 152–154, 155–156, 159,
162, 163, 164; and China, 159;
creation of, 152; Executive
Committee of (ECCI), 156, 157,
159; fifth congress of, 156; first
congress of, 152; fourth congress
of, 156, 157; July Theses of, 153;
presidium of, 156; third congress
of, 156, 159; second congress of,
153, 155–156; seventh congress
of, 156, 157; sixth congress of,
156; united front strategy of,
160, 161
Communist Party of the Soviet
Union (CPSU), 165, 183n; and
Chinese Communist Party (CCP),
173–174; eighteenth congress of,
159n; seventh congress of, 148;
and Soviet-Yugoslav dispute,
164; Tito and, 164n; twentieth
congress of, 165, 166, 168, 171,
180; twenty-first congress of, 171,

174; twenty-second congress of,
174n, 175, 180
community, 24, 35, 38, 367, 369.
See also international community,
international society, society,
universal community of mankind
Concert of Europe, 340n–341n
conflict of laws, 300n
Congo, 5, 231, 233, 248, 267
Congress of Soviets, Second, 145;
Seventh, 150; Sixth, 149; Third,
146
Congress (of United States), 117,
120, 124, 131, 133n, 134, 136,
137, 138n, 189, 191, 208, 210,
215, 223, 224, 312n
Congress of Vienna, 59, 341. *See
also* Vienna Settlement
Congress System of Diplomacy, 73,
82, 84, 85, 89
conservative international theory,
73–74, 340n, 341
Constantinople, 49, 50
constitutional government, 71n, 78,
84, 89, 91, 92, 95, 97, 122–123,
127
contagion, doctrine of, 289, 305,
341
containment, 191–192, 228
continental solidarity, American
doctrine of, 193, 196, 207
Cooper, C. L., 226n
Coplin, W. D., 334n
Corcyra, 11
Corfu Channel case, 313–314
Corinth, 11
Corsica, 66
Costa Rica, 269n
Cottam, R. W., 370n, 371n, 372n
Council of People's Commissars
(Sovnarkom), 147, 150n, 151,
152
counterinsurgency, 361
counterintervention, 53, 132, 262n,
291–292, 317, 320, 322n, 323,
341; and balance of power, 342;
Canning and, 87–88, 89; Castlereagh and, 79; and Cold War,
305; and interbloc noninterven-

nental tradition of, 20–21; communist views of at United Nations, 237, 238, 248–251, 264–266, 274; and debate on status of United Nations General Assembly resolutions, 238n, 242, 243, 244, 259–260, 275, 276; definition of, 33, 36–37, 37–38; denial of, 25, 31, 296; derivation of principle of nonintervention in traditional, 20–44; French Revolution and, 65, 66, 69; function of, 16, 99n, 334–335; of human rights, 296, 306–310, 344–349; independence as foundation of, 30, 283; and individual, 24, 29, 58, 296, 306–310, 344–349; international society and, 384, 385–386; and intervention, 11–12, 20–44, 91, 245, 281–293, 394; Latin American states on at United Nations, 255–257, 269–271; as law of civilized states, 55, 125; "legislation" in, 376; and multinational corporations, 374; and municipal law, 15, 41, 58, 296, 311; nationality in, 65, 66; "new," 240–241, 250, 254–255, 256, 260, 315, 361–362; of nonintervention, challenges to, 294–310; of nonintervention, contemporary, 275–277, 310–326; of nonintervention, traditional, 13–14, 20–44, 53, 54, 64, 102–103, 140–141, 281–293, 387–388; and order, 375–385; and peace, 57; of peace, 293, 300n; of peaceful coexistence, 182–186, 248–251, 315; purpose of, 397; rules of, 376; science of, 20, 28, 35, 43, 295, 311; and sovereignty, 40, 296–303; and Spanish Civil War, 160–161; Spanish school of, 30; Soviet, principle of nonintervention in, 145, 182–186; subjects of, 4n, 22–24, 55, 66, 155n, 256; Third World views of at United Nations, 238, 251–255, 266–269, 274–275; of United

Nations Charter, 234–237; in United Nations practice, 237–277; United States and, 112, 136n, 205–206, 222–225, 230–231; vocabulary of, 23; Vietnam War and, 222–225, 318–323, 376–377; of war, 293; Western views of at United Nations, 237, 257–261, 271–274, 275. *See also* enforcement, law, intervention, nonintervention

International Law Commission, 39n

International organizations, 296, 303–306, 310, 318, 325, 349, 352n, 365–366, 378, 379, 383–384, 389

international peace and security, 262n, 263, 264, 265, 267, 270, 272, 303, 393, 394, 399

international police, 9, 203n, 292

international socialism, 153, 154, 162

international society, 38, 57–58, 61, 261, 296, 339, 371; and balance of power, 290–291; and civil war, 285, 286–287, 316–323, 358–361; and collective intervention for order, 292–293; and collective intervention to uphold nonintervention, 291–292; consensus in, 308, 369; and democracy within states, 384; distinguished from international community, 389; and domestic jurisdiction, 262; and human rights, 306–310, 344–349; and individuals, 288, 296, 306–310, 344–349; and international anarchy, 231, 329–330; and international law, 385n; justice in, 307; membership of, 24, 25, 29, 40, 294, 317, 351, 380, 381; order in, 53, 330–333, 341n; and principle of nonintervention, 43, 294–310, 325, 327–328; positivists' conception of, 294; and principle of self-determination, 380–381; rudimentary nature of, 294, 303, 383, 384; sovereign

443

BOOKS WRITTEN
UNDER THE AUSPICES OF THE
CENTER OF INTERNATIONAL STUDIES
PRINCETON UNIVERSITY

Gabriel A. Almond, *The Appeals of Communism* (Princeton University Press 1954)

William W. Kaufmann, ed., *Military Policy and National Security* (Princeton University Press 1956)

Klaus Knorr, *The War Potential of Nations* (Princeton University Press 1956)

Lucian W. Pye, *Guerrilla Communism in Malaya* (Princeton University Press 1956)

Charles De Visscher, *Theory and Reality in Public International Law*, trans. by P. E. Corbett (Princeton University Press 1957; rev. ed. 1968)

Bernard C. Cohen, *The Political Process and Foreign Policy: The Making of the Japanese Peace Settlement* (Princeton University Press 1957)

Myron Weiner, *Party Politics in India: The Development of a Multi-Party System* (Princeton University Press 1957)

Percy E. Corbett, *Law in Diplomacy* (Princeton University Press 1959)

Rolf Sannwald and Jacques Stohler, *Economic Integration: Theoretical Assumptions and Consequences of European Unification*, trans. by Herman Karreman (Princeton University Press 1959)

Klaus Knorr, ed., *NATO and American Security* (Princeton University Press 1959)

Gabriel A. Almond and James S. Coleman, eds., *The Politics of the Developing Areas* (Princeton University Press 1960)

Herman Kahn, *On Thermonuclear War* (Princeton University Press 1960)

Sidney Verba, *Small Groups and Political Behavior: A Study of Leadership* (Princeton University Press 1961)

Robert J. C. Butow, *Tojo and the Coming of the War* (Princeton University Press 1961)

Glenn H. Snyder, *Deterrence and Defense: Toward a Theory of National Security* (Princeton University Press 1961)

Klaus Knorr and Sidney Verba, eds., *The International System: Theoretical Essays* (Princeton University Press 1961)

Peter Paret and John W. Shy, *Guerrillas in the 1960's* (Praeger 1962)

George Modelski, *A Theory of Foreign Policy* (Praeger 1962)

Klaus Knorr and Thornton Read, eds., *Limited Strategic War* (Praeger 1963)

Frederick S. Dunn, *Peace-Making and the Settlement with Japan* (Princeton University Press 1963)

Arthur L. Burns and Nina Heathcote, *Peace-Keeping by United Nations Forces* (Praeger 1963)

Richard A. Falk, *Law, Morality, and War in the Contemporary World* (Praeger 1963)

James N. Rosenau, *National Leadership and Foreign Policy: A Case Study in the Mobilization of Public Support* (Princeton University Press 1963)

Gabriel A. Almond and Sidney Verba, *The Civic Culture: Political Attitudes and Democracy in Five Nations* (Princeton University Press 1963)

Bernard C. Cohen, *The Press and Foreign Policy* (Princeton University Press 1963)

Richard L. Sklar, *Nigerian Political Parties: Power in an Emergent African Nation* (Princeton University Press 1963)

Peter Paret, *French Revolutionary Warfare from Indochina to Algeria: The Analysis of a Political and Military Doctrine* (Praeger 1964)

Harry Eckstein, ed., *Internal War: Problems and Approaches* (Free Press 1964)

Cyril E. Black and Thomas P. Thornton, eds., *Communism and Revolution: The Strategic Uses of Political Violence* (Princeton University Press 1964)

Miriam Camps, *Britain and the European Community 1955–1963* (Princeton University Press 1964)

Thomas P. Thornton, ed., *The Third World in Soviet Perspective: Studies by Soviet Writers on the Developing Areas* (Princeton University Press 1964)

James N. Rosenau, ed., *International Aspects of Civil Strife* (Princeton University Press 1964)

Sidney I. Ploss, *Conflict and Decision-Making in Soviet Russia: A Case Study of Agricultural Policy, 1953–1963* (Princeton University Press 1965)

Richard A. Falk and Richard J. Barnet, eds., *Security in Disarmament* (Princeton University Press 1965)

Karl von Vorys, *Political Development in Pakistan* (Princeton University Press 1965)

Harold and Margaret Sprout, *The Ecological Perspective on Human Affairs, With Special Reference to International Politics* (Princeton University Press 1965)

Klaus Knorr, *On the Uses of Military Power in the Nuclear Age* (Princeton University Press 1966)

Harry Eckstein, *Division and Cohesion in Democracy: A Study of Norway* (Princeton University Press 1966)

Cyril E. Black, *The Dynamics of Modernization: A Study in Comparative History* (Harper and Row 1966)

Peter Kunstadter, ed., *Southeast Asian Tribes, Minorities, and Nations* (Princeton University Press 1967)

E. Victor Wolfenstein, *The Revolutionary Personality: Lenin, Trotsky, Gandhi* (Princeton University Press 1967)

Leon Gordenker, *The UN Secretary-General and the Maintenance of Peace* (Columbia University Press 1967)

Oran R. Young, *The Intermediaries: Third Parties in International Crises* (Princeton University Press 1967)

James N. Rosenau, ed., *Domestic Sources of Foreign Policy* (Free Press 1967)

Richard F. Hamilton, *Affluence and the French Worker in the Fourth Republic* (Princeton University Press 1967)

Linda B. Miller, *World Order and Local Disorder: The United Nations and Internal Conflicts* (Princeton University Press 1967)

Wolfram F. Hanrieder, *West German Foreign Policy, 1949–1963: International Pressures and Domestic Response* (Stanford University Press 1967)

Richard H. Ullman, *Britain and the Russian Civil War: November 1918–February 1920* (Princeton University Press 1968)

Robert Gilpin, *France in the Age of the Scientific State* (Princeton University Press 1968)

William B. Bader, *The United States and the Spread of Nuclear Weapons* (Pegasus 1968)

Richard A. Falk, *Legal Order in a Violent World* (Princeton University Press 1968)

Cyril E. Black, Richard A. Falk, Klaus Knorr, and Oran R. Young, *Neutralization and World Politics* (Princeton University Press 1968)

Oran R. Young, *The Politics of Force: Bargaining During International Crises* (Princeton University Press 1969)

Klaus Knorr and James N. Rosenau, eds., *Contending Approaches to International Politics* (Princeton University Press 1969)

James N. Rosenau, ed., *Linkage Politics: Essays on the Convergence of National and International Systems* (Free Press 1969)

John T. McAlister, Jr., *Viet Nam: The Origins of Revolution* (Knopf 1969)

Jean Edward Smith, *Germany Beyond the Wall: People, Politics and Prosperity* (Little, Brown 1969)

James Barros, *Betrayal from Within: Joseph Avenol, Secretary-General of the League of Nations, 1933–1940* (Yale University Press 1969)

Charles Hermann, *Crises in Foreign Policy: A Simulation Analysis* (Bobbs-Merrill 1969)

Robert C. Tucker, *The Marxian Revolutionary Idea: Essays on Marxist Thought and Its Impact on Radical Movements* (W. W. Norton 1969)

Harvey Waterman, *Political Change in Contemporary France: The Politics of an Industrial Democracy* (Charles E. Merrill 1969)

Richard A. Falk and Cyril E. Black, eds., *The Future of the International Legal Order*, Vol. I, *Trends and Patterns* (Princeton University Press 1969)

Ted Robert Gurr, *Why Men Rebel* (Princeton University Press 1970)

C. S. Whitaker, Jr., *The Politics of Tradition: Continuity and Change in Northern Nigeria, 1946–1966* (Princeton University Press 1970)

Richard A. Falk, *The Status of Law in International Society* (Princeton University Press 1970)

Henry Bienen, *Tanzania: Party Transformation and Economic Development* (Princeton University Press 1967, rev. ed. 1970)

Klaus Knorr, *Military Power and Potential* (D. C. Heath 1970)

Richard A. Falk and Cyril E. Black, eds., *The Future of the International Legal Order*, Vol. II, *Wealth and Resources* (Princeton University Press 1970)

Leon Gordenker, ed., *The United Nations in International Politics* (Princeton University Press 1971)

Cyril E. Black and Richard A. Falk, eds., *The Future of the International Legal Order*, Vol. III, *Conflict Management* (Princeton University Press 1971)

Harold and Margaret Sprout, *Toward a Politics of the Planet Earth* (Van Nostrand Reinhold Co. 1971)

Francine R. Frankel, *India's Green Revolution: Economic Gains and Political Costs* (Princeton University Press 1971)

Cyril E. Black and Richard A. Falk, eds., *The Future of the International Legal Order*, Vol. IV, *The Structure of the International Environment* (Princeton University Press 1972)

Gerald Garvey, *Energy, Ecology, Economy* (W. W. Norton 1972)

Richard H. Ullman, *The Anglo-Soviet Accord* (Princeton University Press 1973)

Klaus Knorr, *Power and Wealth: The Political Economy of International Power* (Basic Books 1973)

Anton Bebler, *Military Rule in Africa: Dahomey, Ghana, Sierra Leone, and Mali* (Praeger Publishers 1973)

Robert C. Tucker, Stalin as Revolutionary 1879-1929: A Study in History and Personality (W. W. Norton 1973)

Edward L. Morse, *France and the Politics of Interdependence* (Princeton University Press 1973)

Henry Bienen, *Kenya: The Politics of Participation and Control* (Princeton University Press 1973)

Gregory Massell, *The Surrogate Proletariat: Moslem Women and Revolutionary Strategies in Soviet Central Asia, 1919-1929* (Princeton University Press 1974)

Library of Congress Cataloging in Publishing Data

Vincent, R   J   1943-
  Nonintervention and international order.
  "Written under the auspices of the Center of International
Studies, Princeton University."
  A revision of the author's thesis, Australian National University.
  Bibliography: p.
  1. Intervention (International law) 2. Sovereignty.
  I. Title.
  JX4071.V55   341.3   72-6526
  ISBN 0-691-05652-8